PRAISE FOR *THE NEXT AMERICA*:

"The broad takeaway from Taylor's outstanding work is that age and ethnicity are reshaping our country, and even our ways of describing each other, rapidly and meaningfully."   —*Washington Post*

"Taylor's book raises big questions about how we've generally managed to get along so well despite wildly divergent expectations and economic differences."   —*Boston Globe*

"The book's greatest strength lies in its detailed analysis of significant trends—from politics to lifestyle choices—among the four generational groups surveyed. . . . Taylor proves a plainspoken translator of . . . survey data, and makes . . . statistical techniques accessible to the lay reader."
                                    —*Publishers Weekly*

"Well-written, fact-packed, neatly graphed, comprehensive description of the contemporary US. . . . Highly recommended."   —*CHOICE*

"An incisive survey of vast recent changes in American society and the ever-wider generation gap between baby boomers and millennials. . . . In this well-written, data-rich book, Taylor . . . examines the demographic, economic, social, cultural, and technological changes that are reshaping the nation. . . . An authoritative report and required reading for policymakers."   —*Kirkus*

"A terrific primer on the key demographic and economic trends that will impact work, family, and political life in the US."   —*Inside Higher Ed*

"The book paints a data-rich portrait how the United States is changing and the coming challenges."   —*Oregonian*

"Showed some peculiar trends never before seen in history."   —*The Source*

PRAISE FOR *THE NEXT AMERICA*:

"The broad takeaway from Taylor's outstanding work is that age and ethnicity are reshaping our country, and even our ways of describing each other, rapidly and meaningfully." —*Washington Post*

"Taylor's book raises big questions about how we've generally managed to get along so well despite wildly divergent expectations and economic differences." —*Boston Globe*

"The book's greatest strength lies in its detailed analysis of significant trends—from politics to lifestyle choices—among the four generational groups surveyed. . . . Taylor proves a plainspoken translator of . . . survey data, and makes . . . statistical techniques accessible to the lay reader." —*Publishers Weekly*

"Well-written, fact-packed, neatly graphed, comprehensive description of the contemporary US. . . . Highly recommended." —*CHOICE*

"An incisive survey of vast recent changes in American society and the ever-wider generation gap between baby boomers and millennials. . . . In this well-written, data-rich book, Taylor . . . examines the demographic, economic, social, cultural, and technological changes that are reshaping the nation. . . . An authoritative report and required reading for policymakers." —*Kirkus*

"A terrific primer on the key demographic and economic trends that will impact work, family, and political life in the US." —*Inside Higher Ed*

"The book paints a data-rich portrait how the United States is changing and the coming challenges." —*Oregonian*

"Showed some peculiar trends never before seen in history." —*The Source*

"An eye-opening and wonderfully written account of how swiftly our country is changing, and how we can preserve our social compact across the generational and ethnic divide. A brilliant analyst of public policy and social trends, Paul Taylor offers a hopeful look at America's future in challenging times—studded with fact, and penetrating and revealing from page to page. *The Next America* is an indispensable book for anyone who wants to know where we are, and where we are going."

—Richard North Patterson, author of the
#1 *New York Times* bestseller *Loss of Innocence*

"Informed by decades of research data, *The Next America* is a lucid exploration of the social, cultural, economic, and demographic trends that are reshaping every corner of our society. Taylor's focus is the fundamental generational shifts that are redefining who we are as a people. His analysis of where we've been and where we're headed is the best and most comprehensive you'll read this year."

—Neil Howe, author of *The Fourth Turn* and *Millennials Rising*

"*The Next America* provides a lively, readable guided tour through the numbers that will influence how well the young adults of today will support the seniors of tomorrow."

—Andrew Cherlin, Griswold Professor of Public Policy
at Johns Hopkins University and author of
The Marriage Go-Round

"A provocative yet balanced assessment of intergenerational relations, filled with invaluable data. Essential reading for citizens and policy-makers alike."

—Stephanie Coontz, author of *The Way We Never Were:*
American Families and the Nostalgia Trap

"Provocative national polling data by the Pew Research Center address such issues as generational differences and similarities in America; the impact of demographic changes; attitudes toward race, religion, and marriage, and more."

—World Wide Work bulletin

THE
NEXT
AMERICA

THE
NEXT
 *AMERICA*

BOOMERS, MILLENNIALS,
AND THE LOOMING
GENERATIONAL SHOWDOWN

PAUL TAYLOR

PUBLICAFFAIRS
New York

To Andy and Stefanie

Published in the United States by PublicAffairs™,
a Member of the Perseus Books Group

PublicAffairs books are available at special discounts for bulk purchases in the U.S. by corporations, institutions, and other organizations. For more information, please contact the Special Markets Department at the Perseus Books Group, 2300 Chestnut Street, Suite 200, Philadelphia, PA 19103, call (800) 810-4145, ext. 5000, or e-mail special.markets@perseusbooks.com.

Library of Congress Cataloging-in-Publication Data
Taylor, Paul, 1949–
    The next America : boomers, millennials, and the looming generational showdown
    / Paul Taylor.—First edition.
        pages cm
    Includes bibliographical references and index.
    ISBN 978-1-61039-350-8 (hardcover)—ISBN 978-1-61039-351-5 (electronic)—ISBN 978-1-61039-619-6 (paperback)—978-1-61039-668-4 (paperback electronic)
1. Baby boom generation—United States.   2. Generation Y—United States.
3. Conflict of generations—United States.   4. Generations—United States.
5. United States—Population.   I. Title.
HN59.T39 2014
305.20973—dc23
                                                                2013036139

10 9 8 7 6 5 4 3 2

CONTENTS

PREFACE

Once you get far enough along in life, you're likely to be struck by the distance between the views in front of you and the ones you can still dimly make out in your rearview mirror. I turn 65 this year. The America of my childhood—with its expanding middle class, secure jobs, intact nuclear families, devout believers, distinct gender roles, polite politics, consensus-building media—is nothing like the country my year-old granddaughter will inherit. Our political, social, and religious institutions are weaker, our middle class smaller, our cultural norms looser, our public debate coarser, our technologies faster, our immigrant-woven tapestry richer, and our racial, ethnic, religious, and gender identities more ambiguous. As a society, we've become more polarized *and* more tolerant—and no matter what we're like today, we're going to be different tomorrow. Change is the constant.

We're also getting a whole lot older, as is almost every other nation on the planet—the fruits of longer life spans and lower birthrates that are each unprecedented in human history. These new demographics of aging mean that pretty soon we won't be able to pay for all the promises we've made to oldsters like me. So we'll have to either shrink their social safety net or raise taxes on their children and grandchildren. This reckoning has the potential to set off a generation war, though it doesn't have to.

This book applies a generational lens to explore the many ways America is changing. It pays particular attention to our two outsize generations—the Baby Boomers, fifty- and sixty-somethings having trouble coming to terms with getting old, and the Millennials, twenty-somethings having trouble finding the road map to adulthood. It looks at their competing interests in the big showdown over entitlement reform that our politicians, much as they might try, won't be able to put off for much longer. It also examines how the generations relate to one another not only as citizens, voters, and interest groups, but as parents, children, and caregivers in an era when the family itself is one of our institutions most buffeted by change.

I don't presume to know how my story ends. Years ago when I was a political reporter I had a weakness for trying to forecast election outcomes. I was about as reliable as a coin flip. Eventually it dawned on me that the future was going to arrive anyway, unbidden by me, and that prediction was something of a mug's game. The only forecasts I'll venture in this book will be about the future we already know—the parts baked in by the demographics and the data. Mostly my aim is to be a tour guide who explains how our nation got from the middle of the last century to the present, then provides some insights about what this breathtaking journey tells us about the changes yet to come. I'll conclude with some thoughts on how to renegotiate the social compact between the generations on equitable terms for all.

Be forewarned: there are a lot of data in this book. Numbers are the coin of the realm at the Pew Research Center, where I've worked since we opened our doors a decade ago. Our staff is a mix of public opinion survey researchers, political scientists, demographers, economists, sociologists, and ex-reporters like me. We call ourselves a "fact tank" and we're fond of the aphorism attributed to Senator Daniel Patrick Moynihan: "Everyone is entitled to his own opinions, but not his own facts." We think good data make good facts, and we're just idealistic enough to believe that a common foundation of facts can help societies identify problems and discover solutions.

We know, of course, that numbers aren't omniscient. And we're aware that public opinion surveys, in particular, can sometimes convey a false certitude that disguises ambiguities of heart, soul, and mind. If you ask Americans whether they favor more assistance to the poor, 65% will say yes. If you ask them whether they favor more spending on welfare, just 25% will say yes. Which finding is "true"? Probably both. "Do I contradict myself?" Walt Whitman once asked. "Very well then, I contradict myself. I am large, I contain multitudes." I sometimes wonder whether he had a peek at our survey findings.

But while we're well acquainted with the limitations of survey research, we also appreciate its value. In the shout-fest that passes for public discourse these days, politicians and pundits frequently claim to speak for the public. Well-designed opinion surveys allow the public to speak for itself. Each person has an equal chance to be heard. Each opinion is given an equal weight. That's the same noble ideal that animates our democracy.

———

A note about the paperback edition. This edition of *The Next America*, published nearly two years after the 2014 hardback edition, contains a new opening chapter on the roots of modern political hyperpartisanship and a new appendix chapter that describes how we conduct public opinion surveys. The rest of the book has been updated to take account of new events, studies, and trend data to emerge in the past two years.

Political Tribes

"**I KNOW THIS IS A HORRIBLE THING** to say," former New York City mayor Rudy Giuliani tantalized guests at a Republican fundraiser in February 2015, "but I do not believe the president loves America." In an era when incendiary political attacks are as routine as a rooster crow at dawn, this one created a furor. Pundits and pols of all stripes said it crossed a line. Giuliani, normally not one to retreat, started walking it back the following day.

Then came the polls. Lo and behold, it turned out that 69% of Republicans agreed that Barack Obama didn't love the country he was twice elected to lead, a view shared by just 6% of Democrats.[1]

Welcome to hyperpartisanship, arguably the most powerful force in twenty-first-century American politics. These days, Republicans and Democrats don't stop at disagreeing with each other's ideas. Increasingly, they deny each other's facts, disapprove of each other's lifestyles, don't live in each other's neighborhoods, impugn each other's motives, question each other's patriotism, can't stomach each other's news sources, and bring different value systems to such core social institutions as religion, marriage, and parenthood. It's as if they belong not to rival parties, but to alien tribes.

Obama, who had burst onto the national stage declaring that "we are not a collection of Red states and Blue states," has often found himself in the crosshairs of these partisan firefights. So did his predecessor, George W. Bush, who'd run for president as "a uniter, not a divider." Once in office, both men pursued policies that proved highly divisive—Bush's Iraq War; Obama's Obamacare. They're hardly the first White House occupants to do so. From Lyndon Johnson's Great Society to Johnson and Richard Nixon's Vietnam War to Ronald

Figure 1.1

The Rising Partisan Gap in Presidential Approval

*Average percentage point gap in approval rating between each president's **own party** and the **other party***

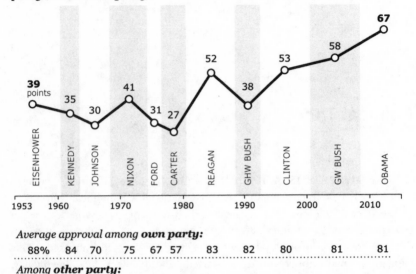

*Average approval among **own party:***

88%	84	70	75	67	57	83	82	80	81	81

*Among **other party:***

49%	49	40	34	36	30	31	44	27	23	14

Note: Data from Eisenhower through George H.W. Bush from Gallup. Because some earlier data did not include partisan leaning, Republicans and Democrats in this graphic do not include leaners.

Source: Pew Research Center's 2014 Political Polarization in the American Public

Reagan's downsizing of government, the past half century has seen plenty of signature presidential initiatives that produced deep schisms in public opinion. Still, none led to the pervasive partisan animosities of the current moment.

Today's hyperpartisanship is as much the handiwork of the American people as it is of their leaders. It is a by-product of the many new ways Americans are sorting themselves—by ideology, age, race, ethnicity, wealth, gender, education, religion, immigrant status, neighborhood—into silos that align with their party affiliation. The sorting is being egged on by politicians and journalists, both of whom now operate in realms where hyperpartisanship flourishes. But the public plays a central role.

Not, however, the *whole* public. One of the paradoxes of this syndrome is that the two fastest-growing political groups in America are hyperpartisans and nonpartisans. That second group is heavily populated by the young, many of whom are mystified by the blood sport that modern politics has become. They are America's most liberal generation by far, but when asked to name their party, fully half of young adults say they are independents. In the eight decades pollsters have posed this question, no generation has ever been so allergic to a party label.

Here's another paradox: hyperpartisanship reigns at a time when most Americans still value the lost art of political compromise. At least that's what they say. If you ask adults of all ages if they would rather that elected officials in Washington, DC, who share their views (1) work with those they disagree with, even if it results in some policies they don't like, or (2) stand up for their positions, even if it means little gets done, most choose (1).[2] As ever, the majority of Americans are pragmatists, ready to meet in the middle.

Yet nowadays these Americans are a silent majority. They don't have the temperament, inclination, or vocal cords to attract attention in a media culture where shrill pundits and 140-character screeds set so much of the tone in the public square. And they punch below their weight at the voting booth, especially during primaries, where their more ideologically driven neighbors turn out in force.

This strident media zeitgeist and these balkanizing electoral dynamics favor congressional candidates who know how to run up the score with their party's respective bases, where grievance runs hot. Other new wrinkles in the ecosystem of modern politics—including the nonstop demands of fund-raising, the emergence of a donor class of billionaire ideologues, the rise of safe-seat partisan gerrymandering, and the growth of economically and ideologically homogeneous neighborhoods—have also helped tilt the campaign playing field toward hyperpartisan candidates.

It's not hard to measure the impact of all these changes on Congress. Republicans and Democrats on Capitol Hill are further apart from one another now than at any point since the end of Reconstruction in the late nineteenth century, according to one widely accepted metric of roll call voting.[3] In the 112th Congress, which ran from 2011 to 2012, every Republican senator and representative voted more conservatively than the most conservative Democrat, and every Democrat was more liberal than the most liberal Republican.[4] This has left the legislative branch of government gridlocked and dysfunctional in the view of its ever more dyspeptic constituents. When confidence ratings for Congress slipped to single digits during one of its threatened government shutdowns, Senator John McCain of Arizona quipped, "We're down to paid staff and blood relatives." It's easy to see why nonpartisans would react to the Beltway catfights by distancing themselves from politics, while hyperpartisans

Figure 1.2

Democrats and Republicans: More Ideologically Divided

Distribution of Democrats and Republicans on a 10-item scale of political values

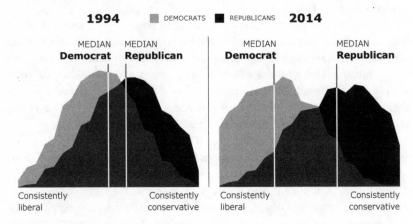

Note: Ideological consistency based on a scale of 10 political values questions. The light grey in this chart represents the ideological distribution of Democrats; the black area of Republicans. The overlap of these two distributions is shaded dark grey. Republicans include Republican-leaning independents; Democrats include Democratic-leaning independents.

Source: Pew Research Center's 2014 Political Polarization in the American Public

would find their animal spirits roused and their outrage amped. And so the cycle perpetuates itself.

As the 2016 presidential race begins in earnest, both sides of this coin have already been on vivid display. Among the candidates who surged during a wildly unpredictable 2015 campaign preseason were a celebrity real estate mogul, a retired neurosurgeon, a female former CEO, and a septuagenarian socialist. Their ideologies are as dissimilar as their resumes. But Donald Trump, Ben Carson, Carly Fiorina, and Bernie Sanders each climbed in the early polls on the strength of a common attribute. All are political outsiders. Whatever their fates in 2016, their unlikely initial success illuminated the restiveness of the American public in an era of stagnant incomes, head-snapping social, cultural, and technological changes, and gruesome global terrorism. It also suggests that hyperpartisanship has created its own contemporaneous counter-force—a populist frustration with conventional politicians of all stripes.

A DEEPER LOOK AT HYPERPARTISANSHIP

The Pew Research Center in 2014 conducted its largest political survey ever to try to better understand this phenomenon. We asked questions that explore people's core political, social, and economic values, their news-gathering habits, and their lifestyle preferences. We interviewed 10,000 adults—roughly 7 times more than we do for a typical political survey—allowing us to generate findings for a wide range of subgroups, from blacks and whites, to young and old, to NPR listeners and Fox News viewers, and so on. We repeated 10 questions we've asked for 20 years that place respondents on a liberal-to-conservative continuum, allowing us to show change over time in the public's ideological and partisan alignments.

The survey found that Republicans and Democrats are more divided along ideological lines—and partisan antipathy is deeper and more extensive—than at any point in at least the last two decades. These trends manifest themselves in myriad ways, both in politics and in everyday life.

The overall share of Americans who express consistently conservative or consistently liberal opinions has doubled over the past two decades from 10% to 21%. And ideological thinking is now much more closely aligned with party affiliation than in the past. As a result, ideological overlap between the two parties has diminished: today, 92% of Republicans are to the right of the median Democrat, and 94% of Democrats are to the left of the median Republican.

Partisan animosity has increased substantially over the same period. In each party, the share with a highly negative view of the opposing party has more than doubled since 1994. Most of these intense partisans believe the opposing party's policies "are so misguided that they threaten the nation's well-being." Among all Democrats, 27% hold this view; among all Republicans, 36% feel this way.

To be sure, most Americans do not view either party as a threat to the nation. Indeed, a majority do not have uniformly conservative or liberal views. Yet many of those in the center remain on the edges of the political playing field, relatively distant and disengaged. On measure after measure—whether primary voting, writing letters to officials, or volunteering for or donating to a campaign—the most politically polarized are more actively involved in politics (see appendix Figure 1A.1). And when we asked respondents about their attitudes toward compromise, most consistent conservatives (57%) and consistent liberals (62%) said the ideal agreement is one in which their side holds out for more of their goals. By contrast, among those with mixed views, a majority

Figure 1.3

How We Identify Conservatives and Liberals

Question wording: I am going to read you a pair of statements ... Tell me whether the first statement or the second statement comes closer to your own views, even if neither is exactly right.

Conservative Position	Liberal Position
Government is almost always wasteful and inefficient	Government often does a better job than people give it credit for
Government regulation of business usually does more harm than good	Government regulation of business is necessary to protect the public interest
Poor people today have it easy because they can get government benefits without doing anything in return	Poor people have hard lives because government benefits don't go far enough to help them live decently
The government today can't afford to do much more to help the needy	The government should do more to help needy Americans, even if it means going deeper into debt
Blacks who can't get ahead in this country are mostly responsible for their own condition	Racial discrimination is the main reason why many black people can't get ahead these days
Immigrants today are a burden on our country because they take our jobs, housing and health care	Immigrants today strengthen our country because of their hard work and talents
The best way to ensure peace is through military strength	Good diplomacy is the best way to ensure peace
Most corporations make a fair and reasonable amount of profit	Business corporations make too much profit
Stricter environmental laws and regulations cost too many jobs and hurt the economy	Stricter environmental laws and regulations are worth the cost
Homosexuality should be discouraged by society	Homosexuality should be accepted by society

Individual questions are recoded as follows: "−1" for a liberal response, "+1" for a conservative response, "0" for other (don't know/refused/volunteered) responses. Respondents are grouped into one of five categories:

Consistently conservative (+7 to +10)
Mostly conservative (+3 to +6)
Mixed (−2 to +2)
Mostly liberal (−6 to −3)
Consistently liberal (−10 to −7)

Source: Pew Research Center's 2014 Political Polarization in the American Public

Figure 1.4

Beyond Dislike

*Democratic attitudes about
the Republican Party*

*Republican attitudes about
the Democratic Party*

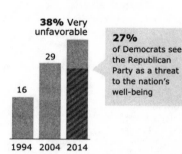

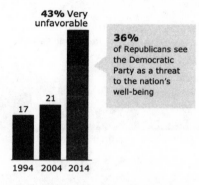

Note: Questions about whether the Republican and Democratic Parties are a threat to the nation's well being asked only in 2014. Republicans include Republican-leaning independents; Democrats include Democratic-leaning independents.

Source: Pew Research Center's 2014 Political Polarization in the American Public

said that Obama and Republican leaders should simply meet each other half-way (see appendix Figure 1A.2).

IDEOLOGY AND EVERYDAY LIFE

These ideological differences also play a role in many other aspects of people's lives, from where they live, to whom they associate with, to how they raise children, to where they look for news.

FRIENDSHIPS. Nearly two-thirds (63%) of consistent conservatives and about half (49%) of consistent liberals say most of their close friends share their political views. By contrast, only 25% of those with mixed ideological values say the same thing about their friends.

SPOUSES. Three in 10 (30%) consistent conservatives say they would be unhappy if an immediate family member married a Democrat; about a quarter (23%) of across-the-board liberals say the same about the prospect of a Republican in-law.

Figure 1.5

Conservatives Prioritize Faith, Obedience; Liberals Value Tolerance, Empathy

% saying each is especially important to teach children

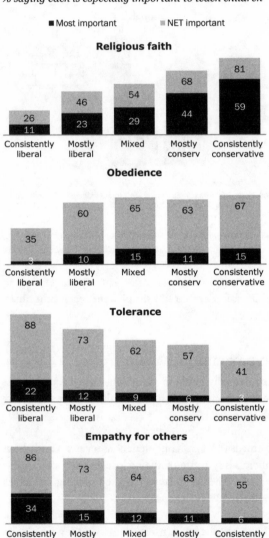

Source: Pew Research Center's American Trends Panel survey, April 29–May 27, 2014

CHILDREARING. Conservatives place more emphasis than liberals do on the importance of teaching children religious values and obedience, while liberals are more inclined to stress tolerance, empathy, creativity, and curiosity. There's broad agreement across the ideological spectrum that it is important for children to learn responsibility (the highest-rated trait of the 12 tested in the survey), independence, hard work, and good manners.

NEIGHBORS. Half of all adults on the right (50%) and about a third on the left (35%) say it is important to them to live in a place where most people share their political views. Just 22% of those with mixed views feel the same way.

MEDIA USAGE. Conservatives and liberals have their own ways of searching for news, with conservatives tightly grouped around Fox News and liberals gravitating toward CNN, NPR, MSNBC, and the *New York Times*. Likewise, in their social media habits, each group tends to cluster around friends and information sources that affirm their worldview.

THE BIG SORT

It's hardly a surprise that these patterns of selective exposure appear in the online world; no medium in human history has made it easier for like to attract like. What's more intriguing is that something similar also appears to be happening in the physical world. In their 2008 book, *The Big Sort*, authors Bill Bishop and Robert Cushing were the first to popularize the idea that more Americans were clustering into think-alike communities. They were careful *not* to claim that political ideology is on people's minds when they choose where to live. As they noted, these decisions are driven by considerations such as cost, community type, family, jobs, schools, shopping, climate, and public amenities. But their thesis is that these sorts of lifestyle preferences are increasingly aligned with people's political ideology.

To make their case, Bishop and Cushing analyzed voting patterns by county in three presidential elections that had all been decided by a few percentage points or less in the national popular vote—1976, 2000, and 2004. They measured partisan clustering at the local level by tallying the number of "landslide counties" in each election—counties where one of the presidential candidates won at least 60% of the vote. In 1976, they found, only about a quarter of all voters lived in a landslide county. But by 2000 and 2004, nearly half of all voters lived in such counties.[5] Thus, they concluded, more people had ideological soul mates as neighbors.

Not so fast, countered political scientists Samuel Abrams and Morris Fiorina. They analyzed trends in party registration over a similar period and found the opposite pattern: there were many fewer "landslide counties" by party registration in 2008 than in 1976. Bishop's rebuttal: those patterns reflect a decline in party affiliation, not a rise in partisan residential heterogeneity.

Other skeptics make a different argument: they say counties are too big to be a useful guide to the often diverse mix of neighborhoods situated within. Yes, comes the response, but counties are typically part of the same media market and regional economy. Most have a distinctive culture, as do most cities and states.

As with many debates waged with competing datasets, this one can't be settled conclusively. But the Big Sort thesis got a nod of support from our survey when we asked people what they were looking for in a place to live. Three-quarters of consistent conservatives said they prefer a community where "the houses are larger and farther apart, but schools, stores, and restaurants are several miles away." By contrast, 77% of consistent liberals said they'd choose to live where "the houses are smaller and closer to each other, but schools, stores, and restaurants are within walking distance."

We also asked the question in a slightly different way—would you rather live in a city, suburb, small town, or rural area?—and found similarly sharp differences by ideology. Some 41% of consistent conservatives said they preferred a rural area, compared with just 11% of consistent liberals. Likewise, 46% of those on the left said they prefer city life, compared with just 4% of those on the right.

And to put in one more plug for the Big Sort, there's this delectable little data nugget cooked up by David Wasserman of the nonpartisan Cook Political Report. After the 2008 election, he found that 89% of the Whole Food stores in the United States were in counties carried by Obama, while 62% of the Cracker Barrel restaurants were in counties carried by John McCain.[6]

ECONOMIC SORTING. While scholars may differ over the extent of ideological sorting by neighborhood, the rise in *economic* sorting by neighborhood is beyond dispute. To study this phenomenon, Pew Research Center analyzed household income trends over a three-decade period in the nation's 74,000 census tracts (the typical tract has about 4,000 inhabitants, meaning it more closely resembles a neighborhood than do any of the nation's 3,100 counties).

The study found that from 1980 to 2010, a growing share of lower-income households were located in a majority lower-income census tract, and a growing share of upper-income households were located in a majority upper-income census tract.[7] Using a slightly different methodology and time frame, Cornell University's Kendra Bischoff and Stanford University's Sean Reardon found a similar trend: in 1970, 65% of US families resided in middle-income neighborhoods; by 2009, that number had dropped to 42%.[8] Income inequality has

Figure 1.6

Rising Residential Segregation, 1980–2010

*% of lower-income households living
in majority **low-income** tracts*

*% of upper-income households living
in majority **upper-income** tracts*

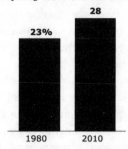

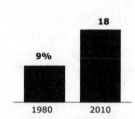

Note: Based on census tracts in the nation's 942 metropolitan and micropolitan statistical areas. In a majority lower-income census tract, at least half the tract's households have a household income below 67% of the metropolitan median household income. In a majority upper-income census tract, at least half the tract's households have a household income above 200% of the metropolitan median household income.

Source: Pew Research Center tabulations of 2006–2010 American Community Survey (ACS) 5-year file and Geolytics 1980 Census data in 2000 boundaries

become one of the defining features of modern American life. As these studies indicate, that trend is now as visible on a map as on a stack of tax returns.

This rise in residential economic segregation doesn't by itself prove that more neighborhoods have turned deep Red or deep Blue. But it's another piece of the puzzle. Throughout our history, the upper rungs of our socioeconomic ladder have tilted conservative, the lower rungs liberal. Now more than ever, these rungs are separated by geography as well as income.

THE MAKING OF THE MODERN MEDIA

Half a century ago CBS anchorman Walter Cronkite wore the crown of "the most trusted man in America."[9] Then, a small, like-minded, and somewhat clubby band of broadcast television networks, wire services, and elite newspapers set the nation's news agenda. Like Cronkite (a closet liberal), they all aspired to a nonideological brand of political reporting, for reasons dictated by the economics, regulations, and technologies of the era. At the top of the food chain, the three national broadcast networks—CBS, NBC, and ABC— effectively enjoyed oligopoly control over the television airwaves (thanks to the physical scarcity of broadcast frequencies). Their business model was to compete among themselves for the biggest slice of a giant audience. Along with attracting eyeballs, their neutral, authoritative "voice of God" journalism engendered trust. When Uncle Walter closed his newscast each night with his reassuring sign-off—"and that's the way it is"—America took him at his word.

Today, the news media have splintered into millions of pieces, some larger than others, but all now operating at a time when new technologies have busted the oligopoly and empowered anyone to be a news disseminator.[10] In this fragmented universe, many news organizations now search for profits by maximizing their appeals to narrow audience niches. And as the American public has grown more politically polarized, the economic case for serving them Red Truth or Blue Truth has grown more compelling.[11]

Rupert Murdoch was the first modern media mogul to seize on this logic when he launched the Fox News Channel in 1996. Its motto is "fair and balanced," but starting with the hiring of former Republican media consultant Roger Ailes to be its chief executive, Fox's mission has been clear: serve a steady diet of right-leaning news and commentary geared toward countering what its viewers see as the liberal bias of the traditional media.[12] Fox has been a huge business success. Twenty years later, it still reigns as the runaway political news leader on cable television. A similar dynamic has played out on talk radio, where conservative talk show host Rush Limbaugh has enjoyed an even longer run atop the ratings heap (although he's been losing listeners lately). There have been lots of efforts to match both of them from the left—in recent years best exemplified by MSNBC's lineup of liberal commentators. All have lagged badly in the marketplace. The conservative explanation is that the mainstream media are already so liberal that there isn't a viable market to its left. The liberal explanation is that grievance and paranoia run hotter on the right.

Either way, these outposts of Red and Blue Truths have transformed the tone, tenor, and norms of modern journalism. Objectivity remains an aspiration at many traditional news organizations, but it no longer has the stage to itself. Many of the newbies in political journalism see their mission as delivering news that rallies the faithful (and incites the enemy). This calls for mixing fact with commentary as a matter of standard practice. And it means choosing stories that depict a version of reality that's often unrecognizable to the other side—sometimes comically so, which explains why the Left's most effective foil to Fox, especially among the young, came in the form of two satirical news programs on Comedy Central: *The Daily Show* and *The Colbert Report*. In this funhouse-mirror media world, the hyperpartisans in the spectators' gallery have no trouble finding their red meat. If you want proof that Obama doesn't love America, probably isn't a Christian, and may have been born in Kenya, Fox is your ticket. If you prefer a running account of the racism, sexism, and homophobia of Republicans, the greed of big business, or the bigotry of the Religious Right, head over to MSNBC. The liberals' war on Christmas? Find it on Fox. The GOP's war on women? That would be MSNBC.

The total audience for these shows is actually quite small—and it's been shrinking since 2009.[13] Nevertheless, University of Pennsylvania political communications professor Diana Mutz argues in *In-Your-Face Politics: The Consequences of Uncivil Media* that they set a tone that seeps into the broader culture, fostering out-group antagonism and undermining institutional trust.[14]

To be sure, as our studies confirm, it's virtually impossible for anyone these days to live in a totally Red or Blue ideological bubble. The modern information ecosystem is simply too all-consuming, nonstop, full throttle, multiplatformed, and mobile. Most Americans rely on an array of outlets—with varying ideological and audience profiles—for political news. Among Millennials, Facebook has become the most widely used conduit for news,[15] and as its influence has grown, scholars have debated the degree to which its algorithms feed stories to users in a way that intensifies the political echo chamber effect. In 2015, Facebook researchers analyzed the

Figure 1.7

Fox News, MSNBC Stir Up Negative Views Among Ideologically Consistent

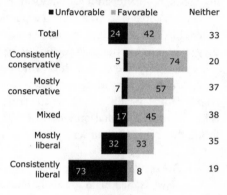

Fox News

■Unfavorable ■Favorable　Neither

	Unfavorable	Favorable	Neither
Total	24	42	33
Consistently conservative	5	74	20
Mostly conservative	7	57	37
Mixed	17	45	38
Mostly liberal	32	33	35
Consistently liberal	73	8	19

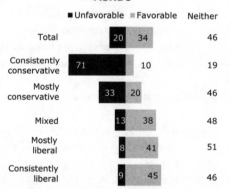

MSNBC

■Unfavorable ■Favorable　Neither

	Unfavorable	Favorable	Neither
Total	20	34	46
Consistently conservative	71	10	19
Mostly conservative	33	20	46
Mixed	13	38	48
Mostly liberal	8	41	51
Consistently liberal	9	45	46

Note: Ideological consistency based on scale of 10 political values questions. "Neither" includes don't know responses. Percentages may not add to 100 due to rounding.

Source: Pew Research Center's 2014 Political Polarization in the American Public

content of news stories that 10 million of its users who self-identified with a political ideology had been exposed to over a six-month period. It found that while people's network of friends and diet of news stories are indeed skewed toward their ideological preferences, users not infrequently encounter opposing views. The study found that 22% of the news stories that Facebook presented to liberals were of a conservative bent, and 33% of the stories shown to conservatives had a liberal slant. Some critics, such as communications scholar Christian Sandvig, were not impressed. Dubbing it Facebook's "it's-not-our-fault study," he said that "selectivity and polarization are happening on Facebook, and its news feed curation algorithm acts to modestly accelerate" the process.[16] Meantime, Mutz notes that news consumers who search for opposing views, no matter in what platform, may have motives other than enlightenment. "People who are really into politics . . . will expose themselves to the other side," she said. "But it could be just to make fun of it, or to know what they're saying to better argue against it, or just to yell at the television set."[17]

Our survey shows that those who occupy the left and right ends of the spectrum have very different ways of staying informed. When we asked respondents how much they use and trust several dozen prominent broadcast, cable, print, and digital-only outlets that cover politics and government, we found that consistent conservatives:

- Are tightly clustered around a single news source, with 47% citing Fox News as their main source for news about government and politics.
- Express greater distrust than trust of 24 of the 36 news sources measured in our survey. At the same time, fully 88% of consistent conservatives trust Fox News.
- When on Facebook, are twice as likely as the typical user (47% versus 23%) to come across political views consistent with their own.

By contrast, consistent liberals:

- Rely on a range of news outlets, with no single source named by more than 15% of consistent liberals.
- Express more trust than distrust of 28 of the 36 news outlets in the survey. NPR, PBS, and the BBC are the most trusted news sources for consistent liberals.
- On Facebook are more likely than other groups (44%, compared with 31% of consistent conservatives and 26% of all users) to block or "defriend" someone because of politics.
- In their Facebook feeds are more likely to follow issue-based groups, rather than political parties or candidates.

Not surprisingly, politics is less of a focus for those in the middle of the ideological spectrum. Their main news sources include CNN, local TV, and Fox News, along with Yahoo News and Google News, which aggregate stories from a wide assortment of outlets. And when they use social media, these adults encounter a mix of views.

Figure 1.8

Evaluations of Press Grow More Negative

*Stories are
often inaccurate*

*Tend to favor
one side*

*Often influenced
by powerful people
and organizations*

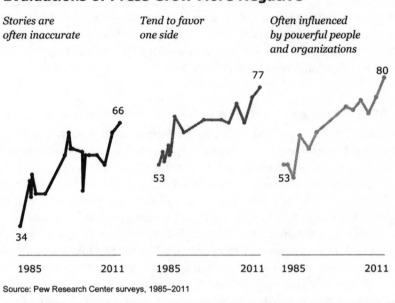

Source: Pew Research Center surveys, 1985–2011

One casualty of this market fragmentation has been the public's trust in media credibility and independence. It has soured badly since Cronkite's day, a process that began before the digital revolution and has continued apace since. Most other key institutions of American life have also suffered sharp drops in public trust, though few have fallen as far as the news media. In keeping with the zeitgeist of our era, the disillusionment is not evenly distributed. Liberals are least trusting of conservative outlets, and conservatives of liberal outlets, as seen in appendix Figure 1A.3.

Dramatic though these changes have been, they aren't new. In many ways, they take American journalism back to its raucous early roots in the late eighteenth and early nineteenth centuries, when newspapers originated as propaganda pamphlets of the political parties. By the middle of the nineteenth century the invention of the telegraph enabled newspaper publishers to expand their readerships by offering real-time reporting from far and wide (the first wire service, the Associated Press, was launched in 1846). This created market incentives to provide neutral, objective news accounts. Those incentives grew stronger in the twentieth century with the invention and commercialization first of radio and then television—the two ultimate "broadcast" platforms. But now the more recent waves of technological innovation, first cable and then digital, have brought journalism full circle back to its narrow-casting origins. It's unclear whether Americans have become better or worse informed as a result. Pew Research surveys taken over several decades suggest that even though the news audience now includes more people wedded to Red or Blue versions of reality, and also more people with higher levels of educational attainment, there's been almost no change in the public's overall knowledge about national and international affairs.[18]

THE DEMOGRAPHICS OF POLARIZATION IN 2016

To recap: Technologies, journalists, and politicians are all promoting polarization, but haven't operated in a vacuum. The public has put its own shoulders into the process. Which brings us to an intriguing question: Why?

A pretty good one-word answer is demographics. The America of the early twenty-first century is undergoing two dramatic demographic overhauls at the same time. Our population is en route to becoming majority nonwhite at the same time a record share is turning gray. Either transformation by itself would be the dominant demographic story of its era. The fact that they are happening simultaneously has created huge generation gaps. We are at a moment in history when young and old don't look alike, think alike, vote alike, form families alike, use technology alike, or share many core social and political values.

All of these gaps have a partisan dimension, which we can track by analyzing voting patterns and party affiliations. Observe, for example, our current electorate through the lens of our four adult generations: Millennials (ages 18 through 35), Gen Xers (ages 36 to 51), Baby Boomers (ages 52 to 70), and the Silent Generation (ages 71 to 88). Millennials are our most racially diverse (about 43% are nonwhite) and most liberal generation. Were it not for their votes, Mitt Romney would be finishing up his first term. Silents are our least racially diverse (about 78% white) and most conservative generation. Millennials are in the worst economic shape of any of the four adult generations; Silents are in the best shape. Millennials are less than half as likely to be married as Silents were back when they were the same age. They are three times as likely to be unaffiliated with any religion. They are far more likely to have given birth to their first child as a single parent. Among Millennials, gender norms are converging, both at home and work—and have traveled quite a distance from the male breadwinner/female homemaker template that prevailed when Silents were coming of age. In all of these dimensions, the transformations have unfolded along a fairly straight chronological continuum, meaning that the attitudes and behaviors of the two generations in the middle—Baby Boomers and Gen Xers—are arrayed in a stairstep pattern between those of younger

Figure 1.9

2014 Partisan Advantages by Year of Birth

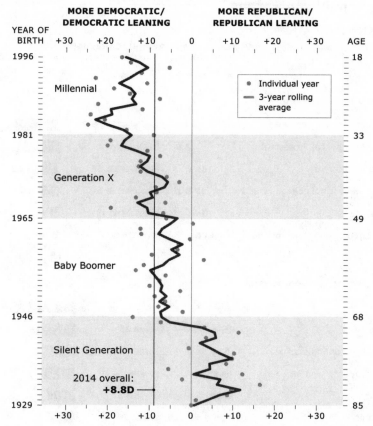

and older cohorts. The same is true for views about many hot-button cultural issues, from same-sex marriage to immigration to marijuana legalization.

These generation gaps are not the only demographic fissure that divides Democrats from Republicans. Here are others, based on more than 25,000 Pew Research survey interviews about partisan affiliation conducted throughout 2014.[19]

RACE AND ETHNICITY. Partisan divisions by race are our oldest and deepest demographic cleavage. What's notable is how big they remain at a time when

Figure 1.10

Strong Groups for the Democratic and Republican Parties

% of each group that identifies as ...

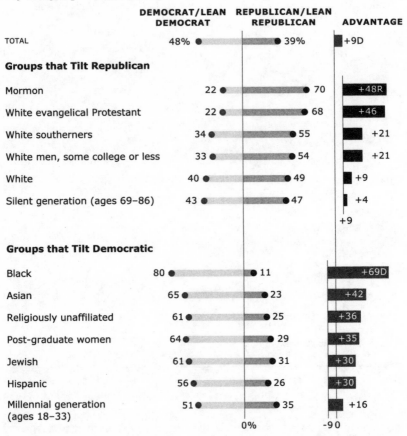

Note: Whites and blacks include only non-Hispanics; Hispanics are of any race. Asians are non-Hispanic and English-speaking only.

Source: Pew Research Center surveys, 2014

our racial tapestry is evolving from black and white to multicolored. Among all white adults who identify with or lean toward a party, Republicans today hold a 49%–40% lead over Democrats. The GOP advantage widens to 21 points among white men who have not completed college (54%–33%) and white southerners (55%–34%). On the flip side, Democrats hold a huge 80%–11% advantage among blacks. They also lead by close to 3 to 1 among Asian Americans (65%–23%) and by more than 2 to 1 among Hispanics (56%–26%)—the two big immigrant groups that are remaking the face of the nation.

GENDER. In a pattern that has persisted for decades, women lean Democratic by 52%–36%, while men are evenly divided (44% Democratic, 43% Republican). Gender differences are evident in nearly all subgroups. For instance, Republicans lead among married men (51%–38%), while married women are evenly divided (44% Republican, 44% Democratic). Democrats hold a substantial advantage among all unmarried adults, but their lead in partisan identification is greater among unmarried women (57%–29%) than among unmarried men (51%–34%).

EDUCATION. Democrats lead by 22 points (57%–35%) in party identification among adults with postgraduate degrees; 20 years ago, there was no gap in this group. The Democrats' edge is narrower among those with college degrees or some postgraduate experience (49%–42%), and those with less education (47%–39%). Across all educational categories, women are more likely than men to affiliate with the Democratic Party or lean Democratic. For example, the Democrats' advantage is 35 points (64%–29%) among women with postgraduate degrees, but only eight points (50%–42%) among postgrad men.

RELIGION. Adults who have no religious affiliation are the fastest-growing and youngest religious group in the population; they lean Democratic by a wide margin (36 points). Republicans lead by even larger margins among one small group, Mormons (48 points), and one large group, white evangelical Protestants (46 points). Younger white evangelicals (those under age 35) are about as likely as older white evangelicals to identify as Republican or lean Republican. Jews lean Democratic by roughly 2 to 1 (61%–31%).

INCOME. Partisan gaps here are not nearly as large as in other categories, mostly because the modern Democratic Party has become an upstairs/downstairs coalition that does best with the poor on one end of the socioeconomic scale and highly educated professionals on the other. Democrats have a sizable edge (54%–31%) among those with family incomes below $30,000.

Republicans have a narrow margin (48%–45%) among those with family incomes of $75,000 and above.

One obvious takeaway from these patterns is that Democrats enjoy a big advantage with what journalist Ron Brownstein dubbed "the coalition of the ascendant"—by which he meant large, growing electoral blocs such as the young, nonwhites, single mothers, and the religiously unaffiliated. Moreover, generational churn ought to be the Democrats' best friend. As more of today's young age into the electorate and more of today's old die off, simple arithmetic would seem to ensure that future elections will turn a deeper shade of blue.

Well, maybe. But these same assumptions have been around since Obama's breakthrough election of 2008, and a funny thing has happened to the age of presumed Democratic demographic dominance. It's been a no show. In fact, when the Democratic Party in 2015 tallied up all election results since Obama was inaugurated in 2009, it found "devastating losses" (its words) at all levels of government. By 2015 there were 69 fewer Democrats in the US House of Representatives, 13 fewer in the Senate, 910 fewer in state legislatures, and 11 fewer in governors' mansions. The GOP hasn't enjoyed such across-the-board majorities since the Hoover-Coolidge era of the 1920s.

What happened? It turns out that the coalition of the ascendant is often the coalition of the unengaged. There's nothing new in the phenomenon of the young turning out to vote in much lower numbers than the old; that seems hardwired into the human life cycle. This turnout gap doesn't amount to much when the generations vote alike, but makes a huge difference when they don't. Nowadays Democrats are especially vulnerable in midterm elections, when turnouts typically fall by nearly half from their presidential year peaks, and when most of the missing voters are from their core voting blocs. For example, a paltry 19.9% of 18- to 29-year-olds voted in the 2014 midterm election, less than half the share that had voted in the presidential race two years earlier. It was the lowest turnout rate for young adults since the voting age was reduced to 18 in 1972. Thus we have the zigs and zags of our last four national elections—Obama's big wins in the presidential years of 2008 and 2012 (when he became the first Democrat since FDR to command a majority of votes in consecutive elections), interspersed around the huge GOP victories in the midterms of 2010 and 2014. Political campaigns are now waged not just in Red and Blue states but in alternating Red and Blue biennials, with demographics the most important difference maker.

To stretch the metaphor into yet another realm, we also now have Red and Blue branches of the federal government, with Democrats winning the popular vote for president in five of the past six elections at the same time Republicans have built their largest majorities in Congress in nearly a century. Nothing like this has ever happened before; again, demographics are a key part of the story. The Senate, with its small-state bias, is an increasingly friendly chamber for Republicans, who have a big edge in rural white sections of the country. Over in the House, Democrats face a growing "wasted vote" dilemma. Their young, nonwhite electoral base is increasingly concentrated in urban districts, where a Democratic candidate can run up 80% or more of the vote. These big margins help give their presidential candidates the boost they need to carry electoral-rich swing states like Pennsylvania, Ohio, Michigan, and Wisconsin. But they add nothing to the Democrats' haul in the House.[20]

All of these electoral dynamics have added a new layer of institutional-ized partisan conflict to the elaborate system of checks and balances that our founders wrote into the Constitution. Given how broken Washington feels these days, some have even begun to wonder if we'd be better off moving to a British-style parliamentary system in which the party that controls the legis-lative branch picks the prime minister. "In a parliamentary system, deadlocks get resolved," Vox Media's Matthew Yglesias wrote in a wistful 2015 essay. "There's simply no possibility of a years-long spell in which the legislative and executive branches glare at each other unproductively."[21]

Practically speaking, any constitutional makeover of that magnitude is, of course, a nonstarter. Moreover, most students of the American system take a more benign view of the constitutional and electoral architecture that has given us three branches of government and two big tent parties. In our dynamic, heterogeneous, and individualistic culture, each party must build a diverse coalition and cater to a wide variety of interests. This has a moderat-ing impact on public policy, as do the checks and balances among the exec-utive, legislative, and judicial branches. This formula has produced the most resilient democracy in human history. Yes, we often lurch down blind alleys or bump into brick walls, but the record shows we eventually figure out how to accommodate majority will, protect minority rights, and find Goldilocks solutions. Our system seems especially dysfunctional at the moment. If history is a guide, this too will pass, perhaps sooner than seems imaginable. Political arrangements are inherently unstable. So are all demographic "locks." There's no reason to expect today's gridlock to be more durable than, say, the FDR coalition that seemed to give Democrats an impregnable hold on power in the 1930s and 1940s, or the rise of the Sunbelt and collapse of the Democratic South that appeared to do the same for Republicans in the final third of the last century. Circumstances change, history surprises, coalitions unravel, parties adapt. Just ask Donald Trump.

But anyone rooting for hyperpartisanship to recede this year has probably picked the wrong election. The 2016 campaign is the seventh presidential race since 1980 to open with a Bush in the field and the fourth since 1992 with a Clinton—making it part *Groundhog Day*, part *Game of Thrones*. Our country has known its share of political dynasties before (Adams, Roosevelt, Kennedy), but we've never had two on the national stage at the same time. The Clinton and Bush families came to prominence in the age of hyperpartisanship, and even though their current standard-bearers aren't from the slash-and-burn school of political combat, both carry family baggage and battle scars accumulated over many decades. They're not the only candidates in the field, of course. As this book went to press, the biggest surprises of the campaign preseason were Trump and Bernie Sanders, who both tapped into a vein of populist disgust with politics-as-usual even though they are each other's ideological and stylistic opposites. As their insurgent candidacies caught fire in 2015, Jeb Bush lamented that "there's been a hollowing out of the center in American politics," adding, "the left is angry and the right is angrier." It will make for an interesting campaign.

LOOKING AHEAD

Even if our political system doesn't break free from the excesses of hyperpartisanship in 2016, it will happen eventually. Looking ahead, these are some of the demographic, economic, and cultural trends in a changing America that will shape elections this year and beyond.

GENERATIONS. "Men resemble their times more than their fathers," goes an ancient proverb. If that bit of wisdom holds, the electoral playing field should indeed grow steadily more hospitable to Democrats. Millennials are our largest and most liberal generation, at ease with the overlapping racial, cultural, social, and technological revolutions of the new century. They're unmoored from traditional organizations such as political parties, but we know from the votes they've cast since coming of age that they are the most Democratic cohort of any in modern history. Moreover, as noted earlier, generational replacement is a double whammy for the GOP. Each year as more Millennials age into the electorate, more members of the Silent Generation, the nation's most conservative age group, will be dying off. In 2012, Millennials made up 25.5% of the age-eligible electorate but only cast about 20% of the votes (enough, however, to rescue Obama from defeat). By 2020, they will be 36.5% of the age-eligible electorate, and, if history is a guide, as they enter middle age, their turnout rates will rise as well. Thus the key question: Will their liberal proclivities stay with them over the life cycle? It's not clear. This is a generation that eschews labels and avoids long-term commitments—to products, employers, organizations, and perhaps ideologies. As children of the digital era, their instinct is to graze, to comparison shop, to wait for the next big thing. So it's possible that the applicable aphorism isn't the one cited above, but the one often attributed to Winston Churchill: "If you're not a liberal at age 20, you have no heart, and if you're not a conservative at age 40, you have no head." Pick your proverb as you keep this in mind: Millennials will be the biggest electoral prize on the horizon for decades to come.

RACE. According to the Census Bureau, the US population will be more than 50% nonwhite by 2044, up from 38% now. The shift will occur in steady steps, with the population becoming nearly 2 percentage points less white in each four-year presidential cycle. Two related demographic forces are driving this racial makeover: more than 8 in 10 of the roughly one million immigrants who come to our country every year are nonwhite, and birthrates among immigrants are nearly 50% higher than among native-born Americans. About half of children born in the US this year will be nonwhite. And sometime in the 2020s, this country's aging white population, which is reproducing at below replacement levels, will decline not just as a share of the whole, but in absolute numbers (that is, deaths among whites will exceed births, and immigration will not cover the difference). For those who think in terms of Electoral College maps, a state-by-state tour tells the story vividly. Today, just four states are majority nonwhite—California, Texas, New Mexico, and Hawaii. By 2060, according to projections by three of the nation's leading political demographers, 22 states will be majority nonwhite and another 10 will have nonwhite populations of at least 40% (see appendix Figure 1A.4).[22] Now toss all these numbers into your mental blender and set them alongside the two most telling data points from the 2012 presidential campaign: 17% and 88%. The first is the share of nonwhites who voted for Mitt Romney. The second is the share of Romney's vote that came from whites. And ask yourself: Which party has more work to do to adapt to the next America?

CLASS. Here's another pop quiz: Which US senator uttered these words in rebuttal to Obama's 2014 State of the Union address: "Today the United States is beset by a crisis of inequality"? Elizabeth Warren, the liberal darling from Massachusetts? Bernie Sanders, the socialist icon from Vermont? No, it was Mike Lee, the Tea Party stalwart from Utah. And his was just one of many signs of a sea change—in oratory if not ideology—the GOP has undergone on this subject since 2012, when Romney was caught telling guests at a GOP fundraiser that his job was "not to worry about the 47% of Americans" who receive government assistance. As a new presidential campaign gets under way, all major Republican candidates are talking about chronic poverty and a shrinking middle class. Like Lee, they define the problem as inequality of opportunity rather than outcome, and they see government as the problem, not the solution. So there's been no grand partisan coming together on a policy response. But just the fact that there's a consensus that we have a problem is noteworthy in itself. So, too, is the fact that a 2014 Pew Research global survey found that adults in the US and Europe saw income inequality as "the greatest threat to the world," ahead of such stiff competition as religious and ethnic hatred, pollution, nuclear weapons, and AIDS and other diseases.[23] The political salience of this issue has been rising for a simple reason: so has income and wealth inequality. These trends have taken hold all over the world in recent decades, but the US leads the wealth inequality sweepstakes by leaps and bounds among rich countries, with our top 10% now taking in 34% of annual income and owning 75% of the nation's household wealth.[24] The last time our economy produced such lopsided gaps was during the Gilded Era of the late nineteenth century. It led to the Progressive movement of the early twentieth century, with its tough antitrust laws, strong labor unions, redistributive income tax, and alphabet soup of regulatory agencies. Nothing of that magnitude looms on the horizon now. The menu of policy responses has been more measured; nowadays labor unions are weak, and the global and technological forces that have produced this inequality are strong. But the center of gravity in the Democratic Party has been moving left on economic issues in recent years, leading front-runner Clinton to strike more populist chords than she and her husband did back in their "triangulating" years in the 1990s. At the same time, however, the familiar smaller government/lower taxes mantra emanating from most Republicans continues to resonate with a public deeply skeptical that government can make things better. Polls show the public is conflicted on these issues. Large majorities now say our economic system is rigged in favor of the rich, and for the past decade about half of American adults have been telling Gallup that the government should "redistribute wealth by heavy taxes on the rich." From 1940, when Gallup first posed that question, until about 2005, most Americans had opposed that idea.[25] But public support for the most redistributive big policy proposal of the modern era—government-guaranteed health care coverage for all—dropped from 69% in 2006 to 45% in 2014, according to Gallup surveys.[26] In short, the public's new enthusiasm for taxing the rich bumps up against its ongoing skepticism over what the government will do with the money. These cross-currents in public opinion set the stage for what's likely to be a spirited economic policy debate in 2016 and beyond.

Figure 1.11

Public's Views About Why Few Women in Top Jobs

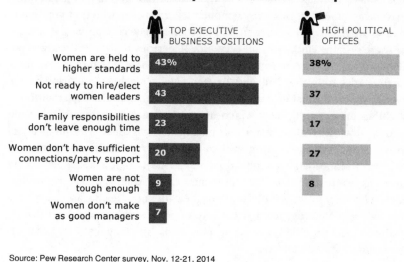

	TOP EXECUTIVE BUSINESS POSITIONS	HIGH POLITICAL OFFICES
Women are held to higher standards	43%	38%
Not ready to hire/elect women leaders	43	37
Family responsibilities don't leave enough time	23	17
Women don't have sufficient connections/party support	20	27
Women are not tough enough	9	8
Women don't make as good managers	7	

Source: Pew Research Center survey, Nov. 12-21, 2014

GENDER. When she first ran for president in 2008, Hillary Clinton chose to downplay the most history-making aspect of her candidacy. This time around, her gender is a—perhaps even *the*—central plank of her platform. No matter how this works out for her in 2016, the tactical shift is of a piece with the steady march of women's empowerment around the world. Just before announcing her candidacy in the spring of 2015, Clinton told a United Nations audience that "there has never been a better time in history to be born female." She was referring mainly to girls in disadvantaged countries who for the first time can get an education, pursue a career, and exercise control over their bodies. But she was also describing the ongoing gender revolution in advanced economies. Today young women in the US are about 25% more likely than their male counterparts to have a college degree, a reversal of gender patterns that had prevailed until a generation ago. They place just as high a value as young men do on career success. Women are the sole or primary breadwinner in 4 in 10 households with minor children, quadruple the share of a generation ago. These transformations have not yet yielded full gender equality. The pay gap has narrowed but persists. And women continue to be underrepresented at the highest levels of politics and business, accounting for only about 1 in 5 members of Congress and just 1 in 20 Fortune 500 CEOs.

Why has the glass ceiling remained so hard to penetrate? The public rejects the explanation that prevailed during the Mad Men era: that women lack leadership traits. Rather, it says the problem is societal and institutional resistance. About 4 in 10 survey respondents say women who try to make it to the top are held to a higher standard than their male counterparts.[27] A similar share says the electorate and corporate America simply aren't ready to put more women in top leadership positions. Only about one in five says these barriers arise from the challenges women face in juggling family and career. Even fewer lay the blame on women's perceived lack of leadership qualities. In fact, the survey found, most Americans find women indistinguishable from men on key leadership traits such as intelligence and capacity for innovation, with many saying they're stronger than men in terms of being compassionate and organized leaders (see appendix Figure 1A.5). There may be better days ahead for women leaders. Fully three-quarters of Americans say they expect to see a woman in the White House in their lifetime. "People are ready for a woman president," says Jennifer Lawless, director of the Women and Politics Institute at American University. The question is: "Are they ready for Hillary as that woman?"[28] We shall see.

CULTURE. Sometimes tipping points arrive in surprising packages. One of the most compelling signals that American culture was on its way to a new normal came in a trio of television ads that aired during the 2014 Super Bowl. A Chevy ad showed a montage of happy families, including one with two dads. A Cheerios ad featured a family with a black father, a white mother, their multiracial daughter, and a baby on the way. A Coke ad had a soundtrack of "America the Beautiful" playing in six different languages as a multicolored array of Americans went about their daily lives. Product advertisers aren't in the business of making political statements. They're certainly not interested in making political enemies, not when each paid $4 million for 30 seconds in front of the biggest audience we assemble each year. All three ads drew backlash in conservative precincts of social and traditional media, some of it quite nasty. The advertisers surely saw this coming; they exhaustively pretest such sensitive ads. Even so, all made the business decision to associate their iconic American brands with our nation's new rainbow of family forms, cultural norms, racial groupings, and sexual identities. The ads foreshadowed big changes not just in culture but in policy. About a year later, there was another telling moment when the legislatures in two conservative states, Indiana and Arkansas, passed religious freedom laws designed to protect vendors who on religious grounds did not want to cater to same-sex weddings. The laws drew the immediate ire of gay rights activists. As their protests mounted, many mainstream corporate pillars, including Walmart, Marriott, and the NCAA, jumped into the fray—but on the side of the gay protesters. Within days, the Republican legislatures in both states backtracked. It's impossible to imagine anything like that happening 10—even 5—years ago. Businesses aren't social change agents, but they do ratify change that's already happened. If Coke, Chevy, Cheerios, Walmart, and Marriott are ready to cast their lot with the next America, the change has already happened. And it's happened in other countries too—witness the 2015 vote in overwhelmingly Catholic Ireland, when by a 62%–38% margin, that country became the first in the world to legalize same-sex marriage via referendum. The sweep and speed of these cultural shifts have been disorienting for many conservatives. As he watched the popular media applaud the gender transition of Olympic champion Bruce Jenner into Caitlyn Jenner, former Reagan administration education secretary and drug czar William Bennett lamented in a 2015 *Washington Post* interview that "people feel like they're under siege and that the terms of the debate are now that you either applaud it or you're a bigot. . . . It's like American culture is being dragged kicking and screaming not only toward acceptance but approval."[29] A few weeks later, in a dramatic confluence of events, rainbow banners were raised across the country on the same day Confederate battle flags started to come down across the South in response to a Supreme Court ruling on same-sex marriage and a massacre by a white supremacist that left 9 dead at a black church in Charleston, South Carolina. Once again, the business community was on the side of change. Some 379 corporations, including many in the Fortune 500, had filed amicus briefs with the Court in support of same-sex marriage. And the move to lower the Confederate flag was led not just by southern politicians, but by the likes of NASCAR and Amazon. These cultural shifts challenge deeply held values among many older, conservative, religious Americans who are a key part of the GOP base. But Bennett is correct—the ground beneath them has moved. And as more and more Republican leaders have begun to acknowledge, if their national candidates want to wage winning campaigns in the next America, they'll have to find a way to honor their traditional values as they open their hearts and minds to the new realities.

ENDURING STRENGTHS

Alexis de Tocqueville was the first to observe nearly 200 years ago that American democracy isn't as fragile as it looks; confusion on the surface masks underlying strengths. On that hopeful note, let's close this opening chapter not by despairing over our hyperpartisanship, but by celebrating the contributions our changing demography can make to our nation's future—if we let it.

Some 43 million foreigners have settled in the United States since we reopened our borders in 1965. Unlike earlier immigration waves that were almost entirely white, this one has been almost entirely nonwhite. The immigrants arriving from Latin America, Asia, Africa, Europe, the Caribbean, and the Middle East are reweaving our racial tapestry into a coat of many colors. Yes, they've contributed to some of the generational and cultural gaps that bedevil our politics and test our social cohesion. The fact that a quarter are living here illegally is an affront to our laws and borders. But as was the case with previous immigration waves, these 43 million newcomers and their children have been rejuvenating our economy. And in a world made smaller by the information revolution, they're deepening our ties of blood and culture to people on every continent of the globe. America is still the world's big dog, making us an object of envy and target of terrorism. Our growing diversity holds out the prospect of mitigating some of those tensions.

Demography isn't the only reason to see our glass half full. We inhabit what's still the world's most enviable slab of real estate, with friendly neighbors north and south, protective oceans east and west, a bounty of energy sources above and below, and a sea-to-shining-sea cornucopia of deep-water ports, navigable rivers, and arable land. These competitive advantages are enhanced by a culture of democratic capitalism that rewards innovation, entrepreneurship, individualism, adaptability, speed, and hard work. It's no accident that most of the major technological and commercial breakthroughs of the digital era have happened on American soil, which, not incidentally, is also home to the world's preeminent (if often reviled) popular culture.

Yet it's easy to lose sight of these assets at a time when our middle class has shrunk, our upward mobility has stalled, our political system has gridlocked, and our sense of mastery over global affairs has diminished. You have to go all the way back to 2004 to find the last time a majority of Americans said the country is heading in the right direction, making these past dozen years the longest stretch of national discontent since the onset of polling.

For most of our history, the American Dream—the idea that everyone here can climb as high as their brains, talent, and drive will take them—has exerted a tug on the imaginations of strivers the world over. Unfortunately the data now describe a different reality.[30] These days if you're born near the bottom, you have a better chance of climbing the ladder of opportunity in Canada and much of Europe than you have here. An updated rendition of the American Dream might go as follows: Choose your parents wisely. The richer they are, the richer you're likely to be.

This isn't a story we enjoy telling ourselves, much less anyone else. For America to prosper in an age of sweeping demographic change, we'll need to find new ways to provide economic opportunity for the young, who've become our most vulnerable generation. And we'll have to do this at a time when young and old don't look alike, which makes the politics more daunting. There

Figure 1.12

For Americans, Hard Work Seen as the Path to Success

Percent who say it is very important ("10" on a 0-10 scale) to work hard to get ahead in life

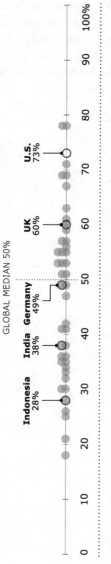

GLOBAL MEDIAN 50%

Percent who disagree that success in life is pretty much determined by forces outside our control

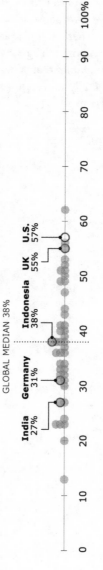

GLOBAL MEDIAN 38%

Source: Pew Research Center survey, 2014

are Red and Blue ways to take up this challenge; that's why we hold elections. The one thing we can't afford is to ignore it. An ancient proverb says societies become great when old men plant trees whose shade they know they will never sit under. Across the ages, we've been a nation of planters. Lately, not so much. Today the inheritance we're leaving future generations increasingly consists of unpaid bills and an unsustainable social safety net. Down this path lies a lesser America.

2

Demographic Destinies

D EMOGRAPHIC TRANSFORMATIONS are dramas in slow motion. They unfold incrementally, almost imperceptibly, tick by tock, without trumpets or press conferences. But every so often, as the weight of change builds, a society takes a hard look at itself and notices that things are different. These "aha" moments are rare and revealing. One occurred on November 6, 2012, the night of President Barack Obama's reelection victory in a campaign that, given the political headwinds stirred by four years of high unemployment, he had every reason to lose.

Instead he won, and rather handily, an outcome that caught a lot of smart pundits and pols by surprise. Republican operative Karl Rove succumbed to a live, on-air mini-meltdown on Fox News that night when he couldn't bring himself to accept the finality of the people's verdict. Michael Barone, the conservative analyst and longtime coauthor of the *Almanac of American Politics*, who probably knows more than anyone else alive about voting patterns down to the county and precinct level, had only a few days earlier predicted an Electoral College landslide for Mitt Romney. So had George Will, the eminence gris of the op-ed pages. As the scope of the Obama victory sunk in, three of the most animated conservative voices in the media—Dick Morris, Bill O'Reilly, and Rush Limbaugh—drew the same conclusion. "This is not your father's United States. This is a United States with a permanently high turnout of blacks, Latinos, and young people," said Morris, who had also forecast a Romney blowout. "The white establishment is now the minority," said O'Reilly. "We're outnumbered," said Limbaugh.

Their demography-is-destiny despair arose from some pretty compelling arithmetic. Had the election been held only among voters ages 30 and older, Romney would have won by 2 million votes instead of losing by 5 million. Had it been held only among men, he would have won by 4 million votes. Had it been held only among whites, he would have won by 18 million votes. Romney carried the white vote by the identical 20 percentage-point landslide that George H. W. Bush had run up among whites a generation earlier. That haul netted the elder Bush 426 Electoral College votes in 1988 and Romney just 206 in 2012. So in the 24 years separating those two elections, whites lost more than half of their Electoral C ollege clout. Aha.

The voters in 2012 were the most racially and ethnically diverse in our nation's history, a trend driven mainly by the tens of millions of Hispanic and Asian immigrants (and their children) who've come across our borders in the past half century and are now showing up at our polling places. But this new multihued electorate is actually a *lagging* indicator of the nation's demographic transformation. In 2012 some 26% of voters were nonwhite—a record—but so was 37% of the population as a whole. Even with their turnout gains, nonwhites still punch well below their weight on Election Day. Many are still too young to vote, many aren't citizens, and many aren't politically engaged. Over time, a mix of demographic and behavioral change is likely to shrink all of these deficits. The US Census Bureau projects that nonwhites will become the majority of the US population in 2044, and by that time, it's a good bet that their voter participation will have closed the gap with their population count.[1]

Romney captured just 17% of the nonwhite vote in 2012, leading one wag to refer to the GOP as the "pale, male, and stale" party, and the Republican leadership itself, in a notably blunt official postelection autopsy, to acknowledge that it too often appears to be a "narrow-minded" collection of "stuffy old men." Elder statesman Bob Dole weighed in with a suggestion that his party hang a "closed for repairs" sign on its front door, and former Florida governor Jeb Bush lamented, "Way too many people believe Republicans are anti-immigrant, anti-woman, anti-science, anti-gay, and the list goes on and on."

The GOP's demographic predicament calls to mind German playwright Bertolt Brecht's puckish advice to his government when it faced similar troubles: dissolve the public and elect a replacement. Political parties can't fire the voters, of course, so they adapt—or try to. Ever since the electoral shock of 2012, Republicans have been engaged in an intraparty civil war, which reached a fever pitch when their congressional Tea Party faction shut down the government for 16 days in the fall of 2013 in an unsuccessful bid to defund Obama's

Figure 2.1

The Changing Face of America, 1965–2065

% of the total population

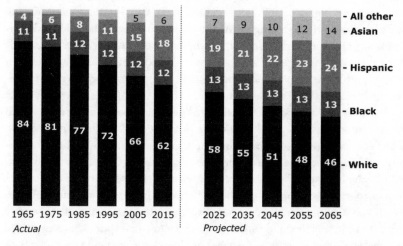

Note: Data labels not shown if less than 4%. Whites, blacks and Asians include only single-race non-Hispanics; Asians include Pacific Islanders. Hispanics can be of any race. Other races and two-or-more races shown but not labeled.

Source: See 2015 Pew Research Center report, "Modern Immigration Wave Brings 59 Million to US, Driving Population Growth and Change Through 2065"

signature legislative accomplishment, the Affordable Care Act. The GOP needs to get past this destructive infighting, and if it wishes to be a party that is competitive in future presidential elections, it also needs to figure out how to become more appealing to the nation's newly diverse electorate. In the meantime, if history is a guide, the demographically ascendant Democrats—now winners of the popular vote in five of the last six presidential elections—have no guarantee of smooth waters ahead. They may find themselves hurt by having to dispense harsh medicine in an age of austerity. They may discover their multiracial base has fissures. Or that ongoing public skepticism about Obamacare creates turbulence for their candidates for years to come. The most reliable rule of American politics is that nothing is static. The pendulum swings.

This book will keep an eye on these partisan dynamics, but its main ambition lies elsewhere. Using a generational frame, it aims to illuminate the demographic, economic, social, cultural, and technological changes that are remaking not just our politics but our families, livelihoods, relationships, and identities. These shifts have left no realm of society untouched. As a people, we're growing older, more unequal, more diverse, more mixed race, more digitally linked, more tolerant, less married, less fertile, less religious, less mobile, and less confident. Our political and media institutions have become more polarized and partisan; so has the public itself. Our economy is producing more low-wage and high-wage jobs, but fewer in between. Our middle class is shrinking. Our median household income has flatlined. Our social class divisions are wider than they've been since the Gilded Age. Wealth gaps between young and old are at levels never before seen in modern times; so are the economic divides between whites, blacks, and Hispanics, and so, of course, is the gap between rich and poor. Our neighborhoods have become more integrated by race but more segregated by income. And more sorted by party. Women have become more economically independent, men less. Gender roles are converging, both at work and at home. Marriage is in decline. The nuclear family is losing its pride of place. The fastest-growing household type in America contains just one person. Not far behind are multigenerational households, in which two or more adult generations live under the same roof, often because that's the only way to make ends meet. Some 4 in 10 newborns have an unwed mother. Half are nonwhite. A teenager has less chance of being raised by both biological parents in America than anywhere else in the world. Young adults are taking longer to grow up, the middle-aged longer to grow old, and the elderly longer to depart this vale of tears. Biases against minorities and gays are diminishing. Today's immigrants—nearly 9 in 10 of whom are not Europeans—look very different from the previous waves of settlers and immigrants who created America. But when it comes to embracing what we think of as traditional American values, it's hard to find more fervent devotees.

Some of these changes are for the better, some for the worse—and some people no doubt will differ over which is which. Most are mutually reinforcing. And all, in one way or another, will have an impact on the immense national challenge that's the central focus of this book: namely, as our population ages, how do we keep our promises to the old without bankrupting the young and starving the future? When we built the social safety net in the twentieth century, the math was easier. We had more workers per retiree, fewer people living to be very old, an economy that seemed to generate new jobs on autopilot, and health care costs that hadn't escalated beyond control. The politics were easier, too. Back then, except for the gray hair and crow's-feet, young and old pretty much looked and thought alike. No more. Our older generation is predominantly white, our younger generation increasingly nonwhite. They have different political philosophies, social views, and policy preferences, as they made clear in 2008 and 2012, when the young-old voting gaps were the widest on record. Many of the young are big-government liberals; most of the old are small-government conservatives (but hands off Social Security and Medicare!). The young are comfortable with the dizzying array of new lifestyles, family forms, and technologies that have made the start of the twenty-first century such a distinctive moment in human history; the old for the most part are disoriented by them. The young are the least religiously connected generation in modern American history; the old are the most devout believers in the industrialized world. The young have been starting their working and taxpaying lives in the worst economy since the Great Depression; the old are finishing theirs off having run up more than $18 trillion in government IOUs that their children and grandchildren will spend their lives paying off. "Mugging Our Descendants" is how a headline on a George Will column toted up the math.

It sounds like the script for a fiscal horror flick, pitting parent against child in offices, hospitals, legislatures, and homes. In the concluding chapter, I'll argue that the drama doesn't have to end in tragedy. If the generations bring to the public square the same genius for interdependence they bring to their family lives, the policy choices become less daunting and the politics less toxic. But this optimistic scenario is by no means preordained. Social Security and Medicare are the most popular, successful domestic programs the federal government ever created. They are a profound expression of the idea that as a nation, we are a community, all in this together. For the best and most compassionate reasons, Americans of all ages oppose reducing benefits to the elderly. Yet as our population grows older and these programs consume an ever larger share of our federal budget, they pose increasingly difficult questions of generational equity. Today's young are paying taxes to support a level of benefits for today's old that they themselves have no realistic chance of receiving when *they* become old. Meantime, the cost of these programs is crowding out investments in the economic vitality of the next generation—and the entire nation. Rebalancing the entitlement programs to adapt to the demographic realities of the twenty-first century will be a massive political challenge. Even more, it will be a test of social cohesion at a time when our generations are divided by race, politics, values, religion, and technology to a degree that's rare in our history.

The story is best told through the prism of the two big generations with competing interests: the Baby Boomers, who'll be crashing through the gates of old age in record numbers for the next two decades, not nearly as well fortified financially for the journey as they'd hoped; and the Millennials, twenty-somethings who have landed back in their childhood homes in record numbers because they haven't been able to get launched in a hostile economy. In the pages ahead, you'll also meet the Gen Xers, who are navigating middle age with mounting economic anxieties about their own old age; and the

Silents, the oldest and most financially secure of our four adult generations, but also the cohort most unsettled by the pace and magnitude of social change.

LONGER LIVES, FEWER BABIES, MORE IMMIGRANTS

The fundamentals of our demography are these: in 2016, about 4 million Americans will be born, roughly 1 million will arrive as immigrants, and about 2.5 million will die. "Generational replacement" is the demographer's term of art for the population change produced by this churn. In some eras the process can be relatively uneventful, but not so in the America of the early twenty-first century, when young and old are so different from each other. Of the myriad forces that bear on these numbers, none has been more inexorable or important than the rise in human longevity. Advances in health care, nutrition, and sanitation have increased life expectancy at birth in the US from 47 years in 1900 to 62 years in 1935 (the year Social Security was enacted) to 79 today to a projected 84.5 by 2050. In the first part of the twentieth century, most of the gains came as a result of improvements in the survival rate of newborns; in the second half, most gains came from medical advances that have prolonged the lives of older adults. And there's more to come. While it sounds like the stuff of science fiction, some biomedical researchers believe that by midcentury, bionic bodies embedded with computer chips and fortified by as-yet-uninvented medications will make life spans of 120 or more years attainable, perhaps even commonplace. If so, just imagine the quality-of-life issues—to say nothing of the retirement finances!—that future generations will need to sort out.

Longer life spans beget lower birthrates. As living standards improve and people grow more confident that their children will survive to adulthood, succeeding generations reduce the number of children they have. In the twentieth century, the world's population grew by nearly fourfold. In this century, however, it is expected to grow only by about 80% before eventually stabilizing at roughly 11 billion.[2] Over the long haul, this is good news for all who worry about the sustainability of the earth's resources. But in the short and medium term, it can create social, economic, and political dislocations, especially in countries like the US that have large cohorts entering old age and smaller cohorts in the workforce. However, all of our biggest economic competitors face even more challenging age pyramids. China's median age will rise from 35 now to 46 by 2050, surpassing the projected median of 41 in the US. Germany's will be 52. And in Japan, where birthrates have been among the lowest in human history for the past generation, the market for adult diapers now exceeds the market for baby diapers. Japan's median age will be 53 by 2050. If present trends continue, there won't be nearly enough Japanese youngsters to care for its oldsters, which helps explain why Japan is the global leader these days in the development and manufacture of caretaker robots.

Globally, the number of people age 60 and older is expected to double by 2050 and triple by 2100, according to a 2015 projection by the United Nations. One way for nations to prevent the economic sclerosis that can occur when their populations age is to replenish their workforce with immigrants. In this realm, the US boasts the world's most enviable demographics. The third great wave of immigration to the US, which began when Congress reopened America's doors in 1965, has brought 59 million new immigrants to our country in the past half century. A record 43 million immigrants are still here (the others have since died or emigrated). With less than 5% of the world's population, the US is now home to about 20% of the worlds' immigrants—4 times more than any other country. Since 1965, new immigrants and their descendants have accounted for more than half of the overall US population growth. And if current trends continue, from now through 2065, future immigrants and their descendants will account for 88% of our population growth and all of our labor force growth. Immigration waves always produce political and cultural backlashes; this one has been no exception, especially since about a quarter of the modern-era immigrants are living here illegally. As columnist Fred Barnes has written, we have a history of hating immigrants before we love them.[3] But no nation has been better served than ours by immigration, and judging by the tens of millions of people from all over the world still clambering to come here, there's every reason to expect our long winning streak to continue.

RACE AND RELIGION

The modern immigration wave has done more than boost our economy. It has given us a racial makeover. Until the middle of the last century, our racial checkerboard was white with a smattering of black. Now it's multicolored, and whites are on a long, steep slide toward losing their majority status. Moreover, in today's America, our old racial labels are having trouble keeping up with our new weddings. About a quarter of all recent Hispanic and Asian newlyweds married someone of a different race or ethnicity; so did 1 in 5 black and 1 in 10 white newlyweds. Not too long ago these marriages were illegal and taboo; now they barely raise an eyebrow. As these couples procreate, what race will society call their children? What will the children call themselves? For centuries we've used the "one-drop rule" to settle such questions—if you're not all white, you're not white at all. Going forward, we'll need a more nuanced taxonomy. America isn't about to go color-blind; race is too hardwired into the human psyche. But race is becoming more subtle and shaded, and most Americans (especially the young) are at ease with the change.

As noted, the new rainbow America has had a big impact on presidential politics. There's an interesting history here. After he lost the Hispanic vote in 1980, Ronald Reagan described Hispanics as "Republicans who don't know it yet." Three decades later they apparently *still* haven't figured it out. To the contrary, they've grown even more Democratic. In 2012, 71% voted for Obama (up from the 56% who voted for Jimmy Carter over Reagan in 1980), as did a record 73% of Asian Americans. Block voting is nothing new among minority groups in America; blacks have supported Democrats by even more lopsided margins for generations. But these new patterns are ominous for the GOP. Hispanics and Asians today comprise 24% of the US population; by 2065 they will make up nearly 40% (while blacks will remain constant at about 13%). They embrace values common to immigrant groups—they're hardworking, family-oriented, entrepreneurial, and freedom loving—all of which, as Reagan rightly observed, could easily make them natural Republicans. Yet they also favor an active government and tend to be social liberals. And many have been put off by the anti-immigrant rhetoric of the GOP in recent years. "If we want people to like us, we have to like them first," said Bobby Jindal, the Indian-American Republican governor of Louisiana, after the 2012 election. The growing partisan divisions by race and ethnicity coincide with the growing schisms by ideology and age. These deep divisions aren't healthy for the polity; they're especially perilous for the Republicans, who find themselves on the wrong side of the new demography.

Race isn't the only demographic characteristic changing before our eyes. Religion is another. In 2012, for the first time ever, not one of the four major party candidates for president and vice president was a white Anglo-Saxon Protestant (one was black, one Mormon, two Catholic). Nor was the Speaker of the House (Catholic), the majority leader of the Senate (Mormon), or any of the nine Justices of the US Supreme Court (six Catholics, three Jews). WASP dominance of our nation's political institutions pretty much peaked at the opening bell in 1776, when 55 of the 56 signers of the Declaration of Independence were white Protestants. It has been falling ever since, and the pace of decline has ramped up in the half century since John F. Kennedy became the first non-WASP president in 1960 and Congress was still three-quarters Protestant (as opposed to 56% now). Like its leaders, the public has also become less Protestant (47%) and less Christian (71%), both record lows. Americans have also become less religious across the board, with 23% of all adults, and more than a third of all Millennials, now saying they are not affiliated with any religion at all. Of these so-called nones, roughly a quarter describe themselves as atheists or agnostics; the remainder believe in God but have no religious affiliation. The US is still the most religiously observant nation among the world's great powers. But led by today's young, it's growing more pluralistic and less connected to traditional religious institutions.

A HOLLOWING OF THE MIDDLE

For the past decade and a half, America's middle class has suffered its worst economic run since the Great Depression. It has shrunk in size, fallen backward in income and wealth, and shed some—but by no means all—of its characteristic faith in the future.[4] Median household income in this country peaked in 1999 and still hasn't returned to that level, the longest stretch of stagnation in modern American history. As for median household wealth—the sum of all assets minus all debt—it has fallen by more than a third since peaking at the height of the housing bubble in 2006. Not surprisingly, an overwhelming share of Americans—85%—say it has become tougher to live a middle-class lifestyle than it was a decade ago. Yet most middle-class Americans say they have a better standard of living than their parents had at the same stage of life (the economic data bear them out) and a plurality expect their children will do even better than they did. The trademark optimism of the American middle class may not be as robust as it was a decade ago, but it hasn't disappeared. It may, however, not be as well founded as it used to be.

This hollowing out of the middle has been accompanied by a sharp rise in income inequality. One standard measure is known as the Gini Index, which ranges from 0 to 1, with 0 representing perfect equality (everyone has equal income) and 1 perfect inequality (one person has all the income). In the US, the index rose to .481 in 2013 (the latest year for which such data are available) from .403 in 1980, an increase of 19%.[5] On the global scale, this means we're not as unequal as many African and South American countries, but we're more unequal than most European and Asian nations. We still think of ourselves as the land of opportunity, but a child born into poverty in Canada and most Western European countries has a statistically better chance of making it to the top these days than does a poor kid in the US.[6] The two decades after World War II were a period of declining inequality in the US—all income groups did well, but in relative terms, those at the bottom did best. Since then, all groups have done less well, and in relative terms, those at the top have done best.

Moreover, when one looks at wealth rather than income, the gaps since the 1980s have ballooned into chasms and are starkly aligned with race and age. As of 2013, the typical white household had 13 times the wealth of the typical black household (up from 8 times in 1983) and the typical older household had 20 times the wealth of the typical younger household (up from 8 times in 1983).[7] There's little evidence from public opinion surveys that Americans

Figure 2.2

Average Annual Change in Mean Family Income, 1950–2010

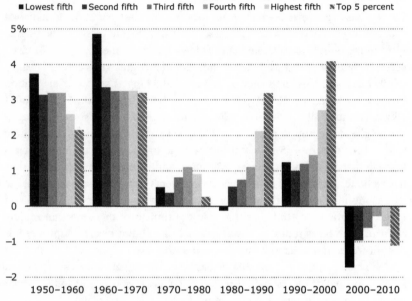

■Lowest fifth ■Second fifth ■Third fifth ■Fourth fifth ░Highest fifth ◣Top 5 percent

Source: Pew Research Center analysis of US Census Bureau, Historical Family Income Tables,
Table F-3 for 1966 to 2010, and derived from Tables F-2 and F-7 for 1950 to 1965

resent the rich. But in growing numbers, they resent the policies and institutions—political as well as economic—that they believe are rigged in favor of the rich.

The rise in inequality is driven in large measure by a workforce that has begun to resemble an hourglass—bulging at the top and bottom, contracting in the middle. The leading culprit is technology. Whole categories of good-paying midlevel white- and blue-collar jobs have been wiped out in recent decades, first by computers and more recently by robots. "The factory of the future will have just two workers," goes the gallows humor in manufacturing towns. "A man and a dog. The man is there to feed the dog. The dog is there to make sure the man keeps his hands off the equipment." This pessimism may prove overwrought. Over time, technological revolutions typically create more jobs than they destroy, and in a 2013 paper, economists Frank Levy and Richard

Murnane counted 3.5 million jobs—software engineers, systems analysts, data experts, and so on—created by computer technology. Most, however, demand more advanced skills and training than the middle-level jobs they replace. In America the key to preserving social and civic cohesion among a diverse population is a dynamic economy that offers plenty of work for a sprawling middle class, with lots of on-ramps from below. Today there are fewer such jobs and on-ramps. At least so far, the digital revolution has left the middle class in worse shape than it found it.

CULTURE, GENDER, MARRIAGE, FAMILY

When the Baby Boomers came of age with a great primal scream of social protest in the 1960s, the electoral backlash was immediate and enduring. In 1968 Richard Nixon won the presidency as the champion of the "silent majority"—by which he meant all the folks who *weren't* protesting. In 1972 he was reelected in a landslide over a Democratic opponent he mocked as the candidate of "acid, amnesty, and abortion." In the ensuing decades the GOP's most effective alliterative attack lines migrated a few notches down the alphabet—to god, guns, and gays—but the basic political calculus never changed. Whenever culture wars flared, Republicans profited—that is, until 2012. In that election

Figure 2.3

Views of Legalizing Marijuana: 1969–2015

% saying marijuana should be ...

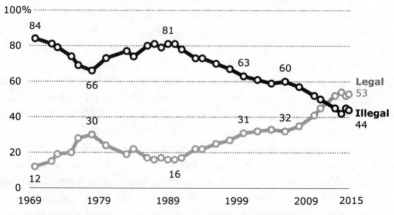

Source: Pew Research Center surveys, 2010–2015; 1973–2008 data from General Social Survey; 1969 and 1972 data from Gallup

year, gay marriage state ballot initiatives, after having gone 0 for 32 during the previous decade, went 4 for 4. Also, voters in Washington and Colorado became the first to legalize the recreational use of marijuana. And in Missouri and Indiana, Republican candidates lost eminently winnable US Senate races because of their tone-deaf remarks about rape and women's reproductive rights. Then in 2015, the US Supreme Court issued the landmark ruling that gave same-sex couples a constitutionally protected right to marry.

To be sure, not all fronts of the culture wars have moved as decisively to the left. More than four decades after the Court's *Roe v. Wade* decision that affirmed a woman's right to choose, abortion remains a fiercely contested issue in states, many of which have enacted restrictive legislation in recent years. However, there's an important generational difference in the politics of these culture-war issues. With abortion, young and old are each divided roughly evenly, pro and con, in their policy views. The same is true for gun control, which is one reason the massacres of schoolchildren in Newtown, Connecticut, and churchgoers in Charleston, South Carolina—horrific as they were—did not generate a sufficient public outcry to build a consensus for new legislation. But when it comes to same-sex marriage, the young are overwhelmingly supportive while the old remain opposed, though they are becoming less so. And even as these cultural issues continue to play out differently in different regions and among different generations, the overall trends in public opinion have put conservatives on notice. As younger adults age into the electorate and older adults age out, the old wedge issues simply don't work the way they once did. "It's not that our message didn't get out," R. Albert Mohler Jr., president of the Southern Baptist Theological Seminary, told the *New York Times* a few days after the 2012 election. "It did get out. It's that the entire moral landscape has changed. An increasingly secularized America understands our positions, and has rejected them."[8]

One casualty of the new economic and cultural order has been traditional marriage, which has suffered a dramatic loss of market share. In 1960, 72% of all adults ages 18 and older were married; by 2013, just 50% were. In the old days, people in all social classes married at roughly the same rate; today marriage is much less prevalent at the bottom than at the top. Pew Research surveys find that adults on the lower rungs are just as likely as others to say they want to marry, but they place a higher premium than others on economic security as a precondition for marriage—a threshold they themselves are unable to cross. These attitudes are self-fulfilling. Marriage brings economies of scale and a heightened commitment to financial responsibility, which means that the growing marriage deficit among poorer adults both reflects and reinforces their growing income deficits. This is worrisome for society. A large body of social science research shows that children born to single parents tend to have a more difficult path in life, even when one holds constant other socio-economic factors.[9] The same holds for elderly adults who don't have a close relationship with their children.

As marriage has declined, gender roles have converged. Today women are the sole or primary breadwinners in 4 in 10 households with children; a half century ago, this was the case in just 1 in 10 such households. A majority of these "breadwinner moms" are unmarried, but a significant share (37%) are wives who earn more than their husbands. Men are having a tougher time than women adjusting to the demands of the modern knowledge-based economy, and it shows in the way they rank their life priorities. A 2011 Pew Research poll found that 66% of young women say that being successful in a high-paying career or profession is a very important life priority for them. That number may not seem remarkable, except for this: just 59% of young men said the same.

This reversal of traditional gender aspirations comes at a time when nearly 6 in 10 college and graduate students are female; nearly half the labor force is female; and working fathers are just as likely as working mothers to say they find it difficult to balance work and family—and more likely to say they don't spend enough time with the kids. The public overwhelmingly supports the trend toward more women in the workforce and more egalitarian marriages. Nonetheless, Americans are cross-pressured on these topics, and many traditional gender norms endure. For example, a 2013 Pew Research survey found that about half of respondents say that children are better off if the mother stays at home and doesn't hold a job, while just 8% say the same about the father. Also, twice as many Americans say it is very important for a prospective husband to be a good provider as say the same about a prospective wife.[10]

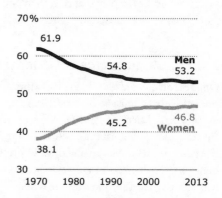

Figure 2.4

Women and Men Approach Parity in Labor Force

Share of labor force that is men, women, 1970–2013

Note: Annual averages based on civilian noninstitutional population age 16 and older. For changes to the Current Population Survey (CPS) over time, see www.bls.gov/cps/eetech_methods.pdf.

Source: Pew Research Center analysis of US Bureau of Labor Statistics, "Women in the Labor Force: A Databook," Table 2, Dec. 2014

In sync with those norms, the decline of marriage has been greatest in the communities where women have the greatest potential to outearn men. For example, fewer than a third of black adults today are married, down from 61% in 1960. As men and women navigate a brave new world of gender convergence, it's not clear how well the institution of marriage will survive.

Families and living arrangements have changed, too. Nearly 3 in 10 households in America today contain just one person, double the share in 1960. Among American women in their early 40s, 15% have never had children, a number 50% higher than the share of women roughly 40 years ago who were childless. A 2013 memoir by comedian Jen Kirkman, *I Can Barely Take Care of Myself: Tales from a Happy Life Without Kids*, serves up an amusing string of anecdotes from the front lines of childlessness. ("Who'll take care of you when you're old?" "Servants!") Demographer Joel Kotkin has coined the term "post-familialism"; others talk about "the new singleism." It's a global phenomenon, having taken root not just in the US but in Canada, much of Europe, and the wealthy countries of East Asia. It's linked to urbanization, secularism, women's economic empowerment, and higher standards of living. There's a lively debate among cultural arbiters over whether it will deliver more or less happiness over the long haul for the people who make these choices. Clearly, though, it poses a dilemma for humankind as a whole. Societies with fewer young people tend to have less energy, dynamism, and innovation. Societies dominated by the old risk becoming sclerotic. The old require the care of the young. If fewer people form families to play that role, then governments will need to fill more of the gap—but this is a burden they already struggle to bear.

POLARIZED POLITICS, PARTISAN MEDIA

One reason elected leaders keep postponing their rendezvous with entitlement reform is that the issue is so partisan and divisive. These days, of course, so is our entire political system. There's no evidence from decades of Pew Research surveys that public opinion, in the aggregate, is more extreme now than in the past. But what *has* changed—and pretty dramatically—is the growing tendency of people to sort themselves into political parties based on their ideological differences. There was a time when our big-tent political parties had room for elected officials who were liberal Republicans and conservative Democrats; nowadays, such political moderates are all but extinct. There are many causes of this political "big sort"—among them the growing tendency of people to live in economically, culturally, and politically segregated neighborhoods; the proliferation of safe-seat congressional gerrymandering; and the rise of a partisan amen chorus in the news media and twittersphere. There's also one unmistakable consequence: government gridlock. The two most recent sessions of Congress have by several measures been the most politically polarized and least productive in modern history, as members (especially Republicans, with their Tea Party base) worried more about staving off ideological challengers from within their own parties than about forging bipartisan compromises across the aisle.[11]

RED TRUTH, BLUE TRUTH. Republicans and Democrats have always had different opinions, but these days they also seem to have different facts. Pew Research surveys in recent years have found a growing partisan gap within the public on such empirical questions as whether the world's climate is getting warmer, whether the national economy has been getting better, whether one's personal finances are improving, and whether the wars in Iraq and Afghanistan were going well.[12] Perception gaps are as ancient as the shadows on the wall of Plato's famous cave. But lately they've taken on an explicitly partisan cast—a development fueled by a change in the norms of journalism, from an era when neutral fact-based reporting was the highest calling to one in which the brightest stars in the media firmament are paid to deliver their facts premixed with partisan commentary. Why were so many smart conservative pundits flummoxed by the outcome of the 2012 election? Perhaps because they'd spent so much time during that campaign in today's version of Plato's cave, trading their "facts" back and forth in a media-saturated echo chamber of think-alike colleagues, readers, tweeters, and viewers. But to be clear, this occupational hazard isn't confined to Red Truthers. A content analysis done in late 2012 by my colleagues at the Pew Research Center's Journalism Project found that MSNBC outdid Fox News by a considerable margin in the share of its news content that was commentary rather than straight news reporting—85% versus 55%. It just so happened that, at least in 2012, the Blue crystal balls had a better grip on reality than the Red ones.

All these data points and trends, squeezed between the covers of one book, can create a sense of foreboding about America's future. They portray a society tugged apart by centrifugal forces. And they show that the two institutions we rely on to be repairers of the breach—the government and the family—are themselves being shaken to their core. Yet this isn't a gloom-and-doom book. There are too many findings from the Pew Research Center's surveys that give voice to the optimism, pragmatism, and resilience of the American public, even in the teeth of dysfunctional politics, rising inequality, frayed families, and anemic labor markets. America *isn't* breaking apart at the seams. The American Dream isn't dying. Our new racial and ethnic complexion hasn't triggered massive outbreaks of intolerance. Our generations aren't at each other's throats. They're living more interdependently than at any time in recent memory, because that turns out to be a good coping strategy in hard times. Our nation faces huge challenges, no doubt. So do the rest of the world's aging economic powers. If you had to pick a nation with the right stuff to ride out the coming demographic storm, you'd be crazy not to choose America, warts and all.

3

Millennials and Boomers

MILLENNIALS AND BOOMERS are the lead characters in the looming generational showdown by dint of their vast number and strategic location in the life cycle. But what gives the drama an almost Shakespearean richness is something more: they're also each other's children and parents, bound together in an intricate web of love, support, anxiety, resentment, and interdependence. Every family, on some level, is a barter between the generations—I care for you when you're young so you'll care for me when I'm old. Every society needs to strike a similar intergenerational compact, then renegotiate the terms if the underlying demographics shift.

That's the challenge ahead. To understand it better, and to explore how these dynamics will play out in both the family and public realms, let's start by concocting a prototypical Boomer. We'll call her Jane Smith. She turned 65 in 2014, one of 10,000 members of the jumbo-sized Baby Boom Generation who'll cross that threshold *every single day* from now until 2030. If the actuaries have her pegged right, Jane's got 20 more years ahead, most of them in good health, during which time she'll collect about half a million dollars' worth of benefits from Social Security and Medicare. Like most people her age, Jane worries about her health, her finances, and her family. But thanks to these programs, she can take comfort in knowing she'll never be penniless in her old age. She'll never fully "outlive her money." She'll never go completely without medical care. And she has a good chance of never becoming a burden to her children and grandchildren. People don't measure their lives in the vast sweep of history—they live in the here and now—so Jane probably doesn't have much occasion to dwell on her good fortune. She might even assume this is what getting old has always been like. She would be wrong. In fact, she and her progeny are the beneficiaries of a radical improvement in old age that's not much older than she is: a publicly financed social safety net that eases some (though by no means all) of the frets and dreads of the golden years.

Of course, nothing in life is free. Some back-of-the-envelope calculations show just who'll be picking up the roughly $500,000 public tab for Jane's old age. During the more than 35 years she worked in various clerical jobs and earned the median wage, Jane paid the equivalent of about $180,000 in Social Security and Medicare taxes, and her employers matched that with another $180,000 (though, by standard economic theory, that share also came out of Jane's pocket in foregone wages). As for the unfunded gap of about $140,000, well, that'll have to be covered by America's taxpayers, today's and tomorrow's.[1]

As it happens, one of them is Jane's youngest child, John Jr., 31. Junior had the bad timing to start his work life just as the national economy went into a tailspin. After bouncing in and out of a run of low-wage, dead-end jobs, he's scraping together a living as a freelance website designer. In 2016 he'll take in about $22,000. Thanks to the deductions he qualifies for, Junior will owe no federal income taxes. Not a penny will come out of his pocket to pay for the nation's soldiers, veterans, food safety inspectors, border patrol agents, diplomats, spies, or cancer researchers. However, Junior *will* have to fork over more than $3,300 in Social Security and Medicare taxes this year to help underwrite the social safety net that he hopes will one day support him in his old age—but that for now supports his mother and the more than 40 million other beneficiaries her age and older.

In his own small way, then, Junior is helping to bankroll Mom. But that's only half their story. Mom is also bankrolling Junior. He boomeranged back to her home four years ago, when the mortgage insurance company where he'd been working as an appraiser's assistant succumbed to the housing bust. He's now living rent-free in his childhood bedroom, amid his faded soccer ribbons, creaky PlayStation, and zany graduation-day photos. This wasn't Plan A, but it has been a pretty useful Plan B. He gets along fine with Mom, even better now than when he was growing up. The refrigerator is stocked, the laundry service free. Plus, he's fortified by an almost eerie certitude that he'll eventually land a good job, launch a career, move into his own place, find a wife, and start a family. In short, all of Junior's dreams are still intact—but on hold.

Had he come of age a generation earlier, it would have been considered strange for Junior to be hunkering down at his mom's home at this stage of life. Nowadays, there's barely a stigma. Thirty percent of all men ages 18 to 34 (and 22% of all young women that age) were living in their parents' homes in 2012, the highest share in modern history. And by 2015, despite years of slow but steady improvement in the labor market, the share of young adults living with a parent remained stable.[2] Call it what you will—post-adolescence, pre-adulthood—it's become so hardwired into the zeitgeist of coming of age in the new millennium that it's already the subject of its own genre of books, movies, sitcoms, reality shows, and PhD dissertations.

But there's not yet a settled take on the phenomenon. Millennial novelist Haley Tanner writes gloomily about her generation "wandering in the purgatorial landscape of postgraduate inertia, premarital indecision, and protocareerist yearning." Most commentators blame the sluggish economy. Boomer author Sally Koslow sees other aggravating circumstances. She goes after Boomer parents who, she believes, are foisting onto their children their own neuroses about getting old. "Boomers' fury at the very idea that we have to age sends a subliminal message that there will always be time for our kids to get another degree or surf another couch, to break up with one more partner or employer, and to wait around to reproduce, while ignoring the reality that opportunities will evaporate," she writes. "If parents aren't old—and who among us doesn't feel 35?—if parents aren't old, with our titanium joints and botox, how can we expect our kids to grow up?" Koslow is the author of *Slouching Toward Adulthood: Observations from the Not-So-Empty Nest*, and also pens advice columns for women who date men who live at home. Meantime, over at the Adult Children Living at Home website, the practical advice is for the parents, not the girlfriends. Rule one: Establish ground rules to cover who pays for what. Rule two: Decide in advance if overnight guests are permitted. Psychologist Carl Pickhardt, author of *Boomerang Kids*, reminds parents that there's a fine line between supporting and enabling. He encourages them to create an atmosphere of "constructive discomfort" by charging their Boomerangers rent and setting a departure date.

Family historian Stephanie Coontz finds some silver linings in the boomerang phenomenon; she argues that young people who postpone the major transitions to adulthood tend to wind up with more durable marriages and more stable careers than their early-maturing counterparts. That analysis gets no love from social commentator Kay S. Hymowitz, who takes a dim view of delayed adulthood, especially when celebrated in movies starring the likes of Adam Sandler, Will Ferrell, Jack Black, Luke Wilson, Vince Vaughn, Zach Galifianakis, Steve Carell, Seth Rogen, or Jonah Hill, whose characters typically flounder around without life scripts, career direction, or the wit to see women as anything other than disposable estrogen playthings. This generation of leading men is a pretty steep downgrade from the glory days of cinema, when

Gary Cooper, Clark Gable, Humphrey Bogart, John Wayne, Jimmy Stewart, and Cary Grant set the cultural norms for manhood. Hymowitz, for one, is unamused. Her terse advice to today's male slackers, whether cracking wise on the silver screen or surfing on their parents' couch: "Man up!"

All of this makes twenty-something romance, courtship, and sex something of a minefield. In *F*ck, I'm in My Twenties*, author Emma Koenig bares her serial heartbreaks ("There should be some kind of loyalty rewards program for getting hurt over and over again"). But it's not just guys who can be commitment-phobic slackers. Amy Schumer has the same struggles with monogamy in her stand-up comedy routines and her 2015 movie, *Trainwreck*. As author Donna Freitas tells it in *The End of Sex: How Hookup Culture Is Leaving a Generation Unhappy, Sexually Unfulfilled, and Confused About Intimacy*, the sex-without-attachment rules apply equally these days to young men and women—and leave both genders emotionally shortchanged. In the hit HBO series *Girls*, the opening scene of the first episode had Hannah (played by show creator Lena Dunham) throwing a fit when her parents announce they're cutting off her monthly checks. The show follows Hannah (the self-described "voice of my generation") and her angst-ridden girlfriends as they navigate awkward sex, dead-end relationships, lousy internships, and oceans of self-pity in the gritty never-never land between childhood and adulthood. Meantime, Aziz Ansari, a comedian, and Eric Klinenberg, a sociologist, provide a how-to on the rules of love in the age of algorithms in their best-selling 2015 book, *Modern Romance*: "Today, if you own a smartphone, you're carrying a 24/7 singles bar in your pocket," they advise. Online dating sites have been around for nearly two decades, long enough to have shed their early stigma as the outpost of the weird and desperate. According to one study financed by eHarmony, a third of recently married couples report having met online.[3] And in recent years, apps like Grindr and Tinder introduced GPS location-based software into the mix, enabling smartphones to provide a digital pathway to one-night stands as well as lifelong soul mates. But the authors warn that too much choice can be paralyzing, and may be one reason marriage rates have plummeted. In focus groups, they heard from scores of twenty-somethings from all over the world who told them they couldn't commit to a partner because someone better might be just a click or swipe away.

Will the Boomerangers ever grow up? Eventually, perhaps, but not just yet. More than 4 in 10 of today's twenty-somethings, like Junior, have returned home to live with their parent(s) at some stage of their young adult lives. As for marriage—for now, fuhgeddaboudit. Back when Jane was the age Junior is now, about half of all twenty-somethings in America were married. Today about 20% are. The Millennials' two seemingly incompatible characteristics—their slow walk to adulthood and their unshaken confidence in the future—are their most distinctive traits. Despite inheriting the worst economy since the Great Depression, despite rates of youth un- and under-employment that are the highest since the government began keeping such records, despite the growing albatross of student loan debt, and despite not being able to think about starting a family of their own, Millennials are America's most stubborn optimists. They have a self-confidence born of coddling parents and everyone-gets-a-trophy coaches. They have a look-at-me élan that comes from being humankind's first generation of digital natives (before them, nobody knew that the whole world wanted to see your funny cat photos).[4] And they have the invincibility of youth. For all those reasons, Millennials are far more bullish than their better-off elders about their financial future. Even as they struggle to find jobs and launch careers, even as nearly half describe themselves as being in the lower or lower middle classes (a higher share than any other generation), nearly 9 in 10 say they already have or one day will have enough money to meet their financial needs. No other generation is nearly as optimistic.

Jeffrey Jensen Arnett, a psychology professor at Clark University in Worcester, Massachusetts, and an expert on twenty-somethings, ascribes their optimism to their lack of life experience. "The dreary, dead-end jobs, the bitter divorces, the disappointing and disrespectful children . . . none of them imagine that this is what the future holds for them," he writes. In an interview with Robin Marantz Henig for a *New York Times Magazine* article, Arnett elaborated: "Ask them if they agree with the statement 'I am very sure that someday I will get to where I want to be in life,' and 96 percent of them will say yes. . . . But despite elements that are exciting, even exhilarating, about being this age, there is a downside, too: dread, frustration, uncertainty, a sense of not quite understanding the rules of the game." Arnett says that what he hears most often from young adults is ambivalence; 60 percent of his subjects tell him they felt like both grown-ups and not-quite-grown-ups.[5]

When it comes to their economic prospects, are they clueless Peter Pans on course for an unhappy rendezvous with reality? There's no shortage of elders who fear exactly that. "We have a monster jobs problem, and young people are the biggest losers," says Andrew Sum, director of the Center for Labor Market Studies at Northeastern University, who predicts the specter of unemployment will "haunt young people for at least another decade. . . . It almost makes you want to cry for the future of our country." Harvard economist Richard Freeman says today's young adults "will be scarred and they will be called 'the lost generation'—in that their careers would not be the same had they avoided this economic disaster." These and other pessimists believe

America's unemployment crisis is as much structural as cyclical—a by-product of a witch's brew of globalization, automation, foreign competition, and a faltering education system. Millennials, they worry, are on track to become the first generation in American history to do less well in life than their parents.

All of these challenges will be exacerbated once the nation has to start coping with the full cost of the retirement of 76 million Boomers. The oldest turned 65 in 2011. By the time the youngest cross that threshold in 2030, America's age pyramid will take on a shape it has never had before. About 1 in 5 Americans will be 65 or older, up from 1 in 7 now. The number of retirees on Social Security and Medicare will rise to about 80 million by 2030, roughly double the figure in 2000. Among them, the fastest-growing cohort will be the "old-old." The number of seniors ages 85 and older is expected to more than triple between now and 2050, to 19 million. Fewer workers supporting more of the old and old-old isn't much of a formula for economic growth, standard-of-living gains, or social comity. "It's like a seesaw—if one side is up, the other side has to be down," says Andrew Biggs, a former deputy commissioner of the Social Security Administration, of the challenge of preserving a safety net for the old without bankrupting the young. "Nobody wants to do the actual things you have to do so you don't screw your kids on this stuff."

THE BOOMERS

At 76 million and 80 million strong, respectively, Boomers and Millennials are the biggest of the four living generations—each significantly larger than the generation that came before. In the case of Boomers, the population bulge is the product of a spike in births that began right after World War II and ended right after the introduction of the birth control pill. Those 19 years were a time when the American economy was a colossus astride the world and its middle class was

Figure 3.1

The Baby Boom

Estimated lifetime births among US women, 1920–2011

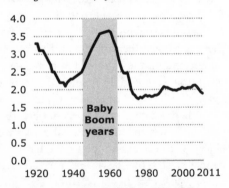

Note: Based on the Total Fertility Rate (TFR). While the TFR is extremely sensitive to shifts in birth timings, it tracks closely with the General Fertility Rate (GFR) throughout this period.

Source: Pew Research Center analysis of National Center for Health Statistics data

living in what was then unimaginable luxury (washing machines! Levittowns! color TVs!). The typical Boomer's mother had three children—one more than the mothers of the previous generation or than any generation since. In the case of Millennials, the big numbers are the product not of high fertility rates but of renewed immigration flows (though immigrant women have about 50% more children than do native-born women, so the two phenomena are related).

As Millennials are entering the workforce, Boomers are entering retirement (although many in both generations will cross these milestones later rather than sooner, thanks to hard times, bad choices, or both). This juxtaposition alone sets up a potential conflict: some of the jobs Boomers aren't leaving are the same jobs Millennials aren't getting.

But the conflict has more to it than that. "Generation Screwed" was the headline on a 2012 *Newsweek* article by demographer Joel Kotkin. The sub-head: "Boomer America Never Had It So Good. As a Result, Today's Young Americans Have Never Had It So Bad." His piece used data from Pew Research and other sources to put a zero-sum-game frame around the diverging economic fortunes of the young and old, the topic of Chapter 5. For now, another element of the Kotkin critique commands attention. Boomers these days are a generation that seems to relish public self-flagellation. A brief sampler, with all of the lashes delivered by Boomers themselves:

> " . . . a grasshopper generation, eating through just about everything like hungry locusts." —Thomas Friedman, *New York Times* columnist

> " . . . squander[ed] the legacy handed to them by the generation from World War II." —Documentary filmmaker Ken Burns

> " . . . the most self-centered, self-seeking, self-interested, self-absorbed, self-indulgent, self-aggrandizing generation in American history." —Paul Begala, TV pundit and former speechwriter for Bill Clinton

> "Thanks to the '60s, we are all shamelessly selfish." —Kurt Andersen, author and social critic

For those who want more, there's always BoomerDeathwatch.com ("Because one day, they'll all be dead") or DieBoomerDie.blogspot.com

("There is no political left or right, only failed baby boomer leadership"). The bashing more typically comes from the Right than the Left, and has ever since the late 1960s, when Boomers held their famous counterculture coming-out party on Max Yasgur's farm near Woodstock, New York, an outdoor rock concert that was either "An Aquarian Exposition: 3 Days of Peace and Music" (so said the iconic poster) or a dystopian homage to drugs, sex, and mud (so said the critics). Boomer culture wars have flared up in fits and starts ever since. But right from the get-go, Boomers themselves have always been on both sides. The same generation that fought the war in Vietnam also stormed the dean's office to protest it (and the military draft that cast such a shadow over their coming-of-age years). The same generation that was in the vanguard of the civil rights, women's rights, and free love movements also gave more votes in 1972 (the first year 18-year-olds could vote) for conservative Richard Nixon than for liberal George McGovern. As columnist Gregory Rodriguez once drily observed, one need only glance at Supreme Court Justice Samuel Alito Jr.'s wonky 1971 Princeton yearbook photo to recall that not all Boomers back then were long-haired hippies. Now fast forward four decades later. When card-carrying Boomer Bill Keller, a columnist and former executive editor of the *New York Times*, labeled his generation an "entitled bunch" and called for them to accept cuts in their retirement benefits, he got an earful from Boomer Leonard Steinhorn, author of *The Greater Generation: In Defense of the Baby Boom Legacy*. Steinhorn wrote:

> In the early 1980s, before most Boomers started raising families, they were called too selfish to have children. Then, when Boomers turned out to be pretty good and selfless parents, they were accused of getting too involved in their kids' lives. Boomers have been accused of creating cultural chaos through moral relativism. Then, when Boomers came of age and declared bigotry of any kind immoral, they were accused of being too politically correct.... When the World War II generation was about to retire, no one blamed them for the Vietnam War, their discrimination against blacks, women, and gays, or their pollution of our waterways and air.

Maybe it's time we navel-gazing Boomers (myself included) declare a cease-fire and stipulate that we all have lots to be proud of—and to be embarrassed by. And to acknowledge that as we've gotten older, the most pressing debates about our generation have evolved from the personal and moral to the political and economic. Many of the old culture wars have died down—and Steinhorn gets that part of the story right. When it comes to promoting tolerance over bigotry, the Boomers won. And because we won, America won. But now the entitlement wars are heating up, and here Keller and his fellow critics have it right. When the oldest Boomers entered the workforce and started to pay taxes in the late 1960s, the national debt was measured in the mere billions. It crossed $1 trillion for the first time in 1981, just as the youngest of the Boomers were graduating from high school. Today it stands at more than $18 trillion and counting. (A better apples-to-apples time trend measures national debt as a share of gross domestic product. This figure peaked at 122% in 1946 as the federal government borrowed heavily to wage World War II. It subsequently dropped to 33% by 1981 but has been rising ever since. It currently stands at about 100% of GDP.) Boomers are by no means the only guilty parties. But this generation, more than any other in American history, has passed through its economically active years not paying the full tab for the goods and services it has asked for and gotten from the government. Its children and grandchildren have been left holding the bill.

A lot of Boomers are angry about this. If it was their passivity and profligacy that allowed the problem to get out of hand in the first place, it's now their frustration over the size of the federal debt that has helped to fuel the Tea Party and the rise of small-government conservatism. "It's not moral for my generation to keep spending massively more than we take in, knowing those burdens are going to be passed on to the next generation, and they're going to be paying the interest and principal all their lives," said 65-year-old presidential candidate Mitt Romney during the 2012 campaign. But as Boomers have grown more fiscally and politically conservative over time, they're also dealing with life-cycle transitions that make them unlikely warriors in the political battle to restrain the growth of the social safety net for seniors. More so than other generations, they're worried about money. And they're just plain downbeat about life.

"Baby Boomers Approach 65—Glumly" is the title of a Pew Research report published on December 20, 2010—12 days before the first of the Boomers turned 65. It began: "The iconic image of the baby boom generation is a 1960s-era snapshot of an exuberant, long-haired, rebellious young adult. That portrait wasn't entirely accurate even then, but it's hopelessly out of date now. This famously huge cohort of Americans finds itself in a collective funk as it approaches old age." The report assembled data on attitudes about life satisfaction, economic mobility, confidence in retirement financing, and optimism about the nation's economic futures to show that, across the board, Boomers were gloomier than other generations. This, despite the fact that most were at or near their peak earning years (at the time, they were ages 46 to 64).

Some of the pessimism is related to the life cycle. For most people, middle age is the most stressful time of life.[6] This has been especially true for

Boomers, who are more likely than previous middle-agers to be juggling the needs of adult children and aging parents. But middle age doesn't appear to be the only culprit. Other longitudinal research, drawn from three decades of data from the General Social Survey, suggests that Boomers have experienced less happiness on average than have other generations over the entire span of their lives. One theory, advanced by University of Chicago sociologist Yang Yang and others, holds that the very size of the Boomer cohort has led to a lifetime of stressful intragenerational competition for a limited share of top spots in schools, colleges, and careers.[7]

It's also possible that the seeds of Boomers' current malaise were planted long ago, but for a different reason: they're having trouble getting their minds around the idea that they aren't young anymore. Remember, this is the only generation in history to become famous just for being born (witness the name). A 1947 *Washington Post* article heralded the start of the nation's post–World War II wave of fecundity as one of the "fruits of demobilization"—and went on to confidently but mistakenly assure readers that it wouldn't last long. Two decades later, Boomers became even more famous just for being young adults; a 1966 *Time* magazine cover story enshrined "Twenty-five and Under" Americans as the Man of the Year, a distinction typically reserved for presidents, generals, inventors, or Nobel laureates. The journalistic instinct was spot-on. Back then, as Boomers reveled in their youth and idealism, they were the world's change agents. In some realms, they've succeeded. In others, life has gotten in the way. But whatever the final score, this much is clear: a generation famous for being young ain't young no more. And it's a bummer.

THE MILLENNIALS

In the decades since Boomers first came bounding onto the national stage, no generation of young adults had made nearly as loud an entrance—until now. Meet the Millennials: liberal, diverse, tolerant, narcissistic, coddled, respectful, confident, and broke.

If timing is everything, Millennials have known a mix of good and bad fortune. By lottery of birth timing, they're the world's first generation of digital natives. Adapting to new technology is hardwired into their generational DNA (more about that in Chapter 11), and while it's impossible to forecast where the digital and social media revolutions will take humankind, it seems safe to predict that Millennials will get there first. They are also the most racially and ethnically diverse generation in American history, a profile that should serve them (and the rest of the US) well in a multicolored world engulfed by cultural, ethnic, and religious divisions (see Chapter 8). On the downside, they're the first generation in American history in danger of having a lower standard of living than the one their parents enjoyed (see Chapter 6). On all these fronts, timing has played a central role.

Millennials' political views (see Chapter 5) have been forged by these distinctive identities and experiences. First, though, a few words about a debate among scholars over a related question: Are they on track to become America's next great civic generation? That was the prediction advanced by generational scholars William Strauss and Neil Howe when they published *Millennials Rising* in 2000, just as the oldest of the Millennials were turning 18. Relying on interviews with teenagers and data about decreases in teen pregnancy, alcohol and drug abuse, dropout rates, crime, and other antisocial behaviors, they posited that the new generation would resemble the Greatest Generation (born before 1928)—a pattern foreordained by the authors' four-phase cycle of history. Millennials would be conformist, socially conservative, involved in their communities, and interested in government. Their book started a genre. Since then, numerous journalists and authors have promoted this civic portrait of Millennials, exemplified by such books as *Generation We* by Eric Greenberg and Karl Weber.

But it hasn't taken long for revisionism to set in. A *Time* magazine cover in 2013 pegged Millennials as "The Me Me Me Generation"—"lazy, entitled narcissists still living with their parents." (In classic newsmagazine style, the cover added a cheeky hedge: "Why they'll save us all.") The "me me me" meme isn't new. It was first put forth nearly a decade ago by Jean Twenge, a San Diego State University psychology professor whose 2006 book, *Generation Me*, analyzed surveys of young people dating back to the 1920s and showed a long-term cultural shift toward high self-esteem, self-importance, and narcissism. In follow-up work, she found that Millennials are less likely than Boomers and Generation Xers had been as young adults to exhibit values such as social trust and civic engagement and behaviors such as contacting public officials or working on political, social, or environmental causes. She did find an overall increase in volunteerism, though she noted it has come at a time when more high schools are requiring their students to do some sort of community service to graduate. Twenge expanded her critique in a 2009 book, *The Narcissism Epidemic*, cowritten with W. Keith Campbell. It cast a jaundiced eye across all precincts of the modern celebrity culture but reserved a particularly disapproving glare for the everyone-gets-a-trophy school of child rearing that has come into vogue in the modern era. Twenge's research found that college students in 2009 were significantly more likely than their counterparts in 1966 to rate themselves above average in writing and math skills—despite the fact that SAT scores decreased slightly during that same period. As she and many others have noted, the parental coddling often persists beyond adolescence. College deans nowadays complain that the hardest part of freshman orientation week isn't getting the new students to feel comfortable staying—it's getting the "helicopter parents" to feel comfortable leaving. Some schools even provide separation-anxiety seminars for Mom and Dad, but that doesn't keep some from calling professors during the academic year to complain about their child's grades.

I'll leave it to the experts to untangle the psychological roots of such behaviors. My own guess is that the mix of global terrorism, digital "stranger danger," the Columbine school shooting, 9/11, Newtown, media hype, and fewer kids per family have thrust parents' biologically normal protective instincts into overdrive. These same factors may also be responsible for the low levels of social trust among Millennials themselves. If you were born in 1984, you were in middle school when the Columbine massacre happened, in high school on 9/11/01, and perhaps just about to become a parent for the first time when the young children of Newtown were struck down. Evil of that magnitude leaves a mark.

Then there's the Internet and social media—the first communication platform in human history that enables anyone to reach everyone. Suppose your buddy shot a video of you bouncing so high on your backyard trampoline that you got stuck briefly in a tree? Back in the dark ages (pre-2005 or so) you might have shown it to a few friends as you yukked it up over some beers. Now you post it on YouTube and Facebook and hope it goes viral. At which point hundreds may see it. Or thousands. Or tens of millions.[8] This outlet for personal expression and empowerment may help to explain their look-at-me tendencies—which find an offline analog in their fondness for tattoos. Back in the day, tattoos were the body wear of sailors, hookers, and strippers. Today they've become a mainstream identity badge for Millennials. Nearly 4 in 10 (38%) have at least one. Gen Xers are not far behind; 32% say they have a tattoo. Only 15% of Baby Boomers and 6% of Silents wear body art. And by the way, for Millennials, one tattoo often isn't enough. Half of all tattooed Millennials have 2 to 5, and 18% have 6 or more.

When it comes to civic engagement, the data on Millennials are mixed. They match their elders on some measures of volunteering and contacting public officials, but lag behind on voting. The voter turnout deficit is largely a life-stage phenomenon; previous generations of young adults also turned out at much lower rates than their elders. In 2008 and 2012, Millennials narrowed the turnout gap—a testament to Obama's strong personal appeal to the young. But in the midterm elections of 2010 and 2014, with Obama not on the ballot, the young stayed home in droves.

As for volunteering, a 2010 Pew Research survey found that 57% of Millennials said they had done so in the past 12 months, compared with 54% of Gen Xers, 52% of Baby Boomers, and 39% of Silents.[9] Pew Research surveys also find that Millennials are about as likely as other generations to say they have signed some sort of petition in the past year, but are less likely than Boomers and Xers to say they've contacted a government official. Once again, there's a life-cycle effect; people start reaching out to their elected officials when they have families, children, jobs, and homes. Lots of Millennials aren't there yet.

That's true of nearly all aspects of this generation's life story. It's still a work in progress. The question is whether their futures will be enhanced or encumbered by choices their elders are making now.

4

Generation Gaps

YOUNG AND OLD IN AMERICA are poles apart. Demographically, politically, economically, socially, and technologically, the generations are more different from each other now than at any time in living memory. Let us count (some of) the ways:

- *They have a different racial and ethnic makeup.* Nearly half of all children in America today are nonwhite. So are more than 4 in 10 members of the Millennial Generation—but just 1 in 5 members of the Silent Generation and about 1 in 4 Baby Boomers.
- *They vote differently.* In 2012 Obama won 60% of the Millennial vote and just 44% of the Silent Generation vote. This young/old voting gap was just a few notches below its historic peak of 21 percentage points in 2008. Throughout the 1980s and 1990s, the age gap was either small or nonexistent. And in the 1992 and 2000 presidential elections, oldsters actually voted slightly more Democratic than youngsters.
- *Their economic fortunes have diverged.* In 1983 the typical household headed by someone 65 or older had 8 times the net worth of the typical household headed by someone under the age of 35. By 2013 that ratio had ballooned to 20 to 1.
- *Their families are different.* In 1960, 6 in 10 twenty-somethings were married. Today just 2 in 10 are married. In 1960 just 5% of children were born to an unmarried mother. Today 40% are.
- *Their gender roles are converging.* Until a few decades ago, becoming a man meant becoming the family breadwinner. Today some 4 in

10 households with minor children have a mother who is either the family's sole or primary breadwinner, up from 11% in 1960. Nearly 60% of college students are women, and in a knowledge-based economy that pays no premium for male strength, women are now nearly half of the labor force, leaving many young men struggling to find careers and life scripts—and many young women faced with a choice of "marrying down" or staying single.

- *They have different ideas about the role of government.* Six in 10 Silents prefer a smaller government that provides fewer services to a bigger government that provides more services. Just a third of Millennials agree.
- *They have a different view of religion.* Some 35% of Millennials are unaffiliated with any religion, compared with 11% of Silents, 17% of Boomers, and 23% of Gen Xers. Millennials are the least religiously connected generation in modern American history.
- *They have different perceptions of global warming.* Six in 10 adults under the age of 30 say the earth's climate is getting warmer because of human activity; just 31% of adults 65 and older agree.
- *They have different military experiences.* Just 3% of Millennial men are veterans, compared with 35% of Silent men when they were the same age, even though both came of age during periods of war (Iraq and Afghanistan for the former, Korea and the Cold War for the latter). The difference, of course, is that the US military no longer uses a draft.
- *They have different views about American exceptionalism.* Two-thirds of Silents say the US is the greatest country in the world; just one-third of Millennials agree. However, Millennials are much more likely than Silents to say that life in America has improved in the past half century.
- *They have a different take on the digital revolution.* Eight in 10 Millennials say the Internet has changed life for the better. Fewer than half of Silents agree.
- *They have different appetites for news.* On a typical day, Millennials spend only about half as much time as Silents consuming news (46 minutes versus 84 minutes). While this is related in part to their phase of the life cycle, Millennials are consuming less news than older generations did when they were younger.

Generation gaps are hardly a novelty. Nearly two centuries ago Alexis de Tocqueville marveled that in America "each generation is a new people."

Figure 4.1

The Young/Old Voting Gap, 1972–2012

% voting for Democratic candidate

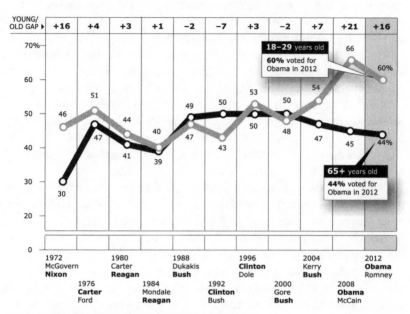

Note: From 1972 through 1988 oldest age category is 60 and older.

Source: Based on exit polls. 1972 and 1976: CBS. 1980–1988: CBS/*New York Times*. 1992: Voter Research & Surveys. 1996 and 2000: Voter News Service. 2004–2012: National Election Pool

More so perhaps than any society in history, our country has always embraced change, making it a hothouse for young adults who have a different worldview from their parents and grandparents. But the current gap is unusually large—and for the reasons spelled out in the previous chapter, potentially fraught. This chapter will look at the new generation gaps through the prism of today's four adult living generations: the Millennials (born after 1980), the Gen Xers (born from 1965 to 1980), the Baby Boomers (born from 1946 to 1964), and the Silents (born from 1928 to 1945).

GENERALIZATIONS ABOUT GENERATIONS

As a branch of demography, generational analysis has always been a bit of a stepchild. It rests on the premise that members of the same generation experience the same historical events at roughly the same stage of their life cycle, and as a result share what might loosely be called a generational persona, one that's also shaped by (and in reaction to) the persona of their parents' generation. In the early twentieth century, Hungarian-born sociologist Karl Mannheim wrote a seminal essay that helped to legitimize generational analysis as a scholarly pursuit. In modern times, American historians Neil Howe and William Strauss expanded on Mannheim's theories by compressing 500 years of Anglo-Saxon history into an overarching generational frame. In their schema, four archetypal generational personas (idealist, reactive, civic, and adaptive) recur in repeating 80-year cycles, with each holding sway for about 20 years before yielding to its successor. They categorize Millennials—America's 14th generation—as civic; Xers as reactive; Boomers as idealistic; and Silents as adaptive. Their work has been popular in part because it helps employers and educators anticipate and plan for the distinctive characteristics of their future workers and students. But it has also attracted critics who find it too rigid and formulaic.

As long as one acknowledges the obvious—that there are as many different personality types *within* a generation as across generations—I see some value in generalizations about generations. All of us know people who bear the marks of their distinctive coming-of-age experiences: the grandmother raised during the Depression who still reuses her tea bags; the uncle who grew up in the 1960s and still sports a ponytail; the kid sister who sends 200 texts a day to her many, many best friends. At the same time, one should bring healthy doses of humility and caution to the exercise. That's because in one sense, it's too easy, and in another, too hard. It's too easy because no one needs a scientific survey to persuade them that the typical 20-year-old, 40-year-old, 60-year-old, and 80-year-old are different from one another. They already know. It's too hard because we can never completely disentangle the many reasons for the differences. At any given moment, they can arise from any of three overlapping processes.

1. Life-cycle effects. Young people may be different from older people today, but they may become more like them tomorrow, as they themselves age.
2. Period effects. Major historical events (wars, social movements, booms, busts, religious awakenings, medical, scientific, and technological breakthroughs) affect all age groups, but the depth of impact may differ according to where people are located in the life cycle.
3. Cohort effects. Period events often leave a particularly deep impression on the young, who are still forming their core values and worldviews.

Generational analysis is weakest at the boundaries. It defies common sense to suppose that everyone born in one year is a member of one generation while everyone born a year later is a member of another. But even if these boundaries are to some degree contrivances—prized more by magazine cover writers than by Census Bureau statisticians—they're useful contrivances. They create a foundation of data that helps us tell the story of ourselves to ourselves, in the imperfect but illuminating language of numbers. For those of us who do this sort of work at the Pew Research Center, they're the tool that facilitates comparisons among the attitudes, values, and behaviors of the young, middle-aged, and old. And because we've asked the same questions over many years, we can also compare today's young with yesterday's young. We can do the same with census, economic, and election data. Taken together, these numbers paint a picture of a society not with generation gaps but with generation chasms. To understand it better, let's start with thumbnail sketches.

THE MILLENNIALS **(BORN AFTER 1980).** Empowered by digital technology; coddled by parents; respectful of elders; slow to adulthood; conflict-averse; at ease with racial, ethnic, and sexual diversity; confident in their economic futures despite coming of age in bad times. Icons: Mark Zuckerberg, Lena Dunham, LeBron James, Carrie Underwood, Jennifer Lawrence, Lady Gaga.

GEN XERS **(BORN FROM 1965 TO 1980).** Savvy, entrepreneurial loners. Distrustful of institutions, especially government. Children of the Reagan revolution—and the divorce revolution. More comfortable than their elders with an increasingly diverse America. Icons: Quentin Tarantino, Will Smith, Adam Sandler, Tiger Woods, Robert Downey Jr.

BABY BOOMERS **(BORN FROM 1946 TO 1964).** As exuberant youths, led the countercultural upheavals of the 1960s. But the iconic image of that era—long-haired hippie protesters—describes only a portion of the cohort. Now on the front stoop of old age, Boomers are gloomy about their lives, worried about retirement, and wondering why they aren't young anymore. Icons: Bill and Hillary Clinton, George W. Bush, Barack Obama, Steve Jobs, Tom Hanks.

SILENT GENERATION **(BORN FROM 1928 TO 1945).** Conservative and conformist, Silents are uneasy with the pace of demographic, cultural, and technological change—and with the growing size of government. But hands off their Social Security and Medicare! Icons: Clint Eastwood, Neil Armstrong, Marilyn Monroe, Tom Brokaw, Hugh Hefner.

Figure 4.2

How the Generations See Themselves

% of each generation saying each attribute describes their generation overall

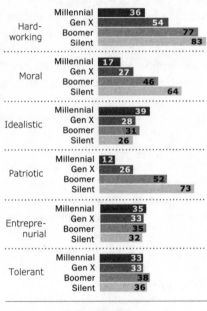

POSITIVE TRAITS

Hard-working	Millennial	36
	Gen X	54
	Boomer	77
	Silent	83
Moral	Millennial	17
	Gen X	27
	Boomer	46
	Silent	64
Idealistic	Millennial	39
	Gen X	28
	Boomer	31
	Silent	26
Patriotic	Millennial	12
	Gen X	26
	Boomer	52
	Silent	73
Entrepre-nurial	Millennial	35
	Gen X	33
	Boomer	35
	Silent	32
Tolerant	Millennial	33
	Gen X	33
	Boomer	38
	Silent	36

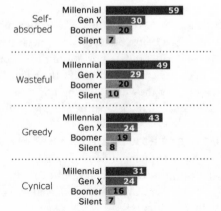

NEGATIVE TRAITS

Self-absorbed	Millennial	59
	Gen X	30
	Boomer	20
	Silent	7
Wasteful	Millennial	49
	Gen X	29
	Boomer	20
	Silent	10
Greedy	Millennial	43
	Gen X	24
	Boomer	19
	Silent	8
Cynical	Millennial	31
	Gen X	24
	Boomer	16
	Silent	7

Source: American Trends Panel (wave 10). Survey conducted Mar. 10–Apr. 6, 2015

Most members of each of these four age groups say their own generation has a unique and distinctive identity, according to a 2010 Pew Research Center survey. But each gives a different set of reasons for their distinctiveness. In response to an open-ended question, Millennials stressed their use of technology. Gen Xers did as well, but many fewer offered that explanation. Boomers cited their work ethic and Silents their shared coming-of-age experience in the Depression and World War II.

A different Pew Research survey, this one taken in 2009, asked Americans of all ages whether they saw a generation gap in America between young and old. About 8 in 10 said yes, nearly identical to the share that had said the same back in 1969, when the generations were famously at each other's throats. But in the modern era, as follow-up survey questions in 2009 and 2012 made clear, the generation gap isn't seen as a source of great friction. Many fewer Americans said they see strong conflicts between young and old than said the same about conflicts between immigrants and the native born, rich and poor, black and white, and Republicans and Democrats. And what generation gaps they do see tend to be focused on technology and lifestyle rather than on the more polarizing terrain of politics (see appendix Figure 4A.1).

Figure 4.3

Group Conflicts

% saying there are "very strong/strong conflicts" between ...

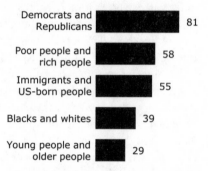

Source: Pew Research Center survey, Nov.–Dec. 2012, N=2,511 US adults

Still another Pew Research survey, this one taken in 2015, explored a wide range of attributes—positive and negative—that different age cohorts ascribe to their own generation. As shown in Figure 4.2, older cohorts rate their own generation more generously than younger cohorts rate theirs, with gaps appearing in a step-wise pattern by age. However, many of these differences may be related more to life stage than to the unique characteristics of a particular generation. People's embrace of attributes such as responsibility, morality, patriotism, and religiosity tends to increase with age—and this has been true over many generations. As for the sizable share of Millennials who view their generation as self-absorbed, wasteful, and greedy, this could be driven to some

degree by young adults regurgitating the negative portrayals of their generation they see in the media. It also may reflect the fact that most older Millennials don't think of themselves as Millennials at all; they're more inclined to say
they are Gen Xers. So their sour assessments may just be another iteration of
the always popular complaint about "kids today."

THE POLITICS OF THE GENERATION GAP

In the past six national elections, generational differences have mattered more
than at any other time in modern history. In each election since 2004, younger
people have voted substantially more Democratic than other age groups, while
older voters have cast more ballots for Republican candidates in each election
since 2008. The greater liberalism of the young and conservatism of the old in
part reflect the differences in their racial and ethnic profiles. Young voters are
more likely than older ones to be nonwhite, and nonwhites are more likely to
be Democrats and liberals. Political polls also find that older generations—
Boomers and especially Silents—do not fully embrace racial diversity. For many
Silents in particular, President Obama himself appears to be an unwelcome
symbol of the way the face of America has changed. Surveys taken in 2011 and
2012 found that feelings of "unease" with Obama, along with higher levels of
anger toward government, are the emotions that most differentiate the attitudes
of Silents from those of the youngest generation. Here's a look at the political
views of the four generations:

Figure 4.4

The Silent Generation

Born: 1928 to 1945

Turned 18 in: 1946 to 1963

Age on Jan. 1, 2016: 71–88

- Conservative views on government and society for most of their lives
- More uncomfortable than younger people with many social changes, including racial diversity and homosexuality
- More likely to rate Social Security as top voting issue
- Favor Republicans on most issues, but not Social Security

Source: Pew Research Center surveys and US Census Bureau data

The Silent Generation

The Silent Generation came of age in the Truman, Eisenhower, and Kennedy years. They had divided partisan allegiances in the 1990s but have become much more Republican in recent years. As the nation's current cohort of older adults, they have all but "replaced" the Greatest Generation (born before 1928), who were more reliably Democratic voters throughout their political lives, but who have now largely passed from the scene.

Silents hold the most consistently conservative views among any generation about government, social issues, and America's place in the world. An overwhelming majority of Silents say they are either angry or frustrated with government. They are a generation that strongly disapproves of Barack Obama, for whom most did not vote. Silents also are the most politically energized generation, as demonstrated by their heavy turnout, relative to other age groups, in the 2010 and 2014 midterm elections.

More often than the younger generations, Silents take the American exceptionalist view that the United States is *the* greatest nation in the world. But fewer older people than young people think that "America's best days are ahead of us."

Figure 4.5

Percent "Angry" with Government

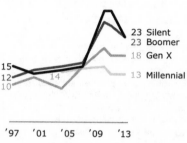

23 Silent
23 Boomer
18 Gen X
13 Millennial

'97   '01   '05   '09   '13

Source: Aggregated data from surveys conducted by the Pew Research Center for the People & the Press, 1997–2013

The political discontent of the Silent Generation is not economically based. A greater proportion of Silents than younger people say they are financially satisfied, and Silents are less likely to say they often don't have enough money to make ends meet.

Race is a factor in their political attitudes. Silents are the whitest of the generations and are the least accepting of the new face of America. Compared with younger generations, relatively few Silents see racial intermarriage and the growing population of immigrants as changes for the better (see appendix Figure 4A.2).

Silents cite Social Security as often as they name jobs as their top voting issue. And while Silents tend to favor the Republican Party on most issues, they are as likely to favor the Democrats as Republicans on Social Security.

The Baby Boomers

Baby Boomers came of age under Presidents Lyndon Johnson, Richard Nixon, Gerald Ford, Jimmy Carter, and Ronald Reagan. They had very little allegiance to the GOP during the 1960s and 1970s but were increasingly drawn to the Republican

Figure 4.6

The Boomer Generation

Born: 1946 to 1964

Turned 18 in: 1964 to 1982

Age on Jan. 1, 2016: 52–70

- Now express as much frustration with government as the Silents
- Particularly concerned about their own financial future
- Uncertainty about retirement security has many planning to delay retirement
- Older Boomers are somewhat more Democratic than younger Boomers
- Nearly half say life in US has gotten worse since the 1960s

Source: Pew Research Center surveys and US Census Bureau data

Figure 4.7

Generation X

Born: 1965 to 1980

Turned 18 in: 1983 to 1998

Age on Jan. 1, 2016: 36–51

- Similar to Millennials on social issues
- Grown more critical of government over the last decade
- Since '09, sharp drop in financial satisfaction
- Older Xers tend to vote more Republican, younger Xers vote more Democratic

Source: Pew Research Center surveys and US Census Bureau data

Party starting in the 1980s. In more recent elections, they've divided their votes between the two parties, with no strong tendency in either direction.

Historically, there has been an age gap within the Baby Boom Generation. Older Boomers, who cast their first ballots in the Nixon elections of 1968 and 1972, have voted more Democratic than have younger Boomers, who came of age under Ford, Carter, and Reagan. In 2008, for example, Obama performed better among older Boomers than among younger ones.

Over the course of several decades, a rising share of Boomers have come to call themselves conservatives, and a majority now favor a smaller government that provides fewer services. When they were in their 20s and 30s, most Boomers preferred big government. On most social issues, their opinions generally fall between those of the Silents and the younger age cohorts. And many Boomers express reservations about the changing face of America.

Most Boomers say they are dissatisfied with their financial situation and many are anxious about their retirement. In 2012 nearly 4 in 10 (38%) said they aren't confident that they will have enough income and assets to last through their retirement years.

Like other generations, Boomers oppose cutting entitlement benefits to reduce the budget deficit. They are also part of a multigenerational majority that supports reducing Social Security and Medicare benefits for seniors with higher incomes. However, unlike Silents, Boomers oppose raising the eligibility age for Social Security and Medicare.

Generation X

Generation X is the in-between generation. They represent the dividing line on many issues between young and old. They came of age politically in the Reagan, George H. W. Bush, and Clinton years, and have never shown a strong allegiance to either party. In 2000 they split their votes between George W. Bush and Al Gore; they narrowly supported Bush in 2004, favored Obama by a clear margin in 2008, but were evenly divided in 2012.

On a range of social issues Gen Xers take a more liberal position than do older voters. They are more likely than both Boomers and Silents to favor legalizing gay marriage and marijuana, and Gen Xers are far more comfortable with the social diversity of twenty-first-century America.

As is true of Millennials and Boomers, jobs have been the number-one voting issue for Gen Xers in recent years. And they are increasingly anxious over their financial futures. Fully 46% say they are not confident they will have enough income and assets to last through their retirement years—the highest percentage in any generation.

The Millennials

Millennials have voted more Democratic than older voters in the past six national elections. They came of age in the Bush and Obama eras and hold liberal attitudes on most social and governmental issues, as well as America's approach to foreign policy.

Just as members of the Silent Generation are long-term backers of smaller government, Millennials, at least so far, are strong supporters of a more activist government.

Figure 4.8

The Millennial Generation*

Born: 1981 to _____
Turned 18 in: 1999 to _____
Age of adults on Jan. 1, 2016: 18–35

- Voted for Obama by two-to-one in 2008, the largest margin within any age group since 1972
- Much less politically engaged than in 2008
- Consistently liberal views on many social and governmental issues
- Experiencing high rates of unemployment, but still upbeat
- Welcome the new face of America

* The cut-off year for the Millennial Generation is not yet determined.

Source: Pew Research Center surveys and US Census Bureau data

They are a racially and ethnically diverse generation, and this diversity helps to explain some but not all of their liberalism on a range of issues. For example, while 57% of all Millennials favor a bigger government with more services, just 44% of white Millennials do. But only about a quarter of whites in older generations (27%) support an activist government.

It's an open question whether the liberalism of Millennials is "baked in" for the long haul or will succumb to the disillusionment many Millennials already feel as a result of their difficult economic circumstances. Polls taken since the 2012 election show falling Democratic allegiance and rising cynicism about politics and government. Millennials were 26% of the age-eligible electorate in 2012, but through the inexorable churn of generational replacement, they will peak at about 36% in 2020.

GENERATIONAL TRENDS IN RED AND BLUE

One way to look at the political leanings of generations is to sort people by the political environment when they became politically engaged. For example, not so long ago, voters 65 and older were predominantly members of the Greatest Generation. Most came of age during Franklin Roosevelt's presidency and were fairly reliable supporters of Democrats even into their later years. As recently as 2004, members of the older cohort supported John Kerry by a greater margin than did all voters in that election. Now, however, the Greatest Generation has mostly passed from the scene, and members of the Silent Generation—most of whom came of age politically during the Truman and Eisenhower presidencies—have come to make up the lion's share of voters 65 and older. They have long voted less Democratic than the Greatest Generation; in 2008 and 2012, both Truman- and Eisenhower-era Silents voted more Republican than did the electorate as a whole.

The Baby Boomers span many presidencies. The oldest, who turned 18 when Lyndon Johnson was president, voted more Democratic than others when they were young, but have become more Republican than average as they have aged. Those Boomers who came of age when Richard Nixon was president for the most part have retained a Democratic leaning. Their votes closely mirrored those of the overall electorate in 2006, 2008, and 2010, but they tilted more Democratic once again in 2012. The youngest Boomers, who mostly came of age in the Ford and Carter years, have been among the most reliable Republican voting groups.

Internal divisions within Generation X are even more notable. The older portion of Generation X who came of age during the Reagan and George H.W. Bush presidencies have voted more Republican than the electorate. In contrast,

Figure 4.9

Generational Voting History

If you turned 18 under president ...	Your age in 2012	Your Generation	Compared with the national average, your cohort was more likely to vote ...									
			'94	'96	'98	'00	'02	'04	'06	'08	'10	'12
Roosevelt	85+	Greatest	D	D	D	D		D				
Truman	78–84	Silent	R			D			D	R	R	R
Eisenhower	70–77	Silent			R	D	R			R	R	R
Kennedy/Johnson	62–69	Boomer	D		D	R				R		R
Nixon	56–61	Boomer	R			D	D	D				D
Ford/Carter	50–55	Boomer	R	R		R	R		D	R	R	R
Reagan/Bush	38–49	Gen X	D	R	R	R		R	R	R		R
Clinton	30–37	Gen X					D	R	D	D	D	D
Bush/Obama	18–29	Millennial						D	D	D	D	D

Note: Light grey boxes represent years in which an age group's vote was roughly equal to the national average. Data from some years not available for oldest and youngest generations due to small sample sizes. Based on likely voters in pre-election polls conducted in each election year. "Your Generation" shows where the majority of that age group is traditionally categorized (e.g., most people who turned 18 under Clinton are Gen X, though the very youngest are classified as Millennials).

Source: Pew Research Center pre-election surveys, 1994–2012

younger Xers, who became active politically during the Clinton administration, mostly have voted more Democratic than average. Millennials largely came of age during George W. Bush's presidency and have consistently voted more Democratic by large margins.

SOCIAL VALUES

On the young-to-old continuum, the younger the generation, the more likely it is to self-identify as liberal, and the older it is, the more likely to identify as conservative. As Figure 4.10 shows, these gaps have been fairly consistent since at least 1996, suggesting that they are driven more by a cohort than by a life-cycle difference. The same pattern appears in appendix Figure 4A.3, which shows trends over 25 years in generational attitudes on an index of questions about family, homosexuality, and civil liberties. Once again, the oldest generation has been the most conservative throughout, and the youngest the most liberal.

Figure 4.10

Self-Reported Ideology by Generation: 1997–2013

Percent

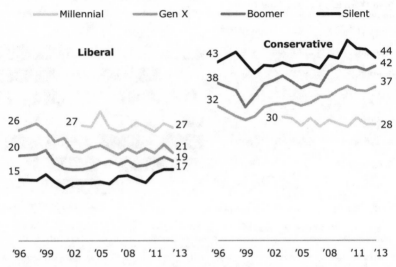

Note: Based on registered voters.

Source: Aggregated data from surveys conducted by the Pew Research Center for the People & the Press, 1996–2013; 2013 data is for January–July only

VIEWS OF BUSINESS

Millennials' views of business are not substantially different from those of older generations. On a three-question index of attitudes about business power and profits, Millennials' opinions mirror those of Gen Xers and members of the Silent Generation and are slightly less critical of business than are the views of Baby Boomers (see appendix Figure 4A.4). Also, Millennials are about as likely as other cohorts to agree that the country's strength is built mostly on the success of American business.

SOCIAL SAFETY NET

Millennials are less skeptical than older age groups about the effectiveness of government, but they are not particularly supportive of an expanded government social safety net. There have been few differences by generation over the past quarter century in views about whether the government has a responsibility to help those in need. Since 2007 there has been a modest decline in the overall proportion favoring more generous assistance for the poor, a downturn that was true for Millennials as well as for older groups.

NATIONAL SECURITY

Members of the Silent Generation tend to be more supportive than other age groups of an assertive approach to national security. At times, Baby Boomers have been more hawkish than the two younger generations, though often the differences among the cohorts have been quite small (see appendix Figure 4A.5).

One of the key questions driving the pattern in the index asks people to agree or disagree with the statement that "the best way to achieve peace is through military strength." With only a few exceptions, Generation X has been significantly less likely than the two older cohorts to agree with this statement. The Millennials first appeared in the 2003 survey, when 47% agreed. That was close to the 45% among Gen Xers who agreed and lower than the 55% of Boomers and 60% of the Silent Generation who did so (see appendix Figure 4A.6).

Another dimension of attitudes about America's relationship with the rest of the world has to do with immigration. Pew Research Center surveys in recent years have found that older adults are more likely than younger adults to say that immigrants have a negative impact on American customs and values.

VIEWS OF THE NATION

Not surprisingly, older generations are also having a harder time than younger ones processing the dramatic demographic, social, and technological changes of the past half century. Among older adults, there is a tension between their belief that America is the greatest country in the world and a sense of pessimism about the country's future. Younger adults are less convinced of America's greatness but more comfortable with the path the country is on.

Figure 4.11

Generational Divide over American Exceptionalism

% saying US is "the greatest country in the world"

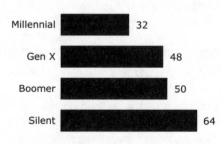

Source: Pew Research Center survey, Sep. 2011, N=2,003 US adults

Overall, 48% of all adults say America is the greatest country in the world, and an additional 42% say it is one of the greatest countries in the world. Fewer than 1 in 10 (8%) say the US is not one of the greatest countries in the world.

There are sharp differences across generations on this question. Millennials are the least likely to say the US is the greatest country in the world—only 32% hold this view. The share rises with each older generation. Nearly two-thirds of Silents (64%) say the US stands above all other nations, a conviction they adhere to despite the discomfort many feel with the societal changes they have witnessed in the past 50 years. Within the Silent Generation it is the oldest members who feel most strongly about America's greatness—fully 72% of those ages 76 to 83 in 2011 said the US is the greatest country in the world.

MORAL VALUES, AMERICA'S FUTURE

The vast majority of American adults—9 in 10 or more across generations—believe that moral values in this country have changed in the past 50 years. However, the generations differ over whether this change has been for the better or the worse. A lopsided majority of Silents (78%), Boomers (77%), and Gen Xers (70%) say it has been a change for the worse, a view shared by about half of Millennials (54%).

There's also a generation gap—albeit a smaller one—on the question of whether America's best days are ahead or behind. Once again, the more upbeat assessments come from the younger generations, with an identical 55% of Millennials and Gen Xers saying our nation's best days are ahead, a view shared by 48% of Boomers and 47% of Silents. The overall balance of opinion tilts positive on this question—with 51% of the American public saying our best days are ahead, 39% saying they are behind us, and the remaining 10% not expressing an opinion one way or the other. That may not be an overwhelming vote of confidence in the future. But neither is it the voice of a public that has lost faith in the national enterprise.

NEWS CONSUMPTION, BY GENERATION

Today's younger and middle-age adults consume much less news in a typical day than do their older counterparts, and long-term trends suggest that they may never match the avid news interest of the generations they will replace, even as they enthusiastically transition to the Internet as their principal platform for news consumption.

A 2012 Pew Research survey found members of the Silent Generation spending 84 minutes watching, reading, or listening to the news the day before the survey was conducted. Boomers did not lag far behind (77 minutes), while

Xers and Millennials spent much less time with the news: 66 minutes and 46 minutes, respectively.

Historically, the pattern has been that a generation's news consumption increases as it ages (see appendix Figure 4A.7). Pew Research surveys give little indication that this has been happening with today's younger generations. In 2004, Xers reported following the news about as often as they did in 2012. The eight-year trend for Millennials has also been flat.

Figure 4.12

Generational Gaps in Time Spent Following the News

Average number of minutes per day following the news by age group*

	Silents	Boomers	Xers	Millennials
2004	88	75	63	43
2006	80	71	63	45
2008	82	72	64	43
2010	83	79	71	45
2012	84	77	66	46

*On the day prior to the survey.

Source: Pew Research Center News Consumption surveys, 2004–2012

This persistently low level of news consumption among the younger generations is likely the result of a variety of factors—such as having more activities and entertainments that compete with the news or fewer compelling major historical events during childhood and adolescence. But one key factor that emerges from our surveys is that older people simply *enjoy* the news more than the young do. Some 58% of Silents and Boomers report they enjoy following the news a lot, compared with 45% of Xers and just 29% of Millennials.

Social media looms as a potential booster of news consumption among the younger generation, albeit a modest one so far. Pew Research's 2012 survey found that a third of Millennials and 20% of Xers said they regularly see news or news headlines on social networking sites. (For more on this, see Chapter 11.) However, only about 35 percent of those who get news from social network sites say they follow up and seek out full news stories.

Traditional news organizations have been forced to cut their reporting staffs by more than a third over the past decade because these changing news habits have eroded their revenue base. Figuring out how to thrive on digital platforms and social media will be essential to their economic survival. But these surveys suggest they may never regain the dominance they once enjoyed in the information ecosystem. The most important raw ingredient—high levels of news engagement among younger generations—isn't there, at least not so far.

5

Battle of the Ages?

IF EVER THERE WAS A MOMENT to gird for a generation war, now would seem to be it. The unsparing arithmetic of a graying population is about to force political leaders to rewrite the social contract between young and old. This will lead to tax increases, benefit cuts, or both. Taking stuff away from people is never popular in a democracy, but it's particularly fraught on this issue at this time, because old and young in America are so different—racially, ethnically, politically. "The question is, how do we re-imagine the social contract when the generations don't look like one another?" asks Marcelo Suarez-Orozco, codirector of immigration studies at New York University.[1] Political analyst Ronald Brownstein worries that the challenge will split the country along a great "gray-brown" age and race divide that could "rattle American politics for decades."[2]

I'm an optimist—not, however, a blinkered one. So let it be said that the pessimists have a pretty strong case, especially when one also considers the diverging economic fortunes of the generations. "Older Americans do not intend to ruin America, but as a group, that's what they're about," writes veteran economics columnist Robert Samuelson, who over many decades has chronicled the way older Americans have used their political clout to grab a growing share of government largesse. Absent changes to current law, more than half of the federal budget will go to Social Security, Medicare, and the nonchild portion of Medicaid by 2022, up from 11% in 1960 and 30% in 1990, according to an Urban Institute study.[3] The federal government now spends about $6 per capita on programs for seniors for every $1 it spends per capita on programs for children. But even as spending priorities have migrated toward the top of the age pyramid, economic need has settled toward the bottom. In 1967, just as the oldest of the Baby Boomers were making their way into the workforce, the poverty rate was nearly three times higher among households headed by an adult age 65 or older than among households headed by an adult below the age of 35 (33% versus 12%). Since then, the ratio has flipped. Today the poorest age cohort of Americans is young adults and their children. The reduction in elderly poverty is largely the handiwork of Social Security and Medicare, and stands as one of the great triumphs of public policy. The benefits of those programs flow to all generations of Americans. But they won't be sustainable unless today's young have the same chance their parents and grandparents did to lead economically productive lives.

So is a Battle of the Ages looming on our horizon? Anything's possible, but there's a lot of evidence to the contrary. In their family lives, the generations are more interdependent now than at any time in modern history. In their attitudes toward the social safety net for seniors, the young are every bit as supportive as the old. And in their basic outlook on life, Millennials seem much more disposed toward cooperation than toward conflict, perhaps because of the nurturing parental norms that guided their upbringing. In response to a survey question, parents of Millennials were only about half as likely to report they often had disagreements with their children as they were to say that, as children themselves, they often fought with their own parents. Our surveys also find that Millennials have a great respect for their elders. Asked which generation has the better moral values, 8 in 10 Millennials pick older adults (as do 9 in 10 Boomers).

It's hard to imagine the Boomers, back when they were coming of age with a great roar of countercultural protest, delivering a similar verdict about their elders. The campus upheavals and street rallies of the late 1960s carried a whiff of generation war. "Never trust anyone over 30," went the popular rallying cry. "We were certain in our convictions, and never more so than in our conviction that our parents were foolish to be certain in theirs," recalled Mark Salter, a longtime speechwriter for Senator John McCain. Those grievances had nothing to do with economic hardship. How could they? In 1969 the US had experienced a record 106 consecutive months of economic expansion. The unemployment rate stood at 3.5%. "I didn't have to look for a job," recalled sociologist Alan Wolfe. "The job looked for me." That was then. In recent years a smaller share of young adults has been employed than at any time since the Bureau of Labor Statistics started tracking such trends in 1948. So it's not surprising that this generation of youthful protesters has a different focus for their grievances: the economy, stupid. But notice the targets they've chosen to demonize. It's all about class, not age. It's 1% versus 99%, not young versus old. Occupy Wall Street, not Occupy Leisure World.

INTERDEPENDENCE

There's another reason this war may never be fought: it would be awkward to storm the ramparts against Mom and Dad when you're a twenty-something still living in your childhood bedroom. The multigenerational family household—an age-old living arrangement that began falling out of favor when the federal government began creating social safety net programs in the twentieth century—has come roaring back. Some 57 million Americans now live in such households, double the number in 1970. The home construction industry, among others, has taken note. Builders like the Lennar Corporation of Florida and Standard Pacific Homes of California are now promoting multigenerational floor plans that feature self-contained suites for Grandma or Junior. Boomers and their live-in Boomerangers aren't the only new family ensemble driving this new market. It also encompasses hard-pressed middle-age adults moving in with relatively well-off elderly parents. Or it's widows in declining health moving in with an adult child. Or it's the new generation of immigrants, who—like their frugal counterparts from other continents and previous centuries—are living in the same house with their extended families, an arrangement that many of them imported from their home cultures. In some cases, multigenerational households are an emergency accommodation to financial hardships or health setbacks. But there's also a happier explanation: longer life spans. According to sociologist Peter Uhlenberg, it's more likely today that a 20-year-old has a living grandmother than it was in 1900 for a 20-year-old to have a living mother.

Even when multiple generations don't live in the same home, they look after one another in other ways. Millions of middle-age adults provide various forms of caregiving to elderly parents, which is one reason the share living in nursing homes has declined over the past several decades. At the same time, millions of well-to-do seniors provide financial assistance to adult children buying homes or to grandchildren going to college. And even if they're not in a position to help out with money, millions of grandparents pitch in with time. An estimated 24% of children under the age of 5 are cared for regularly by a grandparent, and about 1 in 10 live with a grandparent.[4] All of these arrangements spread well-being up and (more typically) down the family tree—almost always in the direction of need. Then, of course, there's the biggest intergenerational family transfer of all—inheritance—which happens when the benefactors are no longer around to take pleasure in the gift of giving. A 2010 study by the Center for Retirement Research at Boston College estimated that Boomers had already inherited $2.4 trillion from their Greatest Generation parents and are in line to eventually take in an additional $6 trillion. And a 2012 report from Accenture calculated that the Boomers themselves, once they go on to their greater rewards, will be in a position to pass along up to $30 trillion to their children and grandchildren.

Those are eye-popping numbers, but they come with equally big qualifiers. The distribution of inheritance is highly skewed toward folks at the upper end of the income and wealth curve. The typical Boomer will receive an inheritance of $64,000, not exactly a ticket to financial paradise. The timing of the receipt is always uncertain; often the money arrives too late to change one's life course. And once you take into account the long-term increases in the cost of living, the gigantic numbers become less impressive. A more downbeat portrait of the financial well-being of Boomers comes from the Employee Benefits Research Institute, which has estimated that nearly half of all Boomers are at risk of not having enough income for basic living and health care expenses in retirement. Boomers themselves share this concern. A 2012 Pew Research survey found that 40% say they aren't confident they'll have enough income and assets to last throughout their retirement years. Yes, some of them eventually will be rescued by fat inheritances. The vast majority won't. Meantime, Boomers are the most "sandwiched" generation in human history—more likely than any previous cohort in its middle age to have (and be supporting or caring for, in some capacity) parents as well as children. Indeed, demographers have a new coinage—"club sandwich"—to evoke the four generations of family members that Boomers can find themselves helping. It's one of the reasons they are staying active in the workforce for an average of three or four years longer than their parents did. And that, in turn, may be one of the reasons Boomerangers are having so much trouble finding jobs and starting careers.

AS THE WORLD TURNS . . . GRAY

Financing the retirement of the Boomers without bankrupting the Boomerangers isn't only an American problem. If it's any solace, the global population boom of seniors will pose far greater stresses in Europe and East Asia. The rolling European financial and unemployment crisis has already forced austerity cuts to the social safety net at the worst possible time, especially in the continent's hard-hit southern nations. Unemployment among young adults hovers around 20% in many countries and tops 40% in Spain and Greece. *Mammismos* (mama's boys) who live at home well into their thirties have been a fixture of family life in Italy and other southern European countries since long before the current economic meltdown, but now the costs to parents and grandparents are spiking as a result. In 2012 the Spanish polling firm Simple Logica found that 40% of Spaniards ages 65 and older said they were supporting at least one younger relative; in 2010 just 15% had said the same.

These age-based economic, social, and political challenges will continue to mount as populations keep growing older. By 2050, half a dozen European nations will have a median age of 50 or older. So will Japan and South Korea. China won't be quite that old, but by 2050 it will be home to 438 million people over the age of 60. If those people were a country unto themselves, they'd trail only India and China itself in population. Some of the same analysts who once foresaw a century of unrestrained economic expansion ahead for China now wonder whether the country will "get old before it gets rich." In the coming decades it will have to cope with the economic and social consequences of its one-child policy, which has created a nation of "inverted family trees" (or, in the Chinese vernacular, 4-2-1 families—four grandparents, two children, one grandchild). In 1975 there were 12 Chinese children for every 2 seniors; by 2035, there will be just 1 Chinese child for every 2 seniors.

As these families age and as China modernizes, the obligations of filial piety so central to the Confucian social order are being severely tested. In 2013 the Chinese government toughened up its "call your mom" law with a stipulation that "family members living apart from the elderly should frequently visit or send greetings." Chinese parents, most of whom still live in rural poverty, now have the right to take legal action against their grown children, most of whom work in urban factories, if they don't stay in touch or send money. In nearby South Korea, Shin Kyung-Sook's bestseller, *Please Look After Mom,* explored filial guilt in children who fail to care for their aging parents; it sold 2 million copies. Countries as diverse as Italy, Spain, Japan, and Russia also confront upside-down family trees—in those cases, driven not by state edict but by a mix of globalization, urbanization, education, and changing gender roles and cultural mores. Fertility rates have plunged to levels never before seen in human history—sinking below 1.5 per woman in many of the world's wealthy nations. Russia is already experiencing the steepest population decline of any major country since the fourteenth century's bubonic plague. In an effort to stem the decline, President Vladimir Putin in 2012 announced he was extending the government's "baby bonus" payments of $8,300 to cover a mother's third child (previously the program had been limited to the first two). After decades of decline, fertility rates have ticked up a bit in recent years in Russia, as they have in countries such as France, Norway, Sweden, Denmark, and Singapore that have also adopted aggressive cash incentive programs for childbearing. (Singapore's package, believed to be the world's most lucrative, is estimated to be worth the equivalent of $135,000 in the first seven years of a child's life.)[5] But even with the increases, the rates in all those countries still fall well short of population replacement level.

PUBLIC ATTITUDES ABOUT SAFETY NETS

In the United States, public opinion surveys offer scant support for the notion that policy challenges presented by an aging society will lead to a generational conflict. Like middle-age and older adults, most Millennials say the government does *too little*, not too much, to support seniors. And young and old alike are more concerned that Social Security and Medicare will run out of money for benefits than about the burden that maintaining current benefit levels puts on future generations of workers and taxpayers.

Those two programs are among the most popular the government ever created. Nearly 9 in 10 Americans say they have been good for the country, and this includes at least 8 in 10 across all generations, young and old (see appendix Figure 5A.1).

However, the generations do differ in their evaluations of the effectiveness of these programs and in their receptivity to changes. A majority of the Silent Generation say they do a good job of serving the people they cover, while most Millennials, Generation Xers, and Boomers rate them as doing only a fair or poor job. Because few in these younger generations are currently drawing benefits from these programs, it's likely that their impressions have been shaped at least as much by media reports and political commentary as by direct experience.

Most Millennials (56%) and Gen Xers (66%) say Social Security needs major changes or a complete overhaul, while most in the Silent Generation (62%) say the system works pretty well. Boomers, many of whom are on the cusp of receiving Social Security themselves, are divided—45% say they think only minor changes are in order, while 50% say major changes need to be made.

Fully 86% of Millennials support changing the system so younger workers can invest their Social Security taxes in private retirement accounts. And 74% of Millennials favor changing Medicare so future participants can use the benefit toward purchasing private health insurance. Support for both of these ideas drops off among older generations and they garner a decidedly mixed reaction from those in the Silent Generation.

When it comes to proposals to gradually raise the eligibility age for these programs, there is substantially more support from those who have already reached retirement age than from those who haven't. About half in the Silent Generation favor gradually raising the Social Security retirement age and the Medicare eligibility age. Majorities across all younger generations oppose this idea. These generational patterns have a distinct flavor of self-interest—cut someone else's benefits, not mine.

A third set of proposals for entitlement changes—means-testing benefits to reduce the amounts that high-income seniors receive—divides the country, but not along generational lines. About half (53%) of Americans favor reducing Social Security benefits for seniors with higher incomes as a way to address financial problems with the system, and there is no difference in levels of support across generational lines. Similarly, 55% of the public, including nearly identical percentages across generations, favor reducing Medicare benefits for higher-income seniors (see appendix Figure 5A.2).

By 58% to 35%, the public says that keeping entitlement benefits as they are is more important than reducing the budget deficit. And by an almost identical 59% to 32% margin, more say that higher priority should be placed on avoiding future Social Security benefit cuts than on avoiding any Social Security tax increases for workers and employers (see appendix Figure 5A.3).

Resistance to benefit cuts increases across generations, but with some variances. Boomers and Silents favor preserving entitlement benefits by a ratio of at least 2 to 1, while Millennials are more evenly divided.

One factor strongly related to attitudes about entitlements is people's reliance—or expected reliance—on these programs. A majority of retired adults (56%) say that Social Security is their main source of income. But among those who are not yet retired, two-thirds (65%) say Social Security will *not* be their main source of income in retirement, while only a 32% minority say that it will. When probed further, nearly a third (31%) of non-retired adults think they will end up getting no money from Social Security in their retirement.

Not surprisingly, experiences with and expectations about Social Security vary significantly across generations. Among those in the Silent Generation—84% of whom are retired—58% cite Social Security as their main source of retirement income. Among these, 28% say it is (or will be) their only source of income in retirement, while 30% have other sources to supplement Social Security.

Millennials have starkly different expectations. More than 7 in 10 (72%) Millennials do not expect Social Security to be their main source of retirement income. In fact, 42% of Millennials think they will get no retirement income from Social Security at all, as do 35% of Generation Xers.

While around 1 in 5 Baby Boomers (22%) say they are already retired, most are not, and their expectations about Social Security are mixed. Fewer than half (42%) of Boomers say that Social Security is or will be their main source of income in retirement, with about a quarter (24%) saying it is or will be their only source of income. A majority (56%) says they will have other sources of income that are more important during retirement, though most of these (35% of all Boomers) say they expect to get at least some income from Social Security to supplement their other sources.

People's dependence, or expected dependence, on Social Security has a significant effect on their attitudes about Social Security policy. In particular, those who say Social Security is or will be their main source of income in retirement overwhelmingly favor maintaining entitlement benefits over deficit reduction as the bigger policy priority. This is particularly true among those in the Silent Generation, who have mostly retired already, but also true among Boomers and younger people as well.

Similarly, those who are counting on Social Security as their own primary income source are far more opposed than others to raising the retirement age for Social Security eligibility. The link between personal need and attitudes on this issue is notably strong among Baby Boomers. Boomers who say Social Security is or will be their main source of income oppose raising the retirement age by more than 2 to 1 (69% oppose, 29% favor), while Boomers who say other sources of income will be more important are divided (52% oppose, 47% favor).

LOOKING AHEAD

Across generations, there is considerable concern that in the future there may not be enough money to provide Social Security and Medicare benefits at their current levels. By contrast, the possibility that keeping these benefits at their current levels may put too much of a financial burden on younger generations is less of a concern—even among young generations themselves.

Majorities of Gen Xers (70%) and Millennials (57%) say they are very concerned that financial shortfalls in Social Security and Medicare may lead to reduced benefits. Fewer Gen Xers (45%) and Millennials (41%) are very concerned that maintaining current benefits may excessively burden young people.

In this regard, Gen Xers and Millennials are in sync with Boomers and Silents; among both groups, more are very concerned about possible benefit reductions than about the possibility that keeping benefits at current levels may place too much burden on younger generations (see appendix Figure 5A.4).

IS THE GOVERNMENT DOING TOO MUCH, OR NOT ENOUGH, FOR SENIORS?

The fact that federal government spending priorities over time have come to favor the old at the expense of the young isn't a concern that registers with the public. To the contrary, a majority of Americans (60%) say the federal government isn't doing *enough* for older people. They say the same about what they consider to be inadequate government spending on programs for the middle class (58%), poor people (57%), and children (57%). On the other hand, nearly two-thirds (64%) say the government does *too much* for wealthy people.

There are few differences by age in these views. More than half of each generation agree that the government does not do enough for older people, including 64% among Baby Boomers and those in Generation X, 55% of Millennials, and 52% of Silents. Notably, majorities of Democrats (69%), Republicans (52%), and Independents (56%) agree that the federal government does not do enough for older people.

The Silent Generation is least likely to say the government does not do enough for children. Just more than 4 in 10 (44%) say this, compared with 64% of Gen Xers, 59% of Baby Boomers, and 57% of Millennials.

On the other hand, the youngest generation is the most likely to say that the government does not do enough for the poor: 62% of Millennials express this view, compared with 53% of the Silent Generation. Nearly 6 in 10 Boomers agree (57%), as well as 54% of those in Gen X (see appendix Figure 5A.5).

Figure 5.1

Government Seen as Shortchanging Old, Young, Middle Class and Poor

% saying government does ...

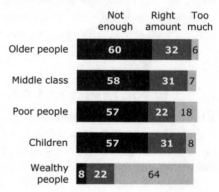

	Not enough	Right amount	Too much
Older people	60	32	6
Middle class	58	31	7
Poor people	57	22	18
Children	57	31	8
Wealthy people	8	22	64

Source: Pew Research Center survey, Sept.–Oct. 2011, N=2,410

WHO SHOULD LOOK OUT FOR OLDER PEOPLE?

The public is divided over whether the government or individuals and their families should be mainly responsible for making sure that retired older adults have at least a minimum standard of living. The differences between generations on this question are relatively small.

Among the public as a whole, about 4 in 10 (43%) say the government is mainly responsible for ensuring at least a minimal standard of living for older people, while 40% say individuals and their families are mostly responsible. Some 14% volunteer that both are equally responsible (see appendix Figure 5A.6).

Millennials and Boomers are nearly evenly divided. The balance among Gen Xers tilts toward the government (47% versus 34%), while the Silents tilt slightly more toward individual responsibility (44% versus 36%).

On this question, the divides are greater across income levels than across generations. Among those with household incomes of $75,000 or more, 51% say individuals should be mainly responsible for making sure older adults are getting a basic level of care, while 33% say the government should be. The numbers are reversed among those with household incomes of less than $30,000 (53% say the government should be mainly responsible, 29% say individuals and their families). Those with incomes between $30,000 and $74,999 are evenly divided (42% each).

When those who say that individuals are mainly responsible are questioned further about whether the government should be responsible if individuals fall short, most agree that the government should be the ultimate backstop. Lopsided majorities across all generations say the government should be mainly or partly responsible for ensuring that retired people have a minimum standard of living.

HOLES IN THE FAMILY NET

If the day comes when entitlement programs for seniors are trimmed, families will have to reclaim some of the caregiving ground they've surrendered to the state. These challenges will be daunting, because the architecture of the American family has changed dramatically since Presidents Roosevelt and Johnson built these programs in the twentieth century. As noted earlier, we are now a society in which 4 in 10 children are born out of wedlock, and in which a teenager has less chance of being raised by both biological parents than in any other country. Between nonmarriage, divorce, and short-term cohabiting unions, family life here is subject to a vast amount of churn. Our nuclear families now share the stage with a wide assortment of stepfamilies and kin networks. What impact will all this have on the bonds of intergenerational family obligation? If fathers aren't around to take care of children when they are young, who'll take care of these absent fathers when they're old? Will they become a generation of elderly orphans? "Over the course of our lives we're accumulating more and more kin to whom we owe less and less," says sociologist Andrew Cherlin, who believes our society is entering uncharted waters. Families are famously adaptive and resilient, but their future is hard to divine. Will kin networks replace nuclear families? Might friends become the new family? Can marriage mount a comeback? How Americans respond—in their public choices as well as their private behaviors—will go a long way toward determining whether the generations spend the coming decades at war or in harmony. And that, in turn, will help shape our nation's destiny in the twenty-first century.

6

Money Troubles

IF JANE SMITH, OUR PROTOTYPICAL BOOMER, is going to have the lifestyle in retirement that she's been hoping for, she'll need something more than the safety net of Social Security and Medicare. Happily, she's got something more—a 401(k). Unhappily, it won't be enough.

Jane is retiring with $120,000 in her 401(k) account. When she combines that with her Social Security check, she'll be able to draw about $24,000 a year in retirement. Trouble is, before she retired, Jane was pulling down the US median annual wage of $41,600. Financial planners say that if you want to enjoy the same standard of living in retirement that you had during your working years, you need to be able to replace roughly 80% of your annual preretirement income. Depending on your circumstances, maybe you can get by on 70%. But once you fall below that level, you'll have to start seriously scaling back. Jane is at 58%.

People tend to have fewer wants, needs, and expenses as they grow older (except, of course, for health care—about which more later). Many can downsize their lifestyles without feeling much of a pinch. But for those, like Jane, who've looked forward to their golden years as a reward after the hard slog of their work lives, it's bound to be a bit of a downer. Before we consider what Jane can do about this, let's first understand why she isn't in better financial shape as she begins this next chapter of her life.

Around the time Jane entered the workforce full-time—in 1984, after the birth of her third child—a pension revolution was just getting under way in America's workplaces. The 401(k), a new retirement savings account known by the section of the IRS code that created it, enabled employees and their employers to contribute money on a pretax basis toward the employee's retirement and have it earn interest, dividends, or capital gains on a tax-deferred basis. Initially the idea was that employers would offer these "defined contribution" plans as a supplement to their traditional "defined benefit" pension plans. The traditional plans guaranteed employees a fixed annual income from retirement until death, typically derived from a formula based on the employee's salary and years of service. But it didn't take long for employers to start treating 401(k)s as a replacement rather than a supplement. These new plans were not only much less expensive than the traditional plans, they also enabled employers to avoid the uncertainties associated with determining how much money to set aside for their obligations to future retirees (risks that many employers have managed spectacularly poorly—witness the more than a trillion dollars' worth of unfunded pension liabilities now on their books). The transition from defined benefit to defined contribution has been anything but smooth; over the years it has been the source of countless labor disputes. But for the most part, it's over. In 1983, among all workers who had some kind of pension coverage, 62% had a defined benefit plan only and just 12% had a defined contribution (401[k]-type) plan only; the remainder had both. By 2010 these shares had flipped—69% had only a defined contribution plan and just 19% had only a traditional defined benefit pension (a smaller remainder had both).[1] Nowadays, traditional defined benefit plans are pretty much confined to the public employee sector, and many of those are being scaled back or eliminated—witness Detroit's 2014 bankruptcy, which resulted in a court-approved reduction in pension payments to both current and future retired city employees. Within the next generation, Social Security is likely to be the only defined benefit revenue stream to the vast majority of America's retirees.

During her 35-year career, Jane worked for three small companies, none of which offered a traditional pension plan. So she spent her entire working life determined to take full advantage of her 401(k)s. She's frugal, has a good head for math, and was quick to grasp the value of using tax-deferred dollars to build her nest egg. Plus, her various employers were contributing 50 cents for every dollar she invested in her plan, so the financial incentives were substantial. But life kept getting in the way—a costly divorce, college tuition for the kids, her daughter's wedding, unexpected medical bills. There were lots of years when she wasn't able to contribute enough of her own money to qualify for the full employer match—meaning she left a chunk of her employer's money on the table. One year she had to take out a hardship loan from her 401(k) savings, subjecting herself to a tax penalty and joining the estimated 1 in 4 workers with such plans who've done the same thing. On top of that, Jane isn't the world's greatest investor. She would periodically move her money into or out of various stock funds in her 401(k) portfolio at what she thought were the market's peaks and valleys, only to find herself wrong-footed. Jane's story, alas, is pretty typical. (Sorry, Jane, that's your fate!) Despite the many attractive features of 401(k)s (tax breaks, personal choice, employer matches), the evidence from the past 30 years is clear: they don't come close to replacing the security and certainty of a defined benefit pension system.

"Basing a [retirement] system on people's voluntarily saving for 40 years and evaluating the relevant information for sound investment choices is like asking the family pet to dance on two legs," writes Teresa Ghilarducci, an economics professor and retirement policy expert at the New School for Social Research. "First, figure out when you or your spouse will be laid off or be too sick to work. Second, figure out when you will die. Third, understand you need to save 7 percent of every dollar you earn. Fourth, earn at least 3 percent above inflation on your investments. Fifth, do not withdraw any funds when you lose your job, have a health problem, get divorced, buy a house or send a kid to college. Sixth, time your retirement account withdrawals so the last cent is spent on the day you die."[2]

Most people can't pull that off. As a result, among all adults who have either a 401(k), an IRA, or some similar tax-advantaged retirement plan and are approaching retirement age (and, by the way, just 60% of households headed by someone on the cusp of retirement have such plans in the first place), the typical balance in these accounts is Jane's $120,000. And they're much better off than those without such accounts. Indeed, if one looks at all Americans on the cusp of retirement, about three-quarters have less than $30,000 in retirement savings, according to the AARP. These levels have risen only modestly in recent years, despite the stock market recovery that began in 2009, and despite the fact that recent cohorts of new retirees have spent more of their working lives in a position to take advantage of 401(k) plans. How far does $120,000 go? Not very. If a 65-year-old married retiree were to convert $120,000 into a standard joint-and-survivor annuity today, it would yield a guaranteed monthly income for life of $575—not exactly a ticket to Easy Street. The modest yield is partly a function of declining interest rates and partly of rising life spans. According to the Society of Actuaries, for a married 65-year-old couple, there's a 45% chance that one of the spouses will live until age 90 and a 20% chance that one will live to age 95. That's good karma for old age, but bad for defined contribution plans. "Many participants are likely to be surprised—and disappointed—when they find out how little their 401(k) plan provides," wrote Alicia Munnell, director of the Center for Retirement Research at Boston College, in 2012. And the disappointments will grow even more acute as retirees discover that Medicare covers only about half of the overall health care bill the typical senior incurs between turning age 65 and the end of life. The rest of the tab—in the form of deductibles, coinsurance, uncovered services, and the uninsured cost of long-term care—will have to come either out of the senior's pocket or from Medicaid. But to qualify for Medicaid, the senior must either be poor or descend into poverty.

IT AIN'T EASY BEING YOUNG

Now here's the really bad news: whatever economic challenges the over-65s are facing these days, they pale by comparison with the money troubles of the young. In the past decade they've been hammered on every front—a difficult job market, runaway college tuition costs, record student loan debt, and a housing market bust that has hit young homeowners much harder than older ones. Worse, this isn't just a Great Recession phenomenon. It's the continuation of a situation that has seen the old prosper relative to the young for many decades. The result has been that Millennials and Xers are not only in far worse financial shape than Boomers and Silents now, they are also in worse shape than these older generations were back when they were the age that Millennials and Xers are now.

Any generational audit should start by looking at the household wealth—the sum of all assets (house, car, stocks and bonds, 401[k]s, etc.) minus all debts (mortgage, car loan, credit card debt, student loan debt, etc.). Unlike income, which can be subject to short-term fluctuations, wealth is a stock of assets, typically accumulated over time, that provides its owner with a foundation of economic well-being—a cushion in the event of short-term economic shocks, funds to purchase big-ticket items, a source of retirement income, and social and economic capital to pass on to one's children and grandchildren. People tend to gather more wealth as they get older, so it's no surprise that there's a big age gap on this measure. What is surprising is how big it has become. In an America that's rapidly going gray, it's not just the people who are migrating north on the age pyramid. It's also money. Back in 1983, the gap in wealth between the typical household headed by an adult age 65 or older and one headed by an adult under the age of 35 was 8 to 1. By 2013, that gap had ballooned to 20 to 1. In the intervening three decades, wealth had gone up sharply for older adults, rising by 75% in inflation-adjusted dollars, and deteriorated badly for younger adults, falling by 31%. (This analysis doesn't factor in the rising share of young adults who are still living in their childhood bedrooms and thus not counted as heads of household.)

How has this happened? When it comes to wealth accumulation, today's young adults have three things going against them. First, they've had a tough time finding work in a high-unemployment economy. Many aren't even trying. For the past four years, an average of just 63% of adults ages 18 to 29 were either employed or seeking employment, the lowest labor force participation rate for this age cohort since women began their march into the workforce four decades ago. In part these low numbers reflect the record shares of 18- to 24-year-olds enrolled in college—41% now, up from 25% in 1980. If history is a guide, today's college grads will earn anywhere from $500,000 to $1 million more over the course

Figure 6.1

Median Net Worth by Age of Householder, 1983 and 2013

In 2013 dollars (unless otherwise noted)

	1983	2013	Change 1983 to 2013
All	$76,614	$81,400	6%
Younger than 35	$15,260	$10,460	−31%
35–44	$88,897	$47,050	−47%
45–54	$123,841	$105,350	−15%
55–64	$150,693	$165,720	10%
65 and older	$120,524	$210,500	75%

Source: Pew Research Center tabulations of Survey of Consumer Finances public-use data

of their lifetimes than their buddies who never went. But at least in the short term, college has been a net financial drag on this young generation.[3]

Average tuition and fees have nearly tripled at public and private colleges since 1980, even after adjusting for inflation. In 2010 a record 40% of all households headed by someone under the age of 35 were carrying student loan debt, up from 17% in 1989. Among households owing such debt, the average balance in 2010 was $28,100, nearly triple the figure (in inflation-adjusted dollars) from 1989.

In standard economic theory, this sort of borrowing enhances human capital and earning power. It qualifies as "good debt"—productive in the long run for both the debtor and society. But Millennials are on a slow walk to the long run. For now, about half of those with student loans say this debt has made it more difficult to make ends meet; about a quarter say it has affected their career choices or made it harder to buy a home; and a small share—about 1 in 13—say it has caused them to delay marriage or parenthood. "The next generation is starting their economic race 50 yards behind the starting line," warned the prologue to *Generation Debt: Why Now Is a Terrible Time to Be Young*, by newly minted Yale University graduate Anya Kamenetz. Her book and that of another Millennial author, Tamara Draut (*Strapped: Why America's 20- and 30-Somethings Can't Get Ahead*), were both published in 2006, *before* the Great Recession deepened their generation's debt woes. As the national economy has

Figure 6.2

Average Student Debt Outstanding Among Households with Student Debt, 1989–2013

In 2014 dollars

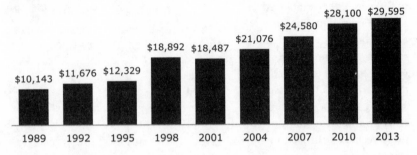

Note: Includes education loans that are currently in deferment and loans in scheduled repayment period.

Source: Pew Research Center analysis of the Survey of Consumer Finances

finally begun to recover, Millennials have led other generations in shedding debt. From 2007 to 2010 their total debt went down by 29%, compared with a drop of 8% for households headed by an adult age 35 or older.[4] But even this seemingly happy statistic has a dark side. The biggest reason Millennials have less debt is that they have fewer homes and cars than their same-age counterparts had in the past. They've downsized their lifestyles.

HOUSING

When the housing bubble burst in 2006, it seized up the financial markets, wrecked lots of people's financial lives, sent millions of homeowners into foreclosure or left them with mortgages that exceeded the value of their home, and plunged the economy into a tailspin from which it is still struggling to recover. That sorry saga is pretty well-known. Less well understood, however, is how much of a generational skew there has been to this housing calamity.

Housing is the most important component of wealth of the typical American. In 2011, despite the collapse of the housing market, home equity (the market value of a house minus mortgage debt) still accounted for about 75% of the total wealth of the median US household. The public's next largest asset—stocks and mutual funds—came in a distant second. But housing has been a much better investment for the old than for the young—largely as a result of nothing more complicated than good timing. A majority of today's older homeowners purchased their present home before 1986, at "pre-bubble" prices. Along with every other homeowner, they were hurt by the housing market collapse of recent years, but over the long haul, the vast majority have seen their home equity rise. Moreover, two-thirds of homeowners ages 65 and older no longer have a mortgage to pay, so they haven't had to worry about going underwater or facing foreclosure. For young adults in their 20s, 30s, and early 40s, no such luck. Among those who are homeowners, most bought at bubble-inflated prices. And when the bubble burst, many were left with negative equity in their homes. Figure 6.3 shows the time trends by age over a quarter century.

The contrast in fortunes could hardly be more stark. The typical household head age 65 or older had 36% more equity in his home in 2011 (in inflation-adjusted dollars) than his same-age counterpart had in 1984, while the typical household head age 44 or younger had only about half the equity in his home that his same-age counterpart had in

Figure 6.3

Change in Median Home Equity, by Age of Householder, 1984–2011

% change

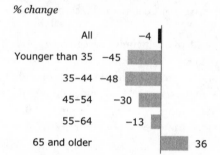

Note: Standardized to 2011 dollars.

Source: Pew Research Center analysis of the Survey of Income and Program Participation data and US Census Bureau P-70, No. 7; Household Wealth and Asset Ownership, 1984: Data from the Survey of Income and Program Participation, Table 5

1984. If there's any silver lining for the younger generation, it's that houses are still selling at a heavy discount from their market peak in 2006. That represents a potential transfer of trillions of dollars in wealth from today's homeowners (who skew old) to tomorrow's home buyers (who skew young). Of course, as the housing market finally begins to recover, these bargains will dry up.

INCOME AND POVERTY

Median household income is yet another measure that illustrates how the old have been prospering relative to the young. Households in all age groups have made gains in annual income compared with their same-age predecessors over the course of the past half century, but the incomes of the oldest households have risen four times as sharply as those of the youngest ones. As a result, incomes of the oldest households, which had been lower than those of younger households, are catching up.

In households headed by adults younger than 35, the median adjusted annual income grew by 28% from 1967 to 2012 (from $40,650 to $51,962). By contrast, in households headed by adults ages 65 and older, median income increased by 108% during the same period (from $21,908 to $45,563; all figures expressed in 2012 dollars and standardized to a household size of three).

As these generational shifts in median income were occurring, Social Security continued to provide a bedrock of stable support for older adults. During the past three decades, it contributed a steady share—about 55%—of the rising annual median incomes of households headed by adults ages 65 and older.

Median income reflects what is happening at the middle of the socioeconomic ladder. Poverty statistics reflect what is happening at the bottom, where the divergence in economic fortunes by generation could hardly be more stark. In 1967, older households were nearly three times more likely than younger ones to be in poverty. Today they are only half as likely. In the intervening years, poverty rates have declined by two-thirds among the old while doubling among the young. These trends result from many factors—government policies that favor the old over the young; structural changes in the economy and labor force; compositional changes in the age pyramid (i.e., a rising share of young adults are historically disadvantaged minorities); and a method of counting poverty that critics say has grown outdated.[5] Whatever the causes, alleviating poverty among the elderly is one of the great success stories of the past half century. But the gains have come, at least in part, on the backs of the young.

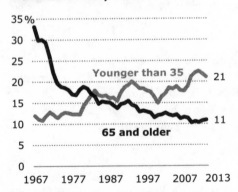

Figure 6.4

Share of Households in Poverty, by Age of Householder, 1967–2013

Source: Pew Research Center analysis of the Current Population Survey Annual Social and Economic Supplement, IPUMS

EMPLOYMENT

The American workforce is graying—and not just because the American population itself is graying. Older adults are staying in the labor force longer, and younger adults are staying out of it longer. According to one government estimate, 93% of the growth in the US labor force from 2006 to 2016 will be among workers ages 55 and older.

Appendix Figure 6A.1 shows the trends. Starting around 2000, the share of young adults who are employed began falling sharply while the share of older adults who are employed began rising. These were both reversals of the patterns that had prevailed in the 1970s and 1980s, when the women's revolution was bringing young women into the workforce in unprecedented numbers. At the same time, the growing aspiration of older adults to retire young was taking more and more of them out of the workforce at younger ages. But young women have reached labor force participation parity with young men, so there are no more dramatic gains to be had from changing gender work patterns. As for older adults, their aspiration to retire early has cooled off markedly in the past two decades. The average age of retirement for men fell to a modern low of 62 in 1995 but has since climbed back up to 64. For decades, the Gallup Poll has been asking working Americans when they expect to retire. In 1996, the average answer was age 60. By 2012, it was 67. Perhaps not incidentally, the age at which a worker can receive the standard Social Security retirement benefit has also been rising gradually, and will eventually reach 67 (up from the traditional 65) for those born in 1960 or later.

It's not only economic necessity that has been keeping more older adults on the job. Attitudes about work also play an important role—in particular, the desire of an aging but healthy population to stay active well into the later years of life. A 2009 Pew Research survey found that a majority (54%) of workers ages 65 and older said the main reason they continue to work is that they want to. Just 17% say the main reason is that they need the paycheck, while about a quarter (27%) say they're motivated by a mix of desire and need. Among workers ages 16 to 64, the pattern was reversed—many more say they work because they need to than say they work because they want to.

When asked to identify specific reasons for working, older workers emphasized psychological and social factors: "to feel useful"; "to give myself something to do"; "to be with other people." Younger and middle-age workers were much more inclined to cite classic pocketbook considerations: "to support myself and my family"; "to live independently"; "to qualify for retirement benefits"; "to receive health care benefits."

Figure 6.5

Work Because You Need To? It Depends on Your Age

% of workers who say they work because they ...

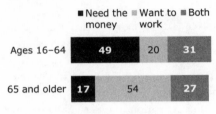

Note: Based on those who work full or part time.

Source: Pew Research Center survey, July–Aug. 2009, N=1,815 residents ages 16 and older

The recession-racked economy of 2009 darkened nearly everyone's calculations about the economics of old age. According to a Pew Research survey that year, nearly 4 in 10 adults who were working past the median retirement age of 62 said they had delayed their retirement because of the recession. And among workers ages 50 to 61, fully 63% said they might have to push back their expected retirement date because of current economic conditions.

Three years later, the economy was slowly climbing out of its ditch, but retirement confidence had yet to stage a recovery. To the contrary, it kept falling. In 2012, nearly 4 in 10 (38%) of all adults said they were not confident they had enough income and assets to last through their retirement years, up from 25% who felt that way in the recession year of 2009. Interestingly, the age group most concerned about financing its retirement is adults in their late 30s and early 40s. It's almost as if, having finally reached the milestones of adulthood—marriage, parenthood, homeownership—this cohort of middle-age Gen Xers suddenly started doing their retirement math and realized that it didn't add up.

Nor is this the only indication from recent Pew Research surveys of the toll the bad economy has taken on the economic self-confidence of young and middle-age adults. As noted in the last chapter, Millennials are strikingly upbeat about their long-term financial prospects; they are more likely than any other age group to say they'll eventually have enough money to live the life they want. That confidence notwithstanding, they are also more likely than any other age group to place themselves in the lower or lower-middle class. Nearly half (46%) do so, up from 25% who said the same in early 2008, as the Great Recession was just beginning. Millennials are much more likely than adults ages 65 and older to place themselves in one of the two lower socioeconomic classes, one illustration of the way the changing economic fortunes of young and old have left a mark on the way these generations view themselves.

Every car salesman knows that Millennials' big-ticket purchasing habits reflect these changes. One of the great mysteries confronting the (otherwise recovering) auto industry these days is: How do you sell a car to a twenty-something? In 2010, adults between the ages of 21 and 34 bought 27% of all new vehicles sold in America, down from a peak of 38% in 1985. "The Young and the Carless" is how one trade publication summed up the trend. Technological change may also be playing a role. "Cars used to be what people aspired to own," says Mark Norman, president of Zipcar, the world's largest car-sharing company. "Now it's the smartphone."[6] Whatever the mix of reasons, Millennials are also buying fewer houses—especially in the car-centric suburbs—than their same-age counterparts did a generation ago.

Figure 6.6

Which Age Group in What Class?

% who say they are ...

	Upper class*	Middle class	Lower class*
All adults	13	47	40
Younger than 30	11	43	46
30–49	13	48	39
50–64	11	48	38
65 and older	17	47	35

*"Upper class" includes those who identify as upper or upper-middle class; "lower class" includes those who identify as lower or lower-middle class.

Source: Pew Research Center survey, Feb. 2015, N=1,504 US adults

Consumer spending drives between 60% and 70% of the US economy, and one reason the recovery has been so sluggish is that so few Millennials are able or inclined to open their wallets. Their low levels of income and wealth and high rates of student debt are likely to put a damper on their economic fortunes for decades to come. They're also facing trillions of dollars in taxes or foregone government goods and services, or both, to pay off the public debt bequeathed to them by their elders. And they'll spend trillions more to finance the entitlement programs for those same parents and grandparents in their old age.

Meantime, where does this leave Jane and her underfunded retirement? For starters, she can be pretty confident that her Social Security and Medicare benefits are safe. No elected official who's compos mentis could look at the public opinion survey findings about those programs and touch the current benefits of current retirees (except, perhaps, the wealthy ones). When Jane compares her economic circumstances at retirement with those of her parents and grandparents at the same stage of life, she knows she's ahead of the game. But when she looks at the economic circumstances facing her kids and grandkids, she knows they're in for a rougher financial ride than she's had. That explains why Junior is living in her house, rent-free. And it's why, now that she's retired, she's spending two days a week caring for young grandchildren, as a way to free up her daughter to work part-time. This wasn't exactly Plan A for Jane's golden years. But as her children have already figured out, it's good to have a Plan B.

The New Immigrants

IMMIGRATION IS THE ENGINE that makes and remakes America. After a long hiatus in the middle of the twentieth century brought on by a social and political backlash, an economic depression, and a world war, the engine is roaring once again. That's good news for anyone who worries about the issue at the heart of this book—how we reengineer the compact between the generations. It's even better news for those who wonder whether the US can remain the world's indispensable nation on into another century. Immigrants are strivers. They have energy, ingenuity, a tolerance for risk, an appetite for hard work, and a faith in the future. Few if any countries have been more enriched by immigrants than ours. And not many are better at weaving them into the social, political, and economic fabric of their new home.

Even so, immigration never starts out easy. Emma Lazarus's inscription on the Statue of Liberty notwithstanding, Americans don't typically welcome newcomers with arms fully extended, especially not when they arrive in large numbers. "Going back to the Founding Fathers—with their formula of limited government, civic equality and tolerance of religious and cultural diversity—each new surge of arrivals has been greeted as a crisis without precedent, only to disappear with unexpected speed as the nation faces new challenges," writes Michael Barone, author of a 2013 book on the impact of immigrants on politics.[1] We worry that they'll take our jobs, drain our resources, threaten our language, mongrelize our race, worship false idols, and import crime and vice. People once said such things about the Irish, Germans, Italians, Poles, Greeks, Slavs, Russians, Jews, and pretty much every other immigrant wave that came ashore, just as today some say the same about Hispanics and Asians.

And throughout history we've hurled insults at new arrivals that make Donald Trump almost sound tame. "The scum of the earth has descended upon us," Thomas E. Watson, a populist congressman, newspaper editor, and (later) senator from Georgia wrote in 1910. "The most dangerous and corrupting hordes of the Old World have invaded us. The vice and crime which they have planted in our midst is sickening and terrifying."

But still they come, chasing dreams, escaping nightmares, and in greater numbers than ever. Today the US is home to a record 45 million immigrants and 38.5 million US-born children of immigrants. If current birthrates and immigration flows continue, an estimated 88% of the population growth in the US between now and 2065 will be accounted for by new immigrants and their descendants, according to a 2015 projection by the Pew Research Center.[2] By 2065, an estimated 159 million Americans, or 36% of the population, will be

Figure 7.1

"Immigrant Stock" Share of US Population, Actual and Projected, 1900–2065

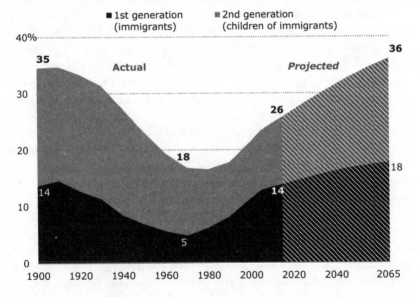

Note: Based on total population, including children and adults.

Source: Data for 1960–2065 from 2015 Pew Research Center report "Modern Immigration Wave Brings 59 Million to US, Driving Population Growth and Change Through 2065"; trends for 1900–1955 from Edmonston and Passel, *Immigration and Ethnicity: The Integration of America's Newest Arrivals*, Washington, DC: The Urban Institute Press, 1994

"immigrant stock" (immigrants themselves or their US-born descendants), equaling the peaks reached in the late 19th and early 20th centuries, when previous immigration waves brought tens of millions of newcomers to a much more sparsely populated America.

The big difference between now and then is who these immigrants are and where they're coming from. Half of all new arrivals in the post-1965 immigration wave have been from Latin America and a quarter from Asia (since 2009, though, Asians have surpassed Hispanics in new arrivals). Europe, which had sent 9 in 10 of America's immigrants during the earlier immigration eras, supplies only about 1 in 10 today. Africa, the Middle East, and other regions account for the remaining 12 percent (see appendix Figure 7A.1).

Because of this shift, immigrants in the twenty-first century are doing more than replenishing our labor force and electorate. They're changing our complexion. America is already one of the most racially and ethnically diverse nations in history, and the modern immigration wave is making our tapestry more intricate with each passing year. In 1965 our population was 84% white; by 2065 it will be 46% white, according to Pew Research projections. How we handle the identity issues that accompany such a sweeping racial makeover is the subject of Chapter 8. Here we focus on the economics, demographics, and politics of immigration, starting with this question: Will the great American story of generational upward mobility—wherein the children of immigrants do better than their parents, and the grandchildren do better yet—play out in the twenty-first century as it did for their counterparts in the nineteenth and twentieth?

In the modern era, lots of immigration scholars and policy-makers have been skeptical. They cite a range of factors: most of today's immigrants are non-European and thus face more deeply entrenched cultural barriers than did their predecessors; about a quarter of all immigrants (the vast majority Hispanic) arrived illegally and thus must navigate lives of stunted opportunity in the shadows of the law; globalization and the digital revolution have eliminated many of the jobs that provided ladders into the middle class for earlier generations of immigrants; the close proximity of the largest sending country (Mexico) and the growing ease of all international travel and communication have enabled today's immigrants to retain their ties to their countries of origin, thereby reducing pressures to adopt America's language, customs, values, and mores.

The worries all have a ring of legitimacy, but increasingly they compete with a growing body of facts on the ground that tell a more upbeat story. The modern immigration wave is mature enough to have produced a sizable adult "second generation" (US-born children of immigrants). In recent years the

Pew Research Center has generated a trove of information about this group, some from our own surveys and some based on our analysis of US Census Bureau data. The headline findings are almost entirely positive. Second-generation Hispanic and Asian American adults are following a well-trekked path in American history—doing better than the immigrant generation on key measures of socioeconomic attainment and cultural adaptation (see appendix Figure 7A.2). Moreover, like their parents' generation, they place more importance than other Americans do on such "traditional American values" as family, hard work, education, and career success.

HISPANICS

There are some blemishes in the story, but first let's register the good news, starting with Hispanics. A decade ago the eminent Harvard historian Samuel Huntington wrote that "the single most immediate and most serious challenge to America's traditional identity comes from the immense and continuing immigration from Latin America, especially from Mexico. . . . The extent and nature of this immigration differ fundamentally from those of previous immigrations, and the assimilation successes of the past are unlikely to be duplicated with the contemporary flood of immigrants from Latin America." Huntington was primarily concerned by what he saw as shortcomings in Hispanic values and culture, which he feared over time would erode this country's Anglo-Saxon work ethic, language, rule of law, individualism—the "American creed," as he called it. Other scholars have focused on more tangible deficits. They worry that the relative paucity of human capital—money, education, job skills—that most Hispanics have brought with them across the border will consign the immigrants and their progeny to economically marginal lives in a knowledge-based economy. Three-quarters of all adult Hispanic immigrants have only a high school degree or less; half are in this country illegally; only a third speak English proficiently.

Such deficits, however, have not condemned their children to a purgatory in the underclass. In 2012, the 7 million Hispanic adults in the second generation had a significantly higher median annual household income[3] than the 17.5 million in the immigrant generation ($48,000 versus $35,000), a higher share with at least some college or more (52% versus 24%), a higher home-ownership rate (50% versus 43%), and a lower poverty rate (16% versus 23%). On all of these indicators, the adult Hispanic second generation still trails the overall adult population of the US, whose 2012 median income for a household of three was $58,000; share with at least some college was 57%; home-ownership rate was 65%; and poverty rate was 13%. But the data suggest a classic progression toward the mean, the more notable because the second generation of Hispanic adults have a median age of just 28, nearly two decades younger than the median age (46) of all American adults (see appendix Figure 7A.3). If history is a guide, median incomes and homeownership rates of second-generation Hispanics will rise as more become middle-age. In the meantime, for the vast majority of Hispanics—first and second generations alike—there's already a strong appreciation for the upward arc of their life journey. Seven in 10 Hispanic adults of the first (71%) and second (67%) generations say their own standard of living is better than their parents' was at the same stage of life. Among all US adults, just 60% say the same.

When it comes to basic measures of social and cultural integration—language, friends, spouses, identity—second-generation Hispanics are much more rooted than immigrant Hispanics in the US mainstream. Fully 93% say they speak English very or pretty well, compared with 48% of the immigrant generation. They are twice as likely as immigrants to say Hispanics as a group get along very or pretty well with whites, blacks, and Asian Americans (52% versus 26%). They are nearly four times as likely to marry a non-Hispanic (26% versus 7% among married adults). They are less likely to say that most or all of their friends come from their family's country of origin (49% versus 64%) and they are almost twice as likely to say they think of themselves as a "typical American" (61% versus 33%).

At the same time, however, second-generation Hispanics retain strong ties to the land and language of their ancestors. Eight in 10 say they can speak Spanish at least pretty well, and more than 9 in 10 say it is important that

Figure 7.2

Generational Differences in Intergroup Relations

% saying their group gets along with each of three other groups "very well" or "pretty well"

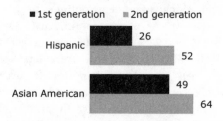

Note: Hispanics were asked how well they get along with blacks, Asians and whites. Asian Americans were asked how well [country of origin] Americans get along with blacks, Hispanics or Latinos, and whites.

Source: Pew Research Center National Survey of Latinos, Sep.–Oct. 2012 (N=1,765 US Hispanic adults), and Pew Research Center Asian-American Survey, Jan.– Mar. 2012 (N=3,511 US Asian adults)

future generations of Hispanics living in the US be able to do so as well. A majority say they most often identify themselves by their family's country of origin (e.g., Mexican American) or by a pan-ethnic label, such as Hispanic or

Latino; just 35% say they most often identify simply as American. That's more than the first generation (8%) and less than the third-and-higher generation (48%), indicating a trajectory of assimilation over time (see appendix Figure 7A.4).[4] However, with only half of third-plus-generation Hispanics saying they typically describe themselves as Americans, assimilation has come to mean something different. Our twentieth-century metaphor was "melting pot." Our twenty-first-century metaphor, in a much more racially and ethnically diverse nation, is "mosaic." Each piece contributes to a whole, but not by losing its distinctiveness.

On values related to work and family, first- and second-generation Hispanics are more similar to one another than to the general public. For example, 78% of both immigrant and second-generation Hispanics say that most people who want to get ahead in life can make it if they're willing to work hard, an optimistic outlook shared by just 58% of the full US public. Both generations of Hispanics are also more likely than the general public to say they place high importance on career success, having a good marriage, and being a good parent, and they're equally likely to place high importance on leading a religious life. In short, they're family-oriented, religious strivers. That's a pretty good summary of what most people mean when they talk about "traditional American values." Far from eroding the American creed, Hispanics are among its most ardent believers.

Not all socioeconomic and cultural indicators are positive. Hispanic educational attainment continues to lag behind that of other racial and ethnic groups by sizable margins. Just 15% of all Hispanic adults ages 25 and older (and 21% of the adult second generation) have a bachelor's degree or higher. The problem isn't aspirational—about 9 in 10 Hispanics say getting a college education is important to success in life. It's economic. Hispanics who dropped out of high school or college, when asked why they didn't continue their education, typically cite a lack of money or the need to support a family.

These education gaps have narrowed sharply in recent years. The Hispanic high school dropout rate has fallen by nearly half since 2000 (1 dropout for every 5 high school graduates now versus 1 for every 3 in 2000). The 2012 National Assessment of Educational Progress showed that over a four-decade span, Hispanic elementary and secondary school students had closed some of their achievement gaps with whites in reading and math (even as rates for all racial groups rose). And in 2012, for the first time ever, a Hispanic high school graduate was as likely as a white high school graduate to enroll in college the following fall. However, for many Hispanic students, college means a two-year rather than a four-year degree. And no matter what kind of college they enroll in, a disproportionate share leave before getting a degree. But while problems remain, the long-term progress has been more impressive than generally understood.

In addition to their education deficits, Hispanics have a deficit of social trust. A classic question in social science research asks respondents: "Generally speaking, would you say that most people can be trusted or that you can't be too careful when dealing with people?" By a whopping 86% to 12% margin (with virtually no differences between the first and second generations) Hispanics say you can't be too careful. Among the general public, caution also trumps trust, but not by nearly as much: 59% say you can't be too careful and 37% say people can be trusted (see appendix Figure 7A.5). In a heterogeneous, fast-paced, risk-taking culture such as ours, social trust helps to keep the gears from grinding.

A third and perhaps most surprising deficit among His-

Figure 7.3

Immediate Entry into College by Race and Ethnicity, 2000–2013

% of recent high school completers enrolled in college the following October

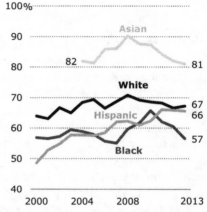

Note: White, black and Asian include the Hispanic portion of those groups. Due to the small sample size for Hispanics, blacks and Asians, a 3-year moving average is used. The 3-year moving average uses the year indicated, the year immediately preceding and the year immediately following. For 2012 a 2-year moving average is used.

Source: US Bureau of Labor Statistics, annual "College Enrollment and Work Activity of High School Graduates" news releases, and National Center for Education Statistics, *The Condition of Education 2012*

panics, especially those in the second generation, has to do with the diminished link between births and marriage. More than half of all births to Hispanic women are to single mothers. Hispanics themselves disapprove in overwhelming numbers of nonmarital births (as do all Americans), but here's a case where norms are in one place and behaviors in another. As Chapter 9 describes in detail, marriage rates have been falling and nonmarital births have been rising among all demographic groups in America for the past half century. The 53% nonmarital birthrate among Hispanics falls between the figure for whites (29%) and that for blacks (71%). The social science findings could not be more clear: all else equal, children born to single mothers tend to do less well in life than those born to married parents. In 2010, a plurality of all poor children in the US were Hispanic. That unhappy milestone is partly a function of population growth and partly of childhood poverty rates that spiked during the recession to 35% among Latinos in 2010, far surpassing that of white children (12%) and nearly equaling the 39% share among black children (see appendix Figure 7A.6).[5] Going forward, the well-being of future generations of Hispanics will depend as much on the families they form—or fail to form—as on the nation's immigration policies or economic trends.

ASIAN AMERICANS

In 2012 the Pew Research Center published a major report on Asian Americans that drew criticism from some of their leading civic and interest groups. Their complaint, in a nutshell: too much good news. Odd on its face, but less so in light of their history and culture. Aside from blacks and Native Americans, no group in this country has been the target of more official discrimination or social stigma. In the late nineteenth century all immigration from China was explicitly prohibited by act of Congress; in the early twentieth century Indian Americans had their official race designation changed from Asian to white and then back again; during World War II 120,000 law-abiding Japanese Americans were rounded up and sent off to internment camps; and it was not until 1952 that Asian-American immigrants were permitted to apply for US citizenship.

That history is enough to make any group wary, but for Asians the reticence about trumpeting success also has a cultural basis. Chinese and Japanese proverbs warn that the nail that sticks out gets hammered down, while a similar American proverb conveys the opposite lesson: the squeaky wheel gets greased. After the report came out, I had a series of spirited exchanges with community leaders. They argued that lots of Asian Americans are struggling, that their community is enormously diverse, and that the patronizing term "model minority" (which the report was careful *not* to use) paints with too broad a brush. So stipulated. But I countered that data are data. And when you gather up all the relevant numbers you can find about this remarkable immigrant group, you wind up with a story that leaps off the page. Here is a condensed version of the overview of the report, which was based on one of the most comprehensive surveys of Asian Americans ever conducted.[6]

Asian Americans are the highest-income, best-educated, and fastest-growing racial group in the US. They are more satisfied than the general public with their lives, finances, and the direction of the country, and they place more value than other Americans do on marriage, parenthood, hard work, and career success.

A century ago, most Asian Americans were low-skilled, low-wage laborers crowded into ethnic enclaves and targets of official discrimination. Today they are the most likely of any major racial or ethnic group in America to live in mixed neighborhoods and to marry across racial lines. When newly minted medical school graduate Priscilla Chan married Facebook founder Mark Zuckerberg in the spring of 2012, she joined the 37% of all recent Asian-American brides who wed a non-Asian groom.

These milestones of economic success and social assimilation have come to a group that is still majority immigrant. Nearly three-quarters (74%) of Asian-American adults were born abroad; of these, about half say they speak English very well and half say they don't.

Asians recently passed Hispanics as the largest group of new immigrants to the US. The educational credentials of these recent arrivals are striking. More than 6 in 10 (61%) adults ages 25 to 64 who have come from Asia in recent years have at least a bachelor's degree. This is double the share among recent non-Asian arrivals, and almost surely makes the recent Asian arrivals the most highly educated cohort of immigrants in US history.

Compared with the educational attainment of the population in their country of origin, recent Asian immigrants also stand out as a select group. For example, about 27% of adults ages 25 to 64 in South Korea and 25% in Japan have a bachelor's degree or more.[7] In contrast, nearly 70% of comparably aged recent immigrants from these two countries have at least a bachelor's degree (for more, see appendix Figure 7A.7).

Figure 7.4

Asian Americans Lead Others in Education, Income

% with a bachelor's degree or more, among ages 25 and older, 2010

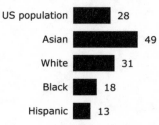

Median household income, 2010

Note: Asians include mixed-race Asian population, regardless of Hispanic origin. Household income is based on householders ages 18 and older; race and ethnicity are based on those of household head.

Source: Pew Research Center analysis of 2010 American Community Survey, IPUMS

Figure 7.5

Meet the New Immigrants: Asians Overtake Hispanics

% of immigrants, by year of arrival, 2000–2014

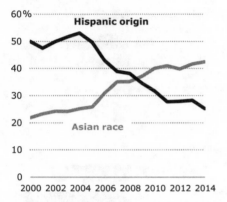

Note: Based on total foreign-born population, including adults and children. Asians include mixed-race Asian population, regardless of Hispanic origin. Estimates derived from information on year of arrival in the US; projection for 2014 based on 2009–2013 trends.

Source: Pew Research Center analysis of 2001–2013 American Community Survey and 2000 decennial census, IPUMS

Recent Asian immigrants are also about three times as likely as recent immigrants from other parts of the world to receive their green cards—or permanent resident status—on the basis of employer rather than family sponsorship (though family reunification remains the most common legal gateway to the US for Asian immigrants, as it is for all immigrants).

The modern immigration wave from Asia is nearly a half century old and has pushed the total population of Asian Americans—foreign born and US born, adults and children—to a record 20.3 million in 2014, or 6.4% of the total US population, up from less than 1% in 1965.

Asian Americans trace their roots to any of dozens of countries in the Far East, Southeast Asia, and the Indian subcontinent. Each country of origin subgroup has its own unique history, culture, language, religious beliefs, economic and demographic traits, social and political values, and pathways into America.

But despite often sizable subgroup differences, Asian Americans are distinctive as a whole, especially when compared with all US adults, whom they exceed not just in the share with a college degree (49% versus 28%), but also in median annual household income ($66,000 versus $49,800) and median household wealth ($83,500 versus $68,529).[8]

They are noteworthy in other ways, too. They are more satisfied than the general public with their lives overall (82% versus 75%), their personal finances (51% versus 35%), and the general direction of the country (43% versus 21%).

They also stand out for their strong emphasis on family. More than half (54%) say that having a successful marriage is one of the most important things in life; just 34% of all American adults agree. Two-thirds of Asian-American adults (67%) say that being a good parent is one of the most important things in life; just 50% of all adults agree.

Their living arrangements align with these values. They are more likely than all American adults to be married (59% versus 51%); their newborns are less likely than all US newborns to have a single mother (16% versus 41%); and their children are more likely than all US children to be raised in a household with two married parents (80% versus 63%).

They are more likely than the general public to live in multigenerational family households. Some 28% live with at least two adult generations under the same roof, twice the share of whites and slightly more than the share of blacks and Hispanics who live in such households. US Asians also have a strong sense of filial respect; about two-thirds say parents should have a lot or some influence in choosing one's profession (66%) and spouse (61%).

Asian Americans have a pervasive belief in the rewards of hard work. Nearly 7 in 10 (69%) say people can get ahead if they are willing to work hard, a view shared by a somewhat smaller share of the American public as a whole (58%). And fully 93% of Asian Americans describe members of their country of origin group as "very hardworking"; just 57% say the same about Americans as a whole (see appendix Figure 7A.8).

By their own lights, Asian Americans sometimes go overboard in stressing hard work. Nearly 4 in 10 (39%) say that Asian-American parents from their country of origin subgroup put too much pressure on their children to do well in school. Just 9% say the same about all American parents. On the flip side of the same coin, about 6 in 10 Asian Americans say American parents put too little pressure on their children to succeed in school, while just 9% say the same about Asian-American parents. (Those numbers help explain why *Battle Hymn of the Tiger Mother,* a 2011 comic memoir about strict parenting by Yale law professor Amy Chua, the daughter of immigrants, touched a nerve among Asian Americans as well as other parents.)

The immigration wave from Asia has occurred at a time when the largest sending countries have experienced dramatic gains in their standards of living. But few Asian immigrants are looking over their shoulders with regret. Just 12% say that if they had to do it all over again, they would remain in their country of origin. And by lopsided margins, Asian Americans say the US is preferable to their country of origin in such realms as providing economic opportunity, political and religious freedoms, and good conditions for raising children (see appendix Figure 7A.9). Respondents rated their country of origin as being superior on just one of seven measures tested in the survey—strength of family ties. (The Pew Research survey was conducted only among Asian Americans currently living in the US. As is the case with all immigration

Figure 7.6

Who's a "Tiger Mom"?

% of US Asians saying (American parents/Asian-American parents)
put ... pressure on their children to do well in school

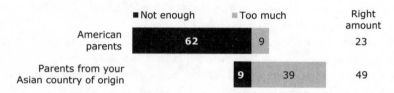

Note: For the bottom bar, respondents were asked about parents from their country of origin group (Chinese-American parents, Korean-American parents, etc.). Those who did not provide a country of origin were asked about "Asian-American parents."

Source: Pew Research Center Asian-American Survey, Jan.–Mar. 2012, N=3,511 US Asian adults

waves, a portion of those who came to the US from Asia in recent decades have chosen to return to their country of origin. However, return migration rates are estimated to be lower for immigrants from Asia than for other immigrants, and naturalization rates—that is, the share of eligible immigrants who become US citizens—are higher.)

Asian-American immigrants have set the bar of socioeconomic success so high that it will be a challenge for the next generation to surpass it. Only about half of the nearly 5 million US-born children of Asian-American immigrants have reached adulthood, so it's early to start drawing up a comprehensive generational score card. Nonetheless, some data are available, and as always, they are instructive. On basic socioeconomic measures such as median household income and college education, the adult children of immigrants resemble the immigrant generation and exceed the general public (see appendix Figure 7A.10). And when it comes to various measures of social integration, they are more likely than immigrants to say they think of themselves as "a typical American," more likely to say they have friends outside their race or country of origin group, and much more likely to marry outside their race (especially women, who are twice as likely as Asian-American men to "marry out"). Out-marriage patterns also differ by Asian country of origin group, with Japanese Americans the most likely to do so and Indian Americans the least likely, a pattern related to the fact that a much higher share of the Japanese were born in the US.

As with Hispanics, the US-born Asian-American adults are much more likely than the immigrants to have children outside of marriage. About 3 in 10 native-born Asian women (this includes both the second generation and third-and-higher generation) who had children in recent years were single, triple the rate among immigrant mothers. Assimilation can be a powerful force—and not always for the better.

ILLEGAL IMMIGRATION

Most of the political and media attention to immigrants in recent years has focused on those who have come illegally. Understandably so—the past few decades have seen the largest influx of such immigrants in the nation's history. The number living in the US more than tripled from 3.5 million in 1990 to a peak of 12.2 million in 2007 before declining somewhat during the 2007–2009 recession. The latest Pew Research Center estimate had 11.3 million here as of 2014,

Figure 7.7

Intermarriage Rates for Asians

% of Asian newlyweds (2008–2010) married to ...

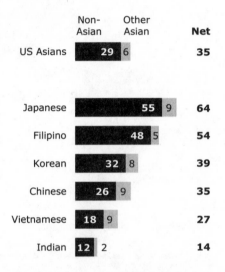

Note: "Newlyweds" refers to people ages 15 and older who got married in the year prior to the survey, and their marital status was "married, spouse present." US Asians and each US Asian group include non-Hispanic single-race Asians who are from only one group; "Non Asian" includes Hispanics and single- or multiple-race non-Hispanics except single-race Asians; "Other Asian" includes non-Hispanics from other single-Asian or multiple-Asian groups.

Source: Pew Research Center analysis of 2008–2010 American Community Survey, IPUMS

which means they accounted for about a quarter of the immigrants in the US that year.[9]

Unauthorized immigrants tend to live in the shadows and avoid contact with government agencies. How do we know how many there are? Mostly thanks to Jeffrey Passel, a brilliant former Census Bureau demographer who decades ago developed something called the "residual method" to estimate the number and characteristics of immigrants who are in the US illegally at any given time. Passel's methodology, which has since been adopted by the

Figure 7.8

Estimates of the US Unauthorized Immigrant Population, 1990–2014

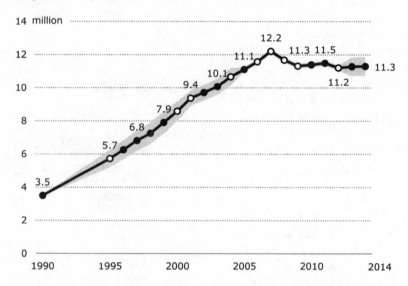

Note: Shading surrounding line indicates low and high points of the estimated 90% confidence interval. White data markers indicate the change from the previous year is statistically significant (for 1995, change is significant from 1990).

Source: Pew Research Center estimates based on residual methodology applied to March supplements to the Current Population Survey (1995–2004, 2013–2014) or American Community Survey (2005–2012)

Department of Homeland Security and other researchers, involves totaling up the number of legal immigrants (computed from administrative data) and the number of all immigrants (computed from census data). The difference between those two numbers—the residual—is presumed to make up the universe of immigrants who are here illegally. It's a bit more complicated than that because various adjustments need to be made for undercounts. Once Passel has established the size of this universe, he can then make educated guesses about the characteristics of unauthorized immigrants. For example, if an immigrant is an accountant, a teacher, or a veteran, it's a pretty good bet he or she isn't here illegally. And so on.

Perhaps the most surprising finding from Passel's research is that a sizeable share of unauthorized immigrants—nearly half—live in a household made up of an adult couple (married or not) and one or more children. This probably isn't the family constellation most people have in mind when they think about a migrant farm worker or a day laborer. However, unauthorized immigrants (46%) are much more likely to be parents of a minor child than are legal immigrants (38%) or native-born US adults (29%). The difference is driven both by the youth of unauthorized immigrant adults, who are typically in the child-rearing and -raising stage of life, and by their relatively high birthrates. It's also a clue to their motives for coming. Yes, they come for work. But they also come to put down roots, start a family, and create a future for their as-yet-unborn children. And it's those kids who are the greatest beneficiaries of their journey. Of the more than 5 million children of today's unauthorized immigrants, about 4 in 5 were born in this country and thus are automatic US citizens, despite the illegal status of their parents. The other 20 percent—the so-called Dreamers, who as young children were brought to this country illegally by their parents—have already been spared the threat of deportation by an Obama administration executive decree in 2012.

As for the roughly 10 million adult unauthorized immigrants, they broke the law, which means they live under the threat of employer exploitation, government deportation, or both. Most work long hours for low wages under lousy working conditions, often doing jobs their US-born counterparts consider beneath them. Tallying up their costs and benefits to society is a complex and subjective exercise. Arguably the greatest harm they do is the illegal way they came to the country—which undermines the rule of law that helps make the US a magnet for immigrants in the first place and is unfair to all who wait their turn to come legally. Once they get here, they tend to be more law-abiding than other Americans because they know any brush with the law could result in deportation. As for their economic impact, it's uneven. Most studies suggest that they depress wages (but only marginally) for the unskilled laborers with whom they directly compete, but raise wages for skilled laborers who benefit from the increased economic activity and productivity associated with their presence in the labor force.[10] For consumers, they're a blessing, as they lower the cost of everything from food to housing to medical care to personal services. They're a net burden on state and local governments, which by law are obligated to educate their children and provide free health care to their indigent. But they're a net benefit to the federal government, mainly because many wind up paying into the Social Security system (up to $15 billion a year, by one estimate)[11] without ever receiving benefits from it.

IMMIGRANTS AND POLITICS

Immigrants—even those who are here legally—typically become workers long before they become voters, and many never take that second step. If an immigrant wants to earn the right to vote, he or she must first become a naturalized US citizen. This is not a casual process. It requires a minimum of five years of continuous residence in the US; $680 in fees; successful completion of English tests and background checks; demonstration of an understanding of US history, government, and constitutional law; and the swearing of a loyalty oath.[12] Among all immigrants who are here legally and thus eligible to naturalize, only about two-thirds (including just 36% of legal Mexican-American immigrants) have done so. The rest remain legal permanent residents, enabling them to work, pay taxes, and receive many government benefits, but not giving them the right to vote.

So, some quick accounting: Of the immigrants currently in the country, about a quarter can't vote because they aren't here legally and an additional quarter can't vote because they aren't citizens. This cuts the potential voter pool among immigrants in half, the vast majority of whom are Hispanics and Asians.

The real electoral muscle of these new immigrant groups lies out in the not-too-distant future. Their children (nearly all of whom, remember, are US born and thus automatically eligible to vote) will be aging into the electorate at the rate of roughly 1 million a year for decades to come. Assuming their voter turnout rates rise over time to the levels of other native-born groups, Hispanics and Asians will be casting up to 25% of all votes in the presidential elections within a few decades, roughly double their share in 2012.

A striking feature of the politics of the modern immigration wave is that the deeper Hispanics and Asian Americans and their adult children have sunk their roots into America, the more Democratic they have become. Ronald Reagan captured 37% of the Latino vote in 1984; Mitt Romney got just 27% in 2012. Likewise, a majority of Asian Americans voted Republican in 1992 and 1996, but just a quarter did in 2012. The progression hasn't always been in a straight line—George W. Bush drew 40% of the Latino vote in 2004—and, to borrow a phrase, past performance is no guarantee of future results. Nonetheless, the trend lines are ominous for the GOP. More than any other factor, it was the big Latino vote for Obama in 2012 that led some Republicans in the US Senate to drop their long-standing opposition to immigration reform. But after a bipartisan immigration bill passed the Senate in 2013, it never even made it to the floor of the Republican-controlled House. Now with another presidential campaign under way, Republicans face a political dilemma. Continued opposition to comprehensive immigration reform will keep the party on its back foot as it tries to mend political fences with Hispanics and Asian Americans. On the other hand, if a bill is enacted that provides for a pathway to citizenship, it could, in the (overheated) calculus of US representative Michael

Figure 7.9

Voter Turnout Rate, by Race and Ethnicity, 1988–2012

% of eligible voters

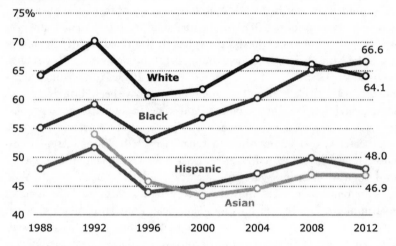

Note: Voter turnout rate for Asians not available prior to 1990.

Source: Pew Research Center analysis of Current Population Survey, November Supplements

Burgess (R-Texas), give "11 million undocumented Democrats" the right to vote.[13] Some GOP strategists have even argued that the party should concentrate less on trying to become competitive with Hispanic voters and more on driving up election turnout among whites, especially the lower-middle-class Republicans most threatened by immigrants. But to many party leaders, including the entire Bush political clan, that's a recipe for slow-motion political suicide. Karl Rove, the architect of George W. Bush's winning campaigns for president and for governor of Texas, wrote in 2013 that if the GOP doesn't find a way to do better with nonwhites, it not only risks extending its losing streak in presidential races, but eventually will put its congressional base at risk as well.[14] As of now, whites make up half the population in the 201 congressional districts represented by Democrats and three-quarters of the population in the 234 districts represented by Republicans. As the nation's underlying demographics grow increasingly nonwhite, the congressional math will move in a Democratic direction unless the GOP finds a way to change the politics.

PARTY IDENTIFICATION

One reason the GOP has fallen so far out of favor with Hispanics and Asian Americans is that its candidates and elected officials sometimes seem to be in a bidding war to see who says the toughest things about immigrants who are in this country illegally. In 2012 Mitt Romney called for them to "self-deport" and one of his rivals for the GOP presidential nomination, Herman Cain, proposed (in jest, he later said) that border fences be electrified. In 2013 Representative Steve King (R-Iowa), likened young illegal immigrants to "drug mules" who have "calves the size of cantaloupes." And in 2015, Trump launched his candidacy with the claim that Mexican immigrants have been "bringing drugs. They're bringing crime. They're rapists. And some, I assume, are good people." These attacks drew rebukes from many GOP leaders, but epithets leave a mark. Pew Research Center surveys show that many legal Hispanic and Asian immigrants have a sense of shared identity and fate with the unauthorized, even if they disapprove of their illegal mode of entry.

Immigrants' differences with the GOP extend well beyond the issue of illegal immigration. They're broadly ideological. Both Hispanics and Asian Americans are more likely than the general public to self-identify as liberals and be supporters of big government. Second-generation Hispanics follow this pattern even more strongly than do Hispanic immigrants.

On social issues such as homosexuality and abortion, second-generation Hispanics and Asians are significantly more liberal than either the general public or the immigrants within their racial and ethnic group. Some but not all of these differences are related to age. Young adults generally are more accepting of homosexuality, but the greater acceptance of homosexuality among second-generation Asian Americans versus those in the first generation remains, even when controlling for age.

THE IMMIGRANT FUTURE

A nation's demographic future is the product of three rates: births, deaths, and immigration. The first two generally aren't susceptible to modification by public policy. The third is—at least by societies such as ours that are in the enviable position of having people from all over the world clambering to get in. With Baby Boomers retiring and birthrates declining, America's fewer-workers-per-retiree future is already upon us. Our old-age-dependency ratio will only grow more problematic with each passing year. The most direct public policy responses—social safety net cuts and tax increases—will be painful. But there's a complementary solution that needn't be: opening our borders in a rational way to more immigrants. It's akin to raising the birth-rate, but its impact is more immediate, because the newcomers arrive ready to work. They tend to have lots of babies, so they're a demographic dividend that keeps giving. Plus, our modern immigration streams are already roughly aligned with the hourglass contours of our workforce needs. We get lots of low-skilled immigrants to do the unpleasant work most native-born American won't do, and we're getting more highly skilled immigrants to pick up the slack in science and engineering, where we're not producing enough homegrown talent. For example, up to two-thirds of the workforce tending to crops and livestock—some 1 million workers—are undocumented Hispanics. (Many are relatively skilled, most have been in the country a decade or more, and some have moved into middle-management jobs.) Meantime, Asian Americans make up less than 6% of the population, but in 2010 collected 45% of all engineering doctorates and 38% of all math and computer science PhDs. Immigrants and their offspring are also heavily overrepresented in the ranks of entrepreneurs—be they sole proprietors or corporate moguls. One-quarter of the high-tech firms launched in the US between 1965 and 2005 were founded by immigrants. And some 40% of all Fortune 500 companies were started by immigrants or their children (the vast bulk of them came during earlier European waves).[15]

In light of all this, it's no surprise that the most enthusiastic proponents of immigration reform are in the business community. Open borders have always been more popular with business elites (who benefit from their economic dynamism) and foreign-heritage interest groups (who want to attract more family members from their ancestral countries) than with the general public (some of whom are directly threatened by the competition for jobs).

The US is already home to four times more immigrants than any other nation in the world.[16] Political backlashes notwithstanding, we have a long and mostly happy history of bringing them in and helping them become American. If we adopt immigration policies that allow us to keep winning the global lottery for newcomers with brains, talent, and drive, we'll go a long way toward ensuring our place as the top dog in the world's economy.

Immigrants are more than units of economic output. They're also our face to the world, and their life stories embody the values our nation holds most dear: pluralism, dynamism, tolerance, entrepreneurship, achievement, optimism. At a time when a rising Asia is flexing its muscles around the globe, having so many successful Asians as part of the new American tapestry is a great calling card on the world stage. Consider the multiple messages conveyed by a small diplomatic flap between the US and China in 2012. On the eve of a visit to Beijing by then-secretary of state Hillary Clinton, a Chinese human rights activist, Chen Guangcheng, escaped house arrest and made his way to the US embassy, where he sought refuge. After a few days of tense negotiations, US authorities agreed to hand him back to the Chinese, but with the understanding that he and his family would soon be permitted to move to the US. The photo that ran in the newspapers the day the crisis was resolved probably did as much as the settlement itself to burnish the US image around the world. It showed Chen being escorted out of the embassy in a wheelchair (blind since childhood, he'd broken his foot while scaling a wall during his escape), accompanied by the two senior US diplomats who'd brokered the deal. One was Gary Locke, the US ambassador to China, a former governor of Washington, a former US secretary of commerce, and a third-generation Chinese American. The other was Harold Koh, then the senior legal adviser to the State Department, a professor of international law and former dean of Yale Law School, and a second-generation Korean American. As the saying goes, only in America.

8

Hapa Nation

WHEN BARACK OBAMA'S PARENTS married in 1961, the best estimates are that perhaps 1 marriage in 1,000 in the US that year was, like theirs, between a black person and a white person. Antimiscegenation laws were still in force in 16 states, and racial intermarriage was a gasp-inducing taboo virtually everywhere else. That was then. Now about 16% of all new marriages in the US are between spouses of a different race or ethnicity from each other. This cultural sea change has been driven not just by blacks and whites, but by a wave of Hispanic and Asian newcomers who've produced a new American tapestry more complex than anything our nation has ever known.

Few families embody this transformation better than the one that resides at 1600 Pennsylvania Avenue.[1] President Obama's wife is a descendant of an African-American slave and a white slave owner. His wife's brother is married to a white woman of Scottish/Irish heritage. His half-sister is an Indonesian American married to a Chinese Canadian. The president himself is the product of an African father raised in Kenya and a white mother raised in Kansas. According to genealogy.com, he too is the descendant of a slave—but on his white mother's side, not his black father's. Obama was born in Hawaii, America's most Technicolor state, where the word "hapa" (half or part) is meant to describe someone of mixed Asian heritage, but colloquially has come to mean a mixed-race person of any kind—a "mutt," as Obama sometimes calls himself.

The fact that no racial label neatly fits our sitting president is in its way fitting for a society that is struggling to find a modern vocabulary for race. Our labels, categories, and classification schemes haven't kept up with our behaviors, attitudes, and weddings. This is new. In one form or another, America has been confounded by race—our original sin—for four centuries. But for most of that history, racial identification had been a simple matter of black or white, with the "one-drop rule" the line of demarcation. The rigidity of this either/or formulation obscured the racial intermixing that has always been a part of our national DNA—but that, of course, was exactly the point. Mixing was deemed to be not just illegal but sinful, so it couldn't be acknowledged above a whisper. Now the stigma is receding. And so too is our exclusively black-or-white racial checkerboard, rendered obsolete by the tens of millions of Hispanic and Asian immigrants who have come to the US since 1965. Today's immigrants and their children are in the vanguard of the modern intermarriage trend. What should we call the children of such marriages? As a society, we don't yet know. No one—not the Census Bureau, not those children themselves, not Americans of different races—has come up with a common vocabulary.

Consider again the man who lives in the White House. Racially speaking, who is Barack Obama? Well, it depends on whom you ask. Given a choice between calling the president black and calling him mixed race, most blacks (55%) say Obama is black; just a third (34%) say he is mixed race. Among whites, the pattern is reversed. Most (53%) say he is mixed race, while just a quarter (24%) say he is black. And among Hispanics (who have their own unique set of challenges finding a racial label that fits their group), 6 in 10 say Obama is mixed race.

Nor is Obama the only object of semantic confusion. When a Pew Research survey asked respondents in 2009 to state what race they themselves are (the choices were white, black, Asian, or some other race) and told they could choose as many categories as they wished, just 1% chose to identify with more than one category. However, later in the same survey, when respondents were asked explicitly if they considered themselves to be mixed race, fully 1 in 6 (16%) said they did,

Figure 8.1

Do You Think of Obama as Black or Mixed Race?

% saying ...

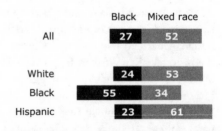

Note: "Both/neither" and "Don't know/Refused" responses not shown. Question wording: Do you mostly think of Obama as a black person or mostly as a person of mixed race?

Source: Pew Research Center survey, Oct.–Nov. 2009, N=2,884 US adults

including 8% of whites, 20% of blacks, and 37% of Hispanics. In short, responses to racial identity questions vary widely depending on wording and context—another sign that our traditional categories aren't very good at capturing our new racial landscape in all of its complexity.

Some groups are more disoriented by and disapproving of all these changes than others—and here's where a big generation gap emerges. As noted in Chapter 4, just 27% of Silents say that "more people of different races marrying each other" has been a change for the better in America. This share rises to 34% among Boomers, 39% among Xers, and 43% among Millennials. And when a similar question is posed in explicitly personal terms—how comfortable would you be if someone in your family were to marry someone of a different race?—the generational differences grow even sharper. Just 38% of Silents say they would be comfortable, compared with 85% of Millennials (see appendix Figure 8A.1).

Whether Americans are ready for them or not, racial and ethnic intermarriages are happening in record numbers.

THE RISE OF INTERMARRIAGE

Some 15.9% of all new marriages in 2013 were either interracial or interethnic, a nearly sevenfold increase over the share in 1960. Looking at all current marriages in 2013, irrespective of the year they began, 9.1% were interracial or interethnic, an all-time high.[2]

There are distinctive patterns by race and ethnicity. Among all newlyweds in 2013, 10% of whites, 19% of blacks, 24% of Hispanics, and 29% of Asians married someone whose race or ethnicity was different from their own.

Even though the rate is lowest among whites, they are still by far the nation's most numerous race group. As such, in

Figure 8.2

Intermarriage Rates, 1960–2013

% of marriages involving spouses of a different race/ethnicity from each other

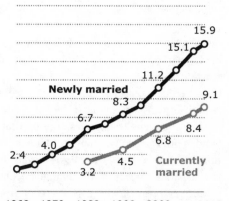

Source: Pew Research Center analysis of 2008–2013 American Community Survey and 1980–2000 census data (IPUMS). For more details see Pew Research Center's "Marrying Out: One-in-Seven New US Marriages is Interracial or Interethnic," June 4, 2010

Figure 8.3

Intermarriage Rates, by Race and Ethnicity, 2013

% of newlyweds married to someone of a different race/ethnicity

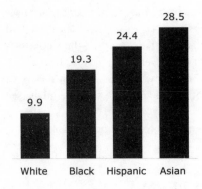

			28.5
		24.4	
	19.3		
9.9			
White	Black	Hispanic	Asian

Note: Asians include Pacific Islanders.

Source: Pew Research Center analysis of 2013 American Community Survey (IPUMS). For more details see Pew Research Center's "Marrying Out: One-in-Seven New US Marriages is Interracial or Interethnic," June 4, 2010

70% of all new mixed marriages in 2010, one spouse was white. Of the approximately 275,500 new interracial or interethnic marriages in 2010, white/Hispanic couples accounted for more than 4 in 10 (43%), white/Asian couples made up 14%, and white/black couples made up 12%. About 3 in 10 new intermarriages were among a mix of different non-white spouses (see appendix Figure 8A.2).

Gender patterns vary widely—and these variances are highly race-specific. Black men are nearly three times more likely than black women to "marry out." By contrast, Asian-American women are more than twice as likely as Asian-American men to marry out. Cultural norms and gender and racial stereotypes help explain these patterns. A 2013 PBS documentary, *Seeking Asian Female,* about a marriage initiated on the Internet between a 60-year-old white American man and his 30-year-old Chinese bride, sparked an animated online debate about the way American pop culture tends to sexualize Asian women and emasculate Asian men. These stereotypes, to some degree, establish the contours of the out-marriage market for Asian Americans of both genders; they also complicate romantic couplings among Asian Americans themselves. The marital dynamics between black men and women are even more fraught. Marriage rates in the African-American community have fallen to their lowest levels in modern history, a trend driven by the disparate impact of the changing economy on black men and women and exacerbated by gender tensions arising from the fact that among the declining ranks of black men who do marry, a record share (more than 1 in 5) choose a bride who is not black. Among whites and Hispanics, by the way, there is no gender difference in intermarriage rates.

There are also distinctive socioeconomic patterns among intermarried couples, based on the race, ethnicity, and gender of the partners. Some of the differences reflect the overall characteristics of these different groups in society

Figure 8.4

Intermarriage Rates of Newlyweds, by Gender, 2010

% of newlyweds married to someone of a different race/ethnicity

No gender difference for these groups ...

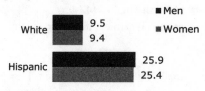

Big gender difference for these groups ...

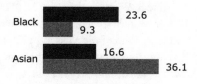

Note: Asians include Pacific Islanders.

Source: Pew Research Center analysis of 2010 American Community Survey, IPUMS

at large, and some appear to be the result of a selection process. For example, among intermarried newlywed couples involving whites, white/Asian couples have the highest combined annual earnings (nearly $71,000), much higher than the earnings of white/Hispanic couples (about $58,000) as well as white/black couples (about $53,000). Also, white/Asian couples have higher combined earnings than either white/white or Asian/Asian couples. Meanwhile, the combined median earnings of white/Hispanic couples are lower than those of white/white couples but higher than those of Hispanic/Hispanic couples. The earnings of intermarried white/black couples fall between those of white/white and black/black couples (see appendix Figure 8A.3).

When it comes to education, white newlyweds who married Asians are more educated than whites who married whites, blacks, or Hispanics. More than half of the white men (51%) and white women (57%) who married an Asian spouse are college-educated, compared with only 32% of white men and 37% of white women who married a white spouse. Also, about 6 in 10 Asian newlyweds who married whites are college-educated.

Newlywed Hispanics and blacks who married a white spouse are more likely to be college-educated than those who married within their group. About 23% of Hispanic men who married a white wife have a college degree, compared with just 10% of Hispanic men who married a Hispanic woman. Likewise, 1 in 3 (33%) Hispanic women who married a white husband are college-educated, compared with about 13% of Hispanic women who "married in." The educational differences among blacks who "marry in" and "marry out" are less dramatic but follow a similar pattern.

Marrying out is much more common among the native-born population than among immigrants. Native-born Hispanics were nearly three times as likely as their foreign-born counterparts to marry a non-Hispanic in 2010. The disparity among native- and foreign-born Asians is not as great, but still significant: nearly 4 in 10 native-born Asians (38%) and nearly a quarter (24%) of foreign-born Asians married a non-Asian in 2010 (see appendix Figure 8A.4).

Among Asian newlyweds, the intermarriage gap between native and the foreign born is much bigger for Asian men than for Asian women. In 2010, native-born Asian male newlyweds were about three times as likely as the foreign born to marry out (32% versus 11%). Among newlywed Asian women, the gap between native and foreign born is much smaller (43% versus 34%). The gender differences are not significant among Hispanic native- and foreign-born newlyweds.

REGIONS AND STATES. Intermarriage in the US tilts west. About 1 in 5 (22%) of all newlyweds in western states married someone of a different race or ethnicity from 2008 to 2010, compared with 14% in the South, 13% in the Northeast, and 11% in the Midwest. At the state level, more than 4 in 10 (42%) newlyweds in Hawaii from 2008 to 2010 were intermarried; the other states with an intermarriage rate of 20% or more are all west of the Mississippi River. For new marriages between whites and Hispanics, states with the highest prevalence rates are New Mexico (19%), Arizona (12%), and Nevada (11%). The highest shares of intermarried white and Asian couples are in Hawaii (9%), District of Columbia (7%), and Nevada (5%). And the top states for white/black intermarried couples are Virginia (3.3%), North Carolina (3.2%), and Kansas (3%).

DIVORCE. Several studies using government data have found that overall divorce rates are higher for couples who married out than for those who married in—but here, too, the patterns vary by the racial and gender characteristics of the couples. An analysis conducted a decade ago found that 10 years after they married, interracial couples had a 41% chance of separation or divorce, compared with a 31% chance among couples who married within their race, according to a study based on the 1995 National Survey of Family Growth (NSFG).[3] A subsequent study that analyzed 2002 NSFG data found that "although interracial marriages overall are more vulnerable to divorce, this reflects the experience of some but not all couples." It found that after 10 years of marriage, interracial marriages that are most vulnerable to divorce involve white females and nonwhite males (with the exception of white females/Hispanic males). Conversely, there is little or no difference in divorce rates among white men/nonwhite women couples, and white men/black women couples are actually substantially less likely than white/white couples to divorce by the 10th year of marriage.[4]

Another study using 1990 to 2001 data from the Census Bureau's Survey of Income and Program Participation (SIPP) found that on the whole, interracial marriages are less stable than same-race, same-ethnicity marriages, but marital dissolution was found to be strongly associated with the race or ethnicity of the individuals in the union. The authors found that "the results failed to provide evidence that interracial marriage per se is associated with an elevated risk of marital dissolution."[5] Mixed marriages involving blacks and whites were the least stable, followed by Hispanic/white couples, whereas mixed marriages involving Asians and whites were more stable than same-race white marriages.

RACIAL IDENTITY AND LABELS

The US is on a demographic track to become a majority nonwhite (or, in the evocative oxymoron, "majority minority") nation sometime between 2040 and 2050. But by then, with an ever rising share of the population likely to be the product of mixed marriages, how much sense will these categories make? History offers some limited lessons. Until a few generations ago, "marrying out" mainly referred to crossing entrenched boundaries of religion or ancestry (race was still beyond the pale). Families would object to—and might sometimes block—marriages between a Protestant and a Catholic, an Italian American and an Irish American, or a Jew and a gentile. Today such unions are so commonplace that they rarely set off family crises and barely attract notice of any kind in the wider society. (A 2013 survey of Jews by the Pew Research Center found that among Jews who have married since 2000, nearly 6 in 10 have a non-Jewish spouse.[6]) Yes, these "mixed" couples and their children have to figure out where to worship and which relatives to visit on which religious holidays, but they don't typically have to confront existential questions about who they are, where they fit, and how society labels them. So one lesson of our history is that identity markers that once seemed impenetrable have a way of becoming porous. And people have a way of adapting.

Race, however, poses a more profound identity challenge than does religion or ancestry. In America, it comes freighted with centuries of slavery and other forms of state-sanctioned discrimination; no other group cleavage in our national life is as deep or painful—or visible. Few people in this country wear their religion in public, but there's no hiding one's race. And nowadays, few seem to want to. Our culture has traded the melting pot for the mosaic. We glory in our distinctive hues. In this new milieu, being mixed race—a stigma not just in our society but in most societies for most of human history—now carries cultural cachet. Pick your favorite mixed-race celebrity, it's quite an A-list: Halle Berry, Beyoncé, Keanu Reeves, Salma Hayek, Derek Jeter, Mariah Carey, Norah Jones, Tiger Woods, Barack Obama.

To be sure, there are still plenty of holdouts from this new racial kumbaya. When General Mills ran a television commercial in 2013 that featured a little girl with a white mom and black dad (the cute plot line had the girl, upon hearing that Cheerios are good for the heart, dumping a bunch of them on the chest of her napping father), two interesting things happened. The first was that the interracial marriage and biracial child were presented without gawking or editorial comment—just your basic TV ad family. The second was that the reaction to the ad got so ugly on the comment section on YouTube that it had to be taken down. (But, as noted in Chapter 1, six months later the same interracial Cheerios family was featured in a new ad on the biggest advertising platform of all—the Super Bowl. General Mills' message could hardly have been more explicit: critics be damned, we're ready to link our brand with the social and cultural changes afoot in America.) There was a similar outbreak of online bigotry when a young woman who is the daughter of Indian immigrants was crowned Miss America in the fall of 2013. Obviously we haven't become a "postracial" society; human beings don't seem to be wired that way. But there are fewer out-and-out bigots than there once were. And increasingly, our new racial landscape is bursting with nuance, shadings, subtleties, possibilities, ironies. A few years ago California-based artist Kip Fulbeck put together the Hapa Project, a photographic exhibition that consisted of a series of portraits of multiracial children and adults. Below each portrait was a short personal statement. "My last boyfriend told me he liked me because of my race," wrote one attractive young woman of middle hue and indeterminate race. "So I dumped him."

A 2015 Pew Research survey of multiracial American adults found they report a generally positive set of attitudes and experiences related to their identity. Six in 10 say they're proud of their mixed-race background and about as many say it has made them more open to other cultures. While 55% say they've been subjected to racial slurs or jokes, just 4% say that having a mixed-race background has been a disadvantage in life. About 1 in 5 say it's been an advantage; the remaining three-quarters say it's made no difference.[7] For this survey, we designated respondents to be mixed race if they reported they were two or more races or were multiracial based on the backgrounds of their parents or grandparents. This enabled us to estimate that nearly 17 million adults, or 6.9% of the adult population, are mixed race. It should be noted that our estimate is much higher than that of the Census Bureau, which reports that 2.1% of US adults are multiracial. The census figure is based on the share of Americans who checked more than one racial category on their 2010 census form. But the disparity between our estimate and theirs is not as great as it appears. In our survey, 61% of those we identified as multiracial (based, remember, on their family lineage as well as self-reports) did *not* consider themselves to be multiracial. Presumably the vast bulk of that subgroup would not check more than one racial box on their census form. The fact that the sizes of these estimates are variable and dependent on vocabulary and context is a reminder of how fluid the boundaries of race have become in the modern era.

There's always been a political dimension to identity labels. In 1997, two of the nation's most powerful civil rights groups, the NAACP and the National Council of La Raza, testified in Congress in opposition to the Census Bureau's proposal to allow people to identify with more than one race on the 2000 decennial census. They feared it would reduce the size of traditionally disadvantaged race groups, thereby "diluting benefits to which they are entitled as a protected class under civil rights law," as the NAACP said in its written testimony. A small group called the Association of Multiethnic Americans countered that the census should concern itself first and foremost with accurate racial identification: "We want a choice in the matter of who we are, just like any other community. [We find it] ironic that our people are being asked to correct by virtue of how we define ourselves all of the past injustices of other groups of people." Another small multiracial advocacy group, Project Race, said in its testimony: "Multiracial children who wish to embrace all of their heritage should be allowed to do so. They should not be put in the position of denying one of their parents to satisfy arbitrary government requirements."

THE HISPANIC IDENTITY CONUNDRUM

Those multiracial groups carried the day back in the late 1990s, but even so, racial and ethnic labeling on the census remains today what it has always been: a confusing maze. No group struggles more with this nation's official race categories than the nation's 57 million Hispanics. They are classified by the federal government as an ethnic group, not a racial group. This is a nod to the genetic reality that Hispanics are a mix of races—with bloodlines flowing from Europe, Africa, and the indigenous Native American tribes of North, Central, and South America. But they all have a connection to Spanish language, culture, and heritage—which are standard markers of ethnicity. The designation of Hispanics as an ethnic group was mandated by Congress in 1976 in response to pressure from Hispanic political and civil rights leaders who wanted official

Figure 8.5

→ NOTE: Please answer BOTH Question 8 about Hispanic origin and Question 9 about race. For this census, Hispanic origins are not races.

8. Is Person 1 of Hispanic, Latino, or Spanish origin?
- ☐ No, not of Hispanic, Latino, or Spanish origin
- ☐ Yes, Mexican, Mexican Am., Chicano
- ☐ Yes, Puerto Rican
- ☐ Yes, Cuban
- ☐ Yes, another Hispanic, Latino, or Spanish origin — *Print origin, for example, Argentinean, Colombian, Dominican, Nicaraguan, Salvadoran, Spaniard, and so on.* ↗

9. What is Person 1's race? *Mark* ☒ *one or more boxes.*
- ☐ White
- ☐ Black, African Am., or Negro
- ☐ American Indian or Alaska Native — *Print name of enrolled or principal tribe.* ↗

- ☐ Asian Indian   ☐ Japanese   ☐ Native Hawaiian
- ☐ Chinese   ☐ Korean   ☐ Guamanian or Chamorro
- ☐ Filipino   ☐ Vietnamese   ☐ Samoan
- ☐ Other Asian — *Print race, for example, Hmong, Laotian, Thai, Pakistani, Cambodian, and so on.* ↗   ☐ Other Pacific Islander — *Print race, for example, Fijian, Tongan, and so on.* ↗

- ☐ Some other race — *Print race.* ↗

data about their community so they could press claims for equal treatment and benefits under the law. This was the first (and so far only) time in US history that an ethnic (as opposed to racial) group had been singled out this way. And it has led to a census form that, for many Hispanics, reads like a riddle.

Race and ethnicity are covered by questions 8 and 9 on the 10-question 2010 census form. Respondents are explicitly instructed to answer BOTH (all caps on the form) questions. Question 8 asks all Americans whether they are Hispanic, and if so, to mark their Hispanic country of origin (Mexico, Cuba, etc.). The question notes that "for this census, Hispanic origins are not races." This is the question that produces the government's official count of Hispanics and—as has been the custom in census-taking since the middle of the last century—it is based entirely on self-identification.[8] Question 9 then asks people to state their race, and provides a total of 15 different boxes (including white, black, American Indian, 11 Asian race boxes, and "some other race"—but not including Hispanic). On the 2010 census, about half (53%) of all those who self-identified as Hispanic in question 8 checked the "white" box in question 9, while 3% checked black and 8% checked mixed race or other—and fully 37% checked "some other race."

Those responses stand as a rebuke to the classification system that produced them. If more than a third of our nation's largest minority group finds itself without a race box to check on the census form, it may be time to come up with a different taxonomy.

For Hispanics, the identity riddle doesn't stop there, however. Four decades after the terms "Hispanic" and "Latino" were affixed to them by the federal government, Hispanics themselves haven't fully embraced those labels. Only about one-quarter (24%) of Hispanic adults say they most often identify themselves by either of those pan-ethnic terms, according to a 2011 Pew Research Center survey. About half (51%) say they identify themselves most often by their family's country or place of origin (using such terms as "Mexican," "Cuban," "Puerto Rican," "Salvadoran, or "Dominican"), and 21% say they use the term "American" most often (a share that rises to 40% among those who were born in the US). The terms "Hispanic" and "Latino" are American confections—they get little use in the 20-plus countries where Spanish is the official language. Plus, many Hispanics in this country are frankly doubtful about just how much they have in common with other Hispanics. In response to another 2011 Pew survey question, about 7 in 10 (69%) Hispanics say that Hispanics in the US have many different cultures; just 29% say they share a common culture. That doesn't mean the labels serve no purpose. They make sense to Hispanic leaders and institutions that want to preserve their power base and to a majority-white host culture that, despite its growing ease with racial diversity, still isn't ready to stop putting labels on people it deems to be different.

One of the most interesting demographic, sociological, and political dramas of the coming century will be whether the Hispanic identity marker recedes over time, as it did for the European immigrants. The answer isn't yet clear. Proximity, modern communication technology, and the relative ease of international travel make it much easier for today's Hispanic immigrants and their children to keep their ties to their ancestral countries and language. Plus, the mainstream culture's new embrace of ethnic diversity reduces the incentives for minorities to shed their ethnic identity. On the other hand, if a quarter of Hispanics continue to marry non-Hispanics, these ethnic identity markers are bound to blur over time.

What boxes will the children of these marriages discover on the 2050 census? If history is a guide, they'll be different from the ones in use now. In fact, several changes are already in the works. In 2015 the Census Bureau began testing a new approach to asking about race, ethnicity, and origin by avoiding those terms. Instead the experimental form asks respondents to indicate which "categories" apply to them, and provides eight proposed boxes to check: White; Hispanic, Latino, or Spanish origin; Black or African American; Asian; American Indian or Alaska Native; Middle Eastern or North African; Native Hawaiian or other Pacific Islander; and Some other race, ethnicity, or origin. Respondents would then be given a follow-up question that asks about their identity based on country of origin, tribe, or other detailed group categories. This is just one of several new approaches under consideration for the 2020 census. In a 2013 report, the bureau addressed the difficulty of racial categorization: "We recognize that race and ethnicity are not quantifiable values," it wrote. "Rather, identity is a complex mix of one's family and social environment, historical or socio-political constructs, personal experience, context, and many other immeasurable factors."

BLACKS IN OBAMA'S AMERICA

The Census Bureau has already decided to drop the word "Negro" from the 2020 form because its surveys have determined that a dwindling share of blacks—mostly older adults living in the South—still use the term. (Going forward, blacks will still be able to check the box "black" or "African American.") No population group has been subject to more classification changes than this one. The first census, in 1790, distinguished between free white persons and slaves. The term "color" (not "race") first appeared in the 1850 census, with three options: white, black, or mulatto. By 1890, census takers had the option of describing nonwhites as "quadroons" or "octoroons." In 1910, census takers were instructed to write "B" for "black only" and "Mu" for mulatto, a category meant to include "persons who have some proportion or perceptible trace of Negro blood." By 1930, these terms had been dropped, replaced by instructions that said that persons who were a mix of "white and Negro blood" were to be counted by census takers as "Negro" no matter how small the share of Negro blood—an explicit affirmation of the long-standing but unofficial "one-drop rule." By 1960, the race box was no longer to be filled out by the census enumerators based on observations from in-person visits; instead, it was to be done by Americans themselves, checking boxes on forms sent to them in the mail. That remains the practice to this day.

Over the years, as different labels have come into and out of vogue, the real problem for blacks comes not from the words themselves, but from the enduring power of the one-drop formula. When President Obama filled out his census form in 2010, he could have checked black, he could have checked white, or he could have checked *both* black and white. He checked black—a decision that disappointed many mixed-race Americans who'd hoped he would use this official declaration of racial identity to signal that it was time to move beyond the old formula. The president's defenders countered that anyone who looks like him has lived the life of a black person, and that it would be a denial of reality to pretend otherwise. Obama's ambiguous racial identity in a one-drop world is one reason he is such a compelling historical figure. Over the years he has been well served by political instincts that have taught him to be wary of the topic of race, but when it comes up—as with the Reverend Jeremiah Wright controversy in 2008, or the arrest of a prominent black Harvard professor at his home in Cambridge in 2009, or the killing of a black teenager in Florida in 2012 by a white/Hispanic neighborhood watch volunteer—Obama is frequently eloquent. He knows that in post–civil rights America, the only way for a black politician to be a national figure is to talk about race in the language of inclusion, not grievance. Here's what he said in 2008 when his candidacy was briefly threatened by a videotape that surfaced of an antiwhite, anti-American tirade delivered by Wright—his pastor, mentor, and friend—from the pulpit of his Chicago church:

> I am the son of a black man from Kenya and a white woman from Kansas. I was raised with the help of a white grandfather who survived a depression to serve in Patton's army during World War II and a white grandmother who worked on a bomber assembly line at Fort Leavenworth while he was overseas. . . . I am married to a black American who carries within her the blood of slaves and slaveowners—an inheritance we pass on to our two precious daughters. I have brothers, sisters, nieces, nephews, uncles, and cousins, of every race and every hue, scattered across three continents, and for as long as I live, I will never forget that in no other country on Earth is my story even possible. It's a story that hasn't made me the most conventional candidate. But it is a story that has seared into my genetic makeup the idea that this nation is more than the sum of its parts—that out of many, we are truly one.

Obama has a complicated relationship with his black constituents. A *Washington Post* article captured a telling moment in 2007 when then-candidate Obama was meeting with a group of black advisers and scholars as he rehearsed for a forthcoming Democratic candidates' debate at predominantly black Howard University.[9] In the article's opening scene, Obama struggles to find the right tone and cadence. "I can't sound like Martin," he finally tells the group. "I can't sound like Jesse." Sometimes his challenge of finding a voice that can straddle the gap between our black and white cultures has produced moments of sweet irony. A few days before his 2009 inauguration, the president-elect stopped by Ben's Chili Bowl, a landmark eatery in Washington, DC's black community, with the usual press gaggle in tow. After paying for his chili dog, Obama was asked by the cashier if he wanted change back from his twenty. "Nah, we straight," he replied.[10] The pool reporter chose to clean up the president-elect's dialect and wrote that he said, "No, we're straight." But a video of the exchange became an Internet hit, especially among blacks who got a kick out of their Harvard-educated president sounding, as one hip-hop commentator put it, "mad cool" with his black street slang.

Throughout most of his presidency, Obama faced a quiet but persistent undercurrent of criticism from black leaders who feel he's been too timid about addressing ongoing racial imbalances in the economy and in society at large. Television host and political activist Tavis Smiley complained during the 2012

Figure 8.6

Blacks' Sense of Progress, 1981–2013

% of blacks who say blacks are better/worse off now than five years ago

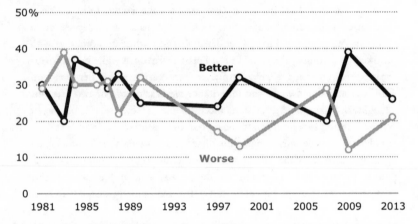

Note: In surveys in 2005 and earlier, blacks include Hispanic blacks. In surveys in 2007 and later, blacks include only non-Hispanic blacks. "Same" response not showed.

Source: Pew Research Center surveys, 1981–2013

campaign that "tragically . . . the president feels boxed in by his blackness." Smiley went on: "It has . . . been painful to watch this particular president's calibrated, cautious and sometimes callous treatment of his most loyal constituency. African Americans will have lost ground in the Obama era."[11] Others say the problem isn't that Obama's boxed in by being black—it's that he's not black enough. Typical of the genre: a headline on a column by black *New York Daily News* columnist Stanley Crouch: "What Obama Isn't: Black Like Me." And for others, Obama's mixed-race heritage is fodder for satire. "The first black president!" black comedian Wanda Sykes marveled at a White House Correspondents' Association dinner in 2009, as the president sat a few feet away on the dais. "I'm proud to be able to say that. That's unless you screw up. And then it's going to be, 'What's up with the half-white guy?'"

As his tenure in office wound down, Obama began talking about race with a passion and purposefulness he'd tiptoed around for most of his political career. His bolder notes rang out with particular force in a 2015 eulogy he delivered for the Reverend Clementa Pinckney, one of nine African Americans massacred by a 21-year-old white supremacist during a Bible study class in a historic black church in Charleston, South Carolina. Obama spoke of racism that expresses itself not just in evil deeds and slurs, but "in the subtle impulse to call Johnny back for an interview but not Jamal," and in laws that "make it harder for some of our fellow citizens to vote." In other settings, those would have been divisive observations, especially coming from the nation's first black president. But in that memorial service, which also saw Obama lead mourners in a verse of "Amazing Grace" to pay tribute to the forgiveness of the families of the dead, his words struck a deep chord of unity and healing. Black leaders praised the president for talking to, rather than lecturing at, their community. And white leaders across the South set aside decades of defiance and began removing the Confederate battle flag from state capitols.

There's no group in America for whom the election of the nation's first black president has had a more positive impact than African Americans. A nationwide Pew Research survey of blacks conducted in November 2009, a year after Obama's election victory, found that across a wide range of measures—satisfaction with the direction of the country, the state of race relations, the pace of black progress, their personal economic circumstances—black attitudes were significantly more positive than in 2007. On many of these measures, blacks were more upbeat than whites, a reversal of patterns that had prevailed for decades.

This spike in attitudes came in the teeth of an economy that had been in a deep recession for those two years, a downturn that hit blacks especially hard. Nevertheless, twice as many blacks in 2009 (39%) as in 2007 (20%) said that the "situation of black people in this country" was better than it had been five years earlier; this more positive view had taken hold among blacks of all ages and income levels. Asked to look ahead, blacks were also more upbeat. More than half (53%) said that life for blacks in the future will be better than it is now, while just 10% said it will be worse. In 2007, 44% said things would be better for blacks in the future, while 21% said they would be worse.

Much of this post-election glow would eventually dim. By 2013, when Pew Research asked blacks those same questions in a new survey, the share who said things had gotten better for blacks over the past five years—26%—had fallen most of the way back to its 2007 level, even though this new five-year assessment period encompassed all of Obama's tenure in the White House.

Then in 2014 and 2015, a string of deadly encounters around the country between unarmed black men and police officers, many captured on cell phone videos, led to widespread protests and sporadic rioting. A nationwide *New York Times*/CBS survey taken in May 2015, shortly after a riot broke out in Baltimore following the death of 25-year-old Freddie Gray while in police custody, found that 65% of blacks and 62% of whites said race relations in the United States were generally bad—by far the most negative assessment of the Obama era. A CNN/ORC survey taken in February of that year found more than twice as many people saying race relations had gotten worse during Obama's presidency as said they had improved.

Those snapshots captured public attitudes at an unusually dark moment, but they laid bare a truth about race that has persisted throughout America's post–civil rights era. For blacks, there is no realm of life in the US more fraught than relations with the police. A nationwide 2014 Pew Research survey taken shortly after the shooting of a black teenager in Ferguson, Missouri, found that just 36% of blacks were at least fairly confident that local police in their community treated blacks and whites equally, compared with 72% of whites. This racial gap in perceptions had been just as wide when the same question was asked in surveys in 2009 and 2007.

It's hard not to be struck by the best-of-times-worst-of-times paradox blacks have lived through during the Obama era. The fact that a black family

Figure 8.7

Blacks' View of Why Many Blacks Don't Get Ahead

% of blacks who say ...

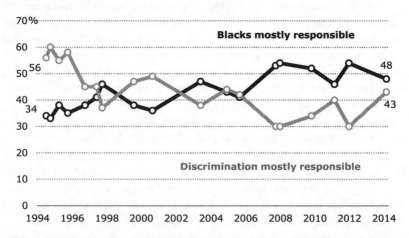

Note: In surveys in 2005 and earlier, blacks include Hispanic blacks. In surveys in 2007 and later, blacks include only non-Hispanic blacks. Question wording: Which of these statements comes closer to your own view—even if neither is exactly right. Racial discrimination is the main reason why many black people can't get ahead these days, OR, Blacks who can't get ahead in this country are mostly responsible for their own condition.

Source: Pew Research Center surveys, 1994–2014

is in the White House speaks volumes about the degree to which old prejudices have receded. Yet huge black-white gaps have persisted (and in some
instances widened) throughout Obama's presidency, in realms from education
to employment to wealth to incarceration.

Our 2013 survey was taken around the time of the commemoration of the
50th anniversary of Dr. King's famous "I Have a Dream" speech on the steps of
the Lincoln Memorial in Washington, DC. It found that just a third of blacks
feel there has been a lot of progress toward reaching racial equality over the
past half century, while 8 in 10 say much more needs to be done. Whites were
more mixed in their assessments. Half said a lot of progress has been made,
and 44% said a lot more needs to be done.

Those mixed views on progress toward racial equality were echoed in
a Pew Research Center analysis of long-term US government trend data on
indicators of well-being and civic engagement, including personal finance, life
expectancy, educational attainment, and voter participation. The data looked
at equality of outcomes rather than equality of opportunity.

Our analysis found that the economic gulf between blacks and whites
that was present half a century ago largely remains. When it comes to household income and household wealth, the gaps between blacks and whites have
widened. On measures such as high school completion and life expectancy, they have nar-
rowed. On other measures, including poverty and home-ownership rates, the gaps are roughly the same as they were 40 years ago (see appendix Figure 8A.5).

FINANCES. Between 1967 and 2011 the median income of a black household of three rose from about $24,000 to nearly $40,000.[12] Expressed as a share of white income, black house-holds earn about 59% of what white households earn, a small increase from 55% in 1967. But when expressed as dollars, the black-white income gap

Figure 8.8

Whites, Blacks Assess the National Economy

% saying national economy is excellent/good

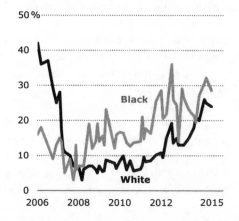

Source: Pew Research Center surveys, 2006–2015

widened, from about $19,000 in the late 1960s to roughly $27,000 today. The race gap on household wealth has increased from $75,224 in 1984 to $84,960 in 2011.

Other indicators of financial well-being have changed little in recent decades, including homeownership rates and the share of each race that lives above the poverty line. The black unemployment rate also has consistently been about double that of whites since the 1950s.

EDUCATION. High school completion rates have converged since the 1960s, and now about 9 in 10 blacks and whites have a high school diploma. The trend in college completion rates tells a more nuanced story. Today white adults ages 25 and older are significantly more likely than blacks to have completed at least a bachelor's degree (34% versus 21%, a 13-percentage-point difference). Fifty years ago, the completion gap between whites and blacks was about 6 percentage points (10% versus 4%). But expressed a different way, the black completion rate as a percentage of the white rate has improved from 42% then to 62% now.

FAMILY FORMATION. The analysis finds growing disparities in key measures of family formation. Marriage rates among whites and blacks have declined in the past 50 years, and the black-white difference has nearly doubled. Today about 54% of whites and 31% of blacks ages 18 and older are married. In 1960, 74% of whites and roughly 6 in 10 blacks (61%) were married. The share of births to unmarried women has risen sharply for both groups; in 2013, more than 7 in 10 births to black women were to unmarried mothers, compared with about 3 in 10 births to white women (71% versus 29%).

INCARCERATION. Black men were more than six times as likely as white men to be incarcerated in federal and state prisons and local jails in 2010. That is an increase from 1960, when black men were five times as likely as whites to be incarcerated.

VOTER TURNOUT. Participation rates for blacks in presidential elections have lagged those of whites for most of the past half century but have been rising since 1996. Buoyed by the historic candidacies of Barack Obama, blacks nearly caught up with whites in 2008 and surpassed them in 2012, when 67% of eligible blacks cast ballots, compared with 64% of eligible whites.

LIFE EXPECTANCY. The gap in life expectancy rates among blacks and whites has narrowed in the past five decades from about 7 years to 4.

In 2014, when a Pew Research survey asked why many blacks have not advanced in this country, about half of black respondents (48%) said those who cannot get ahead are mainly responsible for their own situation, whereas about 4 in 10 (43%) said that racial discrimination is the main reason. Fifteen years before, most blacks blamed discrimination. Multiple surveys taken since 1994 show that this shift in blacks' perceptions has occurred in fits and starts over time, and that the change predates Obama's election.

In one of the most intriguing findings of the 2009 survey, most blacks joined with most whites in saying that the two racial groups have grown more alike in the past decade, both in their standards of living and their core values. Seven in 10 whites (70%) and 6 in 10 blacks (60%) said that the values held by blacks and whites have become more similar in the past 10 years. Similarly, a majority of blacks (56%) and nearly two-thirds of whites (65%) said the standard-of-living gap between whites and blacks has narrowed in the past decade.

In fact, most of the racial gaps in key personal finance indicators widened during the 2007–2009 recession and have remained at elevated levels since. But when it comes to race and economics during the Age of Obama, reality is one thing, perception another. In 2013, blacks were still only about half as likely as whites to rate the national economy as poor, and twice as likely to say things will be better in the coming year. They were also more upbeat than whites in their perceptions of the housing market and the job market.

All of these attitudes suggest that Obama's presidency has had a salutary impact on African Americans that's hard to measure but impossible to ignore. Not on their economic circumstances, obviously, but on their sense of belonging. I was a reporter in South Africa for three years in the mid-1990s during the transition from apartheid to democracy. Despite surface similarities, that country's racial dynamics are completely different from ours. No matter what the white settlers had done over the centuries in South Africa, blacks there have always known it was their country, their place—the land of their ancestors. The same can't be said of blacks in America; their ancestors arrived in chains. For them the color line has been more than an instrument of discrimination; it has been a badge of un-belonging. But when 130 million of their fellow Americans take part in two successive elections that choose Barack Obama as the nation's leader, that badge loses some of its oppressive power. The black-white divide is still America's deepest cleavage, and Obama's presidency hasn't made it go away. But it has made it smaller. To paraphrase Dr. King, the arc of our history is bending toward inclusion.

Whither Marriage?

SIXTY YEARS AGO *Ladies' Home Journal* launched "Can This Marriage Be Saved?," an advice column that has become the longest-running and most widely read standing feature in magazine publishing history. Its "riveting true stories" about marriages in trouble chronicle the everyday stresses that take their toll on the world's most enduring social institution: "He's Always Obsessing About Money"; "The Holidays Make Me Crazy"; "Our Sex Life Is Stale"; "My Stepdaughter Is Ruining Our Marriage"; "We Can't Get Pregnant"; "He Told Our Secrets Online"; "Home Renovations Are Wrecking Us"; and so on. The column is a cornucopia of commonsense advice, but if its mission has been to save marriages, it has been a massive bust. Back when it launched, nearly three-quarters of all adults in the US were married. Now just half are.

Lots of particular marriages fail for lots of particular reasons. But nowadays it's the institution itself that's in big trouble. And the biggest problem isn't that people who try marriage are failing at it. It's that fewer are trying at all.

Marriage's loss of customers has occurred among all age groups, but it's most acute among Millennials. Today just 18% of adults ages 18 to 29 are married, compared with 59% in 1960. During the past half century, the median age at first marriage has risen by about six years for both men and women.

Are today's young adults abandoning marriage or merely delaying it? The weight of history would suggest the latter. In one form or another, marriage has been a social foundation upon which virtually all of the world's cultures and civilizations have been built. Institutions that have endured for thousands of years don't disappear overnight—do they?

Figure 9.1

Marriage Loses Market Share, 1960–2013

% of adults 18 and older, by current marital status

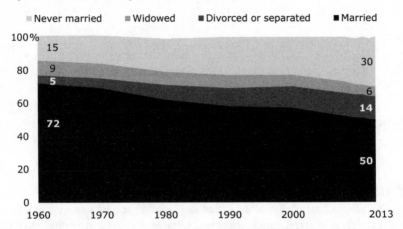

Source: Pew Research Center analysis of Decennial Census (1960–2000) and American Community Survey data (2008–2013), IPUMS

Time will tell. For now, it's notable that marriage is in retreat not just in the US but in nearly all developed (and some less developed) countries across the world. The trend is most advanced in Scandinavia, where cohabitation has for all intents and purposes replaced marriage. (But cohabiting unions there are much more durable than those in the US—so much so that a child born to cohabiting parents in Sweden has less of a chance of experiencing his or her parents' breakup than does a child born to *married* parents in the US, according to sociologist Andrew Cherlin.)

In the US, meantime, large swaths of the public—led by Millennials—express doubts about the long-term viability of the institution. In a 2010 Pew Research survey, nearly 4 in 10 (39%) Americans—and 44% of Millennials—agreed that marriage is becoming obsolete. When the same question was posed to voters by *Time* magazine back in 1978, when divorce rates were peaking, just 28% agreed.

This doesn't mean that today's young people don't want to marry. Most still do. If history is a guide, most eventually will. That same 2010 survey also found that 70% of unmarried Millennials say they would like to get married one day. So what's holding them back?

To borrow an old joke about politics: three things—money, money, and I can't remember the third. The retreat from marriage is above all a class-based phenomenon. Back in 1960, there was just a 4-percentage-point gap (76% versus 72%) in marriage rates between college graduates and those with a high school diploma or less. By 2013, the gap had ballooned to 18 percentage points (63% versus 45%). The same disparities are found by income and race; over the past half century the greatest declines in marriage rates have been among minorities and those at the lower end of the income scale—categories that overlap (see appendix Figure 9A.1).

It's not that people in these groups lack the motivation to marry. If anything, it's that they place marriage on too high a pedestal. The Pew Research survey found that among the unmarried, there are no differences by education or income in the desire to get married. But the survey also found that the less education and income people have, the more likely they are to say that to be a good marriage prospect, a person must be able to support a family financially. In effect, they create an economic prerequisite for marriage that they themselves can't meet.

Their doubts can be self-fulfilling. Marriage has always been associated with positive economic outcomes—not just because it's an efficient way to allocate and combine labor (yes, two can live more cheaply than one), but because the marital commitment itself tends to promote values and behaviors associated with economic success—constancy, responsibility, persistence, an inclination for pragmatic compromise. On top of that, our tax laws and Social Security rules provide substantial benefits to married couples. When people from all walks of life get married in roughly equal shares, marriage spreads these economic and behavioral rewards in roughly equal measure up and down the socioeconomic ladder. But in a world where a disproportionate share of those who tie the knot

Figure 9.2

Share Married, by Educational Attainment

% of adults 18 and older

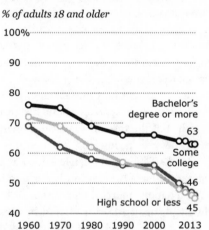

Source: Pew Research Center analysis of Decennial Census (1960–2000) and American Community Survey data (2008–2013), IPUMS

enter marriage already enjoying the head start of a good education and healthy economic prospects, it's easy to see how the marriage gap and the income gap reinforce each other. That's exactly what has been happening for decades.

Demographers estimate that 8 in 10 adults will eventually marry, but the typical American today spends less of his or her adult life in a marriage than at any time in modern history—and a record 28% of all US households are now headed by a single person. Marriage, in short, has lost its cultural hegemony. It was once the mandated path to adulthood; it's now a lifestyle choice.

The shift is most visible among Millennials, who value marriage somewhat less than the next youngest adult generation, the Gen Xers, did back when they were the age Millennials are now. Just 30% of Millennials say having a successful marriage is one of the most important things in life. Back in 1997, 35% of Gen Xers felt that way about marriage. And there's an even bigger disparity between the two generations in their views of parenthood—but that one runs in the opposite direction. Some 52% of Millennials say being a good parent is one of the most important things in life, compared with 42% of Gen Xers who said the same back when they were the age Millennials are now.

Our entertainment culture mirrors and reinforces these changes. In the first several decades of television, the family sitcom ruled the ratings roost. All of the iconic shows—*Ozzie and Harriet, Leave It to Beaver, My Three Sons, Father Knows Best, The Cosby Show,* etc.—revolved around the foibles of everyday life in a tight-knit nuclear family. Dad was both the authority figure and the butt of endless jokes about his clumsiness in matters of the heart and hearth. But the humor was always loving, and it was impossible to miss the meta-message: people, this is how you're supposed to live!

In more recent times, television has done an about-face on marriage. With the exception of the hilariously dysfunctional *Simpsons,* it has been a long time since a happily married nuclear television family grabbed and held the prime-time zeitgeist. Instead television has served up a steady diet of relationship shows, buddy shows, and parenthood shows—*Friends, Seinfeld, Sex and the City, Desperate Housewives, The Good Wife, Two and a Half Men, Parenthood.* When marriage appears at all on the small screen, it's usually as a bridge too far, a cautionary tale, or a full-on calamity.

One need not sentimentalize marriage. The good old Ozzie and Harriet marriages included a lot of relationships that were loveless, or worse. In the days when adults felt overwhelming social pressure to get and stay married, the rate of domestic violence within marriage was an estimated 30% higher than now.[1] And while the great majority of 1950s-era wives never faced that sort of abuse, many felt trapped in other ways. The women's liberation movement drew much of its energy from women who wanted more from life than a wife-as-homemaker marriage.

Half a century later, adults of both genders have their doubts that a person needs to be married to lead a fulfilling life. A 2010 Pew Research survey asked respondents whether they thought it was easier for a married person or a single person to find happiness. About 3 in 10 (29%) said it was easier for married people while just 5% said it was easier for single people. But a sizable majority—62%—said it makes no difference. Even among married people, a majority said marriage has no bearing on one's prospects for happiness.

These findings are notable for a couple of reasons beyond their decidedly lukewarm embrace of the joys of married life. One is a big gender disparity. Some 38% of men say it's easier to find happiness as a married person, compared with just 22% of women—providing some data underpinnings to the folk wisdom and social science that say marriage is a better deal for men than for women.

Even more intriguing, however, is that the public appears to be undervaluing the contribution marriage makes to happiness. Pew Research surveys often begin by asking respondents, "Generally, how would you say things are these days in your life—would you say you are very happy, pretty happy, or not too happy?" In the survey profession, this is known as a door-opener question; its main goal is to get respondents comfortable with doing the interview. But because there's quite a cottage industry these days in happiness research, the responses have value in their own right, especially since we can deconstruct the nationwide sample to analyze the various correlates of happiness.

It turns out that happiness and marriage make a great couple. In one recent survey, 36% of married people said they are very happy, while just 22% of unmarried people said the same. These results rarely vary by more than a few percentage points from survey to survey. But they should be kept in perspective. Marriage is correlated with other traits that are also correlated with happiness—such as high income, religiosity, and good health. In other words, the kind of people inclined to be married are the kind of people inclined to be happy.

However, this still leaves open the possibility that marriage in and of itself also helps in life's happiness sweepstakes. One way to test that proposition

Figure 9.3

Is Marriage Bliss?

% "very happy" by marital status

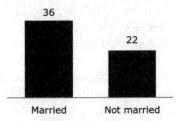

Source: Pew Research Center survey, Nov. 2012, N=2,511 US adults

is through a statistical technique known as regression analysis, which measures the strength of the linkage between a variable of interest (in this case, marriage) and an outcome of interest (in this case, happiness), while holding all other variables constant. Our regression analysis finds that, all else being equal, marriage increases one's likelihood of being very happy—by 12%. That might not sound like much. But consider: Gender, race, ethnicity, education, and age are among the many characteristics that have no independent statistical impact whatsoever on a person's likelihood of being very happy. Marriage is among a small circle of traits—including good health, high income, and strong religious observance—for which there is an independent impact.

The irony, of course, is that the very public that affirms a link between marriage and happiness doesn't seem to be reading its own memos. Marriage helps make people happier, yet fewer people are marrying. Why?

WHY IS MARRIAGE IN RETREAT?

Most theories about the decline of marriage start with the impact of structural changes to the economy. The most important of these—the movement of women in the workforce—undid the equilibrium of the male breadwinner/female homemaker template for marriage that had prevailed since the industrial era. At the same time, the development of a postindustrial, knowledge-based economy has diminished the job prospects and earning power of less educated men, creating a "marriage market mismatch" at the lower end of the socioeconomic scale. In the old marriage marketplace, a woman needed a husband for financial security. In the new marriage marketplace, fewer women have that need, and fewer men can cater to it.

Other theories focus on the more intimate realms of marriage. Until not too long ago, marriage was the only socially and morally acceptable gateway to sexual partnerships. The introduction of the birth control pill in the early 1960s helped to pry much of this regulatory authority over sex away from marriage. Adultery remains a taboo, but in an era of "friends with benefits," sex among unmarried or never-married adults carries little if any stigma. This has complicated the case for marriage—and not just because sexual desires can now be respectably accommodated without lifetime commitments, but also because it has increased the demand on marriage to provide something even more precious than sex. More so than ever, people want a spouse to be their lifelong companion, emotional soul mate, partner in the journey toward self-fulfillment. Marriage, in a word, is supposed to be built on love (see appendix Figure 9A.2).

But as social historian Stephanie Coontz has observed, love may be the undoing of marriage.[2] At the very least, it has injected an unstable element into the suddenly fragile heart of an age-old institution. For most of its 5,000-year history, marriage had little to do with love. Across cultures and centuries, it thrived as a way to propagate the species, establish people's place in the social and economic order, acquire in-laws, organize productive activity along gender lines, extract labor from the young, and distribute resources from parents to children. Only in the eighteenth century, with the spread of market economies and the Enlightenment, did love and mutual self-fulfillment start to enter into the marital bargain. Today, arguably, they're the dominant part. But love can be fickle and self-fulfillment a high bar. Can an institution built on love be as durable as one built on the stouter stuff of economic self-interest? As a society, we're conducting that experiment right now. So far, the answer appears to be no (see appendix Figure 9A.3).

In the middle of the twentieth century, the anti-Nazi German theologian Dietrich Bonhoeffer sent a congratulatory letter to some newlyweds of his acquaintance. It contained an aphorism about marriage that reflected an old-fashioned view of the institution. "It is not your love that sustains the marriage," he wrote, "but from now on, the marriage that sustains your love." Today one would be hard-pressed to find that sentiment expressed anywhere in Western literature or culture. "If you were to write the same letter to newlyweds now, I don't think they'd have a clue what you were talking about," said David Blankenhorn, founder and president of the Institute for American Values, a nonpartisan think tank whose mission, among others, is to try to restore what he calls the "fractured" institution of marriage.

Other groups have also taken up that challenge, but their contributions so far have been mainly in the realm of

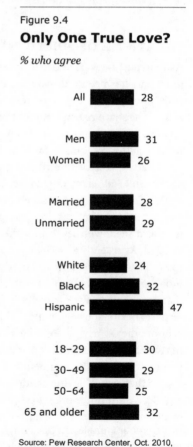

Figure 9.4

Only One True Love?

% who agree

All	28
Men	31
Women	26
Married	28
Unmarried	29
White	24
Black	32
Hispanic	47
18–29	30
30–49	29
50–64	25
65 and older	32

Source: Pew Research Center, Oct. 2010, N=2,691 US adults

diagnosis, not cure. A 2013 research paper, "Knot Yet: The Benefits and Costs of Delayed Marriage," did a wonderful job showing how young adults view marriage as a "capstone" rather than "cornerstone" arrangement—"something they do after they have all their other ducks in a row, rather than a foundation for launching into adulthood and parenthood."[3] Given this new cultural framework for marriage, it's no surprise that it's the high-achieving young adults who are most likely to get hitched. "Marriage has become a status symbol," writes Cherlin, "a highly regarded marker of a successful personal life. . . . Something young adults do after they and their live-in partners have good jobs and a nice apartment."[4] He noted that in 2012, according to a study by *Brides* magazine, 36% of newlyweds paid the entire cost of their wedding receptions, and an additional 26% contributed to the cost.

THE STIGMA OF SINGLE PARENTHOOD

As marriage rates have declined, the reaction of the American public for the most part has been a do-your-own-thing shrug of acceptance. That's not the case, however, for the most important consequence of the decline in marriage—the sharp rise in births outside of marriage. Of all the structural changes on the marriage and family front in recent decades, this one has drawn the most negative reaction by far from the public.

In 2014, 40% of all births in the US were to unmarried mothers, up from just 5% in 1960. Many might assume this has been driven by a surge in teenage births. To the contrary, the teen birthrate (births per 1,000 women ages 15 to 19) in the US today has dropped by more than 60% from its peak in 1957; it is now at the lowest level since the US government started tracking such data in 1940. As recently as 1990, teenage girls accounted for more births in the US than did women ages 35 and older. Now the reverse is true. Teenage mothers today give birth to about 10% of all babies, and 18% of babies born outside of marriage. They may or may not be having more sex than their same-age counterparts of previous generations, but thanks to the widespread use of contraception, they're having fewer kids. It's one reason that in 2014, for the first time in two decades, the share of births to unmarried mothers ticked down slightly, to 40% from 41% the year before.

So then, who's having children out of wedlock? Mostly, women in their 20s and 30s. Until not too long ago, marriage and parenthood were linked milestones on the journey to adulthood. And if they happened out of sequence—that is, if a single woman got pregnant—a "shotgun wedding" was the culturally prescribed remedy. This custom now seems quaint. Nowadays an estimated 6 in 10 single mothers have live-in boyfriends when they give birth, about double the rate among unmarried mothers a generation ago. However, these cohabiting unions tend to be of short duration—only about half survive until the child's 5th birthday.

Nonmarital births have also soared in many of the world's other developed countries, for many of the same reasons. But the US is an outlier in its combination of high nonmarital birthrates, high divorce rates, and high turnover in cohabiting relationships. As a result of all these trends, Cherlin says that a teenager in the US has a smaller likelihood than a teenager in any other country in the world of living in a household with both biological parents.

Figure 9.5

Share of Births to Unmarried Women, 1960–2014

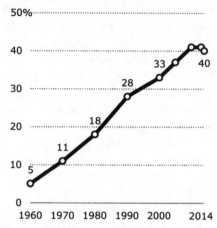

Source: National Center for Health Statistics data; 2014 data is preliminary

A large body of social science research shows that, on average and controlling for other factors, children have better outcomes in life if raised by both parents than if raised by just one. They are healthier, do better academically, get into less trouble as adolescents, are less likely to drop out of high school or become teenage parents, are less prone to substance abuse or criminal behavior, and are more successful in their jobs and careers.[5]

Policy experts of all ideological stripes accept these findings—and so, as we'll see in a moment, does the public. Yet the topic of single parenthood gets very little public attention these days. It has been politically and racially fraught for decades, ever since Daniel Patrick Moynihan penned the controversial 1965 report "The Negro Family: The Case for National Action." Moynihan, who went on to become UN Ambassador, a US senator from New York, and one of the nation's leading public intellectuals, was at the time a young assistant secretary of labor in the Johnson administration, which was pressing ahead with its ambitious civil rights agenda and its "War on Poverty." Moynihan's thesis was that progress toward racial equality would be held back because so many black children were being raised by single mothers. He argued that such families were a by-product not just of the "tangle of pathologies" in poor communities, but of a matriarchal family culture among blacks that traced its roots to slavery.

Critics denounced the report for what they deemed its "blame-the-victim" take on poverty and racial inequality; supporters welcomed it as an unvarnished dose of truth. The Johnson administration went ahead and ramped up funding for Aid to Families with Dependent Children, a welfare program that provided cash support to poor single mothers. But the program quickly became a lightning rod for conservatives who said it created incentives for nonmarital motherhood and promoted a culture of dependence. Ronald Reagan, among many others, inveighed against "welfare queens" to good effect on the campaign trail. In 1996 President Bill Clinton joined with a Republican-controlled Congress to kill AFDC and enact a stripped-down replacement, a move that has taken much of the toxicity out of the political debate over welfare policies. Since then, the national conversation about single parenthood has pretty much disappeared.

But single parenthood itself hasn't. Indeed, what's notable about this brief retrospective are the data that attracted Moynihan's notice in 1965. He sounded the alarm because the out-of-wedlock birthrate among blacks had risen to an estimated 25%. Half a century later, the rate is 71%. Among Latinos, the rate is 53%. Among whites, 29% (see appendix Figure 9A.4). What once seemed shocking has become mainstream. Perhaps that's why it draws so little public attention. Or perhaps it's that elites—mindful of the stir the Moynihan report triggered decades ago—find the whole subject to be uncomfortable. "I know of no other set of important findings [about the poor outcomes of children raised by single parents] that are as broadly accepted by social scientists . . . and yet are so resolutely ignored by network news programs, editorial writers for the major newspapers, and politicians of both political parties," wrote conservative scholar Charles Murray in his 2012 book, *Coming Apart*.[6]

The overall verdict from the public about the rise of single parenthood is an emphatic thumbs down. Asked in 2010 whether each of seven demographic changes affecting the composition of families was good or bad for society, 69% said the rise in single women having children was bad, while just 4% said it was good—by far the most negative reading on any of the trends. In 2013, when the question was asked in a slightly different form, 64% said the rising number of children born to unmarried mothers was a big problem for society, 19% said it was a small problem, and 13% said it was not a problem.

However, there are some notable generational differences in these attitudes. Among adults ages 50 and older, 74% say unwed motherhood is a big problem; among adults 18 to 29, just 42% say the same. Along these same lines, a majority of the public (61%) believes that a child is more likely to grow up happy in a home with both a mother and a father, but there are generational differences here too. Silent Generation adults are more likely than Millennials (75% versus 53%) to say this. Also, men are more likely than women (67% versus 54%) to feel this way. And more Hispanics (72%) and blacks (65%) say this than do whites (57%)—more evidence that when it comes to single parenthood, attitudes and behaviors do not always move in sync with one another.

Nonmarital births aren't the only reason more children are being raised by single parents. Divorce has become much more prevalent over the past half century, a trend most experts trace to the same mix of economic and cultural factors that have produced the delayed marriage phenomenon: if marriage is supposed to be mainly about finding love and self-actualization, it's a destination that some share of the married population won't be able to reach.

Divorce is never a happy outcome, but Americans cast a much less disapproving eye on it than they do on nonmarital births. A majority (58%) of the public say that divorce is preferable to maintaining an unhappy marriage, and an even bigger majority—67%—say that if a marriage is very unhappy, the children are better off when the parents get divorced.

Contrary to public perceptions, divorce rates have been declining for several decades. Part of this is simple math: people can't divorce if they don't marry. But rates of divorce have also declined somewhat among married couples. This is likely related to the aging of the population and other changes in the demographics of marriage. Divorce rates have always been highest among couples who marry young and couples at the lower end of the socioeconomic ladder. There are fewer of those marriages now. Many young couples today choose to cohabit rather than marry, and while these relationships often break up, it can't be a divorce if it was never a marriage. Among couples who do go ahead and marry young, a greater share than in the past live in the land of the "haves," where the rate of divorce has always been lower.

GRAY DIVORCE

At the same time, however, there has been a sharp rise in "gray divorce"—a Boomer-driven phenomenon exemplified by the breakup in 2010 of the 40-year marriage of former vice president Al Gore and his wife, Tipper. A half century ago, only 2.8% of adults older than age 50 were divorced; by 2011, that share had risen to 15.4%. For the first time in history, more Americans ages 50 and older are divorced than widowed (13.5%).[7]

Family scholar Susan L. Brown has done research showing that divorce has been migrating north on the age pyramid for several decades. Just 1 in 10 people who got divorced in 1990 were age 50 or older, she reports; now more than 1 in 4 new divorcees are in that age group. Boomers have been at the heart of the divorce explosion throughout all phases of their adult lives. Forty years ago they tended to marry young and divorce young. Now they're more likely than previous generations to divorce later in life (in part because their remarriages are at a relatively high risk of ending in divorce). Given all this, Brown finds that 1 in 3 Boomers are currently single—which leaves many of them economically and socially vulnerable on the cusp of old age.[8]

But gray divorce may also be a by-product of more positive social trends—for example, advances in the quality of life of older adults and changes in women's roles, opportunities, and expectations. "The extension of the active, healthy life span is a big part of this," said Coontz. "If you are a healthy 65, you can expect another pretty healthy 20 years. So with the kids gone, it seems more burdensome to stay in a bad relationship, or even one that has gone stale." Most divorces among older adults, as among younger adults, are initiated by women, leading Coontz to observe: "Another big factor is that with their increased work experience and greater sense of their own possibilities, [women] are less willing to just 'wait it out.' We expect to find equality, intimacy, friendship, fun and even passion right into what people used to see as the 'twilight years.'"[9]

SAME-SEX MARRIAGE

As marriage is in broad retreat among the general public, it has been embraced by gays and lesbians as the crown jewel of their quest for civil rights and social acceptance. The irony of gays rushing toward marriage while straights seem to be running away hasn't been lost on the commentariat, especially conservatives who see an explicit connection between the opposing trends.

Until not too long ago, the case against same-sex marriage was based at least in part on the notion that it would have the socially undesirable effect of weakening the link among matrimony, procreation, and child rearing. However, as more straight adults are themselves breaking the link, this becomes a much more difficult case to make. "The conservative argument still has serious exponents, but it's now chuckled at in courtrooms, dismissed by intellectuals, mocked in the media and (in a sudden recent rush) abandoned by politicians," wrote *New York Times* columnist Ross Douthat in March 2013, a few days after a pair of same-sex marriage cases were argued before the US Supreme Court.[10]

The near-collapse of the elite argument against same-sex marriage is mirrored by an equally dramatic change in the views of the general public. Indeed, it's hard to think of any other social/moral/political issue in modern history that has seen such a large swing in prevailing attitudes in such a short time period. As recently as the 2004 presidential campaign, public sentiment against same-sex marriage was so intense that GOP strategists went out of their way to put the issue on state ballots in key swing states, knowing it would help drive up turnout among social conservatives. Back then, according to Pew Research surveys, just a third of adults supported same-sex marriage. Now more than half do. There's still a big generation gap on this issue, with 73% of Millennials favoring the legalization of same-sex marriage, compared with just 39% of Silents. George Will among others has stressed the generational replacement component of the shift in public attitudes. "Quite literally the opposition to gay marriage is dying," he noted on ABC's *This Week* in 2012. But along with the demographic dynamics, support has been growing among all age groups.

What has caused the change? Our surveys show that it has little or nothing to do with new attitudes about marriage and everything to do with new attitudes about gays. Among supporters of same-sex marriage in 2013, fully 28% said they were once opponents. Asked why they changed their minds, no one cited changing attitudes about marriage. Instead, the most common response was that familiarity had led to acceptance. Nearly 9 in 10 Americans (87%) now say they know someone who is gay or lesbian, up from 61% in 1993, and about half (49%) say a close friend or family member is gay or lesbian. In a separate 2013 Pew survey of lesbian, gay, bisexual, and transgender (LGBT) adults, more than 9 in 10 said they believe social acceptance of their community has grown in the past decade; they, too, cite "people knowing someone who is LGBT" as the primary driver of change.

Clearly a feedback loop has taken hold: as the social stigma recedes, more gays come out of the closet, and as more gays come out of the closet, the stigma recedes still more. But it hasn't disappeared—not even close. As of 2013, almost half of Americans (45%) said that engaging in homosexual behavior is a sin, a view highly correlated with frequency of religious attendance and other measures of religiosity. And 40% of adults say they would be upset if they learned they had a gay or lesbian child—down from the 60% who felt this way in 2004, but a sizable minority nonetheless.

Our surveys also toss cold water on the premise that gays are rushing toward marriage while straights are running away. Among LGBT survey respondents, 60% said they are either currently married or would like to marry one day; among the general public, that figure is 76%. Even in its troubled state, marriage hasn't fallen off its pedestal. It remains a life aspiration for the vast majority of Americans—"a status symbol, a highly regarded marker of a successful personal life," in the words of Andrew Cherlin. Indeed, in his majority opinion for the US Supreme Court in the ruling that struck down

Figure 9.6

Sharp Rise in Support for Same-Sex Marriage

Allowing gays and lesbians to marry legally ...

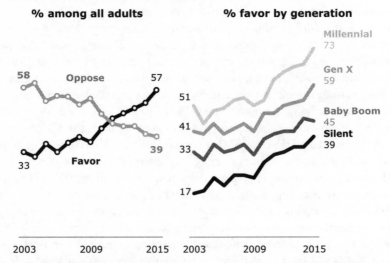

Source: Aggregated data from surveys conducted by the Pew Research Center for the People & the Press, 2003–2014; 2015 data from May 2015 survey only

the Defense of Marriage Act (DOMA), Justice Anthony Kennedy paid homage to the symbolic importance of marriage. He ruled that the federal government's refusal to recognize legal same-sex marriages imposed a "stigma" that "demean(s)" gay couples and "humiliates" their children. DOMA, he wrote, deprives a group of people their Fifth Amendment rights not only because they cannot get access to the many tangible federal benefits that accrue to married couples, but because the law is telling them that their marriages are somehow "less worthy" than those of straight couples.

WHAT'S A FAMILY?

As marriage has receded, family forms have changed. Back when *Ladies' Home Journal* launched its advice column, the preeminent family unit of the mid-twentieth century—mom, dad, and the kids—pretty much had the stage to itself. No longer. Families now come in all shapes, sizes, and constellations:

single parent, multigenerational, same sex, different race, step, blended, tangled.

Given the breadth and sweep of these changes, it's reasonable to ask: Just who belongs in the family album these days and who doesn't? As Figure 9.7 shows, a majority consider most of the constellations discussed in this chapter to be a family. Not surprisingly, traditional marriage and parenthood top the list. However, the public is also ready to confer family status on groupings it doesn't always approve of. For example, nearly 9 in 10 say a single parent with a child is a family, and more than 6 in 10 say the same about a same-sex couple raising a child. Younger adults are more expansive than older adults with all of these definitions. Thus, the broader boundaries of family would seem to be both culturally and demographically ascendant.

But that doesn't mean all relatives are created equal. In 2010, Pew Research did a survey in which we asked people how obligated they would feel to provide either financial help or caregiving to a relative who had a serious problem. (Each respondent was asked only about the category of relative he or she has, as determined by questions asked earlier in the survey.)

Obviously, these are highly individual matters, but as Figure 9.8 illustrates, some overall patterns emerge. The biblical injunction to honor thy mother and

---

Figure 9.7

Is This a Family?

% saying each grouping is ...

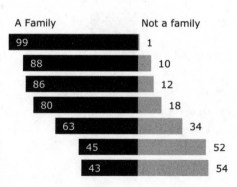

	A Family	Not a family
Married couple w/ children	99	1
Married couple w/o children	88	10
Single parent w/ children	86	12
Unmarried couple w/ children	80	18
Same-sex couple w/ children	63	34
Same-sex couple w/o children	45	52
Unmarried couple w/o children	43	54

Note: Question wording: "As I read you a list of different arrangements, please tell me whether you consider each to be a family or not?"

Source: Pew Research Center survey, Oct. 2010, N=2,691 US adults

father hasn't been lost on the American public: parents top the list (we didn't ask about young children because we took it as a given that everyone would say they are obligated to help them). From there the rankings descended in a crisp stair-step pattern: grown child, grandparent, sibling, in-law. Steprelatives don't fare as well as biological relatives. But all rank above "your best friend"—which was the lone nonrelative on the list.

Figure 9.8

Ranking the Relatives

% who say they feel "very obligated" to provide needed financial assistance or caregiving to their ...

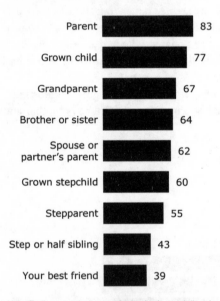

Parent	83
Grown child	77
Grandparent	67
Brother or sister	64
Spouse or partner's parent	62
Grown stepchild	60
Stepparent	55
Step or half sibling	43
Your best friend	39

Note: Each respondent was asked only about relatives he or she has. Question wording: "Suppose someone you know had a serious problem and needed either financial help or caregiving. How obligated would you feel to provide assistance if that person were your [NAME ON LIST]: Would you feel very obligated, somewhat obligated, not too obligated or not at all obligated?"

Source: Pew Research Center survey, Oct. 2010, N=2,691 US adults

All of this suggests that in the face of massive social and demographic change, kinship is still a preeminent element of people's lives. Yes, the institution of marriage is in retreat; yes, the makeup of families is changing; and yes, the public disapproves of the decoupling of marriage and parenthood. But through it all, family remains the center of most people's universe.

Three-quarters of adults say their family is the most important element of their lives. There are very few differences by demographic group. And when asked about the future of the institution of marriage and family in this country, two-thirds say they are optimistic—again, with little variance in responses by age, race, or gender. That same question tested the public's optimism about other key institutions, values, and behaviors that impact the nation's well-being. None rose to the level of family and marriage.

However, the public's upbeat view of the future of marriage finds few takers in the community of scholars and policy advocates who track its faltering fortunes. "I suspect marriage as we have known it is not coming back," writes Isabel V. Sawhill of the Brookings Institution.[11] Social commentator Kay S. Hymowitz concurs, noting that even if a national movement to take up the challenge of restoring marriage were to somehow emerge, "the policy levers are few."[12] At a subdued Brookings symposium in 2013 built around the "Knot Yet" report, Douthat of the *New York Times* struck the closest thing to a hopeful note. He pointed out that over the past several decades, as family instability has grown, many of the dire social consequences that were presumed to be an inevitable by-product—youth crime, high school dropouts, teen pregnancy, etc.—have ameliorated rather than worsened. "[The decline of marriage] may have a negative impact on human flourishing," he said, "but it hasn't dragged us into the kind of abyss that scolds and conservatives usually like to threaten people with." That's not exactly a ringing endorsement of the status quo, but it's a useful reminder of the resilience of the human spirit and human institutions. Looking ahead, as the Boomers grow older and the social safety net grows smaller, that resilience will be put to the test as the nation struggles to figure out how best to care for its elderly at a time when a growing share will have fractured families to which they are only loosely attached.

Nones on the Rise

O N THE EVE OF THE 2004 presidential primaries, David Brooks traced the faith journeys of three of the leading candidates.

"George W. Bush was born into an Episcopal family and raised as a Presbyterian, but he is now a Methodist," Brooks began his *New York Times* column.[1]

"Howard Dean was baptized Catholic, and raised as an Episcopalian. He left the church after it opposed a bike trail he was championing and now he is a Congregationalist, though his kids consider themselves Jewish.

"Wesley Clark's father was Jewish. As a boy he was a Methodist, then decided to become a Baptist. In adulthood he converted to Catholicism, but he recently told Beliefnet.com, 'I'm a Catholic, but I go to a Presbyterian church.'"

In most of the world, such faith-hopping would be unheard of. In America it's practically routine. Some 42% of American adults have a different religious affiliation from the one they were raised in, and an additional 9% left their childhood religion at some point in their lives but have since returned to the fold, according to Pew Research Center surveys in 2008 and 2014.

Restlessness has been hardwired into America's religious metabolism from the get-go. The *Mayflower* was full of pilgrims who broke from the Church of England in the early 1600s and set sail for a new world so they could practice a devout but nonconformist brand of Christianity. Fire-and-brimstone Puritans like Jonathan Edwards—who sermonized about "Sinners in the Hands of an Angry God"—set the tone for spiritual life in the new colonies. But if America has always been a place for the devout, it has also always been devout in its belief in religious freedom. Our Declaration of Independence pays homage to God as the endower of our unalienable rights; our Constitution forbids the state from establishing a religion and guarantees all Americans the freedom to practice any religion they wish—or none at all. This seemingly incompatible mixture attracted the notice of our most astute early visitor, Alexis de Tocqueville, who marveled that Americans were deeply religious, yet didn't seem to take offense if their neighbors held false versions of the faith.

For much of this country's history, the combination of devoutness and pluralism led to a steady rise in religious institutions of all kinds—schools, universities, hospitals, orphanages, and above all, houses of worship of nearly every conceivable variety, from storefront Pentecostal churches to Roman Catholic cathedrals, Mormon temples, and independent Jewish *havurot.*

According to historical estimates, the share of Americans who were "churched"—who belonged to some congregation—doubled from 17% in 1776 to 34% in 1850 and then climbed steadily after the disruption of the Civil War to 62% in 1980, when it leveled off.[2] Since the 1990s, church membership and self-reported rates of church attendance have either held steady or declined modestly—about 6 in 10 US households still belong to religious congregations and more than 1 in 3 US adults continue to say they attend religious services once a week or more.

But at the same time, a major new trend has emerged: disaffiliation. Despite the relative stability in church membership, the number of Americans who do not identify in surveys with any religion—the "nones"—has been growing at

Figure 10.1
The Churching of America

Rates of church membership, 1776–2000

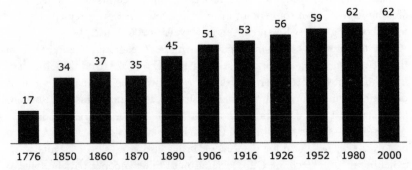

Source: Roger Finke and Rodney Stark, *The Churching of America 1776–2005: Winners and Losers in Our Religious Economy* (Rutgers University Press, 2005)

a dramatic pace. As of 2014, more than one-fifth of the US public—and more than a third of Millennials—were religiously unaffiliated, the highest percentage ever in Pew Research Center polling. From 2007 to 2014 alone, the unaffiliated increased from just over 16% to just under 23% of all US adults. Their ranks now include more than 17 million self-described atheists and agnostics (7% of the US adult public) as well as nearly 39 million who say they have no particular religious affiliation (16%).[3]

Not surprisingly, this large and growing group of Americans is less religious than the rest of the public on most conventional measures, including frequency of attendance at religious services and degree of importance they attach to religion in their lives (see appendix Figure 10A.1). But it would be a mistake to think of them as completely secular. A 2012 survey found that roughly two-thirds of the country's 46 million unaffiliated adults believe in God (68%); more than a third classify themselves as "spiritual" but not "religious" (37%); and 1 in 5 (21%) say they pray every day. With few exceptions, though, the unaffiliated say they are *not* looking for a religion that would be right for them. Overwhelmingly, they think that religious organizations are too concerned with money and power, too focused on rules, and too involved in politics.

The growth in the number of religiously unaffiliated Americans is driven largely by generational replacement, the gradual supplanting of older generations by newer ones.[4] Young adults today are more likely than older adults to have no religious affiliation. And Millennials are also much more likely to be unaffiliated than previous generations were when they were young.

In addition, Generation Xers and Baby Boomers have become somewhat more religiously unaffiliated in recent years. In 2014, 23% of Gen Xers and 17% of Baby Boomers described themselves as religiously unaffiliated, up slightly (but by statistically significant margins) from 19% and 14%, respectively, since 2007.

According to longer trends from the General Social Survey (GSS), the percentage of Americans who were raised without any religious affiliation has been rising gradually, from about 3% in the early 1970s to about 8% in the past decade. However, the overwhelming majority of today's adult "nones"—78%—were raised with an affiliation, according to the 2014 Pew Research Center survey.

TRENDS IN RELIGIOUS COMMITMENT

Despite these trends, the US remains a highly religious country—particularly compared with other advanced industrial democracies—and some measures of religious commitment in America have held remarkably steady over the years. For instance, the number of Americans who currently say religion is very important in their lives is little changed since 2007 and remains considerably higher than in Britain, France, Germany, or Spain.[5] And over the longer term, Pew Research surveys find no change in the percentage of Americans who say that prayer is an important part of their daily life. It was 76% in 2012, exactly the same as 25 years earlier, in 1987.

But on some other measures, such as attendance at worship services, there is evidence of a gradual decline in religious commitment. Numerous studies indicate that people tend to report going to church more often than they really do, so these numbers are perhaps best understood not as measuring how many Americans actually are in the pews each week, but as gauging whether Americans *think of themselves* as regular attenders. At the high end of the spectrum, there is relative stability: 37% of US adults reported in Pew surveys in 2012 that they go to religious services at least once a week, about the same as in 2003 (39%). But at the low end, there is a small but statistically significant change: in 2003, 25% of US adults indicated they seldom or never attend religious services; by 2012, that number had ticked up 4 points, to 29%.

Figure 10.2

The Religiously Unaffiliated, by Generation

% saying they are unaffiliated ...

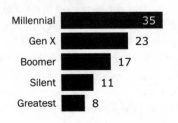

Source: Pew Research Center survey, June 4–Sept. 30, 2014

Similarly, the percentage of Americans who say they never doubt the existence of God has fallen modestly but noticeably over the past 25 years. In 1987, 88% of adults said they never doubt the existence of God. As of 2012, this figure was down to 80%.

In addition, the percentage of Americans who say the Bible should be taken literally has fallen in Gallup polls from an average of about 38% of the public in the late 1970s and early 1980s to an average of 31% since.[6] And based on analysis of GSS data, Mark Chaves of Duke University has found that Americans born in recent decades are much less likely than their elders to report having attended religious services weekly at age 12. Young adults are also less likely than older adults to report that when they were growing up, their parents attended religious services regularly.

Figure 10.3

Importance of Religion   Morality and Belief in God*

% saying "very important"   *% saying, in order to be moral, it is ...*

*Question: "Which one of these comes closest to your opinion, number 1 or number 2? ... #1 – It is not necessary to believe in God in order to be moral and have good values or #2 – It is necessary to believe in God in order to be moral and have good values."

Source: Pew Research Center survey, Mar.–May 2011, N= 27,130 adults in 23 countries

Chaves recently summarized trends in American religion by noting that "there is much continuity, and there is some decline, but no traditional religious belief or practice has increased in recent decades."[7]

RELIGIOSITY AND DISAFFILIATION

How can church membership, self-reported attendance at religious services, and other key measures of religiosity in America be holding fairly steady or declining only modestly while disaffiliation is rising dramatically? The answer is that the growth of the unaffiliated is mostly among people who are *already at the low end* of the religiosity spectrum (see appendix Figure 10A.2). In the past many of them might have retained a connection to a religious tradition, even if it was only nominal. Now they identify as "nones."

In 2007, 38% of people who said they seldom or never attend religious services described themselves as religiously unaffiliated. In 2012, 49% of infrequent attenders eschewed any religious affiliation. By comparison, the percentage describing themselves as unaffiliated has been flat among those who attend religious services once a week or more often.

THE RISE OF THE UNAFFILIATED

What accounts for the rise of the "nones"? There are four leading theories:

1. Political Backlash

Several leading scholars contend that Americans—and younger adults, in particular—have turned away from organized religion because they perceive it as deeply entangled with conservative politics and do not want to have any association with it. University of California, Berkeley, sociologists Michael Hout and Claude S. Fischer first suggested in 2002 that "part of the increase in 'nones' can be viewed as a symbolic statement against the Religious Right."[8] In their recent book, *American Grace: How Religion Divides and Unites Us*, Robert Putnam of Harvard University and David Campbell of Notre Dame marshal evidence from various surveys that supports this thesis. From the 1970s through the 1990s, they argue, "religiosity and conservative politics became increasingly aligned, and abortion and gay rights became emblematic of the emergent culture wars." The result, they write, was that many young Americans came to view religion as "judgmental, homophobic, hypocritical, and too political." It should be noted, however, that the percentage of religiously unaffiliated people has risen among Republican voters as well as among Democratic voters (though the increase is greater among Democrats).

2. Delays in Marriage

Some sociologists, including Robert Wuthnow of Princeton University, attribute the overall decline in church attendance since the 1970s to broader social and demographic trends, such as the postponement of marriage and parenthood by growing numbers of young adults.[9] Aggregated data from Pew Research Center polls are broadly consistent with this theory. They show that among adults under 30, the married are more likely than the unmarried to have a religious affiliation. But an analysis of religious affiliation patterns by generation suggests that Americans do *not* generally become more affiliated as they move through the life cycle from young adulthood to middle age and retirement.[10] Rather, the percentage of people in each generation who are religiously affiliated has remained stable, or decreased slightly, as that generation has aged.

In the past half century, religious intermarriage has become more common. Among married adults who wed before 1960, 19% have a spouse with a different religion from their own. Among those wed since 2010, fully 39% have

Figure 10.4

Recently Wed Americans More Likely to Marry Outside the Faith

Based on those who are currently married, by year married

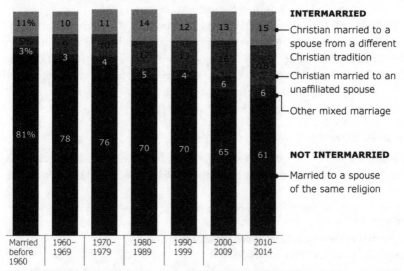

INTERMARRIED

—Christian married to a spouse from a different Christian tradition

—Christian married to an unaffiliated spouse

Other mixed marriage

NOT INTERMARRIED

—Married to a spouse of the same religion

| Married before 1960 | 1960– 1969 | 1970– 1979 | 1980– 1989 | 1990– 1999 | 2000– 2009 | 2010– 2014 |

Note: Evangelical Protestantism, mainline Protestantism, and historically black Protestantism are treated as separate religions. "Christian married to an unaffiliated spouse" includes unaffiliated respondents married to a Christian.

Source: Pew Research Center survey, June 4–Sept. 30, 2014

a spouse with a different religion. This trend is likely related to the broader pattern of disaffiliation, perhaps as both cause and effect.

3. Broad Social Disengagement

Yet another theory loosely links the rise of the unaffiliated to what some observers contend has been a general decline in "social capital"—a tendency among Americans to live more separate lives and engage in fewer communal activities, famously summed up by sociologist Robert Putnam as "bowling alone."[11] In this view, the growth of the religious "nones" is just one manifestation of much broader social disengagement.

Various Pew Research Center surveys offer support for this hypothesis. Young adults, the age group that is least likely to be affiliated with a religion, are also the group least trusting of their fellow human beings. On the other side of the same coin, a survey by the Pew Research Center's Internet & American Life Project found that the 40% of Americans who describe themselves as "active" in religious organizations—a higher bar of commitment than affiliation with a religious group—are more likely than other Americans to be involved in all types of volunteer and community groups, from sports leagues to arts groups, hobby clubs, and alumni associations.

And a 2012 Pew Research Center survey found that religiously unaffiliated Americans are less inclined than Americans as a whole to feel that it is very important to belong to "a community of people who share your values and beliefs" (28% of the unaffiliated say this is very important to them, compared with 49% of the general public).

4. Secularization

Finally, the rise of the unaffiliated in the US also has helped to breathe new life into theories that link economic development with secularization around the

---

Figure 10.5

Wealthier Nations Are Less Religious; US a Prominent Exception

% saying religion plays a very important role in their lives (2011–2013)

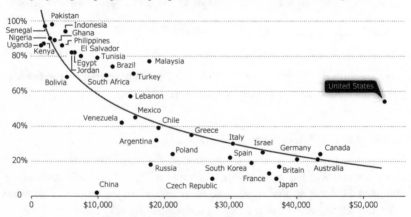

Estimated 2013 GDP per capita (PPP, current international $)

Note: The curve represents the logarithmic relationship between GDP per capita and the percentage saying that religion plays a very important role in their lives. Germany, France, Britain percentage data from spring 2011; U.S., Japan percentage data from spring 2012.

Source: Pew Research Center surveys, Spring 2011, 2012, 2013 and IMF World Economic Outlook Database, Apr. 2014

globe. Back in the 1960s, when secularization theories first achieved high visibility, they were sometimes accompanied by predictions that religion would wither away in the US by the twenty-first century.[12] The theories social scientists propound today are more subtle—contending, for example, that societies in which people feel constant threats to their health and well-being are more religious, while religious beliefs and practices tend to be less strong in places where there is more "existential security."[13] In this view, gradual secularization is to be expected in a generally healthy, wealthy, orderly society.

Pew Research Center surveys have asked people in many countries about the importance of religion in their lives, how often they pray, and whether they think it is necessary to believe in God to be a moral person. Throughout much of the world, there is a negative correlation between these measures of religiosity and a country's national wealth: publics in countries with a high gross domestic product (per capita) tend to be less religious, while publics in countries with a low GDP tend to be more religious. Americans, of course, are a major exception to the rule, because the US has both high GDP per capita and high levels of religious commitment.[14] Nonetheless, some theorists view the rise of the unaffiliated as a sign that secularization is advancing in America.[15]

MYTHS ABOUT THE UNAFFILIATED

While the root causes of disaffiliation are still open to debate, Pew Research Center surveys can lay to rest some common misperceptions and establish some baseline truths about the "nones."

First, disaffiliation has taken place across a wide variety of demographic groups, including both men and women; whites, blacks, and Hispanics; college graduates and those without a college degree; people earning $75,000 or more and those making less than $30,000 annually; and residents of all geographic regions of the country. This phenomenon isn't confined—as some have mistakenly suggested—to college campuses, the East and West Coasts, or the affluent (see Appendix Figure 10A.3).

Second, the unaffiliated are far from uniformly secular (see appendix Figure 10A.4). One-third say religion is at least somewhat important in their lives. Two-thirds believe in God (though fewer than half say they are absolutely certain of God's existence). And although a substantial minority of the unaffiliated consider themselves neither religious nor spiritual (42%), a majority describe themselves either as religious (18%) or as spiritual but not religious (37%).

Nor are the "nones" uniformly hostile toward organized religion. They are much more likely than the public overall to say that churches and other religious organizations are too concerned with money and power, too focused on rules, and too involved in politics. But at the same time, a majority of the unaffiliated clearly think that religious institutions can be a force for good in society. Three-quarters say religious organizations bring people together and help strengthen community bonds (78%), and a similar number (77%) say they play an important role in helping the poor and needy (see appendix Figure 10A.5).

Like most of the US public, a solid majority of the unaffiliated think religion as a whole is losing its influence on American life. But they are less inclined than the general public to view this as a bad thing—only 26% say it is, compared with half of the public at large. And atheists and agnostics overwhelmingly view religion's declining influence as a *good* thing for society (see appendix Figure 10A.6).

Another common misperception is that religiously unaffiliated Americans are "seekers" who haven't yet found the right church for them. In fact, very few are in the market. Leaving aside atheists and agnostics, just 10% of those who describe their current religion as "nothing in particular" say they are looking for a religion that is right for them; 88% say they are not.

Nor are the ranks of the unaffiliated predominantly composed of practitioners of New Age spirituality or alternative forms of religion. Generally speaking, the unaffiliated are no more likely than members of the public as a whole to have such beliefs and practices (see appendix Figure 10A.7).

POLITICAL COUNTERWEIGHT TO WHITE EVANGELICALS

When it comes to politics, the religiously unaffiliated have a distinct identity. They are heavily Democratic in their partisanship and liberal in their political ideology. More than 6 in 10 (63%) describe themselves as Democrats or say they lean toward the Democratic Party (compared with 48% of all registered voters), while just 26% identify with the

Figure 10.6

Partisanship and Ideology

% among registered voters

	All registered voters	Unaffiliated
Party identification	%	%
Dem/lean Dem	48	63
Rep/lean Rep	43	26
Independent/ other – no lean	9	11
Ideology		
Conservative	39	20
Moderate	36	38
Liberal	21	38

Source: Aggregated data from surveys conducted by the Pew Research Center for the People & the Press, Jan.– Jul. 2012

GOP. And there are roughly twice as many self-described liberals (38%) as conservatives (20%) among the religiously unaffiliated. Among voters overall, this balance is reversed.

The liberalism of the unaffiliated extends to social as well as political issues. Nearly three-quarters (72%) of religiously unaffiliated Americans say abortion should be legal in most or all cases, compared with 53% of the public overall. And 73% of the religiously unaffiliated express support for same-sex marriage, compared with about half of the public at large. But the portion of the unaffiliated who say they would prefer a smaller government providing fewer services to a larger government providing more services (50%) is similar to the share of the general public (52%) who take the same view (see appendix Figure 10A.8).

In recent elections, the religiously unaffiliated have become among the most reliably Democratic segments of the electorate. In 2008 fully three-quarters of the religiously unaffiliated voted for Barack Obama over John McCain, and they were as strongly Democratic in their vote choice as white evangelicals were Republican. Obama's margin of victory among the religiously unaffiliated was 52 points; McCain's margin of victory among white evangelical voters was 47 points.

Moreover, the religiously unaffiliated constitute a growing share of the Democratic electoral base. Back in 2007 there were about as many religiously unaffiliated Democratic and Democratic-leaning registered voters as there were white mainline and white Catholic Democratic voters. And the religiously unaffiliated were only slightly more numerous among Democratic and Democratic-leaning registered voters than were black Protestants (17% versus 14%).

Today the religiously unaffiliated are significantly more numerous than any of these groups within the Democratic coalition (24% unaffiliated, 16% black

Figure 10.7

Presidential Vote of the Religiously Unaffiliated, 2000–2012

% voting for each candidate

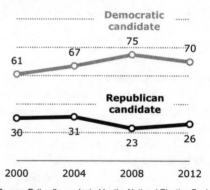

Source: Exit polls conducted by the National Election Pool, 2000, 2004, 2008 and 2012

Figure 10.8

Changing US Religious Landscape, 2007–2014

% of adults who are ...

	Change
26.3% → 25.4% Evangelical Prot.	-0.9
23.9 → 22.8 Unaffiliated	+6.7
20.8 Catholic	-3.1
18.1	
16.1	
14.7 Mainline Protestant	-3.4
4.7 → 5.9 Non-Christian faiths*	+1.2

2007   2014

* Includes Jews, Muslims, Buddhists, Hindus, other world religions and other faiths. Those who did not answer the religious identity question, as well as groups whose share of the population did not change significantly, including the historically black Protestant tradition, Mormons, and others, are not shown.

Source: Pew Research Center survey, Jun. 4–Sep. 30, 2014

Protestant, 14% white mainline Protestant, 13% white Catholic). By contrast, Republican and Republican-leaning registered voters are only slightly more likely to be religiously unaffiliated today than in 2007 (11% versus 9%).

CHRISTIANS IN DECLINE

The growth in the ranks of the unaffiliated is not the only big change in America's religious landscape in recent years. There has been an equally large shrinkage in the Christian share of the adult population—from 78.4% in 2007 to 70.6% in 2014. As with the rise of the "nones," the drop in Christian affiliation is particularly pronounced among young adults but is occurring among Americans of all ages. It is also occurring among other major demographic groupings—whites, blacks, and Latinos; college graduates as well as those with only a high school education; women as well as men. During this same time period, the share of Americans who identify with non-Christian faiths has inched up, from 4.7% in 2007 to 5.9% in 2014. Growth has been especially notable among Muslims and Hindus, albeit from a very low base (see Appendix Figure 10A.9).

The drop in the Christian share of the population has been driven mainly by declines among mainline Protestants and Catholics. Each of those large religious traditions has shrunk by approximately 3 percentage points since 2007. The evangelical Protestant share of the US population has also dipped, but at a slower rate, falling by about 1 percentage point since 2007.[16]

Even as their numbers decline, American Christians—like the US population as a whole—are becoming more racially and ethnically diverse. Whites now account for smaller shares of evangelical Protestants, mainline Protestants, and Catholics than they did seven years earlier, while Hispanics have grown as a share of all three religious groups. Racial and ethnic minorities now make up 41% of Catholics (up from 35% in 2007), 24% of evangelical Protestants (up from 19%), and 14% of mainline Protestants (up from 9%).

DISAFFILIATION AND PLURALISM IN THE AMERICAN CONTEXT

One way to reconcile the three seemingly incompatible strands of American religion today—continued devoutness despite rising pluralism and increasing disaffiliation—is to keep in mind that even religious Americans typically take a non-exclusivist view of the path to salvation. According to a 2008 Pew Research survey, 65% of *religiously affiliated* adults say

Figure 10.9

Who Achieves Eternal Life?

% among respondents who are affiliated with a particular religion

My religion is the one, true faith leading to eternal life	29
Many religions can lead to eternal life	65
Don't know/Refused	6

What Determines Eternal Life?

% of adults saying ...

One's belief	30
One's actions	29
Combination of actions/beliefs	10
Other	10
Don't believe in eternal life	7
Don't know/Refused	14

Source: Pew Research Center survey, Jul.–Aug. 2008, N=2,905 US adults. For more information, see Pew Research Center's Religion & Public Life Project, "Many Americans Say Other Faiths Can Lead to Eternal Life," Dec. 18, 2008

many religions can lead to eternal life, while just 29% say theirs is the one true faith leading to eternal life.

That poll also found that roughly equal numbers of Americans say that whether a person achieves eternal life is determined by the person's beliefs (30%) as say it depends on a person's actions (29%). An additional 1 in 10 Americans say the key to obtaining eternal life lies in a combination of belief and actions. The remaining one-third of the public says that something else is the key to eternal life, or that they don't know what leads to eternal life, or that they don't believe in eternal life.

Who Can Go to Heaven?

The view among religious believers that there are many paths to salvation isn't limited to Christians of one denomination accepting Christians of a different denomination. It's more expansive.

Among non-Protestants who say that many religions can lead to eternal life, roughly three-quarters (74%) say that Protestantism can lead to eternal life. A similar proportion of non-Catholics who believe that many religions lead to eternal life (73%) say that Catholicism leads to salvation.

The numbers are only slightly lower for Judaism, with the overwhelming majority (69%) of non-Jews who say many religions can lead to salvation saying that Judaism can bring eternal life. A slight majority of non-Muslims (52%) also say Islam can lead to eternal life, and a similar number (53%) of non-Hindus say the same of Hinduism.

Taken as a whole, these responses reveal that most American Christians, including evangelicals, have more than just other Christian denominations in mind when they say there are many paths to salvation. For example, among white mainline Protestants (85%), black Protestants (81%), and white Catholics (88%), more than 8 in 10 of those who say many religions can lead to eternal life include at least one non-Christian religion.

Significant numbers of white evangelical Protestants also believe various non-Christian religions can lead to eternal life, though these figures tend to be lower than those seen among other religious groups. Nearly three-quarters (72%) of evangelicals who say many religions can lead to salvation name at least one non-Christian faith that can do so. White evangelicals who say that many faiths can lead to salvation are just as likely as other groups to cite Catholicism. However, evangelicals are less likely than other groups to say that non-Christian faiths can lead to eternal life. About two-thirds of evangelicals (64%) who see multiple paths to salvation say that Judaism, for example, can bring eternal life, lower than the 73% among mainline Protestants and the 77% among white Catholics who say this. And only about one-third of evangelicals who say there are multiple paths to salvation say that Islam (35%) or Hinduism (33%) can lead to eternal life, with 26% saying that atheists can achieve eternal life (see appendix Figure 10A.10).

CHURN

All of these surveys portray an American religious marketplace in its familiar state of churn. The decline of affiliation is a relatively new phenomenon, but the restless search for a true path is as old as the Pilgrims. And so is Americans' live-and-let-live attitude toward people with different faiths. Those who worry that America is heading toward a European future of institutionalized secularism and empty cathedrals would do well to reflect on the resilience that religion in the US draws from this genius for tolerance and reinvention. Americans have never launched crusades or inquisitions; we've never gone to war over God. And so we haven't felt the need to suppress religion out of fear of its destructive furies. At the same time, our organized religions have always understood they need to adapt to survive. The fact that "nones" are on the rise indicates that religious institutions have some work to do. In modern times, American religion has become "more personalized and individualistic, less doctrinal and devotional, more practical and purposeful," in the words of sociologist Alan Wolfe.[17] Those are the market-driven impulses behind the evangelical mega-churches that now dot the American landscape, often offering an I'm-OK-You're-OK-Jesus-Loves-You theology of affirmation and self-help. Their message is a far cry from "Sinners in the Hands of an Angry God." They aren't for the whole American flock; nothing ever is. But they're animated by a restlessness that's uniquely American, and that keeps religion more vibrant here than perhaps in any other advanced country on earth.

Living Digital

NATALIE MARKS'S DIGITAL COMING-OUT moment came when she was in sixth grade.[1] It was 2000; she was 11 years old and had just heard about online chat rooms from a classmate. So one day after school she went over to her best friend Leigh's house, where the two of them navigated the beeping and buzzing of the dial-up modems of that long-ago era, created AOL user names, and started chatting up the world.

If her parents had known what Natalie was up to, they would have been worried sick that their little girl chose an online handle that was a bit saucy and unmistakably female. They would have been borderline apoplectic if they had known that, from her earliest postings, Natalie encouraged strangers of unknowable age, sex, and location to believe that she was interested in meeting them in person. "I didn't have many friends at school, and it was a fun way to act older and have weird personalities," she recalled. "I'd try to imagine myself as a 23-year-old and talk to people in that voice. I actually never told anyone exactly where I lived and I usually played pranks on the ones who got too aggressive. I'd write, 'meet me at this mall,' but I'd never show up. I was kind of a bully about that and I was different from the way I really acted at school."

Natalie is a digital native—a member of the first generation in history for whom digital technology platforms are the essential mediators of social life and information acquisition. Her parents and grandparents use many of the same gadgets and social networks she uses—and do so with increasing ease and frequency. But Natalie and her fellow Millennials are different. Their relationship with digital technology is unique precisely because it's *not* something they've had to adapt to. It's all they've ever known. It has played a fundamental role in shaping the nature of their friendships, the structure of their social networks, the way they learn, their provision and acceptance of social support, the way they interact with groups and institutions, their posture toward the wider world, and the way they allocate their time. During the course of Natalie's adolescence, thanks to the likes of Google and Facebook, she migrated from a digital universe where the Web didn't have a clue who she really was to one where it seems to know everything about her—and everyone else. What kind of adults will these digital natives become? We'll speculate on that at the end of this chapter. First let's follow the trail of Natalie's technology biography.

Once she entered middle school, Natalie's social circumstances changed radically. She developed lots of friends and her online life switched from chat rooms to instant messaging (IM). She was on AOL Instant Messenger constantly, with multiple screens open. Each contained a different conversation and each contained the seeds of five-star drama. The last thing she and her friends did at school each day was to figure out which pals to IM after the short trip home from school. "The transition from 8th period class to continuing the gossip at home was effortless," she recalled. "Our conversations never, ever ended, and it was 'mean girl' kinds of stuff. You'd have your phone to your ear and your hands on the keyboard and you'd repeat to everyone else the secret that had just been told you on the phone. And then you'd watch everybody trash everybody else."

Sometimes Natalie was the tormenter; sometimes the tormented. A common strategy among her peers was to lure someone into saying something catty and intimate, then to cut and paste the exchange into another IM conversation, or—better yet—to print it out and show it around school. "You had no privacy and you were constantly in arguments about the things you said or that were said about you," she said. Cliques were identified by her classmates' profiles. The ever-changing profiles, with their evolving keyword clues and announced alliances and feuds, often identified the newest social faction that the tribal school groups had assembled. Those left out or not in-the-know usually were outraged. "Away messages were the play-by-play of people's lives," said Natalie. "Kids were annoying in how much detail they shared. 'Going to take a shower now.' And they used away messages to break up with someone or ask someone out. Every day brought screaming and crying battles over some IM away message issue. I lost tons of friends doing those things, but I wasn't often bored. Basically, we had a lot to say about nothing."

An equal share of distress accompanied the school-wide habit of sharing IM account passwords. It was a sign of "true love" when students did that and it almost invariably led to heartbreak when the relationship soured and the scorned party—usually—decided to make the scorner suffer for causing the breakup. At times, third parties learned the password through these networks. Natalie was burned when an unknown someone pretended to be her and posted lies about her sex life. "I was mortified and had no way to disprove the rumors," she said.

The most spectacular social debacle at her school occurred when an upper-class girl filmed a bedroom episode with her boyfriend and sent it to him, thinking it would stay private between them. But he forwarded it to some friends, and eventually it found its way to members of the town's school board. His motives were not clear. Some classmates thought it was a prank that was supposed to be funny. Others thought he did it for revenge—or to spice up their relationship. Still others thought it was an accident. Whatever the case, the girl "vanished from the face of the earth," Natalie recalled. "Everyone in the school saw it within 24 hours of his e-mail. She was gone—and untraceable." This episode came before youthful "sexters"—people who share risqué photos via cell phones—started to get arrested on accusations they were trafficking in child pornography when they shared such photos.

With less melodrama, Internet use also became the dominant venue for homework for Natalie and her classmates. "The meaning of the word 'research' was 'type keywords into Google,' and neither teachers nor parents could force us to crack open a reference book," she said. Students turned to the Internet first to do the legwork for major research projects. Most used online Spark-Notes to complete class assignments. It was a free online service akin to Cliffs Notes, which at the time was a fee-based service. (By 2013, Cliffsnotes.com was ad-supported and free.) Teachers soon enough caught on and used the increasingly sophisticated search engines of the early 2000s to grab blocks of text from student papers and see that they were copied word for word from SparkNotes and other "term paper" services. The younger teachers were the first to catch on and train the older teachers.

THE TEACHERS' TAKE

To find out what teachers make of the digital revolution and its impact on education, the Pew Research Center teamed up with the College Board and the National Writing Project in 2012 to survey 2,462 middle and high school teachers about the research habits of their students.[2] This wasn't a nationally representative sample; all respondents had either taught Advanced Placement courses or participated in a summer institute sponsored by the National Writing Project. Overall, 77% said the impact of digital technologies had been mostly positive. Yet when asked whether they agreed or disagreed with specific assertions about how the Internet is impacting students' research, their views were decidedly mixed.

On the plus side, virtually all (99%) AP and NWP teachers agreed that the Internet enables students to access a wider range of resources than would otherwise be available, and 65% also agreed that the Internet makes today's students more self-sufficient researchers.

At the same time, however, 76% of teachers surveyed "strongly agreed" with the assertion that Internet search engines have conditioned students to expect to be able to find information quickly and easily. Large majorities also agreed that the amount of information available online today is overwhelming to most students (83%) and that today's digital technologies discourage students from using a wide range of sources when conducting research (71%). Fewer teachers, but still a majority of this sample (60%), agreed with the assertion that today's technologies make it harder for students to find credible sources of information.

Some of the teachers who took part in focus group sessions reported that for their students, "doing research" has shifted from a relatively slow process of intellectual curiosity and discovery to a fast-paced, short-term exercise aimed at locating just enough information to complete an assignment. Here, in descending order, are the sources teachers in our survey said students are "very likely" to use in a typical research assignment:

- Google or other online search engine (94%)
- Wikipedia or other online encyclopedia (75%)
- YouTube or other social media sites (52%)
- Their peers (42%)
- SparkNotes, CliffsNotes, or other study guides (41%)
- News sites of major news organizations (25%)
- Print or electronic textbooks (18%)
- Online databases such as EBSCO, JSTOR, or Grolier (17%)
- A research librarian at their school or public library (16%)
- Printed books other than textbooks (12%)
- Student-oriented search engines such as Sweet Search (10%)

What kind of employees and adults will these students become? The consensus view, expressed by a diverse group of 1,021 technology stakeholders, scholars, and experts interviewed as part of a different Pew Research survey in 2011, is that today's teens and young will be nimble, quick-acting multitaskers who treat the Internet as their external brain and who approach problems in a different way from their elders.[3] But the respondents were evenly divided as to whether their hyperconnectivity and always-on lifestyles will prove to be a net positive or negative. For each expert who said that Millennials' use of digital technologies would empower them to learn more than previous generations and become more adept at finding answers to deep questions, a different expert worried that this generation will exhibit a thirst for instant gratification and quick fixes, a loss of patience, and a lack of deep-thinking ability due to what one referred to as "fast-twitch wiring."

CELL PHONES AND SOCIAL NETWORKS

By the middle of Natalie's high school career in the mid-2000s, cell phones and social networking sites such as Facebook became integral parts of students' lives. Each produced changes in Millennials' behavior. In Natalie's world, the story arc for arrival of cell phones in a household usually went like this: Parents would buy their teen a cell phone in the name of safety and logistical convenience. They were comforted they could talk to their child wherever she was and that it made life easier to be able to coordinate transportation, meal planning, and errand running on the fly. But within a few months, a darker side would emerge. There would be a major family blow-up as teens discovered texting and parents discovered how many hundreds of dollars they had to pay for the extra thousands of texts when the teen exceeded the limits on the data plan for the family phone. In Natalie's case, a "texting shock" bill of $200 one month triggered her parents' rage. Her phone was confiscated. She was grounded. Negotiations ensued. Limits were set. An all-you-can-eat data plan was eventually purchased. "That kept the peace," she said.

Then texting became the norm for her and her peers. By mid-2009, research by the Pew Internet Project had found that when it came to contact outside school with their friends, teens treated texting as their primary form of daily communication. It surpassed voice calling, face-to-face contact, e-mail, and instant messaging[4]—and the trend line has continued to move in an upward arc ever since.

Why? Natalie explains: Texting is private and covert, even when you're in a crowd. Texting is efficient when basic information is exchanged. "Why waste time talking?" she asks. Texting is "less rude"—or, as communications scholars would say, it's asynchronous. You can send your messages when you want and check your messages on your timetable, rather than being interrupted by a phone call or annoying someone else. Yet, it also has the advantage of being immediate. The query-reply transaction can be completed in seconds.

The rise of mobile connectivity tracked with the explosion of social media in 2005–2009. Some Millennials had been interested in blogging in the early

2000s, but their embrace of social media was much more widespread once social networking services emerged. Friendster (launched in 2002), MySpace (launched in 2003), and Facebook (launched in colleges in 2003, in high schools in 2005, and among the general public in 2006) brought waves of Millennials into the world of building technological social networks and sharing content with the friends in those networks (see appendix Figure 11A.1). Their parents and grandparents lagged in their adoption of the sites, but became fairly avid users over time. The differences between the generations now are more qualitative than quantitative. But Millennials continue to be the early adopters of the social media universe, which by 2013 meant they were the first to register a dose of Facebook fatigue. In a Pew Research survey and set of focus groups conducted that year among 12- to 17-year-olds, a staggering 94% reported using Facebook, but some expressed waning enthusiasm for the platform. The culprits: too much drama, too much oversharing of the minutiae of life, and too many adults on the site. Some teenagers also reported being stressed by the need to constantly tend to their online reputation, but nearly all said they had to be on the site so as not to miss out.

Natalie was a bit behind her classmates in starting on Facebook, but she reports that she became "addicted" as she prepared for college. She was accepted at a prestigious southern university and like many of her classmates joined a Facebook group of incoming freshmen to the school. The school offered a personality test to the Facebook group and Natalie joined the many classmates who took it, posted her results in her profile, and began chatting on the site with others about their test results. There was one girl whose personality type seemed a good match with Natalie's and whose narrative answers in the test struck Natalie as "cool." The girl and Natalie launched an epic discussion thread during the early summer and decided to room together because they hit it off so well. "Big mistake," Natalie remembers. "She was a completely different person online than offline. I got totally fooled. And we hated each other."

Figure 11.1

Texting, by Generation

Among cell phone owners, the % who send or receive text messages

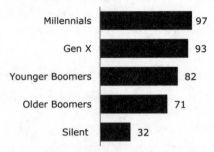

Millennials	97
Gen X	93
Younger Boomers	82
Older Boomers	71
Silent	32

Source: Pew Research Center survey, Aug.–Sep. 2013, N=1,636 US adult cell phone owners

They parted ways after a tense year together, but that did not diminish Natalie's enthusiasm for Facebook. She quickly amassed several thousand "friends" and spent a great deal of time on the site almost every day because it answered perhaps the central question of any young person's life: What are my friends doing and saying now? "It was a never-stop bull session with enough news and comedy and tragedy to be worth sticking around" (see appendix Figure 11A.2).

As time passed, Natalie developed a better sense of how different kinds of people acted on Facebook and which of them were likely to be long-term friends. She became a quick skimmer of her news feed, pausing to read only a few of the most interesting items. She tried to write her own updates more thoughtfully, crafting them as items she would want to read or watch if they had been posted by one of her friends. "I got tired of knowing too much and trying too hard to keep up," she said.

As Natalie neared her graduation, she became hypervigilant about her reputation. She deleted hundreds of pictures of her at parties or tailgates and even vacations. She carefully checked all the references to her and occasionally got into fights with people who would not take down a post that she felt reflected poorly on her. She knew that people were judging her based on how she was represented on Facebook and she wanted to present well.

Still, a Facebook search for her as this chapter was being written showed that she has a pretty public status. And the featured picture has her in a pink wig. "This type of picture isn't something I would have chosen while job hunting, but now that I've been at my job for 10 months, and I'm pretty positive they like me, I feel it's OK for me to be myself," she said. "I'm Facebook friends with some of my coworkers who are in their 40s and 50s but they know that I'm a little weird and I feel close enough with them in real life that I don't mind them seeing what I'm like outside of work. I've already proven that I work hard, so it's OK for them to see that I play hard too."

WORKING IN A CONNECTED WORLD

After graduating from college in 2011, Natalie returned to her home in the Northeast for a few months but felt the tug to return to her southern college town. She found her first job there through the Craigslist classifieds working for a dance troupe doing marketing, especially via social media. Both Natalie and her prospective employer checked each other out on Facebook before Natalie showed up at the employer's home in a not-so-nice part of town. They also did enough Googling ahead of time to have a decent sense of each other. "She [the employer] looked legit and she told me that I didn't come off as too weird in my profile," Natalie said. "That's the basis of moving ahead in relationships these days." So, they advanced to the face-to-face meeting and got along well enough that Natalie was offered the post on the spot.

That job was only part-time, so Natalie kept looking and was alerted (via a Facebook friend) that a very hot Internet company was hiring. The job interview was a group interview in a local bar and it featured several group activities to test the "social intelligence" and sociability of the participants. She got the job and became a "glorified brand ambassador" at the firm's events around the city for clients. She met a lot of people that way and, soon enough, one of them offered her a job at the big professional sports team in town working on game days. Then another friend from her short-lived job with the Internet startup helped her connect to an events planning job for a local racetrack.

Natalie's search for employment obviously isn't the prescribed route into a career in law, medicine, science, engineering, or other professions, but most twenty-somethings, like her, find themselves hunting for jobs rather than careers. "The job-searching scene is a blur of friends and connections and tips and false leads," she said. "It's gossip over drinks, quick little text messages, occasional trips to jobs websites, scans of [Facebook] news feeds, anything that might produce useful material." She noted that the process, much like the information exchanges on other subjects, takes place in multiple kinds of channels (face-to-face, phone, electronic) on multiple screens using multiple apps. It has the feel of dipping into and out of streams of information, rather than a comprehensive review of a centralized, single source of information. Media companies and those with goods, services, and ideas to promote are eager to know which channels matter most to this hyperconnected generation. Millennials insist that is the wrong way to think about how they acquire and share created information. Asking Millennials whether Facebook matters to them more than texting or whether apps on their smartphones are more useful than searches on their computers only prompts puzzled looks. "It's all of the above," Natalie said. (See appendix Figure 11A.3.)

NETWORKED INDIVIDUALS
USING NETWORKED INFORMATION

Millennials like Natalie function in networks. Their elders do, too. But the avid embrace of technology by Millennials has particularly affected how they use those networks and how those networks shape their lives. A new "social operating system" has been emerging for several generations but has accelerated in recent decades due to widespread broadband adoption, ubiquitous mobile connectivity, and the rise of technological social networks.[5] Sociologist Barry Wellman coined the term "networked individualism" to describe the way loose-knit networks of people—especially Millennials—are overtaking more tight-knit groups and large hierarchical bureaucracies as the most prevalent relationship structure. The defining features of networked Millennials are:

They enjoy more personal freedom but need to expend more personal effort to meet their needs

In the world of networked individuals, it is the person who is the focus; not the family, not the work unit, not the neighborhood, and not the social group. Many meet their social, emotional, and economic needs by tapping into loosely knit networks of diverse associates rather than relying on tight connections to a relatively small number of core associates. This means that networked individuals can have a variety of social ties to count on but are less likely to have one surefire "home" group of protectors and observers.

Often individuals rely on many specialized relationships to meet their needs. For example, a typical social network might have some members who are good at meeting local, logistical needs (pet-sitting, watering the plants), while others are especially useful when medical needs arise. Yet others (often sisters) provide emotional support. Still others are the ones whose political opinions carry more weight, while others give financial advice, provide restaurant recommendations, or suggest music and books to enjoy.

This social operating system gives people new ways to solve problems and meet social needs through wider and more diverse networks and use of new media, as Natalie did in finding jobs. It offers more freedom to individuals than people experienced in the past, because now they have more room to maneuver and more capacity to act on their own.

At the same time, life as networked individuals requires that people develop new strategies and skills for handling problems. People like Natalie must devote more time and energy to the art of networking. They need to expend effort and sometimes money to maintain their ties near and far; choose whether to phone, visit, or electronically connect with others; remember which members of their network are useful for what sorts of things (including just hanging out); and forge useful alliances among network members who might not have known each other previously. In short, networked individualism is both socially liberating and socially taxing. Paradoxically, the technology that promises to connect us also threatens to overload us with extra work.

The new media are the new neighborhood

More than two-thirds of American adults and more than 80% of Millennials create content through social networking sites, other social media, and their various rankings, ratings, commenting, and remixing applications. In an environment where most are "publishers" and "broadcasters" and where powerful search technologies make it easy to find such content, people can easily locate and connect with others who share their tastes, lifestyles, political beliefs, spiritual practices, health conditions, hobbies, or professional quests. The act of creating on new media is often a social—and networking—activity, in which people work together or engage in short- and long-term dialogues.

People still value their neighbors, because living nearby remains important for everyday socializing and for dealing with emergencies large and small. Yet, neighbors are only about 10% of people's significant ties.[6] As a result, people's social routines are different from those of their parents or grandparents. Although people see their coworkers and neighbors often, most of their important contacts are with people who live elsewhere in the city, region, nation—and abroad. The Internet, either mobile or wired, is especially valuable for those kinds of connections.

Networked technology has also changed the social point of contact from the household (and work group) to the individual. Each person also creates her own Internet, tailored to her needs. Each person builds and maintains her own network and maintains it through her own address book and individually controlled e-mail address(es), screen name(s), social and technological filters, and mobile phone number.

Networking works best with lots of information disclosure. One consequence is less privacy

A moral and practical imperative of successful networking is to follow the Golden Rule—if you expect people to share their information with you, you need to share yours with them. Similarly, the acquisition of social capital depends on the expenditure of social capital. As Natalie put it, "I want to be findable and I want to make my share of [content] contributions. To me, that's how things get done." People cannot build networks without describing who they are, what talents or skills they possess, what they know, and what their needs are. There is also some pressure for deliberate, considered disclosure in social media when people cannot fall back on close, long-term friends who perpetually stand ready to help them. Finally, there is encouragement to be connected. People cannot easily ask for help from their networks without using digital tools, and they cannot be available to help others if they are off the grid.

The cost of more transparency and connectedness will be additional transparency and connectedness, whether people like it or not. This level of personal transparency produces a loss of privacy and the perhaps unwanted commercialization of personal information that others can capture. As former

Google CEO Eric Schmidt boasted, "We know where you are. We know where you have been. We can more or less know what you're thinking about."

For all these reasons, Millennials are buffeted by cross-pressures on the subject of privacy in the digital era. Nearly 9 in 10 agree that people generally share too much information about themselves online. Millennials themselves, of course, are the leading offenders. But they are also the prime beneficiaries. Their "overshare" lifestyle online has generated a gusher of digital data that have enabled start-ups like Uber and Airbnb, as well as traditional businesses in virtually every realm of commerce, to more effectively target services and products to end users. "Most people's life experiences teach them that revealing their private information allows commercial (and public) organizations to make their lives easier, whereas the detrimental cases tend to be very serious but relatively rare," writes Bob Briscoe, chief researcher in networking and infrastructure for British Telecom.[7]

At the same time, the vast majority of Americans say they are concerned about their lack of control over data collected about them online. A 2015 Pew Research Center report found that while 93% of Americans say it is important to be in control of such personal information, just 31% are confident that government agencies and landline telephone companies keep their records private, and only 38% say the same about credit card companies. This concern hasn't led to widespread use of enhanced defensive techniques, however. Just 1 in 10 Americans say they have taken steps such as encrypting phone calls, texts, and e-mail, or using a service that allows them to surf the Internet anonymously.[8] Many Internet users routinely engage in less sophisticated privacy measures, such as clearing cookies or browser history (59%) or refusing to provide personal information not relevant to a transaction (57%).

THE REVOLUTION'S REACH

It's not just the social life of Millennials that has been shaped by the digital revolution. Other domains of their life—learning, work, and leisure—have been affected as well. A brief rundown:

Time use and media consumption

The Kaiser Family Foundation reported several times in the 2000s on the media consumption of Natalie's cohort, which it called Generation M[2] (the "M" stood for "media").[9] In 2009, it found that those ages 8 to 18 were exposed to 10 hours and 45 minutes of media of all kinds during a typical day and spent 29% of that time multitasking with several kinds of information in front of them at the same time.[10] Technology analyst Linda Stone calls this a state of "continuous partial attention" and Millennials are in this state more often than their elders.[11]

There is conflicting evidence about whether this is harmful, specifically in the sense of whether people perform tasks well and completely when they are dividing their attention among various input sources. But this certainly reflects the reality Natalie described as she discussed the way she dips into different media and social information streams at various points during her day. Some wags have suggested that this instinct to try to monitor things constantly is the result of FOMO—"fear of missing out." Natalie doesn't object to that characterization, but says she also multitasks because it sometimes feels efficient and urgent to try to juggle a variety of things at the same time.

"I'm constantly staring at my phone and so are my friends even when we're all together," Natalie said. "We're all extremely addicted and even though I don't want to be, I'm not doing anything to change it because ultimately I like feeling like I'm in touch and know what's going on at all times. I'm always checking the usual apps—Facebook and [photo-sharing service] Instagram— even if someone is trying to have a conversation with me. I see other people do it to me. I'll be telling a story and they're nodding along with one-word semi-responses but I know that half of my story has been lost because their attention is mostly focused on whatever they're texting about or reading on the screen. It's irritating but I know I do it, too."

Long-running studies by the Pew Research Center have shown sweeping changes in news consumption patterns since the mid-1990s. Most are tied to technology and there are notable differences by generation.[12] Millennials now are less likely to get news on a given day than their Gen X predecessors were in the mid-1990s at their same age. Compared with all their elders, Millennials who do get news are more likely to use the Internet, their cell phones, mobile apps, and tablet computers. They are more likely to say they get news from social networking sites (see appendix Figure 11A.4). They are less likely to get news from newspapers, TV either in broadcast or cable stations, radio, or magazines. They are more likely to say that comedy cable shows are a source of news. "I do not miss *The Daily Show* [with Jon Stewart] and *The Colbert Report,* if I can help it," Natalie said. "I get all of my pop-culture from PerezHilton.com (my guilty pleasure) and general information from *Huffington Post*. I'm also constantly kept up-to-date from just signing into Facebook. If something is 'trending,' then my entire news feed will be filled with links to articles or YouTube videos."

In addition, Millennials are more likely to say they graze for news at various times of the day, rather than consume it at set time periods. Natalie says she feels a responsibility as a citizen to stay up with news, but that doesn't mean she engages in active searches. "My feeling is that if I'm constantly checking things, the most interesting stuff or most important news will cross my path, rather than me thinking it's my responsibility to be an active searcher for it," she said. But she acknowledges that her news consumption strategy is better at harvesting cat videos and Kardashian sightings than at updates on poverty or global warming, which is one reason that Millennials (like their same-age counterparts in the past) are much less well informed than their elders about public affairs.

Other Pew Research studies show Millennials are more likely than older Americans to participate in news by sharing links, contributing comments, and posting their own material.[13] They are more likely than their elders to judge news operations—especially Web-based offerings—based on the willingness of a news organization to allow comments and contributions from users and to be transparent about its operations. Millennials are more likely to say search engines and social media steer them to local news and information on a variety of topics, including most dimensions of civic news such as local government, political news, and educational news.[14]

Patterns of influence and decision making

In an environment of information overabundance, social networks have become a tool that helps people figure out how to drink from the proverbial fire hose. A mantra for many is, "If news is important, it will find its way to me." For Millennials, this is a primary reason to check their social networking spaces with some regularity. Half of Millennial users of social networking sites check them multiple times a day, compared with fewer than a third of Boomers who do so. In addition, people often turn to their social networks to help them evaluate the new information they encounter. For example, Millennials are the most likely generation to use online social spaces to discuss and share health information and stories, though they still rely on doctors and other health providers when they need to make health decisions.[15] Also, about 3 in 10 social networking Millennials say they have gotten more involved in a political cause after discussing it or reading about it in social networking spaces, compared with about 1 in 4 social networking Boomers.[16] But on the flip side of the same coin: Millennials are also twice as likely as Boomers to say they have become less active in a cause after reading what their friends said about it on social networking sites.

As more and more people become content creators, it is increasingly common for Millennials to assume that when they discover something, they will share it with their broad network. This is part of the ongoing process of building and maintaining a vibrant social network; reciprocal sharing is the way Millennials build their social capital and reputations. "When I discover a story that I think is hilarious or a new song, I want everyone to know about it so we can talk about it and laugh or sing along with them," Natalie said.

There are several other ways that the technological environment especially affects Millennials' decision making. One is crowdsourcing. Millennials over-perform when it comes to creating and reading user reviews and comments online as they make up their minds about where to eat and drink, what movies and musical acts to see, and what Web content to access. They are also ripe targets for the algorithms that many popular websites use to organize their content. Search engines are particularly potent gatekeepers and arrangers of information for Millennials; social networking sites follow close behind. Not only does this apply to the main content of the site, but it also applies to the advertisements that surround that content—more and more of which are sorted by the websites' understanding of what matters to users, based on their previous use of the site and other material that is collected about them and added to their data-based profiles.

Networking literacy

The most successful Millennials thrive because they have a set of new literacies that amount to mastery of networking and troves of information—social and otherwise—that stream into their lives.[17] Networking literacy starts with *graphic literacy* that recognizes that life is experienced as communications, media, and data on screens. They can interpret this material and feel comfortable contrib-uting to it. Successful networking also requires *navigation literacy,* a sense of Internet geography that allows them to maneuver through multiple informa-tion channels and formats. They understand the changes that have occurred as information has become networked—by links, by continual editing, by algo-rithmic authority. Beyond that, Millennials have *context and connections liter-acy* that helps them weave together the information and chatter that are flowing into their lives at a quickening pace. Even if the tidbits they gather are disaggre-gated from any larger context, they have the wherewithal—often with help from the network helpers—to puzzle through the material they collect.

Millennials also have mastery over their own attention, a kind of *focus liter-acy*: that is, the capacity to minimize distractions and complete what they need to do. Natalie speaks of how she has learned through trial and error when it is essen-tial to be connected and when to disengage. "There are times to need to be quiet to recharge and figure things out," is how she puts it. Yet, despite their focus, they also have *multitasking literacy*: the ability to do several things (almost) at once. With multiple inputs from family, friends, work, and institutions—and multiple in-person, Internet, and mobile sources provide these inputs—thriving network-ers such as Natalie have gained the ability to attend to them without lots of fuss.

The age of information overload also requires *skepticism literacy*. Inter-net veteran Howard Rheingold says people need a fine-tuned sense of "crap detection" to evaluate what they encounter online. This means weeding out the media and people who have outdated, biased, incomplete and agenda-driven, or just dead-wrong ideas to promote.

Identity and ethics

The technology-mediated environment has created new conditions under which Millennials form and re-form their identities and ponder what it means to be a moral actor. Media scholar danah boyd argues that many people—and most Millennials—live in "networked publics" organized around networked information that has four properties:

- It is *persistent*: people's online creations and material about them is automatically recorded and archived.
- It is *replicable*: people's content can easily be duplicated and passed along to others.
- It is *scalable*: content about people can be visible in all kinds of public and networked places.
- It is *searchable*: content in networked publics can be easily found and displayed through search engines.[18]

She argues that this new kind of individualized publishing power and communication capacity has led Millennials into a new world where (1) invisi-ble audiences can observe what people are saying and doing; and (2) the barri-ers between public and private are porous.

These four properties structure network publics and the interactions that take place in them. Many of these properties are not unique to networked publics—oral histories made stories persistent, the printing press replicated content with ease, broadcast media scaled the visibility of live acts, and li-brarians have long invested in approaches to searching for information. Yet in networked publics, these properties are a part of the environment by de-fault and are interconnected in new ways. Furthermore, because they play a role in all mediated interactions and because networked publics play a significant role in the lives of many teens, teens who participate in social network sites must account for these properties during everyday acts and interactions.[19]

Millennials are the generation most affected by these changes because they grew up knowing no other platform for social commerce. Like all teens and young adults since the beginning of time, they're constantly trying to figure out their identity, social status, group affiliations, and passions. The only reality they've known is one in which the boundaries are blurred between private and public, work and play, present and absent, and home and school. Inevitably, they'll be the ones setting the social mores of the new digital age. When is it rude to look away from someone to check out the latest text message on your smartphone? When is it appropriate to pass along a communication or keep it closely held? When should you share your real name or make one up? When to lurk and when to engage? When to declare a relationship or abandon it? All of those norms are still works in progress, but it's the Millennials who'll be making up the rules.

WHAT'S NEXT?

The Pew Research Center's Internet Project periodically tries to gaze into the future by teaming with researchers at the Imagining the Internet Center at Elon University on opt-in online surveys of technology experts and scholars. We typically ask them to weigh in on the probability that one of two opposite scenarios will unfold—a technique known as assessing a "tension pair." In 2011, after a spate of magazine articles raised the "Is Google Making Us Stupid?" question, we asked about the following two scenarios. The first posited:

- In 2020 the brains of multitasking teens and young adults are "wired" differently from those over age 35 and overall it yields helpful results. They do not suffer notable cognitive shortcomings as they multitask and cycle quickly through personal- and work-related tasks. Rather, they are learning more and they are more adept at finding answers to deep questions, in part because they can search effectively and access collective intelligence via the Internet. In sum, the changes in learning behavior and cognition among the young generally produce positive outcomes.

Some 55% of the 1,021 respondents agreed with that statement, while 42% agreed with the opposite statement, which posited:

- In 2020 the brains of multitasking teens and young adults are "wired" differently from those over age 35 and overall it yields baleful results. They do not retain information; they spend most of their energy sharing short social messages, being entertained, and being distracted away from deep engagement with people and knowledge. They lack deep-thinking capabilities; they lack face-to-face social skills; they depend in unhealthy ways on the Internet and mobile devices to function. In sum, the changes in behavior and cognition among the young are generally negative outcomes.

Many who chose the upbeat scenario made it clear that it was more their hope than their best guess, and a number said the most likely outcome is a combination of both. So the real result here is probably closer to 50/50. By the way, to encourage a spirited discussion, respondents were given no middle-ground choice, nor were they offered another alternative altogether—that young people's brains would *not* be wired differently. Some of the respondents made that argument, positing that people's patterns of thinking will likely change but that their mechanisms of brain function won't.

Survey participants did offer strong, consistent predictions about the most desired life skills for young people in 2020. Among those they listed were public problem-solving through cooperative work, the ability to search effectively for information online and to be able to discern the quality and veracity of the information one finds and then communicate these findings well, synthesizing (being able to bring together details from many sources), being strategically future-minded, the ability to concentrate, and the ability to distinguish between the "noise" and the message in the ever-growing sea of information.

Futurist John Smart, president and founder of the Acceleration Studies Foundation, recalled an insight of economist Simon Kuznets about the evolution of technology effects known as the Kuznets curve: "First-generation tech usually causes 'net negative' social effects; second-generation 'net neutral' effects; by the third generation of tech—once the tech is smart enough, and we've got the interface right, and it begins to reinforce the best behaviors—we finally get to 'net positive' effects," he noted. "We'll be early into conversational interface and agent technologies by 2020, so kids will begin to be seriously intelligently augmented by the Internet. There will be many persistent drawbacks, however. The biggest problem from a personal-development perspective will be motivating people to work to be more self-actualized, productive, and civic than their parents were. They'll be more willing than ever to relax and remain distracted by entertainments amid accelerating technical productivity.

"As machine intelligence advances," Smart continued, "the first response of humans is to offload their intelligence and motivation to the machines. That's a dehumanizing, first-generation response. Only the later, third-generation edu-cational systems will correct for this."

Barry Chudakov, a Florida-based consultant and a research fellow in the McLuhan Program in Culture and Technology at the University of Toronto, wrote that by 2020,

> technology will be so seamlessly integrated into our lives that it will effec-tively disappear. The line between self and technology is thin today; by then it will effectively vanish. We will think with, think into, and think through our smart tools but their presence and reach into our lives will be less visi-ble. Youth will assume their minds and intentions are extended by technol-ogy, while tracking technologies will seek further incursions into behavioral monitoring and choice manipulation. Children will assume this is the way the world works. The cognitive challenge children and youth will face (as we are beginning to face now) is integrity, the state of being whole and un-divided. There will be a premium on the skill of maintaining presence, of mindfulness, of awareness in the face of persistent and pervasive tool exten-sions and incursions into our lives. Is this my intention, or is the tool incit-ing me to feel and think this way? That question, more than multitasking or brain atrophy due to accessing collective intelligence via the Internet, will be the challenge of the future.

No one knows what the future holds, but it's clear that Natalie's informa-tion ecosystem and social platforms are vastly different from those of her fore-bears. The ever-changing digital landscape is likely to keep those generation gaps quite wide for the foreseeable future. It may even change the very nature of what it means to be human and to grow old.

Getting Old

AMERICANS ARE GETTING OLD and, before too long, they may be getting *very* old. A Methuselah drug awaits its inventor, but scientists at major universities and research institutions are hard at work. Some believe it may be only a matter of decades before someone in a lab coat makes a breakthrough that leads to an entirely new aging paradigm, one that replaces the generally accepted limits of human longevity with wondrous new possibilities. Merely imagining such a prospect raises mind-bending questions. Will radically extended life spans be the path to nirvana or dystopia? Will the extra years be available only to those who can afford them? What becomes of family bonds, medical costs, retirement finances, and social safety nets when America is awash with 120-year-old great-great-grandmas?

Aging and dying have always fascinated, haunted, and ultimately defined human beings. But the boundaries between the two have shifted dramatically over the centuries. For most of human history, life was "nasty, brutish and short," in the memorable synopsis of Thomas Hobbes, the seventeenth-century British philosopher. A newborn in the Roman Empire could expect to live to be about 25. As recently as 1900, the typical American lived to be just 47, with averages yanked down by the appallingly high share of newborns and infants who succumbed to infectious diseases. Even in ancient times, however, living into old age, while rare, was not unheard of. The Bible speaks of people living to be "three score and ten" (70 years) or even "four score" (80 years). And early American history is full of famous people who led famously long lives. When they died within hours of each other on the Fourth of July, 1826, Thomas Jefferson was 83 and John Adams was 90.

In the modern era, life expectancy at birth in the US has been increasing by about a year every six years.[1] The typical American baby born today can expect to live an average of 78.7 years, up from 75.4 years two decades ago—steady progress but not as rapid as the rise in many other developed countries, leading the US to slip from 20th to 27th in the rankings for life expectancy among the world's 34 OECD countries. During the same two-decade period, the number of centenarians in the US grew by about 50%, to more than 50,000. By the middle of this century, according to Census Bureau forecasts, close to a half million people in the US will be at least 100 years old. (The oldest person on record—Frenchwoman Jeanne Calment—lived to be 122.[2])

Even today, scientists don't know exactly why people age and die. They understand many of the mechanisms that lead the body to break down and stop working over time, but the underlying causes of aging are still a mystery. One popular theory holds that humans are essentially programmed to die after they are no longer needed to raise the children they produce. According to this theory, evolution has ensured that people are strong and vigorous during their fertile years, so they can have and rear offspring, but this bodily vigor subsides after people's reproductive and parenting years are over.[3]

Despite the unknowns about human longevity, a host of companies these days are offering a variety of treatments, from human growth hormones (HGH) to testosterone, aimed at helping people to slow down the aging process. Drugs such as resveratrol and rapamycin and experiments with new genetic combinations have the allure of a magic bullet: take a pill or flip a genetic switch and live an extra 20, 30, or even 40 healthy years. These therapies have largely been shunned by the mainstream medical community and, so far, they have not been scientifically shown to increase a person's life span in any meaningful way.

Some in the anti-aging movement believe that real gains will not be made by ingesting one compound but through a combination of medical therapies. Aubrey de Grey, a former Cambridge University researcher and now the chief science officer at an anti-aging think tank in Mountain View, California, called the Strategies for Engineered Negligible Senescence (SENS) Foundation, says aging will be conquered through a variety of "rejuvenation biotechnologies" that will repair and maintain the body indefinitely, much in the way a good mechanic can keep a vintage car running indefinitely. Under this scenario, various treatments including stem cell and gene therapies would be applied at the cellular level to halt the damage to the body caused by aging. "I'd say we have a 50/50 chance of bringing aging under what I'd call a decisive level of medical control within the next 25 years or so," de Grey said in 2010.[4]

Other experts believe that aging ultimately will be conquered by engineers and computer scientists rather than biomedical researchers. Ray Kurzweil, an American computer scientist and inventor whose work has led to the development of everything from checkout scanners at supermarkets to text-reading machines for the blind, says that what might seem outlandish today eventually will become possible because technological change is exponential rather than linear. "The reason information technology grows exponentially is that we use the latest technology to create the next," he said in a recent interview. "So each new generation of technology grows exponentially in capability and the speed of that process accelerates over time."[5]

Soon, Kurzweil predicts, it will be possible to place powerful machines in the human body that replace or improve existing biological systems. Machines, from pacemakers to cochlear implants, already play a huge role in medicine, and you don't need to be a science fiction writer or a professional futurist to see that the role of technology in medicine will continue to grow. But Kurzweil and other scientists say that greater computing power combined with extreme miniaturization (nanotechnology) will allow scientists to put microscopic machines in the body—at first to protect and maintain people's organs and ultimately to effectively replace them. In essence, Kurzweil says, scientists will "reverse engineer" bodily systems so that they can be replaced with much more reliable machines. He doesn't stop at this "bionic man" scenario. Eventually, he claims, human beings will achieve immortality by fully merging with machines. Kurzweil predicts that scientists will one day find a way to reverse engineer the brain and download human consciousness into it. Blood, bone, skin, and organs (what he and others call "wetware") will no longer be necessary.[6]

A Baby Boomer who turned 66 in 2014, Kurzweil makes it clear he has a very personal stake not just in the development of these new technologies, but in how quickly they come onstream. He believes that if he hangs on for another 15 years, he'll have a shot at immortality. "I'm right on the cusp," he told a *Wall Street Journal* reporter in 2013, then added some words of encouragement to his fellow Boomers: "I think some of us will make it through." As for the concern that only the wealthy will have access to such technologies, he noted with a dismissive shrug that people not too long ago said the same about cell phones.[7]

If the public policy questions raised by radical life extension are dizzying, the social and ethical questions are even more complex. Would it change the way we view marriage and children? Would it alter our sense of what it means to be human? Leon Kass, who chaired the President's Council on Bioethics under President George W. Bush, has observed that one of the "virtues of mortality" is that it instills a desire to make each day count. Knowledge that one will soon die "is the condition . . . for treasuring and appreciating all that life brings," he says.[8] Along these same lines, Stanley Hauerwas, a theologian at the Duke University School of Divinity, says that without death, love as we know it would cease to exist because it is the finite nature of life that prompts people to wholly commit themselves to others. "Death . . . creates an economy that makes love possible," he says. "If you lived forever there would not be the necessity of loving this one not that one. You could love them all." But others see the possibility of significantly longer life spans as a blessing—one that people will embrace, just as they have all previous social and technological advances. De Grey says that people fear much longer life spans only because they have talked themselves into believing that death is natural, and even good. He calls this a "pro-aging trance," which he says was "a sensible way of coping with the inevitability of aging" when it was inevitable. But now that aging and dying might not be inevitable, this mind-set "becomes part of the problem."[9]

PUBLIC ATTITUDES

It's only been in the past few years that the issue of radical life extension has begun to attract the notice of the mainstream press; before that it had been pretty much consigned to the realm of scientists, futurists, and ethicists. The May 2013 cover of *National Geographic* featured a picture of a newborn with the attention-grabbing caption: "This Baby Will Live to Be 120." In September 2013, a *Time* cover asked: "Can Google Solve Death?" Still, most of the American public is either unfamiliar or uncomfortable with the subject. In the spring of 2013, a majority (54%) of respondents to a Pew Research survey said they'd heard nothing about radical life extension. When prompted, respondents voiced ambivalence. Our survey asked, "If new medical treatments slow the aging process and allow the average person to live decades longer, to at least 120 years old, do you think that would be a good thing or a bad thing for society?" Respondents were closely divided; about half (51%) said bad while 41% said good. Follow-up questions produced more uncertainty. When asked if they themselves would want such medical treatments, a majority (56%) said they would not. But when asked if they thought most people would want such treatments, two-thirds (68%) said yes, most others would.

Men are more likely than women to say they want such treatments for themselves, blacks and Hispanics more likely than whites, and the young more likely than the old—but all of these demographic differences are relatively modest (see appendix Figure 12A.1). There's a much bigger gap in personally desiring treatments between those who think that extending longevity will be good for society

(71% in this camp said they would want the treatment for themselves) and those who think it would be bad (just 13% said they would want the treatments).

The public is skeptical that such medical advances are coming anytime soon; only a quarter think these therapies will be available in 2050. In comparison, many more believe that by mid-century, scientists will be able to bring back extinct species by cloning (50%), there will be a cure for most forms of cancer (69%), and artificial arms and legs will perform better than natural ones (71%).

Even though 4 in 10 Americans say life-extending therapies would be good for society, large majorities fear negative impacts of one kind or another. For example, while about 8 in 10 say "everyone should be able to get these treatments if they want them," two-thirds say that only wealthy people would have access to treatments. Two-thirds also say they believe that "longer life expectancies would strain our natural resources" and that "medical scientists would offer the treatment before they fully understood how it affects people's health."

And about 6 in 10 (58%) say that "these treatments would be fundamentally unnatural." Opinion is divided over whether the economy would be more productive because people could work longer: 44% say it would and 53% say no (see appendix Figure 12A.2). Views on many of these questions are related to beliefs about the overall effect of radical life-extension treatments on society. For example, among those who think the economy would be more productive with longer life spans, 70% think new medical treatments to radically extend life would be a good thing for society, while just 25% say it would be a bad thing.

Figure 12.1

Do You Want to Live to Be 120 Years Old?

% saying (they/most people) would or would not want medical treatments that slow the aging process and allow the average person to live to at least 120 years

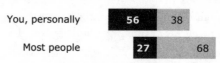

Note: Half of survey respondents were asked about their personal option and half were asked about "most people."

Source: Pew Research Center survey, Mar.–Apr. 2013, N=4,006 US adults

GETTING OLDER, FEELING YOUNGER

Aging is life's great mystery. Whether or not radical life extension comes to pass, virtually everyone wonders what it will be like to grow old. When the Pew Research Center did a national survey on the subject among adults of all ages, we found a striking dissonance: Getting old isn't nearly as bad as people think it will be. Nor is it quite as good.

On aspects of everyday life ranging from mental acuity to physical dexterity to sexual activity to financial security, the survey showed a sizable gap between the expectations that young and middle-age adults have about old age and the actual experiences reported by older Americans themselves.

These disparities came into sharpest focus when respondents were asked about a series of negative benchmarks often associated with aging, such as illness, memory loss, an inability to drive, an end to sexual activity, a struggle with loneliness and depression, and difficulty paying bills. In every instance, older adults report experiencing them at lower levels (often far lower) than younger adults report expecting to encounter them when they grow old.

At the same time, however, older adults report experiencing fewer of the benefits of aging that younger adults expect to enjoy when they grow old, such as spending more time with their family, traveling more for pleasure, having more time for hobbies, doing volunteer work, or starting a second career.

These generation gaps in perception also extend to the most basic question of all about old age: When does it begin? Survey respondents ages 18 to 29 believe that the average person becomes old at age 60. Middle-age respondents put the threshold closer to 70, and respondents ages 65 and above say that the average person does not become old until turning 74.

Other potential markers of old age—such as forgetfulness, retirement, becoming sexually inactive, experiencing bladder control problems, getting gray hair, having grandchildren—are the subjects of similar perceptual gaps. For example, nearly two-thirds of adults ages 18 to 29 believe that when someone "frequently forgets familiar names," that person is old. Less than half of all adults ages 30 and older agree (see appendix Figure 12A.3).

However, a handful of potential markers—failing health, an inability to live independently, an inability to drive, difficulty with stairs—engender agreement across all generations about the degree to which they serve as an indicator of old age.

The survey findings would seem to confirm the old saw that you're never too old to feel young. In fact, it shows that *the older people get, the younger they feel*—relatively speaking. Among 18- to 29-year-olds, about half say they feel their age, while about a quarter say they feel older than their age and another quarter say they feel younger. By contrast, among adults 65 and older, fully 60% say they feel younger than their age, compared with 32% who say they feel exactly their age and just 3% who say they feel older than their age.

Moreover, the gap in years between actual age and "felt age" widens as people grow older. Nearly half of all survey respondents ages 50 and older say they feel at least 10 years younger than their chronological age. Among respondents ages 65 to 74, a third say they feel 10 to 19 years younger than their age, and 1 in 6 say they feel at least 20 years younger than their actual age.

In sync with this upbeat way of counting their felt age, older adults also have a count-my-blessings attitude when asked to look back over the full arc of their lives. Nearly half (45%) of adults ages 75 and older say their life has turned out better than they expected, while just 5% say it has turned out worse (the remainder say things have turned out the way they expected or have no opinion). All other age groups also tilt positive, but considerably less so, when asked to assess their lives so far against their own expectations.

Figure 12.2

Markers of Old Age

% saying that a person is old when he or she ...

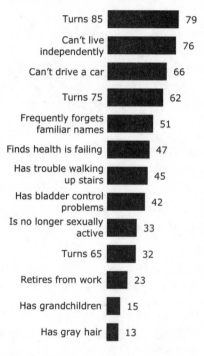

Turns 85	79
Can't live independently	76
Can't drive a car	66
Turns 75	62
Frequently forgets familiar names	51
Finds health is failing	47
Has trouble walking up stairs	45
Has bladder control problems	42
Is no longer sexually active	33
Turns 65	32
Retires from work	23
Has grandchildren	15
Has gray hair	13

Source: Pew Research Center survey, Feb.–Mar 2009, N=2,969

THE DOWNSIDE OF GETTING OLD

Of course, there are burdens that come with old age. About 1 in 4 adults ages 65 and older report experiencing memory loss. About 1 in 5 say they have a serious illness, are not sexually active, or often feel sad or depressed. About 1 in 6 report they are lonely or have trouble paying bills. One in 7 cannot drive. One in 10 say they feel they aren't needed or are a burden to others.

But when it comes to these and other potential problems related to old age, the share of younger and middle-age adults who report expecting to encounter

Figure 12.3

The Gap Between How Old We Are and How Old We Feel

Averages for actual age vs. felt age, by age group of respondent

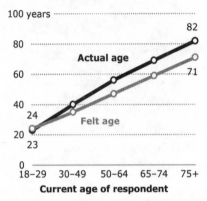

Note: Responses of "Don't know/Refused" not included in averages.

Source: Pew Research Center survey, Feb.–Mar 2009, N=2,969

them is much higher than the share of older adults who report actually experiencing them.

These problems are not shared equally by all groups of older adults. Those with low incomes are more likely than those with high incomes to face these challenges. The only exception to this pattern has to do with sexual inactivity; the likelihood of older adults reporting a problem in this realm of life is not correlated with income.

Not surprisingly, troubles associated with aging accelerate as adults advance into their 80s and beyond. For example, about 4 in 10 respondents (41%) ages 85 and older say they are experiencing some memory loss, compared with 27% of those ages 75–84 and 20% of those ages 65–74. Similarly, 30% of those ages 85 and older say they often feel sad or depressed, compared with less than 20% of those who are 65 to 84. And a quarter of adults ages 85 and older say they no longer drive, compared with 17% of those ages 75 to 84 and 10% of those who are 65 to 74.

But even in the face of these challenges, the vast majority of the "old old" in our survey appear to have made peace with their circumstances. Only a miniscule share of adults ages 85 and older—1%—say their lives have turned out worse than they expected. It no doubt helps that adults in their late 80s are as likely as those in their 60s and 70s to say they are experiencing many of the good things associated with aging—be it time with family, less stress, more respect, or more financial security.

THE UPSIDE OF GETTING OLD

When asked about a wide range of potential benefits of old age, 7 in 10 respondents ages 65 and older say they are enjoying more time with their family. About two-thirds cite more time for hobbies, more financial security,

Figure 12.4

The Challenges of Growing Older

It's not as bad as younger adults think

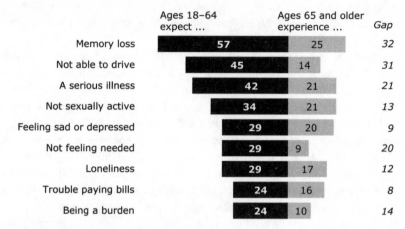

	Ages 18–64 expect ...	Ages 65 and older experience ...	Gap
Memory loss	57	25	32
Not able to drive	45	14	31
A serious illness	42	21	21
Not sexually active	34	21	13
Feeling sad or depressed	29	20	9
Not feeling needed	29	9	20
Loneliness	29	17	12
Trouble paying bills	24	16	8
Being a burden	24	10	14

The Benefits of Growing Older

Reality doesn't measure up to expectations

	Ages 18–64 expect ...	Ages 65 and older experience ...	Gap
More time for hobbies/interests	87	65	22
More time with family	86	70	16
Volunteer work	80	52	28
More travel	77	52	25
More financial security	67	64	3
Less stress	65	59	6
Not working	58	66	−8
More respect	56	59	−3
Second career	39	14	25

Source: Pew Research Center survey, Feb.–Mar 2009, N=2,969

and not having to work. About 6 in 10 say they get more respect and feel less stress than when they were younger. Just over half cite more time to travel and to do volunteer work. As Figure 12.4 illustrates, older adults may not be experiencing these "upsides" at quite the levels that most younger adults expect to enjoy them once they grow old, but their responses nonetheless indicate that the term "golden years" is something more than a syrupy greeting card sentiment.

Of all the good things about getting old, the best by far, according to older adults, is being able to spend more time with family members. In response to an open-ended question, 28% of those ages 65 and older say that what they value most about being older is the chance to spend more time with family, and an additional 25% say that above all, they value time with their grandchildren. A distant third on this list is having more financial security, which was cited by 14% of older adults as what they value most about getting older.

When, exactly, does old age begin? The aggregated wisdom of our survey respondents is at age 68. But that average masks a wide, age-driven variance in responses. More than half of adults under 30 say the average person becomes old even before turning 60. Just 6% of adults who are 65 or older agree (see appendix Figure 12A.4). Moreover, gender as well as age influences attitudes on this subject. Women, on average, say a person becomes old at age 70. Men, on average, put the number at 66.

Even if the public has decreed that the average person becomes old at age 68, you won't get too far trying to convince people of that age that the threshold applies to them. Among respondents ages 65 to 74, just 21% say they feel old. Even among those 75 and older, just 35% say they feel old.

The survey found that the average age that people aspired to live to was 89. One in 5 would like to live into their 90s, while just 8% say they would like to surpass the century mark. The public's verdict on the most desirable life span appears to have ratcheted down a bit in recent years. A 2002 AARP survey found that the average desired life span was 92.

The same factors that predict happiness among younger adults—good health, good friends, and financial security—by and large predict happiness among older adults. However, there are a few age-related differences. Most notably, once all other key demographic variables are held constant, although being married is a predictor of happiness among younger adults, it is not so among older adults (perhaps because a significant share of the latter group is made up of widows or widowers, many of whom presumably have "banked" some of the key marriage-related correlates of happiness, such as financial security and a strong family life).

Aging is more than a human drama. It's also a societal drama. Between now and midcentury, even absent any breakthroughs in life extension, the graying of the world's population will put enormous stress on economies, families, and governments in the US and around the world.

13

Empty Cradle, Gray World

A NYONE REMEMBER THE JAPANESE MIRACLE? A genera-
tion ago the phrase ricocheted around the world wherever political and
economic elites gathered. As the US struggled with recessions, inflation, and
energy crises, Japan was busy building the world's best cars and coolest electronic gadgets. It boasted a soaring GDP, productive workforce, efficient factories, clean streets, and virtually no crime. Its banks had become the world's
biggest. Its corporations were scooping up iconic chunks of America, from
Rockefeller Center to Columbia Pictures to Pebble Beach to 7-Eleven, leading
one US congressman to worry that "the United States is rapidly becoming a
colony of Japan." In 1979 Harvard sociology professor Ezra Vogel published
Japan as Number 1: Lessons for America, in which he described how an insular island nation had risen phoenix-like from the self-inflicted catastrophe of
World War II by reengineering its political, economic, and social institutions.
The book was an international bestseller.

Japan is still a global economic powerhouse, but the triumphalism of that
bygone era has been replaced by a declinism nearly as pervasive. Not only
did its economy never become number one, it's now no longer number two:
in 2010, Japan relinquished that spot to its once and future nemesis, China.[1]
Its GDP per capita, which had surpassed that of the US in the early 1990s,
has since fallen significantly behind. Its Nikkei average stands at about half of
its 1989 peak; its land prices are at 1975 levels; its government debt has ballooned above 200% of GDP, more than double that of most other advanced
nations. What went wrong? Lots of things: speculative bubbles, unproductive

investments, crony capitalism, weak governance. But one factor exacerbates all others: demographics.

Japan has the oldest population in the world, and as scores of other countries are about to discover for themselves, aging societies have trouble maintaining their economic vitality. The active share of the population needs to support the inactive share, and older folks simply don't have the energy, imagination, entrepreneurship, and drive that younger ones do. Going forward, the age pyramid in the Land of the Rising Sun will only grow more top-heavy. Japan's median age is 45 today. By 2050 it will be 53. By 2060, 37% of its population will be 65 or older. No country in history has ever had to cope with that old a population. The challenges go well beyond economic growth; they go to the very fabric of the nation's social, family, and political life. The Japanese have a word, *kodokushi,* to describe the phenomenon of older, often childless adults who die lonely deaths, sometimes at their own hand. It is a growing problem. As of 2010, some 4.6 million elderly Japanese lived alone, and the share who died at home grew by 61% between 2003 and 2010, according to Japan's bureau of social welfare and public health. In early 2013, Japan's finance minister, Tara Aso, 72, caused a stir when he suggested at a meeting of a national council on social security reforms that the elderly "hurry up and die" to ease the strain on the nation's finances.[2] He later said his remarks were inappropriate, but over the years he has also talked about "doddering pensioners" and "tube people." In any case, Japan's government continues to chip away at the social safety net for seniors.

Longevity, however, isn't the main cause of Japan's demographic winter. The real problem is too few births. If present trends were to continue—which they won't—Japan would eventually un-breed itself into extinction. Today its population is 127 million. By 2100, if you believe the United Nations projection, it will be down to 84 million, and if you believe the Japanese government's own worst-case projections, it could fall as low as 47 million. "I am the last Japan optimist," muses Jesper Koll, an American economist who has lived in Tokyo since the Miracle era. "[People here] say, 'Oh, in 600 years there will be 480 Japanese left.'"[3] Japan's fertility rate—1.4 per woman—is among the lowest in the world and far below the 2.1 level that most developed societies must maintain to keep from depopulating over time.

How did this happen? Many Japanese tell some version of the following story: After the real estate and stock market bubbles burst in 1990, the Japanese essentially lost some of their faith in themselves and their collective future. The ensuing decades of economic stagnation, coming so hard after the go-go decades, which came so quickly after the war years, have rattled this proud, ancient, and still somewhat xenophobic society to such a degree that many of its young have turned inward. In an age of declining expectations, Japan's Millennials are setting their life compasses on individual fulfillment—getting what they can for themselves. They're delaying marriage and childbearing, or abandoning it altogether. There's even some suggestion that they're losing their appetite for sex. According to one recent survey, one-third of young men ages 16 to 19 express no interest in sex, a puzzling sentiment reportedly shared by 60% of young women that age.[4] It hasn't helped that Japan's day care centers are too expensive for most families. In 2013 the *New York Times* ran a feature story about a pregnant Tokyo woman who had toured 44 day care centers in a desperate search to find an affordable one that met her standards. Such expeditions have their own name—*hokatsu*—and as a source of stress are said to be on par with the notorious job searches of newly minted Japanese college graduates.[5]

Japan's baby bust is the most acute in the world, but similar dynamics are taking hold on every continent. The demographic term of art is "sub-replacement-level fertility." It first emerged in Scandinavia in the 1970s and is now common throughout Europe, Russia, East Asia, and some South American, Caribbean, and Middle Eastern countries. It's most prevalent in the wealthy countries of "old Europe"—Germany, France, Italy, and Spain—as well as in the Asian Tigers of Japan's neighborhood: China, South Korea, Singapore, Hong Kong, and Taiwan. But this is not merely a phenomenon among the affluent. More than 20 Muslim countries have had fertility declines of at least 50% since the late 1970s, with the sharpest drops in Iran, Oman, the United Arab Emirates, Algeria, Bangladesh, Tunisia, and Libya. The typical Iranian woman had nearly 7 children as recently as the late 1970s; now she has about 2. Halfway around the world, Mexico has seen its fertility rates plunge by a similar order of magnitude over roughly the same time period. In fact, Mexican women now have a lower fertility rate than Mexican-American immigrants. According to UN projections, some 49 countries are now producing so few children that they will see their populations decline between now and 2050; about a third are "developing" economies and two-thirds are more affluent economies.

All of this marks an unprecedented turning point in human history. Until a few centuries ago, the prevailing demographic paradigm consisted of high birthrates, high infant mortality, and relatively short life expectancy. In modern times, advances in sanitation, nutrition, medicine, and public health dramatically reduced infant mortality and increased longevity. This produced a huge demographic and economic dividend for the world, at least initially. More children surviving into adulthood meant more producers and consumers—more units of economic activity. Starting around 1900, the world's population expanded more rapidly than ever before, growing fourfold in the twentieth century alone, to more than 7 billion today. Standards of living also rose dramatically, especially in the developed world. But not everyone saw these trends as a cause for celebration. In 1968, just as the oldest of America's Baby Boomers was entering the workforce, sociologist Paul Ehrlich published *The Population Bomb,* which began on this attention-grabbing note: "The battle to feed all of humanity is over. In the 1970s hundreds of millions of people will starve to death in spite of any crash programs embarked upon now. At this late date nothing can prevent a substantial increase in the world death rate." Ehrlich, who was channeling the apocalyptic visions conjured up two centuries earlier by British scholar Thomas Malthus, called for a wide range of population control measures to mitigate the looming disasters of overpopulation. His book, like Vogel's, became an international bestseller.

How times change. Today's demographic doomsday scenarios tend to revolve around too few, not too many. Yes, there are still "explosionists" concerned that an overpopulated planet will deplete the earth's resources, but they now share the stage with "implosionists" troubled by a world of too few young supporting too many old. These compositional shifts in the global age pyramid are the result of what has been dubbed the "second demographic transition." The old paradigm of high birthrates, high infant mortality, and short life expectancy has been replaced by a new paradigm of low birthrates, low infant mortality, and long life expectancy. For the most part, these changes weren't driven by public policy edict. Rather, they're a natural adaptation to improvements in medical science and public health. In olden days, people felt they needed to have lots of kids to ensure that some would survive to take care of them in their old age. Now they feel safe having fewer. Other social changes—secularization, urbanization, the women's revolution, modern media—contributed to the trend. In advanced societies, the less religious tend to have, on average, about half a child less than do the religiously observant; as religiosity has declined around the world, so has childbearing. Urbanization has raised the cost and reduced the economic rewards of child rearing; not many family farms need tending in Shanghai, London, or Mexico City. Meantime, the movement of women into the workforce has upped the opportunity cost of baby-making; nowadays, if a woman chooses to be a stay-at-home mom, it typically means she's forgoing income. Then there are the norms set by a media-saturated popular culture. In Brazil, where television began being introduced sequentially into the provinces a few generations ago, researchers found a correlation between the arrival of television and the decline of birthrates, prompting demographer Phillip Longman to observe: "Discuss among yourselves whether this was because of what's on Brazilian television—mostly soap operas depicting rich people living the high life—or simply because a television was now on at night in many more bedrooms."[6]

When birthrates tumble, there's a short-term economic dividend for society. Children are expensive—not just for their parents but for the governments that underwrite the cost of their education and health care. Over time, however, the cost-benefit equation shifts. Small cohorts of children grow up to become small cohorts of workers—at which point there aren't enough of them to keep the economy humming. During the 20th and now 21st centuries, different countries around the world have experienced these phases at different times, but the sequence and trajectory are the same. And the pattern is now sufficiently universal that the world is on the cusp of a milestone that would have astonished explosionists from Malthus to Ehrlich: the growth in the population of children is about to grind to a halt. Between now and midcentury, according to UN estimates, the number of children under age 15 will grow by just 10%. In this same period, the global population of seniors (ages 65 and older) will nearly triple as today's middle-age bulge matures and as medical science extends the human life span. Graying populations create financial stress for social insurance systems. They have a tendency to trigger unproductive changes in public investments, such as the reallocation of resources from the needs of children to the needs of seniors. And of course, they exert financial pressures on the elderly themselves, as well as their families.

In all of these trends, the US is an outlier. The fertility rate here is among the highest in the wealthy world (just under 2 per woman), so our median age won't rise nearly as fast. Ours is 38 now; by 2050, it is projected to be 42. The global median age, by contrast, is expected to climb from 29 in 2010 to 36 in 2050.[7] The overall US population is projected to increase at a faster rate than average, thanks to births and immigration. By 2050, it is expected to be about 400 million, up from today's 320 million. The world's population is projected to rise from about 7 billion now to 9.6 billion by the middle of the century, before leveling off at around 11 billion in 2100 (though projections that far into the future should be treated with caution).

The vast bulk of the global growth will come in the poor countries of Africa and Asia, while most of today's economic powers will, like Japan, see their populations shrink or flatline. Germany, for example, has not had a single year since 1972 in which births exceeded deaths. Even with an ongoing stream of immigration from Turkey and other neighbors, it will see a significant population decline by midcentury. Meantime in China, where the official government estimate is that the one-child policy has prevented 400 million births over the past 30 years, there are growing worries about a graying population, a shrinking labor force, a skewed gender ratio (118 baby boys for every 100 baby girls, the most lopsided ratio of any country in the world), and a radically attenu-ated kinship structure.[8] China's population is projected to remain flat through midcentury. In 2015, after having spent more than a decade phasing out the one-child policy, the Chinese government scrapped it all together. When the policy was first put into effect in the 1970s, the conventional wisdom was that it represented an enlightened form of state-enforced family planning (at best) or a necessary evil (at worst). Now, roughly half a billion abortions and steril-izations later, it has become the target of bitter resentment throughout much of China, in part because it's viewed as an affront to a basic human right, in part because it has been applied unevenly, and in part because it has created a generation of "little emperors" who've grown up without brothers and sis-ters and whose children will grow up without cousins, aunts, uncles, nephews, or nieces. A recent paper by Chinese demographers attacked the policy with unusual fervor:

> The One-Child Policy will be added to other deadly errors in recent Chinese history, including the famine in 1959–61 . . . and the Cultural Revolution of the late 1960s and early 1970s. While those grave mistakes both cost tens of millions of lives, the harms done were relatively short-lived and were cor-rected quickly afterward. The One-Child Policy, in contrast, will surpass them in impact by creating a society with a seriously undermined family and kin structure, and a whole generation of future elderly and their children whose well-being will be seriously jeopardized.[9]

No other country has gone to China's extremes to limit births. None has felt the need. In most countries, the decline has come without official prod-ding. One way to think about population decline is that it is a price societies pay for modernity and prosperity. However, it's a bit more complicated than that. As already noted, some of the steepest birthrate declines have come in poor or developing countries, including many in the Muslim world. Mean-time, in Western Europe and other industrialized countries, there's now a pos-itive correlation between female labor force participation and high birthrates, a trend reversal that first appeared about two decades ago. Relatively high-fertility countries like Sweden, Norway, Iceland, and Denmark now have more women employed than do low-fertility countries like Italy, Spain, Greece, and Germany. This may be related to the Calvinist work ethic of Northern Europe, or to their robust network of day care and other social support systems for children, or to the economic woes of Southern Europe. Pick your hypothe-sis. Meantime, in the US the sharpest declines in fertility since the onset of the Great Recession have been among women on the lower rungs of the socioeconomic ladder (in particular, immigrants and women with only a high school degree or less). Today women with a college degree in the US are more likely to give birth than those with a high school diploma or less, and women in their 30s are giving birth at a higher rate than women under the age of 20. On this demographic front as on so many others, the US finds itself in better shape than any of its major economic and geopolitical competitors.

DEPENDENCY RATIOS

The principal economic implication of an aging population is that it potentially reduces the share of the population that is in the prime of its working life. This can slow overall economic growth, absent a compensating rise in productivity. At the same time, the share of the population that depends on those at work may increase. The "dependent" population includes most seniors who, in addition to their savings, depend on family transfers, private pensions, and social insurance. Children, of course, are principally dependent on their parents.

The potential burden on the working-age population to provide for the dependent population is measured by the dependency ratio, which can be expressed by three different metrics. The old-age dependency ratio is defined as the ratio of the population ages 65 and older to the working-age population (ages 15 to 64). The child dependency ratio is the ratio of population younger than age 15 to the working-age population. Finally, the total dependency ratio is the ratio of the overall population of dependents (those younger than 15 or older than 64) to the working-age population.[10]

The old-age dependency ratio in the US is projected to nearly double, from 19.5 in 2010 to 35.5 in 2050. That will mostly be due to the aging of the Baby Boomers. However, because the child and middle-age populations in the US are expected to increase at about the same pace, the child dependency ratio in the US will be about the same in 2050 (30.1) as in 2010 (29.6). Thus, future increases in the total dependency ratio in the US—from 49 in 2010 to 65.6 in 2050—are driven entirely by aging.

The increase in the old-age dependency ratio in the US is not a new phenomenon. The ratio previously rose from 12.8 in 1950 to 19.5 in 2010. However, the child dependency ratio fell sharply in the past, from 41.7 in 1950 to 29.6 in 2010. That was the consequence of tumbling birthrates in the wake of a Baby Boom–fueled bulge in the middle of the US age distribution. Thus, despite an overall aging of the population, the total dependency ratio in the US had fallen from 54.5 in 1950 to 49.0 in 2010.

Old-age dependency ratios in the world overall are lower than in the US but they are rising faster, projected to more than double from 11.7 in 2010 to

Figure 13.1

Dependency Ratios in the United States

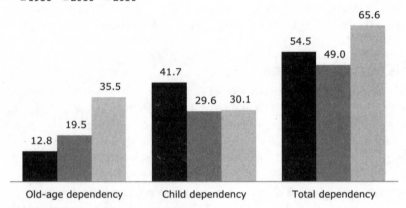

■1950 ■2010 ■2050

Old-age dependency: 12.8, 19.5, 35.5
Child dependency: 41.7, 29.6, 30.1
Total dependency: 54.5, 49.0, 65.6

Global Dependency Ratios

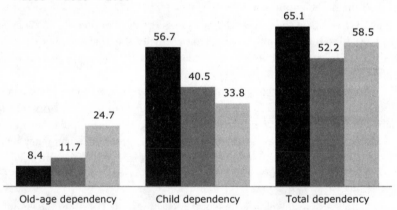

■1950 ■2010 ■2050

Old-age dependency: 8.4, 11.7, 24.7
Child dependency: 56.7, 40.5, 33.8
Total dependency: 65.1, 52.2, 58.5

Note: The old-age dependency ratio is the population age 65 and over divided by population age 15–64. The child dependency ratio is the population age 0–14 divided by population age 15–64. The total dependency ratio is the population age 65 and over plus population age 0–14, divided by population age 15–64.

Source: United Nations, Department of Economic and Social Affairs, *World Population Prospects: The 2012 Revision*, June 2013

24.7 in 2050. However, global increases in old-age dependency are balanced by steep declines in the child dependency ratio, from 40.5 in 2010 to a more US-like level of 33.8 in 2050. This means that the total dependency ratio in the world is expected to increase from 52.2 in 2010 to 58.5 in 2050, a much smaller increase than in the US.

Old-age dependency ratios are also expected to rise in all major regions of the world—Asia and Oceania, Africa, the Americas, and Europe. In all regions but Africa the old-age dependency ratio will at least double from 2010 to 2050. As old-age dependency ratios increase, there are expected to be countervailing decreases in the child dependency ratios in all regions except Europe, with the sharpest decline in Africa.

In Asia and Oceania and the Americas, the expected reductions in child dependency are not sufficiently large to make up for the growing numbers of seniors. The result is an increase in total dependency from 2010 to 2050— from 47.7 to 54.8 in Asia and Oceania and from 51.7 to 61.0 in the Americas. Europe, where only the population of seniors is growing, is projected to experience the sharpest increase in the total dependency ratio, from 46.5 to 73.2. In other words, in 2050, there will be about 73 dependents for every 100 people in the prime of their working years in Europe, almost a 1 to 1 ratio.

Africa is the only region where dependency ratios are projected to decline. With the prime working-age population growing rapidly, the total dependency ratio in Africa is expected to decrease from 80.4 in 2010 to 61.5 in 2050. Thus, by 2050, there will be almost 20 fewer dependents per 100 working-age people in Africa. That is a potentially very favorable demographic tailwind for economic growth in Africa (see appendix Figure 13A.1).

THE G7 AND THE BRICS

This section analyzes demographic projections for two prominent blocs of countries—the G7 and the BRICS—which together account for roughly two-thirds of the global economy. The G7 includes the US, UK, Germany, France, Italy, Japan, and Canada. These seven countries accounted for 38% of global output in 2012, half of which originated from the US alone. BRICS refers to five of the world's major emerging economies: Brazil, Russia, India, China, and South Africa. These five countries accounted for 27% of world output in 2012, with China alone responsible for more than half of that contribution.[11]

The G7 and BRICS also include the three most populous countries in the world—China, India, and the US. Collectively, the G7 countries were home to 743 million people in 2010, or 11% of the world population. The BRICS carried much greater heft, being home to nearly 3 billion people in 2010, or 43%

of the global population. This section reports on the demographic future for six of the G7 countries—the original G6—and the five BRICS.[12]

Most G6 and BRICS countries face significant demographic headwinds between 2010 and 2050. Their populations are projected to grow at below-average rates or to decline, several will age to unprecedented levels, and most will experience large increases in their dependency ratios. Within this general landscape, the US in the G6 and India and South Africa within the BRICS will experience the most favorable demographic outcomes.

Population Change

Only the US and India are expected to see notable gains in population from 2010 to 2050. The growth in India (34%) will be slightly lower than the global increase of 38%. The US will lag behind a bit, its population increasing by 28% from 2010 to 2050. Other countries will either grow at about half the global pace (UK, France, Brazil, and South Africa) or actually shrink in size (Japan, Germany, Italy, and Russia). These trends point to the US increasing its demographic influence and its relative economic power within the G6, and India doing the same within the BRICS (see appendix Figure 13A.2).

Median Age

The G6 countries are among the oldest countries in the world today. Three of them—Japan, Germany, and Italy—are projected to reach median ages of 50 or higher by 2050. The US is the youngest country in this group and will retain that distinction in 2050, aging up modestly from 37 in 2010 to 41 in 2050.

The BRICS, with the exception of Russia, are currently among the younger countries in the world. As of 2010, the median age in India and South Africa is only 26 and 25, respectively, and Brazil, too, is quite young with a median age of 29. However, these countries are projected to age rapidly. By 2050, median ages are expected to rise to 37 in India, 34 in South Africa, and 44 in Brazil. Among the BRICS, only India and South Africa will be younger than the G6 economies in 2050. Brazil, Russia, and China will look more like "old" Europe (see appendix Figure 13A.3).

Dependency Ratios

The total dependency ratio is projected to increase significantly in all G6 countries. The most notable case is Japan, where the ratio is expected to climb to 96, meaning Japan will have almost as many dependents as those in the workforce in 2050. Russia and China are also projected to experience sharp increases in the total dependency ratio—from 39 to 60 in Russia and from 36 to 63 in China. By contrast, the ratio is expected to decrease in India and South Africa, signaling a greater potential for economic growth as a result of the so-called demographic dividend. Even so, the old-age dependency ratio is projected to double in both countries.

Within the G6, the US is projected to see an increase in the old-age dependency ratio, from 19 in 2010 to 36 in 2050. Japan and Italy are expected to double the old-age dependency ratio to 72 and 62, respectively, and Germany will see its ratio increase to 60. By this measure, these three countries will greatly outdistance their G6 counterparts (see appendix Figure 13A.4).

PUBLIC ATTITUDES ABOUT AGING POPULATIONS

Depending on the country, there are vastly different views about the gravity of the challenges posed by aging populations; for example, 87% of the public in Japan say it is a major problem for their country, while just 23% of Egyptians say the same. As appendix Figure 13A.5 illustrates, Americans are near the bottom of the pack, with just 26% saying that aging is a major problem in this country.

Respondents in 21 countries were also asked who should bear the greatest responsibility for people's economic well-being in their old age—their families, the government, or themselves? Once again, the Americans stand out. Nearly half (46%) say people themselves should be mainly responsible, second only to the 53% of South Koreans who feel the same way. The Germans (41%) and Brits (39%) aren't far behind, but beyond those four, in the vast majority of countries surveyed, only a small sliver felt that people themselves should be mainly responsible. This is a question that evokes the creed of self-reliance. Who should care for me when I'm old and creaky? In effect, the Americans say: I'll do it myself. The Russians, Italians, and Israelis nominate their government, and the Pakistanis and Brazilians volunteer their families.

Not all Americans are rugged individualists, however. About a quarter of the survey respondents in this country said the government should be primarily responsible, while a fifth said the job should fall mainly to the families of the elderly. But here, too, American public opinion is an outlier. In other countries, many more said this is a government rather than a family responsibility, typically by ratios of 2 to 1 or more. Americans rank second to last (behind only Pakistanis) in the share who think the responsibility lies mainly with government (see appendix Figure 13A.6).

Notably, the American penchant for self-reliance doesn't translate into a particularly robust belief that everything will be just fine for them in their golden years. When the survey asked people around the world how confident they are that they'll have an adequate standard of living in their old age, US respondents finished a bit above the middle of the pack, with more than 6 in 10 saying they are very (24%) or somewhat (39%) confident.

The Chinese and Brazilians are the most confident, followed by the publics of the three African countries that were part of the survey—Nigeria, South Africa, and Kenya. Given that none of those countries has a robust public pension program or a high standard of living, the confidence would appear to be based on family and cultural factors rather than simple economics.

At the other end of the spectrum, the countries where people are the least confident they'll have a good standard of living in their retirement are Russia, Italy, and Japan. That is hardly a surprise, given their looming demographic winter (see appendix Figure 13A.7).

IS DEMOGRAPHY DESTINY?

How closely linked are a country's demographic and economic destinies? Obviously, when a country's workforce grows relative to its youth and elderly populations, the stage can be set for rapid economic growth. But these outcomes aren't inevitable. Countries that reap the benefits of the so-called demographic dividend tend to have complementary factors at play, such as good governance, high saving rates, investments in schooling and public health, policies promoting gender equity, and openness to trade and foreign investments.[13] Thus, many of the countries on the cusp of the demographic dividend—India, Pakistan, Egypt, Nigeria, and Kenya—can't automatically assume that economic benefits will flow. India, for example, ranks very low on indicators of nutrition, health, and education for its youth population and has regressed in recent years. And as Egypt's leaders have discovered, having a young, well-educated, but unemployed labor force can be a recipe for unrest, even revolution.

By the same token, it's not inevitable that the aging of a country's population portends gloom for its economic prospects. As labor will become scarcer and more expensive, employers can try to raise productivity through capital deepening or innovation. Japan, for example, has become a global leader in the fast-developing field of robotics (including robots that learn how to care for the elderly). It's also possible to boost the size of a workforce through immigration, though that will require some cultural adjustments in societies, such as Japan's, that have a history of closing themselves off to foreigners. And workers themselves may choose to work longer in aging countries, especially since life expectancy and health outcomes are improving at older ages. In the US, for example, labor force participation among those 65 and older has risen from a low of 10.8% in 1985 to 18.5% in 2012, according to the Bureau of Labor Statistics.

Among all of the world's countries, Japan has the most experience trying to figure out how to maintain its vitality while going gray. After 30 years and counting, the returns aren't very encouraging. It's true that the Japanese economy and public mood brightened somewhat in 2013 with the return to power of Prime Minister Shinzo Abe, a hard-line nationalist who has pushed through a popular progrowth economic agenda that's been dubbed Abenomics. Nonetheless, the country's demographic challenges persist. In 2012 the *New York Times* ran a fascinating story about the clash of generations in Onagawa, a community wiped out by the 2011 tsunami that destroyed one of the country's nuclear power plants.[14] Like hundreds of other small communities throughout rural Japan, this one had been losing population and growing older for decades—long before the natural disaster hit. In the wake of the tsunami, the question before the town council was how and where to rebuild. The mayor proposed a reconstruction plan that would consolidate its 15 tiny fishing villages into a central location in the hope of saving money and giving the area a more sustainable future. Younger residents supported the plan, but they were vastly outnumbered by their elders, who wanted to live out their remaining years in their small ancestral villages. The mayor was summarily ousted. His successor is rebuilding all 15 villages, including one that has 22 residents. This is not an isolated case. For decades the Japanese government has been pouring resources into big rural infrastructure projects to try to stem the economic decline. It has been a boon for the politically connected construction industry, but the hinterlands haven't come back. Now they're filled with deserted train stations, empty resorts, bridges to nowhere, and schoolhouses built for thousands that serve dozens.[15] All of this has left the government with a huge overhang of debt that the Japanese will be paying off for generations. There may not be many children in Japan's schoolhouses these days, but as they grow up, they'll have plenty of bills to pay.

The Reckoning

IDA MAY FULLER, A NEVER-MARRIED legal secretary from Brattle-boro, Vermont, was the first person in the United States to retire on Social Security. Her initial monthly check, bearing the auspicious number 00-000-001, arrived in the mail on January 31, 1940, shortly after her 65th birthday. It was for $22.54. Being of sturdy New England farm stock, Ida proceeded to live for 35 more years. The checks just kept coming. By the time she died at age 100, she'd drawn $22,888.92 from Social Security.

Doesn't sound like much? Well, consider this: Ida had only started to pay Social Security taxes in 1937, the year the program began. Her total contribution during those three years amounted to a princely $24.75. Her employer kicked in another $24.75. Which means that Ida received a nearly five hundred–fold return on those combined contributions, courtesy of younger generations of workers and taxpayers who supported the system during her retirement years.

If you're inclined to think of Social Security as a giant government-run Ponzi scheme, Ida's good fortune is a good place to start your story.[1] Her windfall was one-of-a-kind, but all beneficiaries of her generation got far more out of the system than they paid in. Over time, as the ratio of workers to retirees has grown less favorable, successive generations have done less well. Still, all of the Silents are enjoying positive returns from their taxes and virtually all Boomers will come out ahead, too. But absent changes to the system, most Gen Xers and virtually all Millennials will get back less in benefits than they contribute in taxes.[2] This will be the case despite the fact that annual spending on Social Security and its sidekick, Medicare, is on track to consume ever larger shares of the federal budget—50% of all noninterest spending in 2030, up from 28% in 1980.[3]

Every single day between now and then, 10,000 more Baby Boomers will turn 65. During the years this pig-in-a-python generation was fully in the workforce, the tax revenues that flowed into Social Security and Medicare not only covered these programs' obligations to older folks who were already retired, they also built up a big surplus that would help prefund the Boomers' own retirement. But in 2010, around the time the oldest of the Boomers began to retire, annual revenues into the system began to fall below annual payouts. This new upside-down arithmetic will persist for as far as the eye can see. Social Security and Medicare will be able to stay afloat for a while by drawing down on the reserves. Eventually, however, the well will run dry. According to Social Security's trustees, the Medicare trust fund will be empty by 2026 and the main Social Security trust fund will be insolvent by 2033.[4] At that point, the trustees say, the policy options are all unpalatable. Either retirees will be hit with a benefits cut of 23%, or workers will have to absorb a massive payroll tax increase of that size, or the two will have to share the pain.

At its core, this is a problem of generational equity. The young today are paying taxes to support a level of benefits for the old that they themselves have no prospect of receiving when *they* become old. Meantime, as a rising share of their tax dollars goes to fund the social safety net for the old, government spending on other priorities, especially on investments that would improve the economic prospects of the young, is being crowded out. Some sort of rebalancing is plainly in order, and every day that elected officials put off the reckoning is a day that generational inequities increase. "Substantial further delay risks further concentrating the burdens of correcting the shortfall on younger workers who already stand to be treated less favorably," wrote the Social Security system's two public trustees, Democrat Robert D. Reischauer and Republican Charles P. Blahous III, in their 2013 annual report.[5]

Before we consider how to take on this challenge, let's spend some time unpacking Social Security. No other government program in history has lifted so many out of poverty or become so integral to so many family budgets—and yet is so poorly understood. This is not an accident. It's the legacy of the political genius who created it, Franklin Delano Roosevelt. When he pushed the Social Security Act through Congress in 1935 as one of the centerpieces of his New Deal, the US and the world were still drowning in the Great Depression. Millions of Americans were homeless, tens of millions had lost their life savings, unemployment hovered around 25%, and poverty was endemic, especially among the elderly. Several decades before, a number of European countries had created the first generation of rudimentary publicly financed national retirement systems—Germany in 1889, England in 1908. Until the onset of the Depression, there hadn't been much appetite for such programs in the US, and Roosevelt understood why: self-reliant Americans scorned them as welfare. However, in the depths of the economic calamity of the 1930s, he saw both need and opportunity. He surmised the country was ready to build a public social safety net for the elderly, provided it was properly designed. To him, that meant one thing above all. It had to be a contributory system; workers would pay wage taxes that would be held by the government and eventually returned to them in the form of a pension. "We put those payroll contributions there to give the contributors a legal, moral and political right to collect their pensions," Roosevelt said. Because of them, he boasted: "No damn politician can ever scrap my Social Security program!"

But right from the get-go, Social Security was never a pure contributory system. Despite the president's misgivings, and sometimes over his objections,[6] FDR's own cabinet worked with Congress (liberals as well as conservatives) to fashion it into something much more akin to a "pay-as-you-go" generational transfer program, in which today's workers are taxed to pay the benefits of today's retirees. What they wound up concocting was a complex hybrid. Beneficiaries receive payments based in part on what they've put in, but in part on other formulas designed to serve a range of social purposes. The taxes are regressive (they land most heavily on those in lower income brackets) while the benefits are progressive (those in lower brackets get the best rate of return), a politically ingenious balancing act that simultaneously disguises and protects its overall redistributionist impact. Other features favor certain categories of recipients. For example, the benefits are far more generous to one-earner married couples than to two-earner couples or single adults. And like all defined pension systems, its best deals go to recipients who, like Ida, are clever enough to live to a ripe old age. It also doubles as a life insurance policy and triples as a disability insurance policy. Of Social Security's roughly 59.5 million beneficiaries (as of mid-2015), 42.6 million are retirees and their dependents, an additional 10.9 million are the disabled and their dependents, and 6 million more are early retirees or survivors of deceased workers.

This all makes for a pretty opaque program, its complexities best understood by those well versed in the actuarial arts. As a layman, I would summarize Social Security's balance sheet as follows: it redistributes wealth in a measured way from young to old, from rich to poor, from the healthy to the infirm, and from everyone to the long-lived. Columnist Robert Samuelson called it "a huge welfare program grafted onto the rhetoric and psychology of a contributory pension," while Nobel laureate Milton Friedman, less charitably, inveighed against the contributions paradigm as a "myth" that Roosevelt and his political progeny sold to a gullible public using "the worst devices of Madison Avenue."[7]

Over the years, the Friedman broadside has been echoed by successive generations of conservative politicians, from Ronald Reagan to George W. Bush to Paul Ryan, who've periodically tried to rally the public behind privatization proposals. Their efforts have never gotten off the ground, even though they poll well among the young. It turns out that Roosevelt may have been disingenuous about the financing of Social Security, but he was spot-on about the politics. To this day Social Security remains the "most sacred of sacred cows," in Friedman's lament. Countless millions of Americans still think of it the way my mother (a child of the Roosevelt era) did: the government takes a bit of money out of your paycheck each week, puts it into a drawer with your name on it, then gives it back to you when you retire, with interest. This accounting fiction is reinforced by every pay stub every wage earner receives; each one meticulously notes how much Social Security and Medicare tax (also referred to as the FICA tax, for Federal Insurance Contributions Act) has been deducted. So: You make your contribution and you earn your retirement benefit. What could be more fair?

Unfortunately, there are plenty of fairness issues, and they've grown more acute as the program itself has aged. As already noted, if one evaluates the system through a generational return-on-investment lens, Social Security has been all downhill since Ida's day. Back when the program first started, 42 workers were making contributions for every retiree drawing benefits. That allowed for windfalls galore, especially for recipients in that first generation, who were eligible for lifetime benefits in retirement even if, like Ida, they had paid just a few years' worth of taxes. But the ratio of workers to retirees has fallen precipitously over the decades. It is currently a bit under 3 to 1 and is slated to drop below 2 to 1 by 2035. To compensate, the Social Security tax (employee plus employer) has been raised time and again, from 2% in Ida's day to 12.4% now. And the cap on wages subject to this tax has gone up even more—from $3,000 then to $118,500 in 2015.

If one were to look just at the income returns on Social Security taxes alone (and take Medicare out of the equation), many of today's 65-year-olds won't get back in lifetime benefits what they and their employers paid in taxes, and negative rates of return will become even more pervasive for tomorrow's retirees, according to an analysis by the Urban Institute's C. Eugene Steuerle.[8] "The bottom line is that the older you are, the more likely that your Social Security benefits exceeded your contributions," says Blahous, a former adviser to President George W. Bush. "The younger you are, the more certain it is that your tax burden will exceed what you ever get out."[9]

But that's not the whole picture. When you widen the return-on-investment lens to take in Medicare as well as Social Security, the payout analysis shifts back to positive territory for nearly all of today's retirees. A 65-year-old single woman retiring in 2014 with median lifetime earnings can expect to get $544,000 in combined benefits from Social Security and Medicare if she lives out her actuarially allotted 20 years in average health. During her working years, she and her employer will have put in about $407,000 in taxes.[10] Current and future taxpayers will cover the remaining $137,000. In short, she's ahead of the game. So are most others her age, though the size of the windfall varies dramatically, depending on a person's demographics, economics, and health. For example, the returns wouldn't be quite as attractive if she were a single man at the median. Because of his shorter life span, he'll get back roughly $60,000 less in benefits. On the other hand, if she were a spouse in a one-earner married couple, the couple would have paid the same $407,000 in taxes, but would get about $910,000 in benefits, thanks to the generous formula for spousal coverage. And if she and her spouse were, say, a two-earner couple with a mix of higher earner and median earner, they would have paid much more into the system (about $1,055,000 by the Urban Institute's estimate) and also gotten back more in benefits (about $1,146,000)—a tidy sum, but not the windfall returns enjoyed by lower-income workers or single-wage-earner couples.

As those examples make clear, payout formulas serve a variety of social purposes. But if they're positive for virtually all current retirees, that leaves today's and tomorrow's taxpayers with a huge and escalating tab. The main driver of the rising costs has been Medicare, which was added to the Social Security system in 1965 by Lyndon Johnson, FDR's political heir, at a time when health costs were impoverishing millions of older adults. The program helps pay for the medical care of nearly everyone age 65 and older. Its tax rate is much lower than Social Security's (1.45% apiece for employers and employees on all wages, an additional 0.9% on individuals for earned income above $200,000). Without increases to this tax base, the Medicare Trust Fund, starting in 2030, will be unable to fully cover promised benefits. Partly that's because of population aging and increased longevity, but it's also because the program provides a guaranteed benefit—health care—whose costs have been rising for decades at a budget-busting pace.[11] Many economists fault Medicare itself for having contributed to these outsized increases. Its fee-for-service payment structure, they argue, creates incentives for doctors and hospitals to keep providing services, sometimes beyond medical need.[12] As is well-known, the US is in its own stratosphere when it comes to health costs. We currently spend 17.6% of our gross domestic product on medical care, roughly double the median share spent by the world's other economically advanced countries.

Medicare and its cousin, Medicaid (the health entitlement program for the poor), have for decades been the fastest-growing major programs in the federal budget. Medicare rose from 4% of federal spending in 1970 to 16% in 2011 and, absent policy changes, is on track to reach 19% in 2035. Medicaid is projected to consume 10% of the federal budget in 2035, up from 1% in 1970 and 8% in 2011.[13] By the time all the Boomers retire, half of the entire federal budget will go to Social Security, Medicare, and the nonchild portion of Medicaid. Much of the rest will go to paying interest on the national debt and maintaining the national defense, which leaves little in the coffers for investments in future economic growth. Fifty years ago, the government spent $3 on public investments that spur economic activity for every $1 it spent on entitlements. Today that ratio has flipped, and within a decade the government will be putting $5 into entitlements for every $1 that goes to roads, education, scientific research, and the like, according to an analysis by Third Way, a centrist public policy think tank.[14]

At this stage of our story, the Ponzi metaphor starts to sound, if anything, too kind. So let's spend a little time rallying to Social Security and Medicare's defense before confronting the generational equity issues they pose. There's a reason both programs are so popular: they're wildly successful. Social Security lifts more than 20 million people out of poverty, two-thirds of them elderly, the rest children, dependents, and the disabled. Without it, more than half of America's seniors would be living in poverty; with it, only about 1 in 10 seniors are poor. It provides 37% of the annual income for all Americans over age 65 and 80% of the income for seniors in the bottom half of the income distribution. Moreover, for the vast majority of retirees, Social Security is their only source of income that's not subject to investment risk, market fluctuations, or erosion by inflation—making it a psychological as well as financial safety valve. Medicare, too, has greatly improved the peace of mind of older Americans; without it, the rising cost of health care would be an even more crushing burden than it already is. And despite the perverse incentives created by its fee-for-service reimbursement system, the program in recent years has begun doing a better job of leveraging its vast market power to negotiate lower prices from health care providers.[15]

These two programs, in short, are in a league of their own when it comes to improving the quality of life of seniors. And because of that, they also improve the quality of life of everyone who loves and depends on seniors— which means virtually everyone. The fact that they've done so without being viewed as welfare is a testament to the enduring popular appeal of FDR's paradigm for Social Security as a contributions-based program. In 2012, in response to an op-ed column in the *New York Times* that proposed that Social

Security benefits be means-tested, Haskel Levi of Oakland, California, wrote a letter to the editor that went to the nub of the matter. "Entitlements without means-testing unites us into one country," he wrote. "Means-testing divides us into rich and poor, each resenting the other."[16] Levi is not alone in worrying that if you whittle away at the universality of the program, you risk bringing down the whole edifice. The old aphorism gets it right: means-testing makes for mean politics.

As both programs come under demographic stress, it's going to take a president with FDR's feel for the psyche of the public and the power of the bully pulpit to preserve them for future generations. The politics will be extremely difficult. There are deep partisan differences in Congress on this issue, with Democrats preferring to target tax hikes and/or benefit cuts on the well-to-do, and Republicans favoring a broad-based benefits cut. About the only thing that leaders of the two parties share is a mutual fear of seniors, the nation's most habitual voters, whose ranks keep growing and whose power to punish politicians who even think of tampering with Social Security or Medicare benefits is the stuff of political legend. But at the end of the day, the equities and the politics will work only if everyone is cajoled into taking a hit (except the neediest, who are the reason to have a safety net in the first place). A few months into his second term, President Obama took a small step in the direction of a comprehensive share-the-pain solution by rolling out a centrist blueprint for entitlement reform that married a slowdown in cost-of-living increases for retirees with an increase in taxes for the wealthy and corporations. Predictably, it provoked howls of protest from leaders in both parties, and Obama didn't put any political muscle into it. But as the math becomes unsustainable, a successor will have to finish the job.

GENERATIONAL EQUITY

When that day comes, Social Security's twenty-first-century saviors will do well to frame the fix around the imperatives of generational equity, a principle with a rich history in American political thought. Aside from the Declaration of Independence, the most famous passage in Thomas Jefferson's writings is the one in which he declares that "the earth belongs to the living, and not the dead," and that therefore no generation has a moral right to bind successor generations with debt. He goes on to say that the natural life span of a generation is 19 years and proposes that all laws—even the constitution itself—should expire "naturally" at the end of that period. This is arguably the most radical of Jefferson's ideas, but he was in some esteemed company. A few years earlier, Thomas Paine, a leading theorist of the Revolutionary era, had written that "it is the summit of human vanity, and shows a covetousness of power beyond the grave, to be dictating to the world to come." Paine believed a generation lasted for 30 years, not Jefferson's 19, but proposed the same remedy: no laws adopted in a democracy should have legal force beyond 30 years. Both Paine and Jefferson lived in a world where kings ruled by divine right. Both were champions of the then-radical notion that the people, not the monarchs, were sovereign. But having recoiled at the excesses of kings, both were keen to put constraints on the excesses of the public, including the bills that one generation might be tempted to leave for the next. As Jefferson put it, laws that had built-in expiration dates would "put the lenders, and the borrowers also, on their guard . . . [and] it would bridle the spirit of war."

His proposal was never put into effect, in part because it suffers from something of a logical fallacy. The public isn't composed of a single same-aged generational cohort whose members will all pass away in 19 (or 30) years; it's made up of people of all ages and life spans. Also, as Jefferson himself acknowledged, not all debts assumed by one generation represent a burden on future generations. Some enhance the future. So he provided for exceptions: "Debts may be incurred for purposes which interest the unborn, as well as the living: such debts are for repelling a conquest, the evils of which descend through many generations," Jefferson wrote. "Debts may even be incurred principally for the benefit of posterity. The term of 19 years might not be sufficient for discharging the debts in either of these cases."

Through the centuries, how has America measured up on this Jeffersonian test of intergenerational equity? The record is mixed. As Figure 14.1 illustrates, national debt as a share of GDP has tended to spike during periods of economic crisis or war, then retreat during periods of normalcy. The troublesome thing about the recent spike (as well as the long-term trend, which tilts upward after smoothing for peaks and valleys) is that the national debt has been approaching the historic World War II level despite the absence of a triggering event of that magnitude. Debt, of course, is not the only measure of the burdens and benefits that each generation leaves for its successors. But applying a broader set of metrics only makes the current picture more problematic. A 2013 cross-national study by a prominent European research institute found that the US ranked worst among 29 advanced countries in the degree to which it imposes unfair burdens on future generations.[17] The study looked at measures such as public debt per child, the ratio of childhood poverty to elderly poverty, and the elderly skew in social spending. An American might quibble with some of the study's inputs and weighting variables, but the story it tells is consistent with what policy analysts of all ideological stripes in the US have been saying for decades: we're robbing the future to pay for the present.

Figure 14.1

US Federal Debt as Share of GDP, 1790–2014

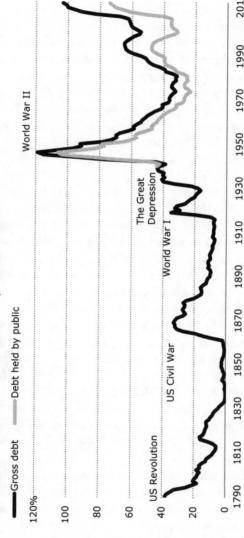

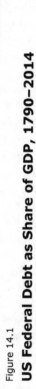

Note: Debt held by the public includes marketable (e.g. Treasury notes) and nonmarketable securities (e.g. savings bonds) issued by the US Treasury to finance government activities and owned by the public. Gross debt is debt held by the public plus securities held by federal trust funds and other government accounts.

Source: Bureau of the Public Debt (http://www.treasurydirect.gov/govt/reports/pd/histdebt/histdebt.htm), Office of Management and Budget (http://www.whitehouse.gov/omb/budget/Historicals), Bureau of Economic Analysis (http://www.bea.gov/national/index.htm#gdp), http://www.measuringworth.com/usgdp/, and Economic Report of the President (2015), Table B-20 (http://www.gpo.gov/fdsys/pkg/ERP-2015/content-detail.html)

GENERATIONAL INTERDEPENDENCE WITHIN FAMILIES

If the day comes when the safety net is downsized, how will the public cope? We can draw some lessons from recent history. Consider all the economic hardships that Americans have endured in recent years: the housing market crash, the persistently high unemployment, the rise in wealth and income inequality, the stagnation in standard-of-living growth. In the face of all this, the public safety net has been a key line of defense, but it hasn't operated in a vacuum. Increasingly, Americans have also turned to what Margaret Mead called "the only faithful human institution": their families. One particularly vivid example: During the worst of the 2007–2009 recession, the number of Americans living in multigenerational family households grew by about 10%, from 46.5 million to a record 51.4 million. Many of those households functioned as an unofficial antipoverty program. People living in them had a lower poverty rate than those who didn't, even though they also had lower incomes, according to a 2011 Pew Research analysis.[18] Multigenerational households come in multiple varieties—Boomerangers waiting for the economic clouds to lift so they can launch themselves into adulthood, grandmothers on nanny duty so their children can earn paychecks that will support the grandkids, middle-age adults who've taken up residence with elderly parents after they've lost a home or job. Robert Frost was more prescient than he knew when he wrote a century ago that "home is where, when you have to go there, they have to take you in."

Of course families, especially poor ones, cannot fully replace the safety net. The scale of the task is simply beyond them. But it's worth remembering that families are humanity's original safety net, and in many ways better suited than governments for the job. Means-testing in the hands of government will always be fraught, pitting group against group. Means-testing within the confines of a family is taken as a given. Without anyone having to spell out the rules, regulations or eligibility thresholds, support flows organically in the direction of need.[19]

For most of human history, this has meant parents caring for children when they're young, and children caring for parents when they're old. But in the modern era, the creation of a government safety net for the old has led most families to reverse the intergenerational flow of support at the latter stages of the life cycle. Now, more older parents support grown children than the other way around. Families remain a bulwark of intergenerational support, but they've adapted to new demographic and economic realities.

The most comprehensive effort in recent times to measure the magnitude and direction of these flows is the Health and Retirement Survey (HRS), funded by the National Institute on Aging and the Social Security

Administration. It has found that among parents ages 51 to 64, between two-thirds and three-quarters (depending on marital status) have given some form of money, time, or residential support to their grown children, while fewer than half reported *receiving* substantial transfers from those same children.[20] These patterns persist even as parents grow older. Among parents ages 65 to 79, more than half have given help in the form of money, care, or co-residence to a child in the past two years, while between 25% and 37% have received any form of assistance from a child during the same period. In a different study, Michael Hurd and his colleagues at the RAND Center for the Study of Aging estimated that the total amount of money (excluding bequests) that the typical parents ages 53 and older will give to their children throughout the remainder of the parents' lives is about $50,000.[21] Grandparents get into the act, too. A 2012 survey by the insurance company Metlife found that more than 6 in 10 (62%) grandparents ages 45 and older have given grandchildren money over the past 5 years and a 2009 Metlife survey indicated that the median amount these grandparents gave was about $3,000.[22]

In addition to these *inter vivos* transfers (those that occur while the giver is still alive), there's a much larger flow that comes in the form of inheritances. Scholars Edward Wolff and Maury Gittleman estimate that roughly 80% of all wealth that's passed down from elderly parents to adult children arrives when the giver has passed away. Boomers are now entering their peak inheritance years; many are in line to receive sizable sums from parents who are part of the wealthiest cohort of elderly adults in history. A Metlife study estimated that two-thirds of Boomers will ultimately receive some type of monetary inheritance. The size of inheritances is highly uneven, but researchers estimate that at the median, they will account for up to 40% of the wealth of the adults in the typical recipient household near the end of their lives.[23]

Turning from transfers of money to those of time and caregiving, here, too, the flow is more downstream than upstream. In any given year, a relatively small share (about 5%) of middle-age children provide substantial care for a parent or parent-in-law—in the form of help with eating, dressing, keeping the household books, or doing household chores.[24] By contrast, an estimated 40% of grandparents provide at least 100 hours of care to a grandchild annually, according to the HRS survey. And a growing share of grandchildren—10%—are actually living with a grandparent.

While families typically direct money and care toward need, they are human institutions, subject to the foibles and frailties of our glorious species. In other words, sometimes these transfers go horribly wrong. In *Someday All This Will Be Yours,* historian Hendrik Hartog explored the legal dramas and emotional traumas unleashed when elderly parents try to use the promise of inheritance to keep adult children in tow as caregivers.[25] If either party reneges on the deal, or if jealous siblings or aggrieved spouses take exception to the terms, all hell can break loose. Hartog dug up the records of probate court cases from the late nineteenth century and compared them with the same genre of litigation in the modern era. He concluded that while Social Security and Medicare may have changed some of the contours of the intergenerational bargain within families, they haven't repealed human nature or rescinded the complexities of the parent-child relationship at the latter stages of the life cycle.

And if human nature isn't unpredictable enough, there's another wild card in the deck—the changes in the structure of the family itself. "Relationships in aging families have become more fluid and less predictable, as reduced fertility and increased rates of divorce, remarriage and stepfamily formation have altered the micro-context in which intergenerational, spousal, and sibling relationships function," write family scholars Merril Silverstein and Roseann Giarrusso.[26] They note that intergenerational exchanges within families have always been driven by a complex mix of altruism and reciprocity, love and guilt, obligation and resentment. These intrafamily exchanges are influenced, too, by a variety of demographic factors—daughters, for example, tend to be more attentive to elderly parents than are sons; elderly blacks and Hispanics tend to compensate for low incomes by providing more downstream support in time and housing. Now, on top of these complications, come the sweeping social, economic, and demographic changes that have shaken the family tree to its roots and that threaten to leave older adults with fewer strong bonds to their younger family members.

THE NEXT COMPACT

Going forward, it's unrealistic to expect families to take on more of the challenge of caring for the elderly; it's quite possible they'll do less. That puts the question that has animated this book squarely in the laps of public policy-makers: how best to honor our commitments to the old without bankrupting the young and starving the future? The most promising answer, in my view, lies with a Jeffersonian approach based on the proposition that *no generation should be asked to provide a level of support for older folks beyond what its members can expect to receive when they grow old themselves.* Or to put it more simply: *every generation should pay its own way.* That ideal puts generational equity where it belongs, at the heart of the effort to modernize Social Security and Medicare. It will infuse some urgency into the issue, because with each passing day, the fixes get harder and the generational skew further out of balance.

Liberals would have to ask themselves how they can justify taxing the hard-pressed young to maintain benefits for the well-to-do old. Conservatives would need to confront the folly of not investing in the nation's future workforce and economic vitality. Leaders from all parts of the ideological spectrum would be able to borrow the most appealing idea in Roosevelt's original sales pitch—you get back what you put in—but apply it to generations rather than individuals.

All of this is easier said than done. Roosevelt had the advantage of selling the public on a benefit. The system's saviors will probably need to sell a retrenchment. Every group except the neediest will likely have to take a hit—young and old, taxpayers and beneficiaries. The cuts to current retirees could be modest (for example, a slowdown in annual cost-of-living adjustments for all, or targeted reductions aimed at the well-to-do) but anything that hurts seniors makes for scary politics. They are deemed to be untouchable not just because elected officials fear them but because their children and grandchildren love them—and benefit from their economic well-being. As the survey findings presented in Chapter 5 make clear, cutting benefits to retirees is the public's least favorite way to reform the system. America's growing racial and ethnic diversity adds to the challenge. In any society, but especially an increasingly heterogeneous one, people are more willing to sacrifice for their own children than for other people's children. That explains why the family is the most resilient safety net.

But this cause is by no means hopeless. The changes explored throughout this book—political, demographic, economic, attitudinal—align in ways that will eventually compel a fix, and perhaps sooner than seems imaginable in today's politically gridlocked Washington, DC. For one thing, the changing demographics of the electorate could create some surprising new alliances on this issue. In years past, the generational equity argument was the near exclusive preserve of small-government conservatives. Now, however, the groups that stand to gain the most from any generational equity-based formula for reform are the young and minorities—the country's most liberal voters. Can fiscal hawks and social policy progressives find common ground on modernizing the safety net? They can if they pursue their overlapping interests.

The absence of any public appetite for generational warfare is another reason for optimism. Despite their many differences, young and old in America aren't spoiling for a fight on this issue. They like each other too much. Their fates are too intertwined. No one needs to explain to them that Grandma's well-being and Junior's are braided together. They know. And they view this interdependence in moral as well as practical terms. If a family or government doesn't provide a safety net for older adults who would

otherwise spend their golden years in poverty, the public believes these enti-
ties have failed a moral test.

But, with Jefferson, Americans of all ages and ideologies also believe it is
wrong for a society to burden its children with excessive debt and diminished
opportunity. They know that every American alive today is the beneficiary of
all the generations that came before—the ones that fought the wars, built the
infrastructure, conducted the scientific and medical research, educated the
children, promoted the entrepreneurship, and nurtured the values that have
made this such an exceptional country. They would like to pass the torch in
similar style.

Moreover, at least among policy elites, there's a much broader consensus on the need to solve this challenge with pragmatic compromise than is
apparent from the relentlessly partisan rhetoric one hears in Congress and
on the presidential campaign trail. Indeed, if bipartisan blue-ribbon panels
or mainstream editorial and opinion writers were magically empowered to
resolve the problem, one suspects the elusive "grand bargain" on entitlements
and taxes would have already been struck. And generational equity would be
a key element of the fix. What these thought leaders *can* do is frame the challenge in generational terms; this has been happening with growing frequency.
For example, in the depths of the manufactured government shutdown crisis
of 2013, a Thomas Friedman column in the *New York Times* was headlined
"Sorry, Kids. We Ate It All." It told the story of an unlikely duo of prominent
Baby Boomers—Stanley Druckenmiller, a billionaire hedge fund manager
and philanthropist, and Geoffrey Canada, the legendary Harlem-based social
activist and educator—who have been touring college campuses and urging
students to get more involved in the political process so they can demand a
more equitable share of government outlays. To critics who say they're foment-
ing a generation war, Friedman quotes Druckenmiller's sharp response: "No,
that war already happened, and the kids lost. We're just trying to recover some
scraps for them."[27] As noted, the war metaphor isn't likely to play well with
any generation. But the equity argument should play well with all of them.
Among the organizations that understand this is the AARP, the massive and
muscular lobby group for adults over the age of 50. It is committed to protect-
ing the interests of today's retirees, but in the past year its leaders have begun
sending public signals that adjustments need to be made to Social Security
and Medicare to preserve those programs for tomorrow's retirees (and the
AARP's future members).[28] Across all realms of society—business, labor, educators, nonprofits, and elected officials from both parties—this consensus is
deepening.

At the end of the day, though, this is a challenge that can only be overcome with presidential leadership. What's needed is someone who can use the bully pulpit to educate the public about the inequities in the status quo. Someone who can explain that FDR's great innovation of the twentieth century—the radical improvement of old age in America—can work for the rising generations in a new century only if the safety net is modernized. The demographics have changed. The old math doesn't work anymore.

ACKNOWLEDGMENTS

As the author of a book built on a bedrock of data, I owe my first thanks to the colleagues at the Pew Research Center who created so much of that data. We work in a highly collaborative setting. Some of these coworkers conceived and carried out the original research, others wrote up the findings, others disseminated it in various formats and media. I'm lucky to count them as friends as well as collaborators. My gratitude to:

Jodie Allen, Richard Auxier, Catherine Barker, James Bell, Anna Brown, Andrea Caumont, Leah Christian, D'Vera Cohn, Alan Cooperman, Claudia Deane, Drew DeSilver, Michael Dimock, Carroll Doherty, Meredith Dost, Bruce Drake, Maeve Duggan, Susannah Fox, Matthew Frei, Richard Fry, Cary Funk, Ana Gonzalez-Barrera, Sara Goo, Elizabeth Gross, Mark Jurkowitz, Michael Keegan, Scott Keeter, Jocelyn Kiley, Donald Kimelman, Rakesh Kochhar, Andrew Kohut, Vidya Krishnamurthy, Amanda Lenhart, Gretchen Livingston, Gustavo López, Mark Lopez, Luis Lugo, Mary Madden, David Masci, Kyley McGeeney, Andrew Mercer, Amy Mitchell, Rich Morin, Seth Motel, Alan Murray, Russ Oates, Kim Parker, Jeffrey Passel, Eileen Patten, Michael Piccorossi, Kristen Purcell, Lee Rainie, Molly Rohal, Tom Rosenstiel, Jessica Schillinger, Elizabeth Sciupac, Aaron Smith, Greg Smith, Sandy Stencel, Renee Stepler, Bruce Stokes, Roberto Suro, Robyn Tomlin, Wendy Wang, Bill Webster, Richard Wike, and Diana Yoo.

A number of them made special contributions to the book that warrant special note. Chapter 11, Living Digital, was written by Lee Rainie. As founder and director of the Pew Research Center's Internet & American Life Project, Lee was responsible for most of the research presented in that chapter; he also interviewed Natalie Marks (a pseudonym), the young woman whose digital coming-of-age story gives the chapter its narrative arc. Chapter 12, Getting Old, draws on portions of a fine 2013 essay about the scientific and ethical dimensions of radical life extension written by David Masci for the Pew Research Center's Religion & Public Life Project. In Chapter 13, Empty Cradle, Gray World, the section that looks at cross-national trends in median age, population size, and dependency ratios is based on the work of Rakesh Kochhar, the center's senior economist. Chapter 10, Nones on the Rise, draws heavily on a report of the same name published by our religion project; Alan Cooperman and Greg Smith worked on the original report and helped me adapt it for the book. Scott Keeter, who was the center's director of survey research from its founding in 2004 until the end of 2015, and continues to serve as a consultant, wrote the Appendix I chapter, How We Know What We Know. Eileen Patten has been indispensable in her role as editorial assistant on this book project, keeping tabs on charts, tables, text, and footnotes while also holding down her day job as a research analyst with the center's Social & Demographic Trends Project. Diana Yoo, the center's art director, helped adapt the charts and tables to book format. I'm grateful to them all.

The terrain covered by this book has been explored by a wide array of scholars, academics, and journalists, many who have far more subject area expertise than I do. Their names appear throughout the book in citations, quotes, and footnotes. Their work has sharpened my thinking as I've looked for meaning in the data. I'm grateful for their intellectual stimulation.

I owe a thank-you to the center's parent organization, the Pew Charitable Trusts, including President and CEO Rebecca W. Rimel and members of the board, for their generous support over the years. And to the Pew Research Center's board, led by Donald Kimelman, a friend of more than 30 years. I'm especially grateful to Peter Bernstein, a Pew Research board member who served as the agent for this book. Thanks as well to the entire team at Public-Affairs, especially Clive Priddle, the publisher, and Melissa Raymond, the managing editor, who handled the manuscript with a sharp pencil and unerring eye.

Finally, a few words about the two people to whom the book is dedicated.

Andrew Kohut, the founding director of the Pew Research Center, was a man of enormous intellectual passion, integrity, curiosity, and entrepreneurship. He figured out decades ago that if you brought social scientists and journalists into the same sandbox and gave them the right tools, values, and mission, you could create a new kind of institution—a "fact tank"—that helps people understand the world around them. Andy and I didn't begin our professional association until I was in my mid-50s, but if anyone were to ask me to name the best teacher I ever had, it would be him. Scores upon scores of his colleagues at the Pew Research Center and the other organizations he led, including Gallup and Princeton Survey Research Associates, share a similar sense of awe and gratitude about Andy. He died on September 8, 2015, at the age of 73, after a long battle with leukemia. Rest in peace, my friend.

And last, Stefanie, forever Stefanie. She and I met at age 3 and married at 21. Now we're on the doorstep of old age (how can that be?) with a family that spans four generations, from our 1-year-old granddaughter to Stefanie's 90-year-old parents. Stef is the hub of this loving family—nanny to the youngest, caregiver to the oldest, touchstone of the whole flock. Better than anyone else I know, she embodies what it means for the generations within a family to live interdependently and in harmony. Thanks for everything, my darling.

APPENDIX I: HOW WE KNOW WHAT WE KNOW

SCOTT KEETER

This book takes a sweeping look at changes in the demographic characteristics, political attitudes, social and religious values, technology and media habits, and economic circumstances of the American public. Most of its data come from surveys conducted by researchers at the Pew Research Center, other organizations, and the federal government, particularly the US Census Bureau.[1]

Accurate and unbiased information about the public is vital to the health of any democracy. Surveys are an important source for that information. As political scientist Sidney Verba put it, "Surveys produce just what democracy is supposed to produce—equal representation of all citizens. The sample survey is rigorously egalitarian; it is designed so that each citizen has an equal chance to participate and an equal voice when participating."[2] This egalitarian aspect of good survey research helps remove, or at least reduce, biases associated with wealth, literacy, education, and other factors that make the voices of some people in the political process louder than others.

But surveys face daunting challenges because changing lifestyles, new technologies, and rising concerns about privacy have made it more difficult for researchers to reach respondents. In recent decades, survey response rates have declined dramatically and the cost of conducting surveys has grown. Despite these challenges, however, well-designed surveys continue to provide accurate data. And digital technology also provides researchers with new and potentially better ways to conduct surveys and gather nonsurvey data about attitudes and behaviors.

Even well-designed surveys have limitations, of course. Studying attitudes and behaviors is a messy business because humans are so complicated. As scientific as survey research strives to be, it remains as much an art as a science.

The goal of this appendix is to pull back the curtain on survey research and provide an unvarnished look at the techniques, challenges, strengths, and weaknesses of our methods. We know (from our own surveys!) that we operate in an era of pervasive skepticism about the veracity of all sources of information, and we believe transparency is the most effective way to build trust among the consumers of our research.

Creating a good survey requires attention to a host of details, most of which can be distilled down to two basic processes that affect the quality of the data produced: *measurement* and *representation*.

> **Measurement** encompasses the questions and questionnaires, the interaction between interviewer and respondent (or the respondent and a paper or Web questionnaire), the collection of any other non-interview data important to the goals of the study (e.g., the voting records of respondents), and the accurate recording and tabulation of the data.
>
> **Representation** refers to steps taken to ensure that data are collected from individuals who collectively are representative of the target population of interest. This includes defining the relevant population, obtaining or creating a means of sampling from it (called a sampling frame), drawing the sample, contacting and interviewing the sampled persons, and making the necessary statistical adjustments to ensure that the resulting sample conforms to the population to which it is being generalized. We will examine how good surveys are designed to provide the most accurate data and minimize the errors in each of these two processes.

The goal of maximizing survey quality in both measurement and representativeness drives many important choices we make in designing a survey project. As with most things in life, there are inevitable trade-offs among quality, speed, and cost that must be considered. Since resources are always finite, decisions must be made about which aspects of the survey would benefit the most from more investment.

MEASUREMENT

"What we've got here is failure to communicate." So said the warden in a classic scene from the movie *Cool Hand Luke*. It's no surprise that many survey research experts consider writing and administering survey questions to be the most difficult and critical part of the survey enterprise, given humankind's long experience with failures to communicate effectively. This is one realm of survey research where science and practical judgment interact most closely. A great deal of scientific research has been done on how to create effective questionnaires and how best to administer a survey, but the process also calls on our instincts and intuition about how language is understood, where idioms may work better than formal words or phrases, and how cultural differences in a population can affect how questions are understood and what reactions they are likely to provoke.

Figure A.1

Your Survey

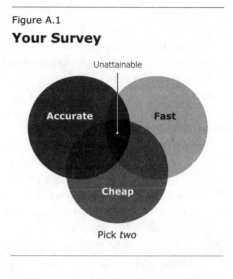

The heart of a good survey is the conversation with the respondent. All of the effort made to obtain a good sample of the population is wasted if the interview does not yield the information it seeks. Different ways of asking about objective facts can make it easier or harder for respondents to recall and report the information being sought. When measuring subjective phenomena such as attitudes, it can be difficult to phrase questions in an unbiased way, especially for controversial topics. Consumers of poll data frequently disagree about whether questions are worded in a way that influences the answer.

Survey Mode

Before a respondent can be asked a question, the researcher must choose a mode of interview. The broad choice is between interviewer administration and self-administration. Within each of these, there are further choices. Interviewer-administered surveys can be conducted in person (sometimes referred to as "face-to-face") or by telephone. Self-administered surveys can use low-tech paper-and-pencil questionnaires or much more elaborate web-based questionnaires with automatic skipping and branching, video clips, and visual aids such as virtual shopping carts. Some surveys use more than one mode. The American Community Survey, a large population survey conducted by the US Census Bureau and the source of much government data used in this book, conducts interviews in person, by telephone, by mail, and on the Web. The use of multiple modes helps the survey achieve a high rate of response at the lowest cost by trying to make contact in different ways (beginning with the mail and Internet, which are less expensive than phone or personal visits) and offering respondents a choice of ways to participate.

The choice of a mode (or modes) depends on many factors. Cost is a big consideration, since interviewer-administered surveys are usually much more expensive than self-administered surveys. But for some subjects and populations, the use of an interviewer is essential. For example, populations with low levels of literacy may struggle with a questionnaire that they have to read and answer. The National Health and Nutrition Examination Survey combines personal interviews with physical examinations that collect clinical data on respondents, such as height, weight, blood pressure, and blood and saliva samples.

The mode of interview is sometimes determined by the type of sampling used in a survey. Telephone surveys are a popular mode in part because telephone numbers can be randomly sampled in a way that ensures that about 98% of households have a chance of being included. Because of the existence of a national database of nearly every valid postal address in the US (the "Delivery Sequence File"), mail surveys have actually become more popular in the past few years because sampling for them is very straightforward.

There are important measurement implications in the choice of a survey mode. Questions that require respondents to choose among a large number of options are difficult in an interviewer-administered mode because people cannot accurately recall more than four or five different things in a single task. Even with just four or five options, certain biases can sometimes affect respondent behavior, such as the tendency to better recall the last options heard (called the "recency" effect). In a self-administered survey, respondents can see all of the options at the same time, potentially reducing the tendency to favor the last items on the list. Additionally, respondents may be more likely to misunderstand certain words when they hear them than when they see them. "Allowed" and "outlawed" sound very similar but obviously mean very different things.

The presence of an interviewer can be beneficial in some situations. Interviewers can manage the pace of the interview, motivate respondents to think carefully about the questions, and provide positive feedback about the respondents' progress through the interview. In some self-administered surveys, respondents may speed through the questions without giving them adequate attention. If respondents become bored or discouraged, they may be more likely to quit the interview when an interviewer is not present.

One of the most important reasons for the popularity of self-administered survey modes is the concern about *social desirability bias*, the tendency of people to try to present themselves in a positive light when describing their attitudes or behaviors to another person. Along the same lines, people may try to avoid responses that create tension in an interview or offend the interviewer. Not surprisingly, characteristics of the interviewers themselves, such as gender or race, have been shown to influence responses. Studies have found that some people will express less opposition to affirmative action when they are interviewed by a black interviewer than by a white interviewer. We will take a deeper look at the phenomenon of social desirability bias below.

Language

According to the US Census Bureau, about 1 in 5 Americans speak a language other than English at home. Though many of these people can speak English, about 8% of the population cannot speak English well enough to participate comfortably in a survey interview. Since most general public surveys are conducted in English, the multilingual nature of the population means that the potential for bias exists if certain groups are unable to participate in the survey because of a language barrier.

Many surveys today, including nearly all of Pew Research's, routinely include a Spanish-language version of the interview and, for interviewer-administered surveys, an interviewer who is bilingual. Because Spanish is the most common non-English language in the US (62% of all non-English speakers), having Spanish versions of our surveys substantially reduces the share of the population we are unable to include because of a language barrier.

Still, for surveys of certain subpopulations in the US, it is essential to include additional languages. Interviews for a 2012 Pew Research Center survey of Asian Americans were conducted in English as well as Cantonese, Hindi, Japanese, Korean, Mandarin, Tagalog, and Vietnamese. Our two Muslim-American surveys were conducted in English, Arabic, Farsi, and Urdu. And when we conduct surveys around the world we, of course, do so in the language or languages of the country in which we are operating.

Asking Good Questions About Objective Phenomena

For the survey researcher, the practical challenge is to write questions that obtain the needed information from respondents with a minimum of error and minimal burden to the respondent. Many considerations inform the choices we make, among them: Do respondents have the cognitive ability and vocabulary to understand the question? Will they all understand it in the same way? Do they have the necessary knowledge to answer it? Will they be willing to answer it—and to answer honestly?

Researchers often take it for granted that respondents understand words the same way they do. But they often don't. During the early days of the AIDS epidemic in the US, researchers at a university were testing questions for a survey on sexual behavior. A middle-age woman was taking part in an in-depth interview that would help researchers see how people understood the terminology to be used in the final survey questionnaire. A critical question was about sexual orientation. The woman was asked, "Are you heterosexual, homosexual, or bisexual?" The woman thought about the question for a moment, and then replied: "Well, it's just me and my husband, so I guess we're bisexual." The researchers decided that the question needed some work.

Sometimes respondents understand the words but interpret them differently. Survey researchers often use so-called vague quantifiers in questions to provide respondents with a shorthand way to summarize their feelings and experiences. As a simple way of distinguishing between people who are familiar with a subject and those who are not, a common Pew Research question asks respondents how much they have heard about a topic, for example: "How much, if anything, have you heard about negotiations between the United States and Iran on Iran's nuclear program? Have you heard a lot, a little, or nothing at all?" The terms "a lot," "a little," and "nothing at all" are undefined and undoubtedly mean somewhat different things to different people, but function effectively in practice to separate those who are engaged with a topic and those who are not.

Vague quantifiers can be helpful when asking about factual matters that are too complex or detailed to be recalled accurately. But they can also lead to trouble. In the movie *Annie Hall*, Alvy (played by Woody Allen) and Annie (played by Diane Keaton) appear in a split-screen scene with their respective therapists, each of whom asks about the frequency of sex that they have. Alvy says, "Hardly ever. Maybe three times a week." Annie says, "Constantly. I'd say three times a week." They agreed on the frequency but not on how to characterize it.

Research on cognitive psychology offers guidance on such matters. Estimates of the frequency of certain activities can differ depending on whether the question is asked in an open-ended way or with categories of ranges. Moreover, the categories offered can affect the results. Asked about daily hours of television viewing, respondents will report higher levels if the categories imply that higher amounts are normal. Similarly, more people will say they did an activity or belong to a specific group if the question is asked in a "yes or no" format than if it is a "check all that apply" one. In 1994, a national exit poll gave voters a list of activities and asked them to check all that applied to them. The poll found that 14% were union members or in a union household; in 1998 the exit poll asked the same question, but in a "yes/no" format, and found that 22%

were from union households. Did union membership among voters increase 8 points in four years? Almost certainly not. The change in format from "check all" to "yes/no" accounts for the increase. The yes/no format requires respondents to focus on each item; the check-all format may encourage respondents to simply scan the list and possibly miss one or more relevant items.[3]

Social Desirability and the Mode of Interview

One of the toughest challenges in polling is ensuring that we get honest answers from people about behaviors and characteristics that are sensitive— because some actions are seen as socially desirable or undesirable. One study found that 94% of people reported washing their hands after using the toilet but an observational study in public restrooms in five cities found that only 68% actually did so.[4] Voting in elections—both past and future—is often overstated. And several studies have found that people understate their weight and overstate their height in telephone surveys.[5]

The presence of an interviewer can influence respondents in ways that may hinder honest reporting. Respondents are aware that they are talking with another person who could judge them or be discomfited by their answers. Reports of illegal drug use, certain sexual behaviors, and cheating on taxes are higher in self-administered than an interviewer-administered surveys. Similarly, reported donations to charity are lower when an interview is self-administered.[6]

In 2014, we conducted an experiment to examine the impact of the mode of interview with our probability-based survey panel, the American Trends Panel.[7] Half of the respondents were assigned to take a survey by phone, while the other half took it online. The groups were nearly identical demographically, so any differences in results should be attributed to the mode of the interview.[8] Significantly more people reported regular conversations with their neighbors when interviewed on the phone (58%) than on the Web (47%). And fewer people reported in a phone interview (20%) that at some point in the past year they did not have enough money to buy food than said this in the Web interview (28%). There was no difference on this question by mode among respondents with higher incomes, but the difference was 12 percentage points among those with incomes below $30,000.

Measuring Attitudes

Polls on matters of public policy can provide important information for the operation of a democracy, but they lose their value if questions are worded

Figure A.2

Fewer Report Financial Troubles on the Phone Than on the Web

% giving answer in each survey mode

Standard of living is somewhat or much worse than parents' at same age

	Phone	Web
All	20	28
Whites	22	26
Blacks	9	29
Hispanics	20	31

Not enough money to buy food

	Phone	Web
All	20	28
$75,000+	5	7
$30,000-$74,999	16	26
Less than $30,000	39	51

Needed to see a doctor but did not because of the cost

	Phone	Web
All	22	28
White	21	22
Non-white	23	40

0   25   50%

Source: Pew Research Center's American Trends Panel survey, Jul. 7–Aug. 4, 2014

in a way that, intentionally or not, puts a thumb on the scale. In this regard, skeptics of survey research have a legitimate concern. However, it is not the case that polls can obtain any result that a pollster desires. Or at least, not a halfway credible pollster.

Much of the work of the Pew Research Center focuses on describing opinions and attitudes about public issues. Our philosophy about opinion measurement draws upon approaches developed by polling pioneer George Gallup and further refined by Pew Research founding director Andrew Kohut during his years at Gallup. It assumes that the public has values and preferences that are important for the government to heed, even if the public does not know all the details about the issues of the day. One implication of this philosophy is that pollsters should not ask people complicated and detailed questions about issues that they may not be familiar with—but also that we should not shy away from asking about important issues, even if not everyone will be an expert about the specifics. A corollary is that it is often valuable to try to gauge knowledge and familiarity with issues and use this information analytically in looking at opinions. For example, people who reported having heard "a lot" about the government's program of collecting communications data as a part of its antiterrorism program were much more likely than those who had only heard "a little" to say that social media sites should not save any information about users' activity on the sites.[9]

Similarly, great caution must be exercised in providing respondents with information in a question (e.g., "As you may know, there have been a series of corruption scandals involving government officials in Washington this past year"); such information has a high potential to influence the responses in unpredictable ways.

This general approach is consistent with a popular perspective in the field of attitude research aptly crystallized by political scientist John Zaller: "[C]itizens do not typically carry around in their heads fixed attitudes on every issue on which a pollster may happen to inquire; rather, they construct 'opinion statements' on the fly as they confront each new issue."[10] For respondents, this process of constructing opinion statements—typically, choosing among options provided by a pollster—relies heavily on ideas that are "top of the mind" for the respondents; hence the concern about pollsters providing potentially biasing information in the question itself.

A different view is that sometimes surveys are measuring "non-attitudes," essentially random responses from uninformed respondents. One implication of this view is that we should not ask opinion questions of people who are uninformed or uninterested in an issue. We sometimes take this advice, particularly when asking for reactions to events that not everyone may have heard about. But for most public opinion topics we poll, past research has shown that even the responses of people who have little familiarity with the issues are meaningful in that they are linked to underlying political values and are reasonably stable over time.

One other good practice in attitude measurement is the use, whenever possible, of multiple measures. It is an axiom of the scientific study of attitudes that every measure contains a mixture of the truth and some random error. By this logic, we should combine multiple measures of any concept of interest because the truth will accumulate and the random errors will tend to cancel each other out. Beyond the scientific logic, it makes sense that many different ways of measuring an attitude will yield insights about it that are unavailable from any single measure.

"Don't Know" Responses

Another aspect of the debate over non-attitudes is the practical question of whether to provide an explicit "don't know" (DK) or "no opinion" option to survey respondents. A long line of research has demonstrated that many respondents will choose a DK option if it is offered to them since it may save them the effort of searching their memory or formulating an opinion. Yet most pollsters choose not to provide an explicit DK option for most questions. Rather, the standard practice is to allow respondents to volunteer that they don't know or have no opinion.

While the presence or absence of a DK option can affect the share of those who express no opinion, it is not the case that everyone will answer any question put to them. For more than a decade, we asked a question about free trade agreements worded as follows: "In general, do you think that free trade agreements like NAFTA and the policies of the World Trade Organization have been a good thing or a bad thing for the United States?" The typical rate of no opinion—volunteered in the telephone interview—was higher than 20%. Questions about international affairs are especially likely to find high levels of DK responses, given the relatively low salience of the topic area for many Americans.

Agree/Disagree Questions

Over the years we have come to be wary of asking questions in an agree/disagree format because of a psychological phenomenon known as "acquiescence bias." This refers to the tendency for survey respondents to agree with statements regardless of their content. The phenomenon is easily demonstrated with some of our own questions.

Public opinion about the use of military force has ongoing political relevance, so the Pew Research Center developed a question in 1987 to measure the public's general orientation toward using force to keep the peace. Asked in a series of agree/disagree questions measuring political values, the question read as follows: "The best way to ensure peace is through military strength." This question typically finds a small majority of the public agreeing. After concerns about acquiescence bias led us in 1994 to change how we polled about political values, this question was converted to a forced choice format. Respondents are introduced to the series with the instruction: "I'm going to read you some pairs of statements that will help us understand how you feel about a number of things. As I read each pair, tell me whether the FIRST statement or the SECOND statement comes closer to your own views—even if neither is exactly right." The question on the use of military force asks respondents to choose between these options: "The best way to achieve peace is through military strength," or "Good diplomacy is the best way to achieve peace." This version produces the opposite result—a majority chooses diplomacy over military strength.

Agree/disagree questions have other problems besides their potential for acquiescence bias. They are cognitively more difficult than questions in other formats and sometimes involve respondents having to think through double negatives. One commonly used question in political science reads as follows: "Public officials don't care what people like me think." If you believe that public officials *do* care, you must disagree with the statement. There is a high potential for confusion.[11]

But these and similar questions also illustrate the practical trade-offs inherent in public opinion research. The trend data from Pew Research's agree/disagree values series (dating to 1987) are very valuable because they allow us to measure change over time in public attitudes. As a result, we began to conduct a parallel series of surveys with the agree/disagree format in order to be able to maintain the long-term trends. This highlights the value of reliable measures in survey research. Reliability refers to the likelihood that a question will obtain consistent results over time. Assuming a person's attitude on a subject has not changed, a reliable question should obtain the same answer at two different points in time. And if the person's attitude *has* changed, a reliable question would detect that change. Even if we have concerns about whether the absolute level of an attitude measured by a particular question is correct (as we do with many agree/disagree questions), a reliable question should reflect changes in the attitude that occur over time. As a consequence, we continue to ask a set of questions that aren't necessarily the best way to measure attitudes, but nonetheless provide useful information about the trend of public opinion.

Figure A.3

Acquiescence Bias

Agree-Disagree Format

The best way to ensure peace is through military strength

(55% agree, 42% disagree)

Forced Choice Format

The best way to ensure peace is through military strength (33%)

OR

Diplomacy is the best way to ensure peace (55%)

Source: Pew Research survey, Sep. and Oct. 1999

Open and Closed Questions

One big choice pollsters face in measuring attitudes is whether to ask open-ended or closed-ended questions. Closed-ended questions are the more familiar, in which respondents are offered a choice among various options as answers to a question. Open-ended questions allow respondents to answer in their own words without the guidance of explicit response options. Familiar closed-ended questions include the following: "Do you approve or disapprove of the way Barack Obama is handling his job as president?" "Are you hearing mostly good news about the economy these days, mostly bad news about the economy, or a mix of both good and bad news?" As open-ended questions, these could ask, "What do you think about the job that Barack Obama is doing as president?" Or, "What kind of news are you hearing about the economy these days?" The open-ended versions would produce much less structured answers and would be interesting but possibly very difficult to categorize and difficult to track over time.

Open-ended questions are very valuable for certain purposes. We use them extensively as follow-up questions to closed-ended questions to understand why people have certain views. They are particularly valuable in measuring opinions about the most important problems facing the country. But open-ended questions have some drawbacks, including the fact that respondents vary in how articulate and verbose they are. Some people may be better able to express their opinion in an open-ended format than are other people. Interviewers also vary in how skilled they are at transcribing responses. And open-ended questions can be very difficult to code and summarize.

Open-ended questions can also lead to different conclusions than closed-ended questions, and it's not always clear which type is more accurate. The exit polls run by a consortium of news organizations in the 2004 presidential election found a plurality of respondents choosing "moral values" as the most important issue in the election, slightly higher than the number who chose the war in Iraq or the economy. This controversial finding led us to conduct an experiment in the days after the election. We asked one group of respondents the exit poll version of the question (with seven options); another group was asked the same question in an open-ended fashion.

The closed-ended version produced a result similar to the exit poll finding: 27% chose moral values, compared with 22% for Iraq and 21% for the economy and jobs. The open-ended version found that "moral values" was indeed important to many voters (14%), but it was not the top issue. Iraq was mentioned by 25%, and the economy was mentioned by 12%.

Why the difference? Among the likely explanations is the fact that "moral values" is a general category of concerns and not a specific issue in the way that the war in Iraq is. As a result, "moral values" may encompass many issues. Indeed, our survey found exactly this when it asked people who selected moral values, "What comes to mind when you think about 'moral values'?" People mentioned many different things, including issues such as gay marriage and abortion, but also the personal qualities of the candidates, religion, and traditional values.

Attitude Measurement and the Mode of Interview

As noted earlier, the mode of interview can affect how people report on their experiences and behavior. But it can also affect the reporting of attitudes for many of the same reasons. Respondents may feel a need to present themselves in a more positive light to an interviewer, leading to an overstatement of socially desirable attitudes and an understatement of opinions they fear would elicit disapproval. Some people may not be concerned with how they appear to an interviewer but are reluctant to express highly negative attitudes because they fear that doing so may make the interviewer uncomfortable.

Some of the largest mode differences in our mode experiment were seen in the ratings of political figures. Public views—on both sides of the political aisle—are considerably more negative when expressed via the Web than over the phone. Hillary Clinton's ratings are a good example of this pattern. When asked on the phone, 19% of respondents told interviewers they have a "very unfavorable" opinion of Clinton; that number jumps to 27% on the Web. Among Republicans and those who lean Republican, fully 53% interviewed on the Web had a

Figure A.4

What One Issue Mattered Most in Your Vote?

% saying the following mattered most to them in deciding how they voted for president

	Fixed List*	Open-end**
Moral values (net)	27%	14%
Moral values	--	9
Social issues^	--	3
Candidate's morals	--	2
Iraq	22	25
Economy/Jobs	21	12
Terrorism	14	9
Health Care	4	2
Education	4	1
Taxes	3	1
Other	4	31
Honesty (integrity)	--	5
Like/dislike Bush	--	5
Like/dislike Kerry	--	3
Direction of country	--	2
Leadership	--	2
Foreign policy	--	2
Don't know	1	5

*First choice among the seven items provided on the exit poll list
** Unprompted verbatim first response to open-ended question
^Abortion, gay marriage, stem cells

Source: Pew Research Center survey, Nov. 2004

"very unfavorable" opinion of Clinton, compared with only 36% of those interviewed on the phone. Very similar differences were seen among Democrats when asked about such Republican figures as Sarah Palin and George W. Bush.

Those who took the phone survey were considerably more likely than those interviewed on the Web to say that gays, lesbians, blacks, and Hispanics face a lot of discrimination, possibly reflecting a feeling on the part of some respondents that they *should* acknowledge that these groups are discriminated against. But black respondents showed the opposite pattern when asked about

Figure A.5

Different Answers on Web and Phone

% giving answer in each survey mode

Very satisfied with your ...	Web	Phone	Diff.
Family life	44	62	18
Social life	29	43	14

There is a lot of discrimination against ...

	Web	Phone	Diff.
Gays and lesbians	48	62	14
Blacks	44	54	10
Hispanics	42	54	12
Women	31	33	2

Very unfavorable opinion of ...	Phone	Web	
Hillary Clinton	19	27	8
Michelle Obama	16	25	9
Sarah Palin	27	40	13
George W. Bush	22	31	9

0   25   50   75%

Source: Pew Research Center's American Trends Panel survey, Jul. 7–Aug. 4, 2014

discrimination against blacks: more of those interviewed on the Web (86%) than on the phone (71%) said that blacks face a lot of discrimination. Perhaps some black respondents may have felt freer to express this sentiment in the comparative anonymity of a Web interview than to another person on the phone.

These examples (and those from our discussion of measures of behaviors and experiences) raise the question of which mode of interview is more accurate. It is difficult to say, but the consensus among experts in this field is that self-administered surveys obtain more accurate answers to sensitive questions. Does this mean that people are even more negative about politicians of the other party than we think, based on years of data from telephone surveys? Possibly, but it's also worth noting that how people express themselves in the presence of others is its own kind of reality. If people who harbor strong prejudices against minorities feel the need to temper their views in interactions with other people, that says something about their attitudes and values.

Building Questionnaires: The Danger of Order Effects

Just as question wording can make a big difference in polling results, so, too, can question order. Each question in an interview can establish the context in which subsequent questions are evaluated. Concern about the impact of prior questions is the reason we and other pollsters typically ask about presidential approval at or near the beginning of an interview. If we were to ask people about other issues before asking whether they approve of the president's performance, their opinions on those issues could influence their evaluation of the president, which is one of the key trend measures in public affairs polling.

One kind of order effect can be seen in responses to open-ended questions. Pew Research surveys generally ask open-ended questions about national problems, opinions about leaders, and similar topics near the beginning of the questionnaire. If closed-ended questions that relate to the topic are placed before the open-ended question, respondents are much more likely to mention concepts or considerations raised in those earlier questions when responding to the open-ended question.

While order effects are often modest in size, the potential impact of them was dramatically illustrated in an experiment that varied the order of questions about the respondent's level of attention to politics and a set of items that actually tested knowledge about the record of their member of Congress. When attention to politics was asked first, 43% of respondents said they follow what's going on in government and public affairs "most of the time." But when first asked difficult questions about their House member's record, just 25% said they follow politics most of the time.[12]

These and similar findings from experiments are a good reminder that the savvy consumer of polls will always examine the questionnaire used, with attention to both the way questions are worded and how they are sequenced.

REPRESENTATION

The best questionnaire and most rigorous measurement techniques will do us little good if we don't interview a representative sample of the population we set out to study. And here's where some of the most serious challenges to survey research lie. It has become increasingly difficult to contact potential respondents and to persuade them to participate. Technological innovations and lifestyle changes make it harder to reach some people with traditional methods such as a telephone survey. The Internet has provided a promising way to interview people, but there currently is no way to select and contact a nationally representative sample on the Internet because there is no complete list of e-mail addresses in the US. Moreover, a portion of the population—though shrinking—remains offline and thus not able to complete a survey on the Internet.

Still, with enough effort and the right methods, it is possible to interview a representative sample of the public. This section describes how samples are created, how random sampling works, how we collect survey data, and what new challenges we face in obtaining representative samples. It also offers an overview of election polling—the most high-profile, and often most controversial, specialty of survey research.

How Sampling Works

A sample is a model of the population, a selection of objects from the population that are meant to represent the population. Representation in surveys is concerned with ensuring that the sample is a *good* model of the population. How that is achieved and how it is assessed are key tasks in survey research.

Probability Sampling and Sampling Error

Statistical science has given us the *probability sample*, commonly known as the random sample. Its most important quality is that it allows us to make inferences about the population with a known degree of accuracy.

Randomness is a ubiquitous feature of life. We're all familiar with the fact that one gets dealt better hands and worse hands in a typical card game. But good card players know the chances of certain combinations of cards appearing—three of a kind, for example. That's the nature of probability. For surveys, the key feature of a probability sample is that all objects in the population have a known chance of being included in the sample. When this is true, we have the ability to ensure that the sample is unbiased (that is, that no characteristic of the population is systematically over- or under-represented). Moreover, it permits us to calculate how likely it is that a given sample differs from the population on any characteristic of interest, and by how much.

These calculations are based on the hypothetical notion of drawing an infinite number of samples of a given size from the population and plotting the results from all of them to see how much they vary from one to the next and from the true population value (which, of course, is what we are trying to discover when we apply these methods). It is possible to summarize this exercise by specifying how certain we wish to be about the result. If we find that in 95% of the samples, the results vary by no more than 6 percentage points overall, we can state that the margin of sampling error is plus or minus 3 percentage points at the 95% level of confidence. Thus we have specified a degree of accuracy (plus or minus 3 points) and a level of certainty (95% of the time) about that accuracy. That is the great power of probability sampling.

In general, bigger samples are generally better samples. If you flip a coin 10 times, it won't surprise you to get 6 or 7 heads out of 10, even though a fair coin will theoretically yield heads half the time. But if you flip the coin 1,000 times, it would be exceedingly strange for you to get 600 or 700 heads. You would wonder if the coin is weighted too heavily on one side. In fact, the same math that allows us to estimate a margin of sampling error for a survey tells us that the chances of getting 600 heads in 1,000 tosses, with a properly balanced coin, are about 1 in 21 billion.

We report a margin of sampling error and a confidence level for the total sample for each survey and sometimes for key subgroups (e.g., registered voters, Democrats, Republicans, etc.). The sampling error for a typical Pew Research Center national survey of 1,500 completed interviews is plus or minus approximately 3 percentage points with a 95% confidence interval. This means that in 95 out of every 100 samples of the same size and type, the results we would obtain will vary by no more than plus or minus 3 percentage points from the result we would get if we could interview every member of the population. Thus, the chances are very high (95 out of 100) that any sample we draw will be within 3 points of the true population value.

The benefits of probability sampling hold even when the sample is a tiny fraction of the population. Hard as it may be to believe, the size of the population is generally irrelevant to the accuracy of a sample. The key is the ability to ensure that everyone in the population has a known, nonzero chance of being selected.

Probability sampling is used in many other fields besides survey research. Businesses randomly sample products on an assembly line in order to measure the incidence of defects. Auditors randomly sample business records to measure accuracy and detect fraud. Random sampling is widely used in agriculture; in fact, many of the sampling approaches used in surveys today were developed for agricultural studies in the early decades of the twentieth century.

Despite the widespread reliance on probability sampling by government, business, medicine, and others, many readers of our work are skeptical that 1,000 or 1,500 people can accurately represent a population of 250,000,000 adults. Sometimes analogies help. We know that good cooks don't have to eat the whole pot of soup to know if it needs salt. Or, a somewhat macabre example: If you don't trust sampling, tell your doctor to draw *all* your blood the next time you need a diagnostic test.

Statistical Significance

Aside from its use in describing the likely accuracy of the poll with respect to the population, the logic of the margin of sampling error plays another important role in survey analysis. Surveys involve comparisons of all kinds: today versus one year ago, men versus women, opinion about one political candidate versus another. The same chance variation described by the margin of sampling error also affects the comparisons we wish to make. If I want to conclude that the president's approval rating is higher today than one year ago, can I be confident that the difference I observe between today's poll and one taken a year ago is real and not simply a function of sampling error in one or both polls? The same statistical methods used in computing sampling error can be used to test the likelihood that a difference in the polls is real and is unlikely to have occurred by chance. This is what is commonly referred to as a *test of statistical significance*.

Sampling error looms large in the mind of some consumers of poll data, but most survey researchers consider it the least of their worries because it's usually a known quantity. That's not to say that we aren't concerned about occasionally getting a strange sample. The laws of probability make it clear that we will: the 95% level of confidence means that for 5% of our samples (1 out of 20), we will have a finding that is more than the margin of error away from true population value. Considering how many polls one comes across during election season, it's not surprising that some anomalous results turn up now and then. Because the findings are unusual, such polls often attract outsize attention. The smart consumer of polls will always ask, "Could this be one of the outliers in the 5% zone?"

Sample Size: How Big Should a Good Sample Be?

It's true that bigger samples are generally better because the margin of sampling error is smaller, but above a certain point an additional sample produces minimal reduction in the margin of error. This is why so many polls have samples of around 1,000 or so. Adding another 1,000 interviews for a total of 2,000 reduces the overall margin of error by only about 1 percentage point.

But bigger samples can be beneficial if the goal of the study is to characterize small subgroups within the population. For example, in a typical survey sample of 1,000 we usually interview around 110 black adults, close to their share of the total adult population (about 12%). Those 110 individuals constitute a good random sample of blacks, but the margin of error for this group will be around 10 percentage points, which may be too large if we want to examine differences *within* the group or try to compare it with other small groups in the sample.

The need to examine very small groups in the population has led us to collect very large samples on occasion. Pew Research Center released its Religious Landscape Study in 2015, based on a national sample of more than 35,000 interviews. This study needed a big sample in order to describe the religious makeup of the nation and of each of the 50 states and the District of Columbia. The survey examines the beliefs and behaviors of both large and small religious groups in the population. For example, atheists make up only about 3% of the population; in a survey of 1,000 adults, only about 20 to 30 will identify as atheist, far too few to analyze on their own. In the Religious Landscape Study, the large sample size produced nearly 1,100 atheists for analysis.

Nonprobability Sampling

Unlike probability samples, a nonprobability sample is one in which the chance that any individual in the population has been selected for inclusion

Figure A.6

Sample Size and Sampling Error

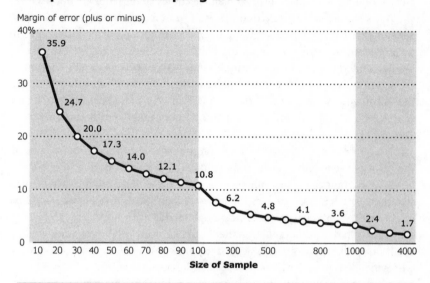

Margin of error (plus or minus)

Size of Sample

is unknown. Lacking this information, we are uncertain as to how well the sample represents the population, and thus how accurate a given finding based on such a sample actually is. But the more convenient and less costly nature of such samples may nevertheless make them useful in cases where the ability to generalize to the population with a known degree of accuracy may be less important. Survey research always entails a balance of considerations among costs, speed, and data quality.

Nonprobability methods are used extensively in marketing research studies (mall intercept studies, opt-in panels), certain kinds of health research (e.g., "case-control" studies and clinical trials), policy evaluation studies, and a growing number of political polls. In 2014, the *New York Times* and CBS News used online nonprobability survey panels from UK-based research firm YouGov as part of their election polling efforts. In addition, nearly all survey researchers employ nonprobability samples in certain circumstances. Most qualitative research relies on convenience samples (so called for the ease of finding and recruiting participants) or purposive samples (where researchers attempt to structure the sample to reflect certain characteristics in the population, such as a balance of age or racial groups). One type of qualitative research commonly used in survey research is the focus group, in which a small number of individuals are brought together to discuss selected topics. These usually employ some type of convenience or purposive sampling rather than probability sampling because the precision and accuracy of the latter are not needed.

But sometimes such research can lead to embarrassment, such as when Senator Bob Dole repeated a finding from a focus group during his campaign for president in 1996. "If something happened along the way," Dole said at a rally, "and you had to leave your children with Bob Dole or Bill Clinton, I think you'd probably leave your children with Bob Dole." Shortly thereafter, the *Washington Post* asked that very question of a nationally representative sample of 1,011 adults and found that 52% preferred Clinton and only 27% preferred Dole.

Nonprobability samples are also commonly used in experiments, where the ability to generalize to the population with a known degree of accuracy is less important than the ability to measure the impact of an experimental treatment or condition (such as the use of certain words in a survey question, or the effect of a video on respondents compared with no video). Detecting the effects of an experimental treatment can be easier with larger samples, and nonprobability panels provide a relatively inexpensive source of respondents who can be assigned to different experimental conditions.

Much of the controversy about nonprobability sampling focuses on opt-in panels. The term "opt-in" refers to the fact that participants can volunteer to be a part of the panel (rather than being scientifically selected for inclusion), or are recruited from a variety of sources that collectively do not constitute the entire population of interest. Panelists are given incentives such as points, prizes, cash, or contributions to charity to join and participate. Once recruited, participants typically complete one or more surveys that collect demographic and other information about them, which can be used in subsequent surveys to select them for inclusion or to weight the results.

Weighting

Even the best probability samples do not produce perfect models of the population. Different kinds of people may be harder than others to contact for a survey or harder to persuade to participate. Sometimes samples are designed in ways that make them somewhat unrepresentative, such as when certain groups are oversampled in order to provide sufficient cases for deeper analysis. An example of oversampling is the inclusion of additional numbers of people who belong to a subgroup in the population (e.g., Hispanics) to ensure that the survey has an adequate number of such people for analysis. To bring the overall sample into alignment with the population, survey researchers use a statistical technique known as weighting. And the practical requirements of conducting surveys mean that we often give some people a greater chance of being included than other people. People who have both a cell phone and a landline phone have a greater chance of being sampled because they could appear in the landline sample, the cell sample, or both.

The logic of weighting is straightforward. Each person in the sample represents a certain number of people like him or her in the population. With a simple random sample in which everyone in the population had an equal chance of being selected, and in which everyone asked to participate did so, everyone in the sample would represent the same number of people in the population. But in practice, some kinds of people are overrepresented and others are underrepresented in the sample. Weighting fixes this by assigning greater weight to some people in the sample than to others.

The proportion of individuals in the sample from a given group is compared with what it should be in the population, usually with information from the US Census or some other definitive source. If the sample contains fewer of such individuals than it should, those cases are given additional weight in the analysis. For example, 22% of the adult population of the US is between 18 and 29 years of age. About 16% of our typical sample will be in this age range, chiefly because young people are more mobile and harder to reach by phone. When this happens, young adults in this age range are given more weight (1.375 in this example), while older adults receive a weight of less than 1.0. This produces a weighted sample that is 22% ages 18 to 29 and 78% ages 30 and older, matching the census parameter for age among adults.

We weight our telephone samples by several characteristics, including gender, age, education, race, Hispanic origin, nativity, region, population density, and type of telephone service. The weighting procedure accounts for the fact that respondents with both landline and cell phones have a greater probability of being included in the combined sample and makes other adjustments for the way the sample was constructed.

Weighting makes samples more accurate but has a small negative impact on the precision (or margin of sampling error) of the sample. Therefore it is important that the computation of sampling errors and statistical tests of significance take into account the effect of weighting, known as the "design effect."

Data Collection

Surveys collect data in many different ways. Here are the principal methods.

Telephone Surveys

The most common data-collection method used by the Pew Research Center is the random-digit-dial (RDD) telephone survey. This method ensures that all telephone numbers in the US—whether landline or cell phone—have a known chance of being included. As a result, samples based on RDD should be unbiased, and a margin of sampling error and a confidence level can be computed for them.

We currently sample landline and cell phone numbers to yield a combined sample with approximately 35% of the interviews conducted by landline and 65% by cell phone (we change the ratio periodically to keep pace with the growing percentage of adults who are reachable only by cell phone—an estimated 48% in the second half of 2015). The design of the samples ensures representation of both listed and unlisted landline numbers (including those not yet listed), as well as all cell phones in service (including pay-as-you-go or "disposable" phones).

Good survey researchers will make multiple attempts to reach and interview the individuals in the sample. This is important because people who are easily reachable and more amenable to the interview are likely to be different from those harder to reach and to persuade to cooperate. Young people are less likely to be at home in the evenings, when much of our calling occurs. Good practice requires that we make numerous calls at different times of the day and on different days of the week in order to ensure that everyone in the sample has a chance to be reached. In addition, we will often try to persuade reluctant respondents to cooperate by calling them again with a special interviewer who is trained in converting refusals. Often, people refuse to participate simply because it is inconvenient at the time of the initial call, but will complete the interview later when given the opportunity.

Web Surveys

The near-ubiquity of the Internet has revolutionized survey research. Most market research surveys are now online, as are a growing number of political surveys. Nearly all surveys of elite populations, such as business leaders, scientists, clergy, academics, and journalists, are now conducted online. As discussed earlier in the section on social desirability bias, self-administered surveys—those with no interviewer present—have many virtues. They are convenient for respondents, who can complete the interview when they are free to do so. Web surveys can be taken anywhere there is an Internet connection (about one-third of Web interviews in our American Trends Panel are taken on a smartphone and an additional 10% on a tablet). And Web surveys also allow researchers to use a host of multimedia elements, such as having respondents view videos or look at graphs and pictures, which are typically not available with other survey modes. In addition, they are usually much cheaper since there is no need for interviewers, who account for a major part of the total cost of telephone and in-person surveys.

But Internet surveys are not without their drawbacks. Unlike studies of elite populations, where nearly everyone has access to the Internet and complete lists of e-mails exist for sampling, surveys of the general population that rely only on the Internet can be subject to significant biases resulting from failure to cover everyone in the population and the absence of any way to draw a sample among those who do. Although Internet access has grown steadily since the Web was invented, about 10% to 15% of the adult population still lacks access, and there are significant demographic differences between those who are online and those who are not. People with lower incomes, less education, living in rural areas, or who are ages 65 and older are underrepresented among Internet users.

There also is no systematic way to collect a traditional probability sample of the general population using the Internet. There is no national list of e-mail addresses from which people could be sampled, and there is no standard convention for e-mail addresses, as there is for phone numbers, that would allow random sampling. Probability-based Internet surveys of the general public therefore must first contact people by another method, such as through the mail or by phone, and ask them to complete the survey online. This is how the Pew Research Center built its American Trends Panel. Respondents to a large national telephone survey were recruited to participate in the panel. Those in the panel with no Internet access are interviewed with a mail survey or by telephone.

Most of the Web surveys being conducted in the market research industry are using nonprobability samples, either from opt-in panels of individuals who have opted in to take surveys in exchange for modest compensation or those who are recruited for a survey on a onetime basis from pop-up ads and other invitations on websites. These surveys are subject to the same limitations facing other surveys using nonprobability-based samples: the relationship between the sample and the population is unknown, so there is no theoretical basis for computing or reporting a margin of sampling error and thus for estimating how representative the sample is of the population as a whole. But in order to take advantage of the large size and low cost of nonprobability samples, many researchers, including those at the Pew Research Center, are experimenting with nonprobability Web samples in hopes of overcoming their limitations.

Mail Surveys

Although decidedly low-tech, mail surveys remain a popular mode of data collection. Mail service is reliable in the US and properly designed survey mailings have a proven track record of being opened and responded to. Pew Research Center's American Trends Panel uses mail surveys for its panelists who do not have access to the Internet. The existence of the postal service's master address database has made sampling for mail surveys much more feasible than in the past. Mail surveys are self-administered, which provides respondents the flexibility to answer when it is convenient to them. It's also possible to include monetary incentives (discussed below) in a mailing, which have been shown to result in higher rates of participation.

In-Person Surveys

In the past, most surveys were conducted in person, face-to-face. That is still the case in much of the developing world, where the communications infrastructure makes it difficult or impossible to conduct telephone or Internet surveys. In-person surveys usually obtain much higher response rates than do other modes. The General Social Survey, a government-sponsored academic survey in the US, still achieves a response rate near 70% with an in-person methodology, and many US government surveys that use personal interviewing have response rates in the 80% to 90% range.

Personal interviews can incorporate aspects of other modes of administration to improve data quality. An interviewer can provide a laptop and headphones to allow a respondent to listen to questions about drug use and other behaviors that would be highly sensitive in an interview. A personal interviewer can reassure a respondent that the data will be used in a responsible way, aggregated with other respondents, and not used to identify or harm the respondent in any way. It is difficult in other modes to provide this reassurance as effectively.

Panel Surveys

Most surveys are onetime encounters with respondents, in which a request for an interview is granted and no further contact is made with the respondent. Panel surveys are different. Respondents join a group of other respondents who have agreed to take multiple surveys over time. Panels allow for the collection of very detailed information about the panelists and make it possible to track attitudes and behaviors over time for the same individuals.

Incentives

Most survey respondents willingly participate in surveys without asking for anything in return. But, not surprisingly, people are usually more willing to participate if they are provided with compensation. Incentives—usually monetary—are widely used in survey research when it is important to obtain cooperation. Pew Research Center routinely offers a $5 reimbursement to people interviewed on a cell phone to compensate them for the cost of the call in the event that they are being charged by the minute for their cell phone time.

In some surveys with an unusually long interview or with rare populations, incentives can be very useful in obtaining cooperation. In our research with the Muslim American population, which constitutes less than 1% of the adult public, locating a Muslim American respondent required enormous effort involving dozens of phone calls to find each potential respondent. When qualified respondents were located, it was very important to obtain their cooperation, and so we offered them $50 to complete the interview.

Threats to Representation: Nonresponse

The percentage of households in a sample that are successfully interviewed—the response rate—has fallen dramatically over the past few decades. At Pew Research, the response rate of a typical telephone survey has fallen from 36% in 1997 to just 9% today. The general decline in response rates is evident across nearly all types of surveys, in the United States and abroad. At the same time, greater effort and expense are required to achieve even the diminished response rates of today. These challenges have led many to question whether surveys are still providing accurate and unbiased information.

Nonresponse to surveys can create bias if the people who do not participate are different from those who do. A high response

Figure A.7

Telephone Response Rates Decline

% of known or assumed households that yield an interview

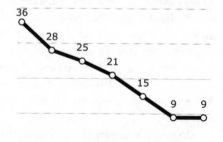

Source: Typical AAPOR Response Rate 3 for telephone surveys conducted by the Pew Research Center

rate is valuable because it limits how different the survey sample can be when compared with the population. The extent of nonresponse bias in a survey depends on two things: the size of the nonrespondent group and how different they are from the respondents. But if respondents and nonrespondents are similar, a low response rate will not lead to biased results.

Fortunately we have good evidence that, for most of the topics we study, respondents and nonrespondents are similar. As a result, surveys still usually produce valid data despite low response rates.[13] How do we know? Pew Research Center has conducted several studies in recent years to assess the representativeness of its surveys, using a variety of techniques. One is to conduct identical parallel surveys, one with the usual level of effort and the other with additional calling, financial incentives for participation, and other factors known to improve response rates. The two surveys produce nearly identical results, despite the difference in response rates. A second technique to assess nonresponse bias is to compare the results of key measures in the survey with identical items in surveys such as the American Community Survey that obtain very high response rates (usually 90% or higher). A third method is to obtain information about sampled households that were not successfully interviewed. Where this has been possible, we have found that characteristics such as home value or partisan affiliation in the interviewed sample were similar to those of all the households in the sample.

None of this is to minimize the concern that high rates of nonresponse pose a serious challenge. One significant area of potential nonresponse bias is that survey participants tend to be significantly more engaged in civic activity than those who do not participate, confirming what previous research has shown.[14] People who volunteer are more likely to agree to take part in surveys than those who do not do these things. This has serious implications for a survey's ability to accurately gauge behaviors related to volunteerism and civic activity. For example, telephone surveys may overestimate such behaviors as church attendance, contacting elected officials, or attending campaign events.

However, the study also finds that the tendency to volunteer is not strongly related to political preferences, including partisanship, ideology, and views on a variety of issues. This helps explain why much of the content of a typical Pew Research Center survey is not seriously affected by the bias related to volunteering.

Despite the generally good news from our studies and those of other researchers, the potential for nonresponse bias is greater when so many people are refusing to participate or can't be contacted. The best way to summarize the extensive scholarly research (and our own) on nonresponse bias is that the response rate is not a good predictor of survey quality. Some studies with low

Figure A.8

Modest Differences on Many Measures but Large Gaps on Civic and Political Engagement

	Pew Research standard survey	US government survey
U.S. Citizen	95%	92%
Homeowner	63	62
Lived at current address 5 or more years	56	59
Married	50	54
Children in household	37	37
Internet user	80	74
Current smoker	22	19
In prior year, received ...		
Unemployment benefits	11	11
Social Security payments	32	27
Food stamps or nutrition assistance	17	10
Registered to vote*	75	75
Contacted a public official in past year	31	10
Volunteered for an organization in past year	55	27
Talked with neighbors in past week	58	41

Note: All government figures are from the Current Population Survey except marital status, smoking and home ownership which are from the National Health Interview Survey.
*Based on citizens.

Source: Pew Research Center methodology study, 2012

response rates have significant biases, while others do not. And even within a given survey, some items may be biased because of nonresponse while others are not.

Regardless of bias, high nonresponse means that the cost of achieving even the lower response rates we get today has risen because the level of effort to obtain an interview has grown. This has made good quality survey research unaffordable for many organizations that need data on the population, leading them to do without or to resort to methodologies that are less proven.

Threats to Representation: Noncoverage

There are other threats to the representativeness of a sample beyond nonresponse. One of the most important is known as noncoverage. If there are

Figure A.9

Growth in the Cell-Only Population

% of each group with wireless service only

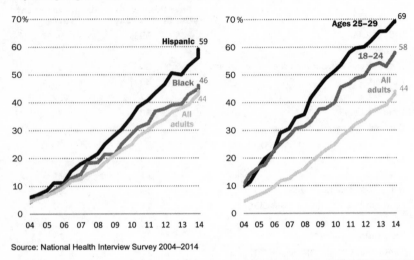

Source: National Health Interview Survey 2004–2014

people who have no chance of being included in our sample, perhaps because they have no telephone, the results of our survey will not represent this portion of the population. Two sources of noncoverage have been of particular interest to survey researchers studying social and political phenomena in the past several years. One is the rapid rise in the share of the population that is no longer reachable on a landline phone and can only be called on a cell phone. Until the latter part of the last decade, most telephone surveys called only landline telephones. But around 2004, the percentage of the adult population described as "cell phone only" began to rise sharply. In 2004, about 5% of adults were cell-only; in 2015, 45% were. Accounting for households with landlines that rarely use them, a majority of the adult population are already functionally cell only. And among certain subgroups in the population, such as young people and Hispanics, sizable majorities are already cell only.

If cell-only adults were similar to those reachable on a landline, the growing share of them would pose little problem for surveys. But cell-only individuals are considerably different demographically and have different attitudes and behaviors than those reachable by landline.

Fortunately, survey researchers responded to this challenge by developing methods for sampling cell phone numbers and including them in their surveys. The Pew Research Center conducted a great deal of research on the feasibility, methods, and consequences of including cell phones. By 2015, 65% of the interviews in a typical national telephone survey were being conducted on cell phones, with just 35% on landlines. Just five years earlier, the ratio was approximately reversed.

Ironically, the rise of cell phones has made it easier to reach certain kinds of people and, as a result, improved the composition of our samples. Cell phones have made telephone service available to some people who previously were unable to afford a landline phone. Consequently, the share of the population with no telephone service is a very low 2%. But interviewing on cell phones comes with a price. Cell phone surveys are more expensive because of the additional effort needed to screen for eligible respondents. A significant number of people reached on a cell phone are under the age of 18 and thus are not eligible for most of our surveys of adults. Cell phone surveys also cost more because federal regulations require cell phone numbers to be dialed manually (whereas auto-dialers can be used to dial landline numbers before calls are transferred to interviewers). In addition, respondents (including those to Pew Research surveys) are often offered small cash reimbursements to help offset any costs they might incur for completing the survey on their cell phone. These payments, as well as the additional time necessary for interviewers to collect contact information in order to reimburse respondents, add to the cost of conducting cell phone surveys.

The Special Case of Election Polls

Polling is never as prominent as it is during elections, especially presidential elections. Election polls slake, if imperfectly, the never-ending thirst we have to know what's going to happen. More important, they help us to understand what the public is saying with its votes. They answer the question of "why it happened"—a much more important question than "what happened," since we ultimately find that out when the votes are counted.

Polls also face a moment of accountability in elections, since the prediction of the outcome can be compared with the reality of what happened. This "final exam" is a source of anxiety for pollsters, but over the decades it has provided a high-profile affirmation of the accuracy of well-designed surveys.

Scientific polling was first introduced to a broad audience in 1936, when George Gallup and Archibald Crossley correctly predicted that President Franklin Roosevelt would be reelected, while the famed *Literary Digest* straw poll incorrectly forecast a victory for Republican Alf Landon, even though it polled more than 2 million people. Despite its huge size, the sample for the

Figure A.10

Public Defeats Pollsters

Polling experienced one of its most embarrassing failures in the 1948 presidential election when polls led pundits and journalists to write off President Harry Truman's chances of reelection – even on election night. Flawed sampling and a failure to poll in the final week of the campaign led to the disaster. This iconic photograph from Truman's victory celebration hangs in the Pew Research Center headquarters as a warning against complacency and hubris.

straw poll was biased, in that wealthier Americans were more likely than others to have received a ballot. In addition, Landon supporters were more likely than Roosevelt supporters to respond to the survey and return their ballots for counting. The combination led to a spectacular failure that discredited straw polls and ultimately contributed to the demise of the magazine.

Since 1936—with the notable exception of 1948—the track record of election polling has been very good. Accurate polls in the 2012 US presidential election made it possible for poll-based models to correctly forecast the outcome of the election in every state. Pew Research Center's presidential election polls have correctly forecast the winner's margin of victory within 1 percentage point in the past three elections.

Still, polling's record in elections is hardly perfect, with some recent high-profile failures in the congressional elections in 2014 and in the 2015 general elections in Israel and Great Britain. In the US, polls in 2014 underestimated the strength of Republican candidates, sometimes by sizable margins. And in Britain in 2015, polls forecast a very close election but the Conservative Party ended up winning comfortably. Election polls face all the challenges that other kinds of surveys face—locating and interviewing a valid sample of the general public, asking questions in a way that obtains accurate information about attitudes and behaviors—but an additional hurdle is estimating who among the people interviewed will actually vote in the election. The problem is that we are trying to describe a population that does not yet exist (except for those who have voted early or absentee). Many more people say they will vote than actually do so. This is not simply a matter of catching the liars; many of those who say they will vote genuinely intend to do so, or they are telling us that they are the kind of person who usually votes. But a lot can happen before or on Election Day to derail a likely voter.

Figure A.11

Trend in Accuracy of Presidential Election Polls

Candidate error (1/2 of total error)

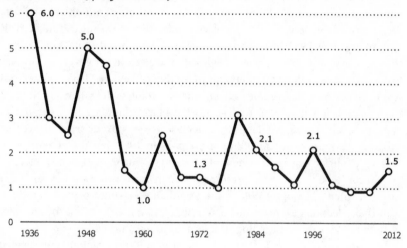

Source: National Council on Public Polls

Election pollsters try to deal with this problem by asking several questions that measure intention to vote, interest and engagement in the election, past voting history, and knowledge of how or where to vote. These questions are typically combined to create a "likely voter scale." But this aspect of polling entails as much art as science, since judgments must be made about how to translate the responses into a turnout forecast. If pollsters guess wrong about the likely demographic composition of the electorate, their election forecasts may be wrong as well. In 2012, some Republican pollsters believed that turnout among minorities would be down significantly from 2008 due to disappointment with President Obama. That did not happen, which is one reason that GOP candidate Mitt Romney and many prominent Republicans were genuinely surprised by the results on election night.

By contrast, polls in the congressional elections in 2014 generally underestimated the vote share captured by Republican candidates. That election saw the lowest turnout in an off-year election since 1942, which may have contributed to the difficulty pollsters had in making forecasts. It is usually the case that habitual voters lean Republican, meaning that they make up a greater share of the total vote in low-turnout elections. Pollsters who expected a some-what higher turnout in 2014 may have included too many Democratic-leaning voters in their samples, thus overestimating the Democratic share of the vote.

One problem that has worried many election pollsters for decades is the concern that voters might not be completely honest about their candidate preference in elections involving a black candidate and a white candidate. This first emerged in 1982 in California when polls predicted that Tom Bradley, the black mayor of Los Angeles, would win the election for governor. Bradley lost a close race to the white Republican candidate, George Deukmejian. Thus was born the so-called Bradley Effect, whereby some white voters are thought to have reported intending to vote for the black candidate in order not to appear racially biased. No definitive evidence was ever produced to prove that this was the reason for the failure of the polls in 1982, but the phenomenon seemed to surface again in several other elections matching black Democrats and white Republicans. Two prominent examples occurred on the same day in 1989, when L. Douglas Wilder and David Dinkins, both black Democrats, won their elections for governor of Virginia and mayor of New York by very narrow margins despite holding sizable leads in most pre-election polls.

Whatever the reason for these polling problems, the phenomenon seemed to disappear by the late 1990s, but pollsters still worried about it when Barack Obama emerged in 2007 as a presidential candidate. With the very prominent exception of the 2008 New Hampshire primary, where all of the polls errone-ously predicted an Obama victory over Hillary Clinton, polling in the subse-quent primaries and general election proved to be accurate, with no sign that Obama's support was overestimated.[15]

NONSURVEY DATA: THE PROMISE OF "BIG DATA"

Not everything we know about people comes from surveys. In fact, a paradox of our era is that as people become more resistant to cooperating with surveys, many are willingly sharing their innermost thoughts and opinions on social media. Others are—perhaps less willingly—leaving behind copious digital evi-dence of their travel habits, purchasing behavior, media consumption habits, and Internet searches. This evidence is sometimes described as "organic data," or just "big data." Former US Census director Robert M. Groves draws the distinction between organic data and "designed data," which surveys produce. Organic data have enlightened us about how the news media cover a variety of topics, how people on Facebook react to the news and whether they retreat to insular islands of like-minded friends, and whether the conversations on Twitter represent public opinion or are a caricature of it.

But we at Pew Research and most social researchers in the field are still grappling with the best ways to use this rich new source of information. It remains a very incomplete resource since much of the data are gathered and owned by private companies who—understandably—worry about liability issues and the possibility of losing the benefits of exclusive access if they make the data available to scholars. The problems of representativeness and coverage that afflict survey samples are even more serious with big data.

But surveys and big data have offsetting strengths and weaknesses. Surveys have lots of variables but a relatively small number of interviews. Properly designed, they can be very representative of the populations they are meant to reflect. In comparison, big data may have millions of data records but only a small handful of measures. And big data are often available for only a portion of the population of interest. But such data provide a view of human activity that is often unavailable from traditional survey methods. Used together, surveys and organic data hold great potential to aid our understanding of social attitudes and processes. As Groves described it, "The challenge to the survey profession is to discover how to combine designed data with organic data, to produce resources with the most efficient information-to-data ratio."[16]

CONCLUSION

As we and other survey researchers grapple with these new challenges, we take comfort in the enduring value of our work. Good democracies require good information. Policy-makers need good information about the populace. They need answers to factual questions like these: What was the impact of the recession on the financial circumstances of different groups? Who is most likely to be victimized by certain types of crimes? How has health care reform affected the rate of health insurance coverage in the US? What share of the public is first-generation immigrants? How many of these individuals are unauthorized? Policy-makers also need to know what people want the government to do (or not do) about the economy, foreign affairs, crime, education, health insurance, immigration, etc. All of this information is gathered through surveys. And the citizenry needs to know more about itself as a people, what other citizens think, and how they live—including those who live on the other side of town.

We don't govern by referendum (or by poll), of course, and most students of democracy consider this a good thing. When scientific polling first came into vogue in the 1930s, Winston Churchill warned that "nothing is more dangerous than to live in the temperamental atmosphere of a Gallup Poll, always taking one's temperature." Public opinion can indeed be volatile, which is one reason we hold elections to choose leaders who, in James Madison's words, can "refine and enlarge the public views" through the prism of their own judgment and experience.[17]

But elections are blunt instruments for divining the public's will, and participation in elections is far from universal. Surveys help leaders and the rest of us to understand the meaning of elections, to discern the existence of mandates, and to determine who took part and who abstained. Between elections, a democracy is well served by an ongoing dialogue between the public and its leaders—and surveys serve this function better than any other tool we have. Ultimately, surveys help everyone in a democracy heed the great Madisonian admonition that "knowledge will forever govern ignorance, and a people who mean to be their own governors must arm themselves with the power that knowledge brings."[18]

Read more about the methodologies used by the Pew Research Center at pewresearch.org/methods

---

Scott Keeter is a consultant to the Pew Research Center, where he was director of survey research from 2005 to 2015. He is a past president of the American Association for Public Opinion Research, and has been an election-night analyst of exit polls for NBC News since 1980. His published work includes books and articles on public opinion, American elections, religion and politics, and survey methodology. A native of North Carolina, he received a BA from Davidson College and a PhD in political science from the University of North Carolina at Chapel Hill.

APPENDIX II

NOTES ON TERMINOLOGY

Here are definitions and explanations of terms used throughout this book:

Race and ethnicity. Blacks, whites, Asians, and other racial groups include only non-Hispanics. Hispanics are of any race. The terms "Latino" and "Hispanic" are used interchangeably.

Nativity. "Native born" refers to persons who are US citizens at birth, including those born in the US, Puerto Rico, or other US territories and those born abroad to at least one parent who is a US citizen. "Foreign born" refers to persons born outside of the US, Puerto Rico, or other US territories to parents, neither of whom was a US citizen.

Immigrant generation. "First generation" refers to foreign-born people. The terms "foreign born," "first generation," and "immigrant" are used interchangeably. "Second generation" refers to people born in the US, with at least one first-generation parent. "Third- and higher-generation" refers to people born in the US, with both parents born in the US. This is sometimes shortened to "third generation."

Generation. The "Greatest Generation" refers to those born before 1928; the "Silent Generation" refers to those born from 1928 to 1945; the "Baby Boom Generation" refers to those born from 1946 to 1964; "Generation X" refers to those born from 1965 to 1980; and the "Millennial Generation" refers to those adults born after 1980. The youngest members of the Millennial Generation are still in their teens. No chronological end point for their generation has yet been fixed, nor has the zeitgeist coined a term for their successor generation.

Educational attainment. "College graduates" refers to those with a bachelor's degree or more. "Some college" includes those with associate's degrees.

"High school graduates" include those with a regular high school diploma or its equivalent, such as a GED.

Additional Notes

- In most figures related to public opinion survey findings, the shares of respondents who said "Don't know" or refused to answer the question are not shown. In some figures, additional voluntary response categories with small shares, such as "Depends" or "Other," may be missing.
- Figures may not add up to 100% because of these missing responses or because of rounding.
- All net figures and change columns are computed prior to rounding.

ADDITIONAL CHARTS AND TABLES

These provide detail and context for the material presented in the book.

Figure 1A.1

Political Activism Gap: Right and Left More Likely to Vote, Donate to Campaigns

 Percent who always vote

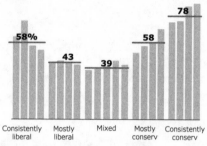

| Consistently liberal | Mostly liberal | Mixed | Mostly conserv | Consistently conserv |

 Percent who contributed to a political candidate or group in the past two years

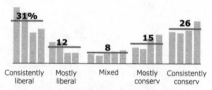

| Consistently liberal | Mostly liberal | Mixed | Mostly conserv | Consistently conserv |

Note: Bars represent the level of participation at each point on an ideological consistency scale of 10 political values questions.

Source: Pew Research Center's 2014 Political Polarization in the American Public

Figure 1A.2

Compromise in the Eye of the Beholder

When Barack Obama and Republican leaders differ over the most important issues facing the country, where should things end up?

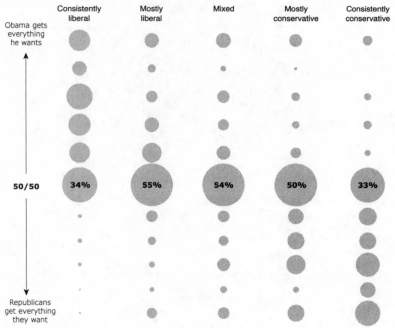

Note: Question asks respondents where, on a scale from zero to 100, Obama and Republican leaders should end up when addressing the most important issues facing the country.

Source: Pew Research Center's 2014 Political Polarization in the American Public

Figure 1A.3

Trust Levels of News Sources by Ideological Group

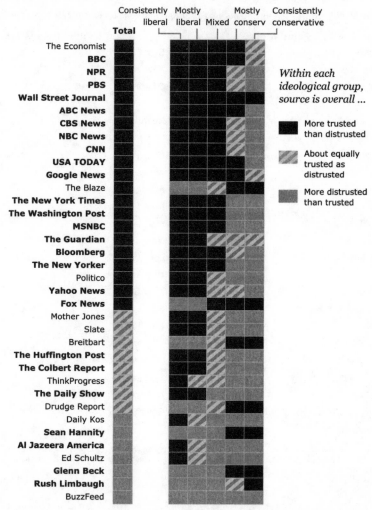

Note: Sources in bold have been "heard of" by at least 40% of web respondents. Based on web respondents. Ideological consistency based on a scale of 10 political values questions. Grouping of outlets is determined by whether the percent who trust each source is significantly different from the percent who distrust each source. Outlets are then ranked by the proportion of those who trust more than distrust each.

Source: Pew Research Center's American Trends Panel (wave 1) survey, March 19–April 29, 2014

Figure 1A.4

Majority-Minority Tipping Years

Year in which states' whole and voting eligible populations become majority-minority

Whole Population		Voting Eligible Population	
State	Year	State	Year
New Mexico	1994	New Mexico	2006
California	2000	California	2016
Texas	2004	Texas	2019
Nevada	2019	Nevada	2030
Maryland	2020	Maryland	2031
Arizona	2023	Georgia	2036
Georgia	2025	Alaska	2037
Florida	2028	Arizona	2038
New Jersey	2028	New Jersey	2040
Alaska	2030	Florida	2043
New York	2031	New York	2045
Louisiana	2039	Louisiana	2048
Illinois	2043	**United States**	**2052**
Mississippi	2043	Illinois	2053
United States	**2044**	Mississippi	2054
Delaware	2044	Oklahoma	2057
Oklahoma	2046	Virginia	2057
Virginia	2046	Connecticut	2058
Connecticut	2047	Delaware	2058
Colorado	2050	North Carolina	2058
North Carolina	2050	Colorado	2060
Washington	2056		

Source: "States of Change: The Demographic Evolution of the American Electorate, 1974–2060," by the Center for American Progress, the American Enterprise Institute, and William H. Frey of the Brookings Institution

Figure 1A.5

Women Seen to Excel at Compromise, Men at Risk-Taking; Overall, Majority of Public Sees Little Difference

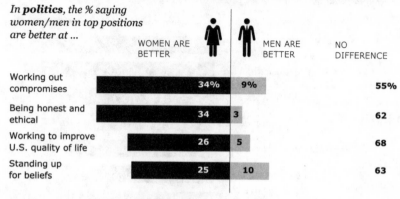

*In **politics**, the % saying women/men in top positions are better at ...*

	WOMEN ARE BETTER	MEN ARE BETTER	NO DIFFERENCE
Working out compromises	34%	9%	55%
Being honest and ethical	34	3	62
Working to improve U.S. quality of life	26	5	68
Standing up for beliefs	25	10	63

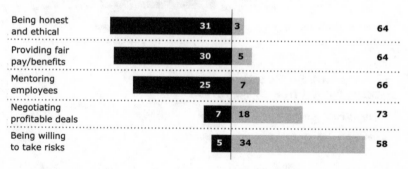

*In **business**, the % saying women/men in top positions are better at ...*

	WOMEN ARE BETTER	MEN ARE BETTER	NO DIFFERENCE
Being honest and ethical	31	3	64
Providing fair pay/benefits	30	5	64
Mentoring employees	25	7	66
Negotiating profitable deals	7	18	73
Being willing to take risks	5	34	58

Note: No answer not shown.

Source: Pew Research Center survey, Nov. 12-21, 2014

Figure 4A.1

The Generation Gap

% saying that young and older people are different in ...

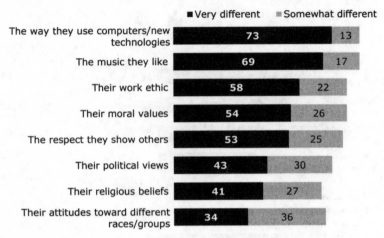

■ Very different   ■ Somewhat different

The way they use computers/new technologies	73 / 13
The music they like	69 / 17
Their work ethic	58 / 22
Their moral values	54 / 26
The respect they show others	53 / 25
Their political views	43 / 30
Their religious beliefs	41 / 27
Their attitudes toward different races/groups	34 / 36

Source: Pew Research Center survey, Jul.–Aug. 2009, N=1,815 US residents ages 16 and older

Figure 4A.2

Silents Not So Positive About New Face of America

% saying each is a "change for the better"

■ Millennial   ■ Gen X   ■ Boomer   ■ Silent

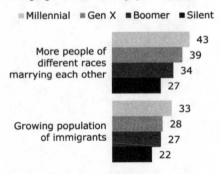

More people of different races marrying each other	43 / 39 / 34 / 27
Growing population of immigrants	33 / 28 / 27 / 22

Source: Pew Research Center survey, Oct. 2012, N=2,008 US adults

Figure 4A.3

Social Conservatism Index

━○━Millennial ━○━Gen X ━○━Boomer ━○━Silent

Conservative views on family,
homosexuality, civil liberties

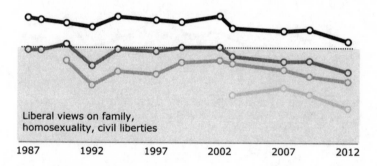

Liberal views on family,
homosexuality, civil liberties

1987 1992 1997 2002 2007 2012

Note: Five-item scale of social attitudes.

Source: Pew Research Center surveys, 1987–2012

Figure 4A.4

Business Attitudes Index

━○━Millennial ━○━Gen X ━○━Boomer ━○━Silent

Businesses make fair profits
and are not too powerful

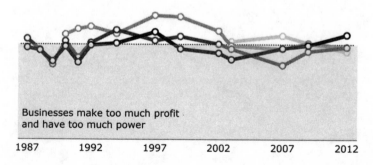

Businesses make too much profit
and have too much power

1987 1992 1997 2002 2007 2012

Note: Three-item scale of attitudes about business.

Source: Pew Research Center surveys, 1987–2012

Figure 4A.5

National Security Index

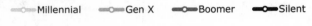

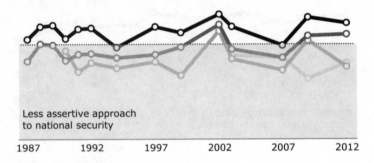

Note: Three-item scale of attitudes about national security.

Source: Pew Research Center surveys, 1987–2012

Figure 4A.6

The Best Way to Ensure Peace Is Through Military Strength

% who agree

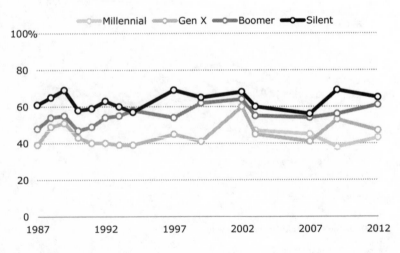

Source: Pew Research Center surveys, 1987–2012

Figure 4A.7

Younger Adults Follow National News Less Closely Than Older Adults

% who very or somewhat closely follow news about political figures and events in Washington

	1996	1998	2000	2002	2004	2006	2008	2012
18–29	49%	58%	50%	58%	57%	51%	58%	43%
30–49	60	67	59	65	70	60	66	56
50–64	64	69	67	74	76	68	71	65
65+	64	69	68	69	71	71	72	70

Note: Question was not asked in 2010.

Figure 5A.1

Generations Agree: Entitlement Programs Have Been Good for Country, Face Financial Trouble

		Total	Millennial	Gen X	Boomer	Silent
Social Security		%	%	%	%	%
Over the years, it has been ...	Good for the country	87	81	88	88	91
	Bad for the country	11	16	10	10	6
Current financial condition	Excellent/Good	18	20	10	18	26
	Only fair/Poor	77	74	86	79	67
Medicare						
Over the years, it has been ...	Good for the country	88	87	89	85	92
	Bad for the country	10	10	10	13	6
Current financial condition	Excellent/Good	18	24	11	16	24
	Only fair/Poor	74	69	79	78	66

Source: Pew Research Center surveys, June 15–19, 2011 (N=1,502) and June 16–19, 2011 (N=1,003)

Figure 5A.2

Younger Generations Support Privatization Proposals

	Millennial	Gen X	Boomer	Silent	Mill.–Silent diff.
% who *favor*	%	%	%	%	%
Changing Social Security to let younger workers put SS taxes in private accounts	86	69	58	52	34
Changing Medicare so people can use benefits toward purchasing private health insurance	74	60	61	48	26

Silents Support Raising Retirement Age

	Millennial	Gen X	Boomer	Silent	Mill.–Silent diff.
% who *favor*	%	%	%	%	%
Gradually raising the Social Security retirement age	40	30	39	51	−11
Gradually raising the Medicare eligibility age	35	35	38	50	−15

No Generational Divide over Means Testing

	Millennial	Gen X	Boomer	Silent	Mill.–Silent diff.
% who *favor*	%	%	%	%	%
Reducing Social Security benefits for higher income seniors	51	57	56	50	1
Reducing Medicare benefits for higher income seniors	54	55	57	56	−2

Source: Pew Research Center survey, Sept.–Oct. 2011, N=2,410

Figure 5A.3

Maintaining Benefits Trumps Deficit Reduction

% who favor ...

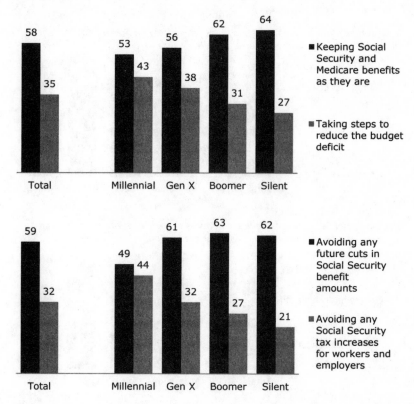

Source: Pew Research Center survey, Sept.–Oct. 2011, N=2,410

Figure 5A.4

More Concern over Keeping Current Benefits Than Burdening Young People

How concerned are you that ... (%)

In the future there may not be enough money to provide Social Security and Medicare benefits at their current levels

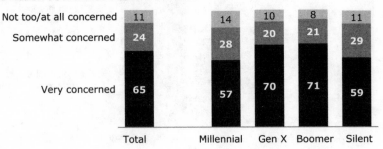

Keeping Social Security and Medicare benefits at their current levels may put too much of a financial burden on younger generations

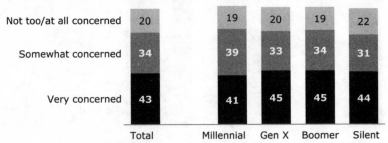

Source: Pew Research Center survey, Sept. 2011, N=2,003

Figure 5A.5

Young and Old Agree: Government Does Too Little for Seniors, Too Much for the Wealthy

	Millennial	Gen X	Boomer	Silent	Mill.– Silent diff.
	%	%	%	%	%
Government doesn't do enough for ...					
Children	57	64	59	44	13
The poor	62	54	57	53	9
The middle class	56	59	62	50	6
Older people	55	64	64	52	3
Government does too much for ...					
The wealthy	62	66	68	63	−1

Source: Pew Research Center survey, Sept.–Oct. 2011, N=2,410

Figure 5A.6

Whose Job Is It to Look Out for Older People?

Who should be _mainly_ responsible for ensuring retired adults have at least a minimum standard of living?	Total	Millennial	Gen X	Boomer	Silent
	%	%	%	%	%
Government	43	44	47	43	36
Individuals and families	40	42	34	39	44
Both equally (Vol.)	14	13	16	14	14
Other/Don't know	3	2	2	3	6
	100	100	100	100	100

If individuals/families mainly responsible ...

If people or families cannot do this, gov't should be responsible	30	33	26	29	30
Gov't should still not be responsible	9	8	7	9	12
Other/Don't know	1	1	1	2	2
	40	42	34	40	44

NET: Government is mainly responsible, jointly responsible, or responsible if families cannot do so themselves	87	90	89	86	80

Source: Pew Research Center survey, Sept.–Oct. 2011, N=2,410

Figure 6A.1

Share of Population Employed, by Age, 1967–2014*

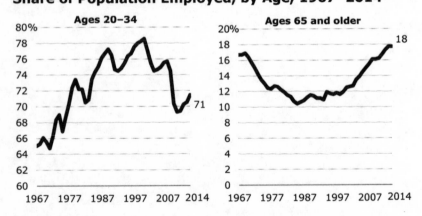

*Note differences in scales along the y-axis.

Source: Pew Research Center analysis of Bureau of Labor Statistics data

Figure 7A.1

Three Great Waves of Immigration to the US

Era and country	Total	%
Modern Era (1965–2015)	**58,525,000**	**100**
Mexico	16,275,000	28
China*	3,175,000	5
India	2,700,000	5
Philippines	2,350,000	4
Korea	1,725,000	3
Vietnam	1,500,000	3
Cuba	1,550,000	3
El Salvador	1,500,000	3
Former USSR	1,450,000	2
Dominican Republic	1,325,000	2
Region totals Latin America	29,750,000	51
South/East Asia	14,700,000	25
Europe, total	6,900,000	12
Africa/Middle East	4,550,000	8
Canada**	1,150,000	2
All other	1,450,000	2
Southern/Eastern Europe Wave (1890–1919)	**18,244,000**	**100**
Italy	3,764,000	21
Austria-Hungary	3,690,000	20
Russia & Poland	3,166,000	17
United Kingdom	1,170,000	6
Germany	1,082,000	6
Ireland***	917,000	5
Region totals Europe, total	16,134,000	88
North/West Europe	4,757,000	26
South/East Europe	11,377,000	62
Canada	835,000	5
Latin America	551,000	3
South/East Asia	315,000	2
Africa/Middle East	332,000	2
Other/Not specified	77,000	<0.5
Northern Europe Wave (1840–1889)	**14,314,000**	**100**
Germany	4,282,000	30
Ireland***	3,209,000	22
United Kingdom	2,586,000	18
Norway-Sweden	883,000	6
Region totals Europe, total	12,757,000	89
North/West Europe	11,700,000	82
South/East Europe	1,058,000	7
Canada	1,034,000	7
Latin America	101,000	1
South/East Asia	293,000	2
Africa/Middle East	5,000	<0.5
Other/Not specified	124,000	1

Note: Population figures rounded to the nearest thousand for 1840–1919, nearest 25,000 for 1965–2015. Data for 1965–2015 include legal and unauthorized immigrants. Data for 1840–1919 include only legal admissions. *Includes Hong Kong, Taiwan, and Macao. **Includes other North America. ***Includes Northern Ireland. Persons from Puerto Rico not included.

Source: Data for 1965–2015 from 2015 Pew Research Center report "Modern Immigration Wave Brings 59 Million to US, Driving Population Growth and Change Through 2065"; for 1840–1919, Table 2 from Office of Immigration Statistics, *Yearbook of Immigration Statistics*, 2008

Figure 7A.2

Comparing Immigrants, the Second Generation and All US Adults, 2012

Median annual household income *(in dollars)*

1st gen.	45,800
2nd gen.	58,100
All US	58,200

College graduates *(% of ages 25 and older)*

1st gen.	29
2nd gen.	36
All US	31

Homeownership rate *(% of households)*

1st gen.	51
2nd gen.	64
All US	65

In poverty *(% of adults)*

1st gen.	18
2nd gen.	11
All US	13

Note: Annual income figure is adjusted and standardized to a household size of three. College graduates include those with a bachelor's degree or more.

Source: Pew Research Center analysis of 2012 Current Population Surveys, IPUMS

Figure 7A.3

Characteristics of Hispanic Adults by Immigrant Generation, 2012

% (unless otherwise noted)

	Generation			
	1st	**2nd**	**3rd+**	**Total**
Population *(in millions)*	17.5	7.0	10.2	34.7
Share of population	51	20	29	100
Median age *(in years)*	41	28	39	38
Married	60	34	41	49
Fertility (*women ages 15–44*)				
Had a birth in the past 12 months	9	7	7	8
Of these, share unmarried	29	52	49	39
Educational attainment (*ages 25+*)				
Less than high school	47	17	21	35
Bachelor's degree or more	11	21	17	15
Median household income ($)	34,600	48,400	43,600	39,200
Average household size (*persons*)	3.5	3.1	2.8	3.2
Homeownership (*householders*)	43	50	49	46
Persons in poverty	23	16	20	21

Note: Unmarried women include those who are divorced, separated, widowed, or never married. Annual income figure is adjusted and standardized to a household size of three.

Source: Pew Research Center analysis of Current Population Surveys, IPUMS; fertility data from 2004–2010 CPS and all other data from 2012 CPS

Figure 7A.4

Which Term Do You Use to Describe Yourself Most Often?

% saying ...

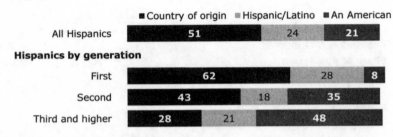

Note: In this figure, first generation includes those born in Puerto Rico. Although individuals born in Puerto Rico are US citizens by birth, they are included among the foreign born because they are born into a Spanish-dominant culture and because on many points their attitudes, views, and beliefs are much closer to Hispanics born abroad than to Latinos born in the 50 states or the District of Columbia, even those who identify themselves as being of Puerto Rican origin.

Source: Pew Research Center National Survey of Latinos, Nov.–Dec. 2011, N=1,220 US Hispanic adults

Figure 7A.5

Trust in People

% in each group who say ...

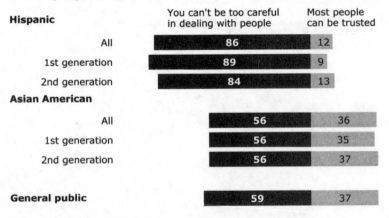

Note: Volunteered responses of "Other/Depends" and "Don't know/Refused" not shown.

Source: Pew Research Center National Survey of Latinos, Nov.–Dec. 2011 (N=1,220 US Hispanic adults); Pew Research Center Asian-American Survey, Jan.–Mar. 2012 (N=3,511 US Asian adults); and Pew Research Center survey of the general public, Apr. 2012 (N=3,008 US adults)

Figure 7A.6

Number of Children in Poverty, by Race and Ethnicity, 1976–2013

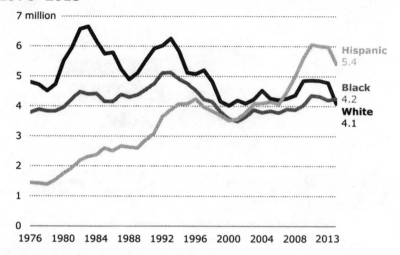

Share of Children in Poverty, by Race and Ethnicity, 2000–2013

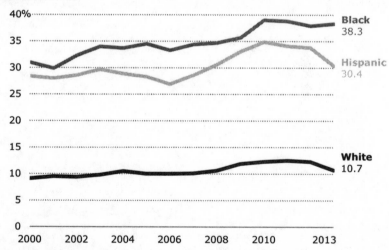

Note: Children include all individuals younger than 18. Whites include only non-Hispanics. Blacks include both Hispanic and non-Hispanic components of the black population. Hispanics are of any race.

Source: US Census Bureau data

Figure 7A.7

Education Characteristics of Recent Immigrants, by Race and Ethnicity, 2010

% among adults

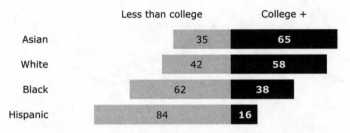

Note: "Recent immigrants" refers to those who came to the US in the past three years prior to the survey date (since 2007). "College +" includes those who are either currently in a four-year college or graduate school or have completed their bachelor's degree or advanced degrees. "Asian" includes mixed-race Asian population, regardless of Hispanic origin.

Source: Pew Research Center analysis of 2010 American Community Survey, IPUMS

Figure 7A.8

Attitudes About Work Ethic

% saying ...

"Most people who want to get ahead can make it if they're willing to work hard."

US Asians	69
General public	58

"Americans from my country of origin group are very hardworking."

US Asians	93

"Thinking about the country as a whole, Americans are very hardworking."

US Asians	57

Note: Those who did not provide a country of origin were asked about "Asian Americans."

Source: Pew Research Center Asian-American Survey, Jan.–Mar. 2012, N=3,511 US Asian adults

Figure 7A.9

For Most Asians, US Offers a Better Life

% saying ...

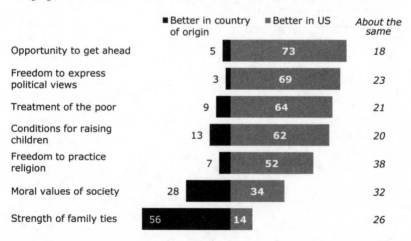

	■ Better in country of origin	■ Better in US	*About the same*
Opportunity to get ahead	5	73	18
Freedom to express political views	3	69	23
Treatment of the poor	9	64	21
Conditions for raising children	13	62	20
Freedom to practice religion	7	52	38
Moral values of society	28	34	32
Strength of family ties	56	14	26

Source: Pew Research Center Asian-American Survey, Jan.–Mar. 2012, N=3,511 US Asian adults

Figure 7A.10

Characteristics of Asian-American Adults by Immigrant Generation, 2012

% (unless otherwise noted)

	Generation			Total
	1st	**2nd**	**3rd+**	
Population *(in millions)*	9.2	2.4	0.9	12.4
Share of population	74	19	7	100
Median age *(in years)*	44	30	43	42
Married	72	37	56	64
Fertility *(women ages 15–44)*				
Had a birth in the past 12 months	8	4	5	7
Of these, share unmarried	10	***	***	16
Educational attainment *(ages 25+)*				
Less than high school	12	7	5	11
Bachelor's degree or more	50	55	53	51
Median household income *($)*	65,200	67,500	91,600	67,400
Average household size *(persons)*	3.1	2.6	2.7	2.9
Homeownership *(householders)*	58	51	65	57
Persons in poverty	12	12	8	12

Note: Includes only single-race Asians, including Hispanics. The symbol *** indicates insufficient number of observations to provide a reliable estimate. Unmarried women include those who are divorced, separated, widowed, or never married. Annual income figure is adjusted and standardized to a household size of three.

Source: Pew Research Center analysis of Current Population Surveys, IPUMS; fertility data from 2004–2010 CPS and all other data from 2012 CPS

Figure 8A.1

Okay with Intermarriage

% saying they would be fine if a family member told them they were going to marry someone of a different race/ethnicity

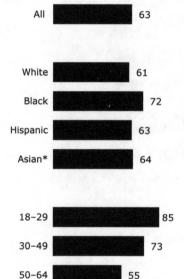

All — 63

White — 61

Black — 72

Hispanic — 63

Asian* — 64

18–29 — 85

30–49 — 73

50–64 — 55

65 and older — 38

Note: Respondents were asked how they would react if a family member was going to marry someone of three racial/ethnic groups other than their own: An African American, a Hispanic American, an Asian American and a white American. Results show those who say they would be fine with a family member marrying all three other racial and ethnic groups.*Sample size for Asian is 86.

Source: Pew Research Center survey conducted Oct. 28–Nov. 30, 2009, N=2,884 US adults

Figure 8A.2

Intermarriage Types, Newly Married Couples in 2010

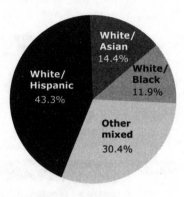

White/Asian 14.4%

White/Black 11.9%

White/Hispanic 43.3%

Other mixed 30.4%

Note: Asians include Pacific Islanders.

Source: Pew Research Center analysis of 2010 American Community Survey, IPUMS

Figure 8A.3

Earnings and Education, Newlyweds in 2008–2010

Median combined annual earnings, in 2010 dollars

		% both college educated
White/Asian	$70,952	41.2
Asian/Asian	$62,000	52.7
White/White	$60,000	23.3
White/Hispanic	$57,900	18.6
White/Black	$53,187	14.5
Black/Black	$47,700	10.2
Hispanic/Hisp.	$35,578	5.4

Note: Asians include Pacific Islanders.

Source: Pew Research Center analysis of 2008–2010 American Community Survey, IPUMS

Figure 8A.4

Intermarriage Among Asian and Hispanic Newlyweds, by Nativity, 2010

% of newlyweds married to someone of a different race/ethnicity

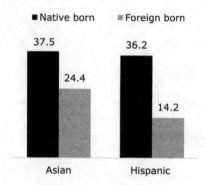

Note: Asians include Pacific Islanders.

Source: Pew Research Center analysis of 2010 American Community Survey, IPUMS

Figure 8A.5

Black/White Gaps Have Narrowed ... and Also Widened

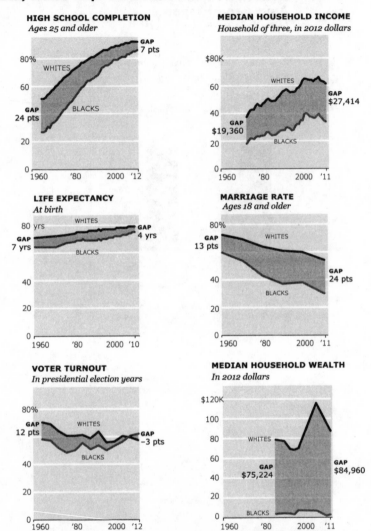

HIGH SCHOOL COMPLETION
Ages 25 and older

MEDIAN HOUSEHOLD INCOME
Household of three, in 2012 dollars

LIFE EXPECTANCY
At birth

MARRIAGE RATE
Ages 18 and older

VOTER TURNOUT
In presidential election years

MEDIAN HOUSEHOLD WEALTH
In 2012 dollars

Source: Pew Research Center analysis of government data. For more details see Pew Research Center, "King's Dream Remains an Elusive Goal; Many Americans See Racial Disparities," Aug. 22, 2013

Figure 9A.1

Share Married, by Race and Ethnicity, 1960–2013

% of adults 18 and older

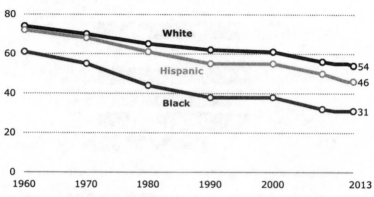

Source: Pew Research Center analysis of Decennial Census (1960–2000) and American Community Survey data (2008–2013), IPUMS

Figure 9A.2

Why Get Married?

% saying "very important" reason, by marital status

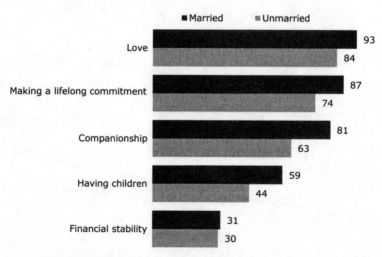

Note: Asked of married (N=1,306) and unmarried (N=1,385) separately.

Source: Pew Research Center, Oct. 2010, N=2,691 US adults

Figure 9A.3

Marriage: It's Not About the Kids

Which of these is closer to your views about the main purpose of marriage? Forming a lifetime union between two adults for … (%)

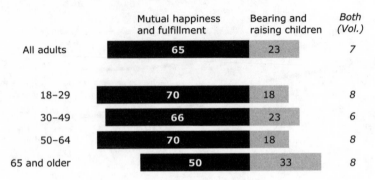

	Mutual happiness and fulfillment	Bearing and raising children	*Both (Vol.)*
All adults	65	23	7
18–29	70	18	8
30–49	66	23	6
50–64	70	18	8
65 and older	50	33	8

Note: Volunteered responses of "Neither" and "Don't know/Refused" are not shown.

Source: Pew Research Center survey, Feb.–Mar. 2007, N=2,020 US adults

Figure 9A.4

Share of Births to Unmarried Women, by Race and Ethnicity, 1960–2013

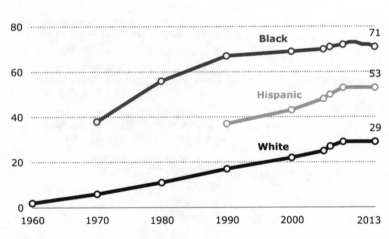

Source: National Center for Health Statistics data

Figure 10A.1

Worship Attendance Among the Unaffiliated and Affiliated

	Unaffiliated		Affiliated	
	2007	2012	2007	2012
Attends worship services ...	%	%	%	%
Weekly or more	7	5	44	45
Monthly/Yearly	25	22	35	36
Seldom/Never	68	72	20	18

Source: Aggregated data from surveys conducted by the Pew Research Center for the People & the Press, 2007 and 2012

Figure 10A.2

Trends in Disaffiliation, by Religious Attendance

% of each attendance category that is unaffiliated

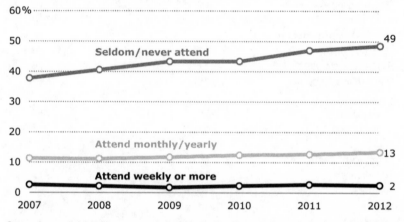

Source: Aggregated data from surveys conducted by the Pew Research Center for the People & the Press, 2007–2012

Figure 10A.3

Trends in Religious Disaffiliation, by Demographic Groups

% who identify their current religion as atheist, agnostic or nothing in particular

	2007	2014	Change
	%	%	
US general public	16.1	22.8	+6.7
Men	20	27	+7
Women	13	19	+6
White	16	24	+8
Black	12	18	+6
Hispanic	14	20	+6
Bachelor's degree or more	17	24	+7
Some college or less	16	22	+6
Annual family income			
$75,000 or more	17	25	+8
$30,000–$74,999	17	23	+6
Less than $30,000	15	22	+7
Married	14	18	+4
Not married	19	28	+9
Region of residence			
Northeast	16	25	+9
Midwest	16	22	+6
South	13	19	+6
West	21	28	+7

Source: Pew Research Center, Religious Landscape Studies, 2007 and 2014

Figure 10A.4

Unaffiliated, but Not Uniformly Secular

	US general public	Unaffiliated	Affiliated
How important is religion in your life?	%	%	%
Very important	58	14	67
Somewhat	22	19	24
Not too/Not at all	18	65	8
Believe in God or universal spirit?			
Yes, absolutely certain	69	30	77
Yes, but less certain	23	38	20
No	7	27	2
Other/Don't know	2	5	1
Frequency of prayer			
Daily	58	21	66
Weekly/Monthly	21	20	22
Seldom/Never	19	58	11
Think of self as ...			
Religious person	65	18	75
Spiritual, but not religious	18	37	15
Neither spiritual nor religious	15	42	8

Source: Pew Research Center survey, Jun.–Jul. 2012, N=2,973 US adults

Figure 10A.5

Views of Religious Institutions

% who agree that churches and other religious organizations ...

	US general public	Unaffiliated	Affiliated
	%	%	%
Are too concerned with money and power	51	70	47
Focus too much on rules	51	67	47
Are too involved with politics	46	67	41
Bring people together/Strengthen community bonds	88	78	90
Play important role in helping the poor and needy	87	77	90
Protect and strengthen morality	76	52	81

Source: Pew Research Center survey, Jun.–Jul. 2012, N=2,973 US adults

Figure 10A.6

Differing Views over the Impact of Religion's Influence on Society

Is religion increasing or losing its influence on American life? Is this a good thing or a bad thing?

	US general public	TOTAL	Atheist/ Agnostic	Nothing in particular
	%	%	%	%
Increasing its influence	25	27	34	24
Losing its influence	66	63	59	65
Good thing	*12*	*28*	*43*	*22*
Bad thing	*49*	*26*	*10*	*32*
Other/Don't know	*5*	*9*	*6*	*11*
Same (Vol.)	2	2	2	2
Don't know	7	7	5	8
	100	100	100	100

The table columns TOTAL, Atheist/Agnostic, and Nothing in particular are grouped under the heading: ----------------Unaffiliated----------------

Source: Pew Research Center survey, Jun.–Jul. 2012, N=2,973 US adults

Figure 10A.7

The Disaffiliated Are Neither "Seekers" nor Especially Inclined Toward New Age Beliefs

	US general public	Unaffiliated
% of "nothing in particulars" who are …	%	%
Looking for a religion that is right for them	n/a	10
Not doing this	n/a	88
% who believe in …		
Spiritual energy in physical things like mountains, trees, crystals	26	30
Astrology	25	25
Reincarnation	24	25
Yoga as a spiritual practice	23	28
% who often …		
Think about meaning and purpose of life	67	53
Feel deep connection with nature and the earth	58	58
% who say it is very important …		
To belong to a community with shared values and beliefs	49	28
% who have ever …		
Had religious or mystical experience	49	30
Been in touch with someone who has died	29	31
Seen or been in presence of a ghost	18	19
Consulted a psychic	15	15

Source: Pew Research Center survey, Jun.–Jul. 2012 (N=2,973 US adults) and August 2009 (N=2,003 US adults)

Figure 10A.8

Social and Political Issues

	US general public	Unaffiliated	Affiliated
Abortion should be ...	%	%	%
Legal in all/most cases	53	72	49
Illegal in all/most cases	41	24	46
Don't know	6	4	6
Same-sex marriage ...			
Favor	48	73	41
Oppose	44	20	50
Don't know	9	7	9
Prefer ...			
Bigger gov't, more services	39	42	38
Smaller gov't, fewer services	52	50	52
Depends/Don't know	9	8	10

Source: Abortion figures from aggregated data from surveys conducted by the Pew Research Center for the People & the Press, 2011–2012. Same-sex marriage figures from aggregated data from surveys conducted by the Pew Research Center for the People & the Press, 2012. Views on role of government from Pew Research Center for the People & the Press survey, January 2012.

Figure 10A.9

Trends in Religious Affiliation, 2007–2014

	2007	2014	Change*
	%	%	%
Christian	**78.4**	**70.6**	**−7.8**
Protestant	51.3	46.5	−4.8
Evangelical	*26.3*	*25.4*	*−0.9*
Mainline	*18.1*	*14.7*	*−3.4*
Historically black	*6.9*	*6.5*	*---*
Catholic	23.9	20.8	−3.1
Orthodox Christian	0.6	0.5	---
Mormon	1.7	1.6	---
Jehovah's Witness	0.7	0.8	---
Other Christian	0.3	0.4	---
Non-Christian faiths	**4.7**	**5.9**	**+1.2**
Jewish	1.7	1.9	---
Muslim	0.4	0.9	+0.5
Buddhist	0.7	0.7	---
Hindu	0.4	0.7	+0.3
Other world religions**	<0.3	0.3	---
Other faiths**	1.2	1.5	+0.3
Unaffiliated	**16.1**	**22.8**	**+6.7**
Atheist	1.6	3.1	+1.5
Agnostic	2.4	4.0	+1.6
Nothing in particular	12.1	15.8	+3.7
Don't know/Refused	**0.8**	**0.6**	**−0.2**

* The "change" column displays only statistically significant changes.

** The "other world religions" category includes Sikhs, Baha'is, Taoists, Jains and a variety of other world religions. The "other faiths" category includes Unitarians, New Age religions, Native American religions and a number of other non-Christian faiths.

Source: Pew Research Center, Religious Landscape Studies, 2007 and 2014

Figure 10A.10

Which Religions Lead to Eternal Life?

% among respondents who are affiliated with a religion and who say "many religions can lead to eternal life"

	All	White evang.	White mainline	Black Prot.	White Catholic
*Can **Catholicism** lead to eternal life?*	%	%	%	%	%
Yes	73	75	77	69	n/a
No	14	14	11	19	n/a
Don't know	13	11	12	12	n/a
Protestantism					
Yes	74	n/a	n/a	n/a	83
No	13	n/a	n/a	n/a	6
Don't know	13	n/a	n/a	n/a	11
Judaism					
Yes	69	64	73	62	77
No	17	21	11	24	12
Don't know	14	15	16	14	11
Islam					
Yes	52	35	55	58	62
No	29	45	26	25	20
Don't know	19	20	19	17	18
Hinduism					
Yes	53	33	57	44	65
No	24	36	20	28	16
Don't know	23	31	23	28	19
Atheists					
Yes	42	26	46	--	49
No	46	68	41	--	38
Don't know	12	6	13	--	13
People with no religious faith					
Yes	56	35	62	--	66
No	31	53	22	--	20
Don't know	13	12	16	--	14

Note: "White Catholic" refers to white, non-Hispanic Catholics. Respondents were not asked about their own religion; e.g., Protestants were not asked if Protestantism can lead to eternal life, Catholics were not asked if Catholicism can lead to eternal life, etc. "Atheists" and "People with no religious faith" was asked of a random half of the sample. Sample size for these items is too small for black Protestants to produce reliable estimates.

Source: Pew Research Center survey, Jul.–Aug. 2008, N=2,905 US adults. See Pew Research Center, "Many Americans Say Other Faiths Can Lead to Eternal Life," Dec. 18, 2008

Figure 11A.1

Social Networking Site Use by Age Group, 2005–2015

% of internet users in each age group who use social networking sites

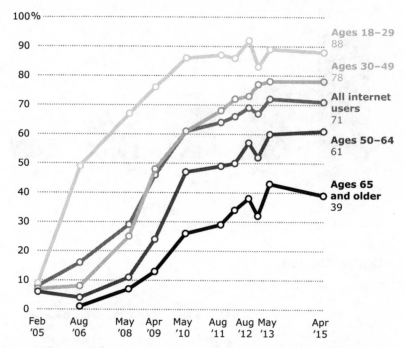

Note: The 2015 question read, "Do you ever use a social networking site or a mobile app for social media like Facebook, Twitter, or Instagram?" Previously, the question read, "Do you ever use the internet to...use social networking sites like Facebook, Twitter, or LinkedIn?"

Source: Pew Research Center surveys, 2005–2015

Figure 11A.2

Mean Size of Facebook Social Networks

(persons)

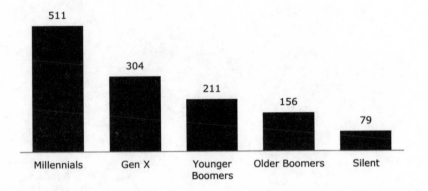

Source: Pew Research Center survey, September 2014, N=1,074 US adult Facebook users

Figure 11A.3

Digital Devices

% of adults who own each device

	All adults %	Millen- nials %	Gen X %	Younger Boomers %	Older Boomers %	Silent %
Cell phone	92	99	95	91	88	75
Desktop/laptop computer	73	77	81	69	71	48
iPod or MP3 player	40	51	50	38	21	12
Game console	40	58	51	32	19	4
e-Book reader	19	17	21	18	20	19
Tablet, like iPad	45	52	55	35	41	24

Source: Pew Research Center survey, Mar.–Apr. 2015

Figure 11A.4

Among Millennials, Facebook Exceeds Any Other Source for Political News

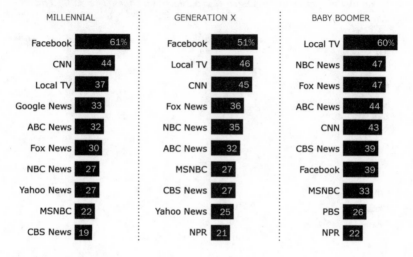

MILLENNIAL

Facebook	61%
CNN	44
Local TV	37
Google News	33
ABC News	32
Fox News	30
NBC News	27
Yahoo News	27
MSNBC	22
CBS News	19

GENERATION X

Facebook	51%
Local TV	46
CNN	45
Fox News	36
NBC News	35
ABC News	32
MSNBC	27
CBS News	27
Yahoo News	25
NPR	21

BABY BOOMER

Local TV	60%
NBC News	47
Fox News	47
ABC News	44
CNN	43
CBS News	39
Facebook	39
MSNBC	33
PBS	26
NPR	22

Note: No answer not shown.

Source: Pew Research Center American Trends Panel survey, Mar. 19–Apr. 29, 2014

Figure 12A.1

Who Wants an Extended Life?

% saying they personally would/would not want treatments for radical life extension

	Would	Would not	Don't know
All adults	**38**	**56**	**6**
Radical life extension			
Good for society	71	24	6
Bad for society	13	83	3
Men	43	52	5
Women	34	59	8
White	34	59	7
Black	46	49	5
Hispanic	46	48	6
18–29	40	57	3
30–49	43	51	6
50–64	35	58	7
65 and older	31	59	10
High school grad or less	41	54	5
Some college	34	60	6
Bachelor's degree or more	37	55	7

Note: This question was asked of half the survey sample, N=2,012.

Source: Pew Research Center survey, Mar.–Apr. 2013, N=4,006 US adults

Figure 12A.2

What Would a Future with Radical Life Extension Hold?

% who agree/disagree with each statement

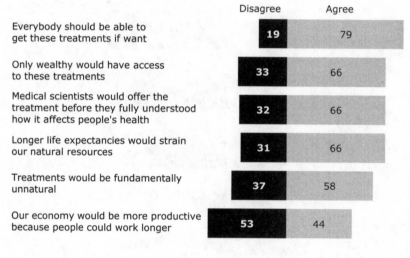

Source: Pew Research Center survey, Mar.–Apr. 2013, N=4,006 US adults

Figure 12A.3

Most Markers of Old Age Differ for Young and Old

% saying that a person is old when he or she ...

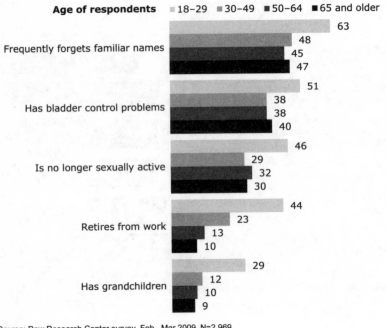

Age of respondents 18–29 30–49 50–64 65 and older

Frequently forgets familiar names
63
48
45
47

Has bladder control problems
51
38
38
40

Is no longer sexually active
46
29
32
30

Retires from work
44
23
13
10

Has grandchildren
29
12
10
9

Source: Pew Research Center survey, Feb.–Mar 2009, N=2,969

Figure 12A.4

At What Age Does the Average Person Become Old?

Mean age

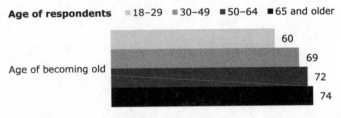

Age of respondents 18–29 30–49 50–64 65 and older

Age of becoming old
60
69
72
74

Source: Pew Research Center survey, Feb.–Mar 2009, N=2,969

Figure 13A.1

Old-age Dependency Ratios, by Global Region

■ 2010   ■ 2050

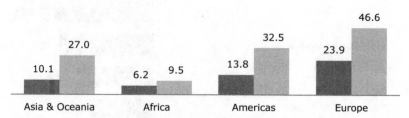

Asia & Oceania   Africa   Americas   Europe

Child Dependency Ratios, by Global Region

■ 2010   ■ 2050

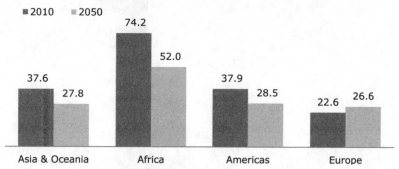

Asia & Oceania   Africa   Americas   Europe

Total Dependency Ratios, by Global Region

■ 2010   ■ 2050

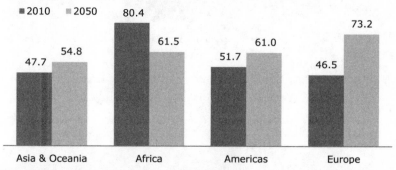

Asia & Oceania   Africa   Americas   Europe

Note: The old-age dependency ratio is the population age 65 and over divided by population age 15–64.
The child dependency ratio is the population age 0–14 divided by population age 15–64.
The total dependency ratio is the population age 65 and over plus population age 0–14, divided by
population age 15–64.

Source: United Nations, Department of Economic and Social Affairs, *World Population Prospects: The
2012 Revision*, June 2013

Figure 13A.2

Population Change in Selected Countries, 2010 to 2050

% change

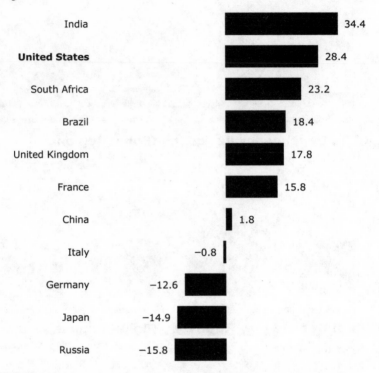

Source: United Nations, Department of Economic and Social Affairs, *World Population Prospects: The 2012 Revision*, June 2013

Figure 13A.3

Median Age in Selected Countries

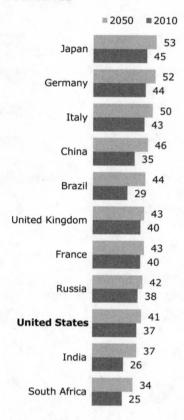

Source: United Nations, Department of Economic and Social Affairs, *World Population Prospects: The 2012 Revision*, June 2013

Figure 13A.4

Total Dependency Ratio in Selected Countries

Old-age Dependency Ratio in Selected Countries

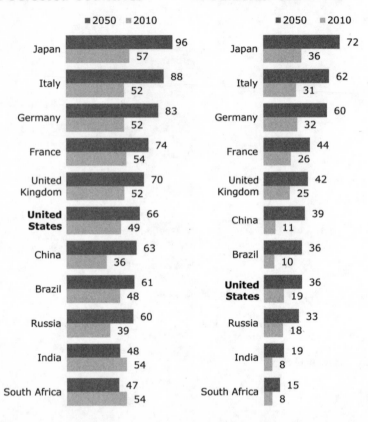

Note: The total dependency ratio is the population age 65 and over plus population age 0–14, divided by population age 15–64. The old-age dependency ratio is the population age 65 and over divided by population age 15–64.

Source: United Nations, Department of Economic and Social Affairs, *World Population Prospects: The 2012 Revision*, June 2013

Figure 13A.5

Is Aging a Problem in Your Country?

% saying it's a "major problem"

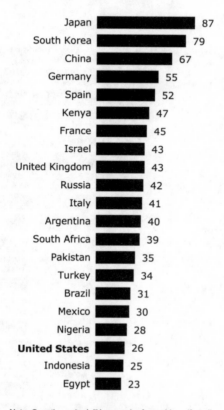

Japan	87
South Korea	79
China	67
Germany	55
Spain	52
Kenya	47
France	45
Israel	43
United Kingdom	43
Russia	42
Italy	41
Argentina	40
South Africa	39
Pakistan	35
Turkey	34
Brazil	31
Mexico	30
Nigeria	28
United States	26
Indonesia	25
Egypt	23

Note: Question asked, "How much of a problem, if at all, is the growing number of older people in (survey country)...." Responses of "Minor problem," "Not a problem," and "Don't know/Refused" are not shown.

Source: Pew Research Center survey, Mar.–Apr. 2013, N=22,425 adults in 21 countries

Figure 13A.6

Who Should Bear the Greatest Responsibility for the Elderly?

% saying ... should bear the greatest responsibility for people's economic wellbeing in their old age

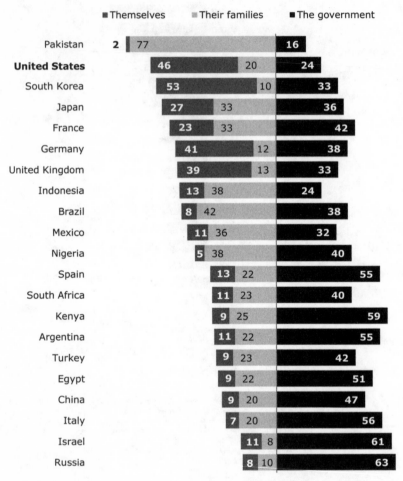

■ Themselves ■ Their families ■ The government

	Themselves	Their families	The government
Pakistan	2	77	16
United States	46	20	24
South Korea	53	10	33
Japan	27	33	36
France	23	33	42
Germany	41	12	38
United Kingdom	39	13	33
Indonesia	13	38	24
Brazil	8	42	38
Mexico	11	36	32
Nigeria	5	38	40
Spain	13	22	55
South Africa	11	23	40
Kenya	9	25	59
Argentina	11	22	55
Turkey	9	23	42
Egypt	9	22	51
China	9	20	47
Italy	7	20	56
Israel	11	8	61
Russia	8	10	63

Note: Volunteered responses of "All equally," "Other," and "Don't know/Refused" are not shown.

Source: Pew Research Center survey, Mar.–Apr. 2013, N=22,425 adults in 21 countries

Figure 13A.7

Will You Have an Adequate Standard of Living in Old Age?

% saying they are "very" or "somewhat" confident they will

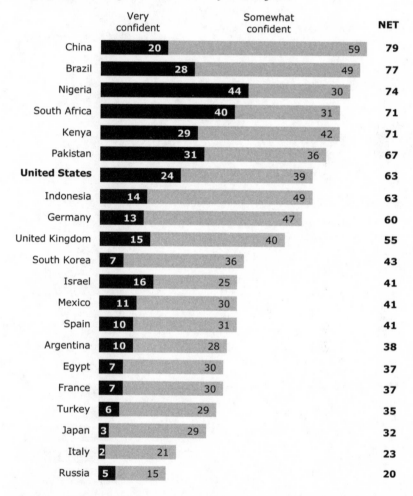

	Very confident	Somewhat confident	NET
China	20	59	**79**
Brazil	28	49	**77**
Nigeria	44	30	**74**
South Africa	40	31	**71**
Kenya	29	42	**71**
Pakistan	31	36	**67**
United States	24	39	**63**
Indonesia	14	49	**63**
Germany	13	47	**60**
United Kingdom	15	40	**55**
South Korea	7	36	**43**
Israel	16	25	**41**
Mexico	11	30	**41**
Spain	10	31	**41**
Argentina	10	28	**38**
Egypt	7	30	**37**
France	7	30	**37**
Turkey	6	29	**35**
Japan	3	29	**32**
Italy	2	21	**23**
Russia	5	15	**20**

Note: Question asked, "Thinking about yourself, how confident are you that you will have an adequate standard of living in your old age..." Responses of "Not too confident," "Not at all confident," and "Don't know/Refused" are not shown.

Source: Pew Research Center survey, Mar.–Apr. 2013, N=22,425 adults in 21 countries

NOTES

CHAPTER 1: POLITICAL TRIBES

1. This HuffPost/YouGov nationwide survey of 1,000 adults, conducted February 20–23, 2015, was one of several taken in the midst of the Giuliani flap; all generated similar numbers. It's possible these results were influenced by the inherently inflammatory context. Nonetheless, the partisan gaps are striking.

2. "Political Polarization in the American Public," Pew Research Center, June 12, 2014.

3. See http://voteview.com/political_polarization_2014.htm.

4. "Political Polarization, Op cit."

5. Bill Bishop and Robert Cushing, *The Big Sort* (Boston, MA: Mariner Books, 2009).

6. Sheryl Gay Stolberg, "You Want Compromise? Sure You Do," *New York Times*, August 13, 2011.

7. Richard Fry and Paul Taylor, "The Rise of Residential Segregation by Income," Pew Research Center, August 1, 2012; http://www.pewsocialtrends.org/2012/08/01/the-rise-of-residential-segregation-by-income/.

8. See http://www.russellsage.org/blog/new-paper-residential-segregation-income-1970–2009.

9. For a skeptical assessment of CBS's oft-cited claim that Walter Cronkite was "the most trusted man in America," see https://mediamythalert.wordpress.com/2012/06/09/cronkite-the-most-trusted-wheres-the-evidence/.

10. One key milestone in this evolution was the 1987 decision by the Federal Communications Commission to drop enforcement of its Fairness Doctrine, which since the dawn of the broadcast era had required radio and television license holders, as a condition of being granted access to scarce public airwaves, to air contrasting views on matters of public interest. Once the rule was dropped, broadcasters were free to offer news and public affairs programming with an ideological slant.

11. Viewership of the three major commercial broadcast network newscasts has dropped by about 30 million viewers, or more than 50%, since Cronkite's heyday in

1980. Newspaper circulation has declined by a similar order of magnitude. During this period many legacy news media organizations have added more eyeballs online than they've lost on air or in print. But the economics of the digital era are quite daunting for them. Online advertising replaces just a small fraction of the ad revenues they have lost on their print and broadcast platforms.

12. For an analysis of the differences in the content of Fox News and MSNBC's political coverage, see "The Master Campaign Narratives in Campaign 2012," Pew Research Center, August 23, 2012; http://www.journalism.org/2012/08/23/2012 -campaign-character-narratives/.

13. See http://www.journalism.org/2015/04/29/cable-news-fact-sheet/.

14. Diana Mutz, *In-Your-Face Politics: The Consequences of Uncivil Media* (Princeton, NJ: Princeton University Press, 2015).

15. Amy Mitchell, Jeffrey Gottfried, and Katerina Eva Matsa, "Millennials and Political News," Pew Research Center, June 1, 2015; http://www.journalism.org/2015 /06/01/millennials-political-news/.

16. Quoted in Caitlin Dewey, "If You Use Facebook to Get Your News, Please—for the Love of Democracy—Read This First," *Washington Post*, June 3, 2015; http://www .washingtonpost.com/news/the-intersect/wp/2015/06/03/if-you-use-facebook-to-get -your-news-please-for-the-love-of-democracy-read-this-first/.

17. Quoted in Farhad Manjo, "Facebook Study Disputes Theory of Political Polarization Among Users," *New York Times*, May 7, 2015; http://www.nytimes.com/2015 /05/08/technology/facebook-study-disputes-theory-of-political-polarization-among -users.html?hpw&rref=technology&action=click&pgtype=Homepage&module=well -region&region=bottom-well&WT.nav=bottom-well&_r=0.

18. See http://www.people-press.org/2007/04/15/public-knowledge-of-current -affairs-little-changed-by-news-and-information-revolutions/. See also http://www .people-press.org/2015/04/28/what-the-public-knows-in-pictures-words-maps-and -graphs/.

19. These party identification figures were computed by adding all those who identified with a party to all those who identified as Independent but said they leaned toward that party. Research indicates very few differences in the views of those groups. Our 2014 figures for the full adult population show 48% are Democrats or lean Democratic and 39% are Republican or lean Republican; this gap has been stable for the past decade. Restricting the sample to registered voters brings the Democratic lead down to 48%–43%. Among likely voters, it falls even more, to 47%–46%. For more detailed breakdowns of demographic groups by party as well as a description of our methodology, see "A Deep Dive into Partisan Affiliation," Pew Research Center, April 7, 2015; http://www.people-press.org/2015/04/07/a-deep-dive-into-party-affiliation/.

20. In 2014, Republican candidates received an aggregate total of 52% of all votes cast in congressional elections nationwide, which resulted in their party winning 57% of all congressional seats. This gap, which has persisted for years, is mainly the result of the overconcentration of Democratic voters in urban districts. Gerrymandering also plays a role.

21. Matthew Yglesias, "American Democracy Is Doomed," Vox, March 2, 2015; http://www.vox.com/2015/3/2/8120063/american-democracy-doomed.

22. Ruy Teixeira, William H. Frey, and Rob Griffin, "States of Change: The Demographic Evolution of the American Electorate 1974–2060," Center for American Progress, February 27, 2015; https://www.americanprogress.org/issues/progressive-movement/report/2015/02/24/107261/states-of-change/.

23. In different regions of the world, different dangers were deemed to be more threatening than income inequality. See http://www.pewglobal.org/2014/10/16/middle-easterners-see-religious-and-ethnic-hatred-as-top-global-threat/#greatest-danger-to-the-world.

24. For income-inequality data, see http://www.census.gov/content/dam/Census/library/publications/2015/demo/p60–252.pdf; for wealth-inequality data, see https://www.cbo.gov/publication/49440.

25. See http://www.gallup.com/poll/182987/americans-continue-say-wealth-distribution-unfair.aspx?utm_source=redistribute wealth by heavy taxes on the rich&utm_medium=search&utm_campaign=tiles.

26. Thomas B. Edsall, "Has Obamacare Turned Voters Against Sharing the Wealth?" *New York Times*, April 15, 2015; http://www.nytimes.com/2015/04/15/opinion/has-obamacare-turned-voters-against-sharing-the-wealth.html.

27. There are gender gaps on these questions, with women more inclined than men to see gender bias as the key factor that keeps women from making it to the top in politics and corporations. To read the full Pew Research report, go to http://www.pewsocialtrends.org/2015/01/14/women-and-leadership/.

28. Quoted in Nia-Malika Henderson, "Hillary Clinton's Gender Tightrope," CNN, April 13, 2015.

29. Robert Costa and Philip Rucker, "Jenner Comes Out, and GOP Fears the Culture War Is Lost," *Washington Post*, June 5, 2015.

30. See, for example, Julia B. Isaacs, "International Comparisons of Economic Mobility," The Brookings Institution, 2008; http://www.brookings.edu/~/media/research/files/reports/2008/2/economic-mobility-sawhill/02_economic_mobility_sawhill_ch3.pdf.

CHAPTER 2: DEMOGRAPHIC DESTINIES

1. The US Census Bureau in 2014 and the Pew Research Center in 2015 published long-term population projections that, while broadly similar, differed somewhat in their portraits of the nation's future racial makeup. The Census Bureau projected that the US population will become majority nonwhite in 2044; Pew Research placed that tipping point around 2050. The Pew Research projections (shown in Figure 2.1 on page 33) also envision a larger Asian-American population and a smaller Hispanic population than does the Census Bureau projection. Both projections analyze current trends in deaths, births, and net migration and project these trends forward in a time series for various segments of the population. One key difference is that the Pew

Research projections rely more heavily on the trends in immigration over the past 15 years, a period when immigration from Asia surpassed immigration from Latin America. The divergent results are a useful reminder that long-term projections can be altered by unanticipated events. In the case of immigration trends, changes in policy have the potential to increase or decrease future flows, as do changes in the economies and demographies of sending and receiving countries. For a description of the methodology Pew Research used to formulate its 2015 projections, go to http://www.pewhispanic.org/2015/09/28/appendix-a-methodology-5/. To read the Census Bureau report on its 2014 projections, go to www.census.gov/population/projections/data/national/2014.html>.

2. All long-term demographic projections in this book should be taken with a grain of salt—and the longer the term, the larger the grain. They're based on the best available data and analysis. But things change. For a summary of the United Nations' 2015 population projection report, go to http://www.un.org/en/development/desa/population/events/other/10/index.shtml.

3. Fred Barnes, "America and Its Immigrants, a Hate-Love Relationship," *Weekly Standard,* July 29, 2013.

4. Pew Research Center, "The Lost Decade of the Middle Class," August 22, 2012. In this report, our analysis of long-term US Census data showed that the share of adults in the middle class declined from 61% in 1971 to 51% in 2011. We defined a "middle class" adult as one living in a household with an annual income between 67% and 200% of the national median—an income range of $39,418 to $118,255 in 2011 dollars (all incomes were scaled to reflect a three-person household). We tested other middle-income boundaries—some wider, some narrower—but always found the same pattern: the middle-income tier has been shrinking steadily for many decades. Our analysis also found that the shares of adults in the upper-and lower-income tiers have each risen steadily over time—the lower tier to 29% in 2011 from 25% in 1971, the upper tier to 20% in 2011 from 14% in 1971. See http://www.pewsocialtrends.org/2012/08/22/the-lost-decade-of-the-middle-class/.

5. A 2011 cross-national analysis by the Organisation for Economic Co-operation and Development (OECD) found that the United States ranked fourth from highest in income inequality among 34 of the world's most advanced economies—behind only Turkey, Mexico, and Chile. That study, which took into account the impact of taxes and public cash transfers, put the US Gini Coefficient at 0.38, lower than the measure of income inequality in the US before taxes and transfers. Both measures have risen more sharply in the US over the past several decades than in all but a handful of the world's other wealthy countries. See www.oecd.org/els/soc/49499779.pdf.

6. Julia B. Isaacs, "International Comparison of Economic Mobility," in *Economic Mobility in America,* Brookings Institution and the Economic Mobility Project of the Pew Charitable Trusts.

7. Based on a Pew Research Center analysis of wealth data from the Census Bureau's Survey of Income and Program Participation (SIPP).

8. Laurie Goodstein, "Christian Right Failed to Sway Voters on Issues," *New York Times,* November 9, 2012.

9. See, for example, Sara S. McLanahan, "Life Without Father: What Happens to the Children?" Center for Research on Child Wellbeing, Princeton, NJ, 2001.

10. Pew Research Center, "The Decline of Marriage and Rise of New Families," November 2010.

11. Ezra Klein, "Good Riddance to Rottenest Congress in History," *Bloomberg,* January 2, 2013. See also Nolan McCarty et al., "Polarization Is Real (and Asymmetric)," May 15, 2012, voteview.com.

12. Researchers at Yale and the University of California, San Diego, conducted a novel experiment and found they could cut the partisan gap on such questions by more than half if they offered survey respondents money for correct answers. Their finding suggests that some Democrats and Republicans know the right answers but choose to answer incorrectly anyway as a way to affirm their beliefs or stick it to the opposition. See www.nber.org/papers/w19080.

CHAPTER 3: MILLENNIALS AND BOOMERS

1. In this calculation by the Urban Institute's C. Eugene Steuerle and Caleb Quakenbush, it is assumed that the taxes paid by employee and employer earn interest each year at a rate 2% above inflation. See http://www.urban.org/UploadedPDF/412945 -Social-Security-and-Medicare-Taxes-and-Benefits-Over-a-Lifetime.pdf.

2. Richard Fry, "More Millennials Living with Family," Pew Research Center, July 29, 2015; http://www.pewsocialtrends.org/2015/07/29/more-millennials-living-with -family-despite-improved-job-market/.

3. See http://www.forbes.com/sites/larrymagid/2013/06/03/a-third-of-recently -married-couples-met-online-and-theyre-more-satisfied-and-less-likely-to-split-up/.

4. It's no surprise that "selfie" was the Oxford Dictionaries' 2013 Word of the Year (see http://blog.oxforddictionaries.com/2013/11/word-of-the-year-2013 -winner/)—91% of American teens report they have posted at least one picture of themselves online. See the Pew Research Center's Internet Project report, "Teens, Social Media, and Privacy," May 21, 2013; http://pewinternet.org/Reports/2013/Teens -Social-Media-And-Privacy/Summary-of-Findings.aspx.

5. Robin Marantz Henig, "What Is It About 20-Somethings?" *New York Times Magazine,* August 18, 2010.

6. Arthur A. Stone et al., "A Snapshot of the Age Distribution of Psychological Well-being in the United States," *PNAS* 107, no. 22 (June 1, 2010).

7. Yang Yang, "Social Inequalities in Happiness in the United States, 1972 to 2004: An Age-Period-Cohort Analysis," *American Sociological Review* 73, no. 2 (April 2008).

8. You never know what will strike the public's fancy online. "Charlie Bit My Finger" was for several years the most viewed YouTube video ever. It was posted in 2007 and by the end of 2012 had attracted more than 500 million views worldwide. The 56-second video features 1-year-old Charlie biting the finger of his 3-year-old brother,

Harry, whereupon Harry announces, "Ouch." That's the whole of it. The young British lads now have their own blogs, video series, and fan clubs. But fame can be fleeting. Their world record has since been surpassed by a number of professional entertainers, among them Psy, the South Korean pop musician and reigning YouTube champ. His "Gangnam Style" video had drawn nearly 2 billion viewers by the end of 2013.

9. Volunteering is a difficult civic engagement activity to measure because measurement depends on survey question framing and context. According to an analysis of the Census Bureau's Current Population Survey September supplement, the Corporation for National and Community Service reports a much lower volunteering rate than the current survey (52%). In 2008, 26.4% of Americans say they had volunteered for an organization in the year prior to the survey (Corporation for National and Community Service, 2009).

CHAPTER 5: BATTLE OF THE AGES?

1. Sabrina Tavernise, "Whites Account for Under Half of Births in US," *New York Times,* May 17, 2012.

2. Ronald Brownstein, "The Gray and the Brown: The Generational Mismatch," *National Journal*, July 24, 2010. Ron has long been one of journalism's most astute observers of these demographic and political trends. He writes and edits a series of articles on this topic in the *National Journal* under the label "The Next America." (Good title! Imitation is flattery, my friend.)

3. Julia Isaacs, Katherine Toran, Heather Hahn, Karina Fortuny, and C. Eugene Steuerle, "Kids' Share 2012," Urban Institute.

4. Lynda Laughlin, "Who's Minding the Kids? Child Care Arrangements: Spring 2011," Current Population Reports, US Census Bureau, Washington, DC, 2013, pp. 70–135.

5. Joel Kotkin et al., "The Rise of Post-Familialism: Humanity's Future?" Civil Service College, Singapore, 2012, p. 29.

CHAPTER 6: MONEY TROUBLES

1. Alicia Munnell, Center for Retirement Research at Boston College, Issue Brief 12-15, August 2012.

2. Teresa Ghilarducci, "Our Ridiculous Approach to Retirement," *New York Times,* July 21, 2012.

3. For Millennials, college may be a financial drag in terms of debt accumulation, but it has already begun to pay off on the employment front. Among young adults ages 25 to 32, the unemployment rate in 2013 was 4% for those with a BA degree or more—compared with 12% for their same-age counterparts with no education beyond a high school diploma—according to a Pew Research Center analysis of US Census Bureau data. Looking back in time, our analysis found that 25- to 32-year-old college graduates of previous generations had even lower unemployment rates—3%

for Gen Xers in 1995, 2% for late Boomers in 1986, 2% for early Boomers in 1979, and 1% for Silents in 1965. (The national unemployment rate was also lower in the past. It stood at 7.6% in 2013, 5.4% in 1995, 7.2% in 1986, 5.8% in 1979, and 4.7% in 1965.)

4. Richard Fry, "Young Adults After the Recession: Fewer Homes, Fewer Cars, Less Debt," Pew Research Center, February 21, 2013.

5. In an effort to respond to critics, the US Census Bureau in November 2011 unveiled a Supplemental Poverty Measure designed, among other things, to make a more comprehensive tally of the noncash government benefits that households receive and the out-of-pocket medical expenses they pay. While these adjustments have had little impact on the overall US poverty rate, they narrow the gap in the poverty rates for younger households and older households, reducing the former and raising the latter. This new supplemental measure represents the biggest change in the way poverty has been calculated since the federal government first began doing so in 1964, but it remains a methodological work in progress. For now, at least, the traditional measure remains the official measure. For more on the supplemental measure, see www.pewsocialtrends.org/2011/11/30/re-counting-poverty.

6. Quoted in Derek Thompson and Jordan Weissmann, "The Cheapest Generation," *Atlantic Magazine,* September 2012.

CHAPTER 7: THE NEW IMMIGRANTS

1. Michael Barone, "A Nation Built for Immigrants," *Wall Street Journal,* September 21, 2013.

2. See "Modern Immigration Wave Brings 59 Million to U.S., Driving Population Growth and Change Through 2065," Pew Research Center, September 28, 2015; http://www.pewhispanic.org/2015/09/28/modern-immigration-wave-brings-59 -million-to-u-s-driving-population-growth-and-change-through-2065/.

3. Median household income figures have been standardized and adjusted to a household size of three so that comparisons can be made on an apples-to-apples basis.

4. In this 2012 Pew Hispanic Trends Project survey, which focused on identity and assimilation (see http://www.pewhispanic.org/2012/04/04/when-labels-dont-fit -hispanics-and-their-views-of-identity/), Puerto Ricans born in Puerto Rico were counted as immigrants, even though they are US citizens by birth. In the typical Pew Research Center survey, Puerto Ricans are not counted as immigrants.

5. Mark Lopez and Gabriel Velasco, "Childhood Poverty Among Hispanics Sets Record, Leads Nation," Pew Hispanic Center, September 28, 2011.

6. The report was based on a Pew Research Center survey of a nationally representative sample of 3,511 Asian Americans, conducted by telephone from January 3 to March 27, 2012, in English and seven Asian languages.

7. Organisation for Economic Co-operation and Development (OECD), Education at a Glance 2011: OECD Indicators. Based on 2009 data.

8. The college data are for adults ages 25 and older. Household income is based on householders ages 18 and older and comes from Pew Research Center analysis of

the Census Bureau's 2010 American Community Survey. Household wealth is based on householders ages 15 and older and comes from Pew Research Center analysis of Wave 7 of the 2008 Survey of Income and Program Participation panel, conducted September–December 2010.

9. See http://www.pewresearch.org/fact-tank/2015/07/22/unauthorized-immigrant -population-stable-for-half-a-decade/.

10. See, for example, Giovanni Peri, "The Effect of Immigrants on U.S. Employment and Productivity," Federal Reserve Bank of San Francisco, August 30, 2010.

11. Adam Davidson, "Do Illegal Immigrants Actually Hurt the US Economy?" *New York Times*, February 12, 2013.

12. In 2013 the US Senate passed a comprehensive immigration bill that included a provision creating a 13-year pathway to citizenship for immigrants who are in the US illegally. As this book was going to press, the fate of that legislation in the US House of Representatives was uncertain.

13. According to a 2012 survey by the Pew Hispanic Center, among Latino immigrants who are not US citizens or legal permanent residents (and therefore likely to be unauthorized immigrants), 54% identify with or lean toward the Democratic Party and 19% self-identify with or lean toward the GOP.

14. Karl Rove, "Immigration Reform and the Hispanic Vote," *Wall Street Journal*, June 6, 2013.

15. Partnership for a New American Economy, June 2011, www.renewoureconomy .org/sites/all/themes/pnae/img/new-american-fortune-500-june-2011.pdf.

16. According to the World Bank, Russia had 12.3 million immigrants in 2010, but the great bulk of them were residents of the former Soviet Union. Germany, with 10.8 million immigrants that year, is a more legitimate number two to the US, which had about 40 million in 2010.

CHAPTER 8: HAPA NATION

1. The de Blasios can give the Obamas a pretty good run for their money on the diversity front. I happened to be in Munich, Germany, last fall, two days after Bill de Blasio was elected mayor of New York City. Both Munich newspapers featured giant front-page, above-the-fold photos of the winning candidate and his striking interracial family—his black wife, Chirlane McCray; their son Dante, sporting his massive Afro; and their daughter Chiara, who adorned her loose, kinky locks with flowers. Interest in the family was even more intense in Italy, the ancestral home of de Blasio's mother, where one restaurant near Naples named a dessert in their honor—a sponge cake filled with hazelnut and white chocolate. See http://www.nytimes.com/2013/11 /15/nyregion/his-roots-in-italy-de-blasio-now-has-fans-there.html?hp&_r=0. Bill de Blasio had started out as a long shot in the mayor's race and wound up winning by a landslide. Some analysts credit the family itself (especially a TV ad featuring Dante and his huge Afro) for the turnaround. It's hard to imagine the New York City

of 1950—or, for that matter, of 2000—embracing that family. But in America, norms change. And the rest of the world watches with fascination.

2. For background information on intermarriage, see Pew Research Center Social & Demographic Trends Project; and see Wendy Wang, "The Rise of Intermarriage," February 16, 2012.

3. M. D. Bramlett and W. D. Mosher, "Cohabitation, Marriage, Divorce, and Remarriage in the United States," *Vital and Health Statistics* 23, no. 22 (2002).

4. J. L. Bratter and R. B. King, "'But Will It Last?' Marital Instability Among Interracial and Same-Race Couples," *Family Relations* 57, no. 2 (2008): 160–171.

5. Y. Zhang and J. Van Hook, "Marital Dissolution Among Interracial Couples," *Journal of Marriage and Family* 71, no. 1 (2009).

6. Pew Research Center's Religion & Public Life Project, "A Portrait of Jewish Americans," October 1, 2013.

7. "Multiracial in America: Proud, Diverse, and Growing in Numbers," Pew Research Center, June 11, 2015; http://www.pewsocialtrends.org/2015/06/11 /multiracial-in-america/.

8. Prior to 1970, the US Census Bureau would have its enumerators make racial judgments about the identities of the people they counted, based on their in-person observations. Since then, Americans have been allowed to label themselves on their census form, and the bureau has adopted a you-are-whoever-you-say-you-are approach to racial labeling. So if an immigrant from Ghana, or a second-generation Chinese American, or a descendant of an Anglo-Saxon family that arrived on the *Mayflower* was, for whatever reason, to choose to identify as Hispanic, that's how he or she would be counted. And if a recent arrival from Mexico City decided to say she wasn't Hispanic, that's how she would be counted.

9. Peter Wallsten, "Obama Struggles to Balance African Americans' Hopes with Country's as a Whole," *Washington Post,* October 28, 2012.

10. Nia-Malika Henderson, "Blacks, Whites Hear Obama Differently," *Politico,* March 3, 2009.

11. Jodi Kantor, "For President, a Complex Calculus of Race and Politics," *New York Times,* October 21, 2012, p. A1.

12. For more information, see Pew Research Center Social & Demographic Trends Project, "King's Dream Remains an Elusive Goal; Many Americans See Racial Disparities," August 22, 2013, http://www.pewsocialtrends.org/2013/08/22/kings-dream -remains-an-elusive-goal-many-americans-see-racial-disparities/#fn-17618-1.

CHAPTER 9: WHITHER MARRIAGE?

1. See Stephanie Coontz, *The Way We Never Were: American Families and the Nostalgia Trap* (New York: Basic Books, 1993).

2. See Stephanie Coontz, *Marriage, a History: How Love Conquered Marriage* (New York: Penguin Books, 2005).

3. Kay Hymowitz et al., "Knot Yet," the National Marriage Project at the University of Virginia, the National Campaign to Prevent Teen and Unplanned Pregnancy, and the Relate Institute, 2013.

4. Andrew Cherlin, "In the Season of Marriage, a Question: Why Bother?" *New York Times,* April 27, 2013.

5. For a summary of findings in this field, see the chapter on marriage (chapter 8) in Charles Murray, *Coming Apart* (New York: Crown Forum, 2012).

6. Ibid., p. 158.

7. Sam Roberts, "Divorce After 50 Grows More Common," *New York Times,* September 20, 2013.

8. Susan L. Brown, "A 'Gray Divorce' Boom," *Los Angeles Times,* March 31, 2013.

9. Coontz was quoted in "Divorce After 50 Grows More Common," by Sam Roberts, *New York Times,* September 20, 2013.

10. Ross Douthat, "Marriage Looks Different Now," *New York Times,* March 30, 2013.

11. Isabel V. Sawhill, "Restoring Marriage Will Be Difficult," Brookings Institution, December 20, 2012.

12. Quoted at a Brookings Institution symposium, March 2013.

CHAPTER 10: NONES ON THE RISE

1. David Brooks, "The National Creed," *New York Times,* December 30, 2003.

2. Roger Finke and Rodney Stark, *The Churching of America 1776–1990* (New Brunswick, NJ: Rutgers University Press, 2005). Note that church membership is different from religious affiliation: a person can identify as a Presbyterian, for example, even if she does not belong to a Presbyterian congregation. Affiliation is measured in Pew Research surveys with the question, "What is your present religion, if any?" followed by a list of response options, such as, "Are you Protestant, Catholic, Orthodox such as Greek or Russian Orthodox, Jewish, Muslim, Buddhist, Hindu, atheist, agnostic, something else or nothing in particular?" Those who say they are atheist, agnostic, or nothing in particular are classified as unaffiliated.

3. See "America's Changing Religious Landscape," Pew Research Center, May 12, 2015; http://www.pewforum.org/2015/05/12/americas-changing-religious-landscape /#fn-23198–7.

4. The term "nones" is often used to describe people who indicate in surveys that they have no religion or do not belong to any particular religion. See, for example, Barry A. Kosmin and Ariela Keysar, with Ryan Cragun and Juhem Navarro-Rivera, "American Nones: The Profile of the No Religion Population, a Report Based on the American Religious Identification Survey 2008," Trinity College, 2009; http://commons.trincoll.edu/aris/files/2011/08/NONES_08.pdf. See also Tom W. Smith, "Counting Religious Nones and Other Religious Measurement Issues: A Comparison of the Baylor Religion Survey and General Social Survey," GSS Methodological

Report No. 110, 2007; http://publicdata.norc.org:41000/gss/documents/MTRT/MR110 -Counting-Religious-Nones-and-Other-Religious-Measurement-Issues.pdf.

5. See the November 2007 report by the Pew Research Center's Global Attitudes Project, "The American–Western European Values Gap: American Exceptionalism Subsides," www.pewglobal.org/2011/11/17/the-american-western-european-values-gap.

6. See Gallup, "In US, 3 in 10 Say They Take the Bible Literally," July 8, 2011, www .gallup.com/poll/148427/say-bible-literally.aspx.

7. See Mark Chaves, *American Religion: Contemporary Trends* (Princeton, NJ: Princeton University Press, 2011), pp. 14, 50–51.

8. Michael Hout and Claude S. Fischer, "Why More Americans Have No Religious Preference: Politics and Generations," *American Sociological Review* 67 (2002): 165–190; www.jstor.org/stable/3088891.

9. Robert Wuthnow, *After the Baby Boomers: How Twenty-and Thirty-Somethings Are Shaping the Future of American Religion* (Princeton, NJ: Princeton University Press, 2007), pp. 51–70.

10. By contrast, some measures of religious commitment—such as frequency of prayer and the degree of importance that people assign to religion in their lives—do tend to rise with age. See the Pew Forum's February 2010 report "Religion Among the Millennials," www.pewforum.org/Age/Religion-Among-the-Millennials.aspx.

11. Robert D. Putnam, *Bowling Alone: The Collapse and Revival of American Community* (New York: Simon & Schuster, 2000). In Robert D. Putnam and David E. Campbell, *American Grace: How Religion Divides and Unites Us* (Simon & Schuster: New York, 2010), p. 127, Putnam and Campbell also consider changing moral and social beliefs to be part of the mix.

12. See, for example, "A Bleak Outlook Is Seen for Religion," *New York Times*, February 25, 1968, p. 3. The article quotes sociologist Peter L. Berger predicting that by the twenty-first century, traditional religions would survive only in "small enclaves and pockets." Berger has since renounced his earlier position.

13. See Pippa Norris and Ronald Inglehart, *Sacred and Secular: Religion and Politics Worldwide* (Cambridge, UK: Cambridge University Press, 2004), pp. 216–217. They argue that "societies where people's daily lives are shaped by the threat of poverty, disease and premature death remain as religious today as centuries earlier. These same societies are also experiencing rapid population growth. In rich nations, by contrast, the evidence demonstrates that secularization has been proceeding since at least the mid-twentieth century (and probably earlier)—but at the same time fertility rates have fallen sharply, so that in recent years population growth has stagnated and their total population is starting to shrink. The result of these combined trends is that *rich societies are becoming more secular but the world as a whole is becoming more religious*" (emphasis in original).

14. See the 2007 report by the Pew Research Center's Global Attitudes Project, "World Publics Welcome Global Trade—but Not Immigration," www.pewglobal.org /2007/10/04/world-publics-welcome-global-trade-but-not-immigration.

15. Norris and Inglehart, *Sacred and Secular,* pp. 89–95. They offer a number of possible explanations for America's exceptional religiosity, asserting in particular that economic inequality and the perception of a porous social welfare net leave Americans feeling "greater anxieties" than citizens in other advanced industrial countries. They also mention "the fact that the United States was founded by religious refugees" and the continuing arrival of new immigrants who bring "relatively strong religiosity with them," pp. 107–108 and 225–226.

16. Evangelical Protestants are defined here as Protestants who say yes when asked, "Would you describe yourself as a born-again or evangelical Christian, or not?" Protestants who do not answer this question affirmatively are categorized here as mainline Protestants. Other research that sorts Protestants into evangelical and mainline categories based on denominational affiliation (e.g., Southern Baptist, United Methodist) finds that the long-term decline in American Protestantism is concentrated primarily among the Protestant mainline. See, for example, Chaves, *American Religion,* pp. 81–93.

17. Alan Wolfe, *The Transformation of American Religion: How We Actually Live Our Faith* (Chicago: University of Chicago Press, 2005).

CHAPTER 11: LIVING DIGITAL

1. Unlike Jane Smith, "Natalie Marks" is the pseudonym for a real person, as are other names in this chapter. Except for the name changes, no other details of their lives have been altered. All the quotes are real.

2. Kristen Purcell et al., "How Teens Do Research in the Digital World," Pew Research Center's Internet & American Life Project, November 1, 2012.

3. Janna Anderson and Lee Rainie, "Millennials Will Benefit and Suffer Due to Their Hyperconnected Lives," Pew Research Center's Internet & American Life Project, February 29, 2012.

4. Amanda Lenhart, Rich Ling, Scott Campbell, and Kristen Purcell, "Teens and Mobile Phones," Internet & American Life Project, Pew Research Center, April 2010, www.pewinternet.org/Reports/2010/Teens-and-Mobile-Phones.aspx.

5. A full explanation of networked individualism and the role of technology in abetting it can be found in Lee Rainie and Barry Wellman, *Networked: The New Social Operating System* (Cambridge, MA: MIT University Press, 2012).

6. These calculations come from the ongoing research of the University of Toronto's NetLab, run by Professor Barry Wellman; http://homes.chass.utoronto.ca /~wellman.

7. Lee Rainie and Janna Anderson, "The Future of Privacy," Pew Research Center, December 18, 2014; http://www.pewinternet.org/2014/12/18/future-of-privacy/.

8. Mary Madden and Lee Rainie, "Americans' Attitudes About Privacy, Security, and Surveillance," Pew Research Center, May 20, 2015; http://www.pewinternet.org /2015/05/20/americans-attitudes-about-privacy-security-and-surveillance/.

9. See www.kff.org/entmedia/8010.cfm.

10. See www.kff.org/entmedia/upload/8010.pdf.

11. See www.poynter.org/uncategorized/71347/our-complex-media-day.

12. See www.people-press.org/2012/09/27/in-changing-news-landscape-even-television-is-vulnerable.

13. See www.pewinternet.org/Reports/2010/Online-News.aspx and www.journalism.org/analysis_report/demographics_mobile_news.

14. See www.pewinternet.org/Reports/2011/Local-news.aspx.

15. See www.pewinternet.org/Reports/2013/Health-online.aspx.

16. Lee Rainie and Aaron Smith, "Politics on Social Networking Sites," Pew Research Center's Internet & American Life Project, September 4, 2012.

17. Much of this framework for new literacies was inspired by the "networked literacy" lecture of Howard Rheingold, University of Toronto, October 2010; the writings of Pam Berger on her Infosearcher blog, "Learning in the Web 2.0 World," http://infosearcher.typepad.com/infosearcher/2007/04/learning_in_the.html; and the work of Henry Jenkins, especially "Confronting the Challenges of Participatory Culture: Media Education for the 21st Century," http://digitallearning.macfound.org/atf/cf/%7B7E45C7E0-A3E0-4B89-AC9C-E807E1B0AE4E%7D/JENKINS_WHITE_PAPER.PDF.

18. Danah Boyd, "Taken Out of Context: American Teen Sociality in Networked Publics," PhD diss., University of California, Berkeley, 2008.

19. Ibid., p. 27.

CHAPTER 12: GETTING OLD

1. See testimony of Dr. Francis Collins before the Senate Appropriations Subcommittee on Labor, Health and Human Services, Education and Related Agencies on May 11, 2011; http://appropriations.senate.gov/ht-labor.cfm?method=hearings.view&id=8a1dcace-6f68-4e35-ad94-4409966e2ffb.

2. Calment (1875–1997) smoked until her 117th year and attributed her longevity to the regular consumption of olive oil, port wine, and chocolate.

3. For more information on this theory, see Tom Kirkwood, *Time of Our Lives: The Science of Human Aging* (Oxford, UK: Oxford University Press, 1999).

4. Quoted in "Who Wants to Live Forever?" *Financial Mirror*, July 6, 2010.

5. Quote from the film *Transcendent Man* (2009); http://transcendentman.com.

6. Joel Garreau, *Radical Evolution: The Promise and Peril of Enhancing Our Minds, Our Bodies—and What It Means to Be Human* (New York: Broadway Books, 2005), p. 104.

7. Holman Jenkins, "Will Google's Ray Kurzweil Live Forever?" *Wall Street Journal*, April 12, 2013.

8. Quoted in Ker Than, "Would Life Extension Make Us Less Human?" MSNBC.com, May 24, 2006, www.msnbc.msn.com/id/12953517/ns/technology_and_science-science/t/would-life-extension-make-us-less-human.

9. Quoted in "Why We Age and How We Can Avoid It," at a July 2005 TED Conference in Oxford, England; www.youtube.com/watch?v=8iYpxRXlboQ.

CHAPTER 13: EMPTY CRADLE, GRAY WORLD

1. Even though China's gross domestic product has surpassed Japan's, the picture is quite different when one accounts for population size. The per capita income of the Japanese is still four times that of the Chinese.

2. Justin McCurry, "Let Elderly People 'Hurry Up and Die,' says Japanese Minister," *The Guardian,* January 22, 2013.

3. Chico Harlan, "A Declining Japan Loses Its Once-hopeful Champions," *Washington Post,* October 27, 2012.

4. Joel Kotkin and Harry Siegel, "Where Have All the Babies Gone?," *Newsweek,* February 15, 2013.

5. Hiroko Tabuchi, "Desperate Hunt for Day Care in Japan," *New York Times,* February 26, 2013.

6. Phillip Longman, "Think Again: Global Aging," *Foreign Policy,* November 1, 2010.

7. The median age divides the population into two equal parts, with 50% of the population older than the median age and 50% of the population younger than the median age.

8. In 2013 the health ministry reported that since the Chinese government introduced the one-child policy in 1971, doctors have performed 336 million abortions and 196 million sterilizations. By comparison, in the US, with a population about one-quarter the size of China's, an estimated 50 million abortions have been performed since the *Roe v. Wade* decision legalized abortion in 1973.

9. Dorinda Elliott, "The End of China's One-Child Policy?" *ChinaFile,* March 15, 2013.

10. Alternative measures of dependency ratios define the working-age population to be either ages 20 to 64 or ages 20 to 69.

11. Estimates of output are from the International Monetary Fund, World Economic Outlook Database, April 2012. Shares are based on purchasing power parity–based evaluations of country gross domestic products.

12. Canada is excluded because it is not one of the countries in which surveys were fielded for this report.

13. See, for example, Robert J. Gordon, "Is U.S. Economic Growth Over? Faltering Innovation Confronts the Six Headwinds," National Bureau of Economic Research, Working Paper No. 18315 (August 2012); David E. Bloom, David Canning, and Günther Fink, "Implications of Population Aging for Economic Growth," National Bureau of Economic Research, Working Paper No. 16705 (January 2011); Richard Freeman, "Is a Great Labor Shortage Coming? Replacement Demand in the Global Economy," National Bureau of Economic Research, Working Paper No. 12541 (September 2006).

14. Norimitsu Onishi, "As Japan Works to Patch Itself Up, a Rift Between the Generations Opens," *New York Times,* February 12, 2012.

15. Alexandra Harney, "Without Babies, Can Japan Survive?" *New York Times,* December 15, 2012.

CHAPTER 14: THE RECKONING

1. Texas governor Rick Perry road-tested the Ponzi metaphor in his campaign for president in 2012. It did not go well.

2. The most authoritative research that compares the return-on-contribution value of Social Security for different generations was done 20 years ago by Dean Leimer, an analyst at the Social Security Administration. His study found that in the aggregate, Americans born before 1938 either already have received, or eventually will receive, a windfall of $8.1 trillion from Social Security—that's the excess of what they'll draw in benefits over the value of their contributions, accrued with interest. Leimer made those calculations based on 1989 dollars; updated to current dollars, that windfall would be valued at $18 trillion, according to a further analysis in 2012 by Sylvester J. Schieber, a former chairman of the Social Security Advisory Board. Who's paid for these windfalls? Leimer and Schieber spell out who: successive generations of taxpayers, in ever escalating amounts. They find that cohorts born from 1951 to 2010 will, in the aggregate, contribute $4.3 trillion more in Social Security taxes, accrued with interest, than they will receive in benefits. And for children not yet born, a $12 trillion bill awaits to help cover the Social Security windfalls that went to earlier generations of recipients. See Dean R. Leimer, "Cohort-Specific Measures of Lifetime Net Social Security Transfers," ORS Working Paper Series No. 59, Washington DC, Social Security Administration. Also see Sylvester J. Schieber, *The Predictable Surprise: The Unraveling of the U.S. Retirement System* (Oxford: Oxford University Press, 2012), pp. 61–64.

3. Congressional Budget Office 2013, "Long-Term Budget Outlook," www.cbo.gov /publication/44521; and Congressional Budget Office Historical Budget Data, August 2013, www.cbo.gov/publication/44507.

4. Another part of the Social Security system, the Disability Insurance Trust Fund, is expected to become insolvent even sooner—in 2016—because the disability rolls have nearly tripled since 1980. Critics say that lax eligibility standards have enabled some people with questionable claims to receive benefits.

5. A summary of the 2013 report of the Social Security and Medicare Board of Trustees, which includes long-term actuarial and financing projections, is available online at www.ssa.gov/oact/trsum.

6. For a compelling history of the political and policy debates over Social Security within FDR's own cabinet, see Schieber, *The Predictable Surprise.*

7. Milton Friedman's 10-minute exposition on "The Social Security Myth" is a YouTube favorite among conservatives, www.youtube.com/watch?v=rCdgv7n9xCY.

8. This 2013 analysis assumes that all contributions made by workers and employers earned 2% interest annually above the rate of inflation. It is based on a hypothetical average worker. The returns of actual Social Security recipients vary widely, depending on a range of factors, including wage levels, years of work, marital circumstances, timing of retirement, and longevity; see www.urban.org/UploadedPDF /412945-Social-Security-and-Medicare-Taxes-and-Benefits-Over-a-Lifetime.pdf. In

2015, C. Eugene Steuerle and Caleb Quakenbush of the Urban Institute updated their projections, resulting in some minor changes to the Figures presented on page 225. To read their 2015 report and analysis, go to http://www.urban.org/research/publication /social-security-and-medicare-lifetime-benefits-and-taxes.

9. Jackie Calmes, "Misperceptions of Benefits Make Trimming Harder," *New York Times,* April 3, 2013.

10. In this example, the contributions are assumed to have earned 2% a year annually above the rate of inflation.

11. Some vivid examples from a 2013 report by the International Federation of Health Plans: an angiogram costs $218 in Switzerland and $914 in the US; bypass surgery is $22,844 in France and $73,420 in the US; hip replacements are $11,899 in Britain and $40,364 in the US.

12. As this book was going to press, the Affordable Care Act, aka Obamacare, was being implemented amid a blizzard of partisan rancor in Congress and many state-houses. Designed to both broaden health insurance coverage *and* reduce medical costs, it represents the largest expansion of the safety net since the 1960s. It's too soon to gauge what impact it will have on the future cost of health care.

13. Estimates from the Peter G. Peterson Foundation, based on data from the Congressional Budget Office; www.pgpf.org/Chart-Archive/~/link.aspx?_id =A0E17E1FEBEE42BFA346F12F51DE4526&_z=z.

14. Jessica Perez, Gabe Horowitz, and David Kendall, "Collision Course: Why Democrats Must Back Entitlement Reform," Third Way, July 2012.

15. A 2011 Congressional Budget Office report estimated that Medicare's market power had enabled it to negotiate health care prices at an 11% discount from what would be available in a market made up only of private insurers. And for reasons that health economists don't fully understand, the overall rate of rise in health care costs has moderated significantly in recent years—perhaps in reaction to the Great Recession, perhaps in anticipation of the implementation of the Affordable Care Act (Obamacare). Whatever the cause, a hopeful sign.

16. Letter to the editor, *New York Times,* February 25, 2013.

17. Pieter Vanhuysse, "Intergenerational Justice in Aging Societies," A Crossnational Comparison of 29 OECD Countries, Bertelsmann Stiftung, 2013.

18. Rakesh Kochhar and D'Vera Cohn, "Fighting Poverty in a Bad Economy, Americans Move in with Relatives," Pew Research Center, October 3, 2011.

19. For an excellent account of how families handled generational relationships in primitive societies through modern times, see chapter 1 by John B. Williamson and Diane M. Watts-Roy in *The Generational Equity Debate,* eds. Williamson, Watts-Roy, and Eric Kingson (New York: Columbia University Press, 1999). They note that in primitive societies, anthropologists found that the question of what share of resources should be consumed by the elderly was sometimes resolved by considerations of power rather than need. For example, the elderly tended to be treated better in societies based on fishing and gathering than in nomadic societies based on herding

and hunting, which placed a higher premium on youth and strength. Societal norms regarding relations between the old and young have shifted multiple times through different centuries and societies, but the overall drift has been toward a veneration of the old because of their moral and practical wisdom and their presumed physical and economic vulnerability.

20. "Growing Older in America: The Health and Retirement Survey," National Institute on Aging, published online March 2007, hrsonline.isr.umich.edu/index.php?p=dbook.

21. Michael Hurd, James P. Smith, and Julie Zissimopoulos, "Intervivos Giving Over the Lifecycle," Rand Labor and Population Working Paper WR-524-1, Santa Monica, California, October 2011; http://www.rand.org/pubs/working_papers/WR524-1.html.

22. "Grandparents Investing in Grandchildren," Metlife Mature Market Institute, New York, September 2012, www.gu.org/LinkClick.aspx?fileticket=jueWk9ubnyE%3D&tabid=157&mid=606; "Grandparents: Generous with Money, not with Advice," Metlife Mature Market Institute, Westport, Connecticut, 2009; www.metlife.com/assets/cao/mmi/publications/studies/mmi-grandparents-generous-advice-money.pdf.

23. This includes transfers from anyone, but the vast majority is composed of transfers from parents or grandparents.

24. Since these estimates are based upon respondents providing at least 100 hours of help, they are underestimates of the total share of respondents who provide help for their parents.

25. Hendrik Hartog, *Someday All This Will Be Yours* (Cambridge, MA: Harvard University Press, 2012).

26. Merril Silverstein and Roseann Giarrusso, "Aging and Family Life: A Decade Review," *Journal of Marriage and Family* 72 (October 2010).

27. Thomas Friedman, "Sorry, Kids. We Ate It All," *New York Times*, October 15, 2013.

28. To read the speech on this subject delivered by AARP CEO A. Barry Rand at the National Press Club on January 15, 2013, go to http://www.aarp.org/politics-society/advocacy/info-01-2013/rebuild-the-middle-class-speech.html.

APPENDIX I: HOW WE KNOW WHAT WE KNOW

1. In this chapter we focus on covering domestic survey research best practices from the US perspective. The Pew Research Center also surveys extensively across the globe. For more on those surveys, see http://www.pewresearch.org/methodology/international-survey-research/.

2. Sidney Verba, "The Citizen as Survey Respondent: Sample Surveys and American Democracy," *American Political Science Review*, 90 (March 1996): 1–7.

3. Richard Morin, "Citing Survey Change, Pollsters Retreat on Estimates of Union Vote," *Washington Post*, November 6, 1998.

4. Sally Squires. "Hand Washing: People Say They Do, But? . . . " *Washington Post*, September 17, 1996.

5. Conrad Hackett, "Do People Lie to Pollsters About Their Physical Characteristics?" Pew Research Center, March 28, 2011; http://www.pewresearch.org/2011/03/28/do-people-lie-to-pollsters-about-their-physical-characteristics/.

6. Roger Tourangeau and Ting Yan, "Sensitive Questions in Surveys," *Psychological Bulletin*, 2007.

7. The American Trends Panel is the Pew Research Center's probability-based, nationally representative survey panel of US adults.

8. Pew Research Center, "From Telephone to the Web: The Challenge of Mode of Interview Effects in Public Opinion Polls," May 13, 2015.

9. Mary Madden, "Americans' Attitudes About Privacy, Security and Surveillance," Pew Research Center, May 20, 2015.

10. John Zaller, *The Nature and Origins of Mass Opinion*, (Cambridge: Cambridge University Press, 1992).

11. W. Saris, M. Revilla, J. A. Krosnick, and E. M. Shaeffer, "Comparing Questions with Agree/Disagree Response Options to Questions with Item-Specific Response Options," Survey Research Methods, 2010.

12. George F. Bishop, Robert W. Oldendick, and Alfred Tuchfarber, "What Must My Interest in Politics Be If I Just Told You 'I Don't Know'?," *Public Opinion Quarterly*, 1984.

13. Pew Research Center, "Assessing the Representativeness of Public Opinion Surveys," May 15, 2012; http://www.people-press.org/2012/05/15/assessing-the-representativeness-of-public-opinion-surveys/.

14. Katherine Abraham, Sarah Helms, and Stanley Presser, "How Social Processes Distort Measurement: The Impact of Survey Nonresponse on Estimates of Volunteer Work in the United States," *American Sociological Review*, 2009.

15. An extensive examination of the causes of the New Hampshire polling failures produced no evidence that the Bradley Effect was to blame. See "An Evaluation of the Methodology of the 2008 Pre-Election Primary Polls," American Association for Public Opinion Research Ad Hoc Committee on the 2008 Presidential Primary Polling, April 2009.

16. Robert M. Groves, "Three Eras of Survey Research," *Public Opinion Quarterly*, 2010.

17. James Madison, *Federalist #10*, November 22, 1787.

18. James Madison, Letter to W. T. Barry, August 4, 1822.

INDEX

Paul Taylor served for a decade as executive vice president of the Pew Research Center, where he directed demographic, social, and generational research. From 1996 through 2003, he served as president and board chair of the Alliance for Better Campaigns, a nonprofit public-interest group that sought to improve the formats and reduce the cost of political communication on television. Before that, he was a newspaper reporter for twenty-five years, the last fourteen at the *Washington Post*, where he covered three US presidential campaigns and served as the *Post*'s bureau chief in South Africa during the historic transformation from apartheid to democracy. Taylor is the author of *See How They Run* (Knopf, 1990) and coauthor of *The Old News Versus the New News* (Twentieth Century Fund, 1992). He twice served as the visiting Ferris Professor of Journalism at Princeton University. He has a bachelor's degree in American studies from Yale University. He and his wife live in Bethesda, Maryland. They have three grown children and two grandchildren (so far!).

PublicAffairs is a publishing house founded in 1997. It is a tribute to the standards, values, and flair of three persons who have served as mentors to countless reporters, writers, editors, and book people of all kinds, including me.

I. F. STONE, proprietor of *I. F. Stone's Weekly*, combined a commitment to the First Amendment with entrepreneurial zeal and reporting skill and became one of the great independent journalists in American history. At the age of eighty, Izzy published *The Trial of Socrates*, which was a national bestseller. He wrote the book after he taught himself ancient Greek.

BENJAMIN C. BRADLEE was for nearly thirty years the charismatic editorial leader of *The Washington Post*. It was Ben who gave the *Post* the range and courage to pursue such historic issues as Watergate. He supported his reporters with a tenacity that made them fearless and it is no accident that so many became authors of influential, best-selling books.

ROBERT L. BERNSTEIN, the chief executive of Random House for more than a quarter century, guided one of the nation's premier publishing houses. Bob was personally responsible for many books of political dissent and argument that challenged tyranny around the globe. He is also the founder and longtime chair of Human Rights Watch, one of the most respected human rights organizations in the world.

•   •   •

For fifty years, the banner of Public Affairs Press was carried by its owner Morris B. Schnapper, who published Gandhi, Nasser, Toynbee, Truman, and about 1,500 other authors. In 1983, Schnapper was described by *The Washington Post* as "a redoubtable gadfly." His legacy will endure in the books to come.

Peter Osnos, *Founder and Editor-at-Large*